Digital Image Security

This book highlights cutting-edge research with a particular emphasis on interdisciplinary approaches, novel techniques, and solutions to provide digital image security for applications in diverse areas. It further discusses important topics such as biometric imaging, big data security and privacy in healthcare, security and privacy in the Internet of Things, and security in cloud-based image processing.

This book

- Presents new ideas, approaches, theories, and practices with a focus on digital image security and privacy solutions for real-world applications.
- Discusses security in cloud-based image processing for smart city applications.
- Provides an overview of innovative security techniques that are being developed to ensure the guaranteed authenticity of transmitted, shared, or stored digital images.
- Highlights approaches such as watermarking, blockchain, and hashing to secure digital images in artificial intelligence, machine learning, cloud computing, and temper detection environments.
- Explains important topics such as biometric imaging, blockchain for digital data security, and protection systems against personal identity theft.

It will serve as an ideal reference text for senior undergraduate and graduate students, academic researchers, and professionals in fields including electrical engineering, electronics, communications engineering, and computer engineering.

Digital Image Security
Techniques and Applications

Edited by
Amit Kumar Singh
Stefano Berretti
Ashima Anand
Amrit Kumar Agrawal

CRC Press
Taylor & Francis Group
Boca Raton London New York

CRC Press is an imprint of the
Taylor & Francis Group, an **informa** business

Designed cover image: Shutterstock

First edition published 2024
by CRC Press
2385 NW Executive Center Drive, Suite 320, Boca Raton FL 33431

and by CRC Press
4 Park Square, Milton Park, Abingdon, Oxon, OX14 4RN

CRC Press is an imprint of Taylor & Francis Group, LLC

ISBN: 978-1-032-40859-0 (hbk)
ISBN: 978-1-032-74378-3 (pbk)
ISBN: 978-1-003-46897-4 (ebk)

DOI: 10.1201/9781003468974

Typeset in Sabon
by SPi Technologies India Pvt Ltd (Straive)

Contents

About the editors

Amit Kumar Singh is an Associate Professor in the Computer Science and Engineering Department, National Institute of Technology Patna, Bihar, India. He has authored over 250 peer-reviewed journals, conference publications, and book chapters. Dr. Singh has been recognized in the "WORLD RANKING OF TOP 2% SCIENTISTS" in "Biomedical Research" (2019) and "Artificial Intelligence & Image Processing" (2020), according to the survey given by Stanford University, USA. Dr. Singh is the associate editor of IEEE Trans. Multimedia, IEEE Trans. Ind. Informat, IEEE Trans. Computat. Social Syst, ACM Trans. Multimedia Comput. Commun. Appl., IEEE J. Biomed. Heal. Informatics, among others. Dr. Singh is the series editor of The IET International Book Series on Multimedia Information Processing and Security. He has edited various international journal special issues as a lead guest editor on publications such as ACM Transactions on Multimedia Computing, Communications, and Applications; ACM Transactions on Internet Technology; IEEE Transactions on Industrial Informatics; IEEE Journal of Biomedical and Health Informatics; IEEE Multimedia; IEEE Access; Multimedia Tools and Applications, Springer; International Journal of Information Management, Elsevier; Journal of Ambient Intelligence and Humanized Computing, among others. His research interests include multimedia data hiding, image processing, biometrics, and cryptography.

Stefano Berretti is an Associate Professor at the Media Integration and Communication Center (MICC) and at the Department of Information Engineering (DINFO) of the University of Florence (UNIFI), Florence, Italy. His research interests are Computer Vision, Artificial Intelligence and Multimedia. During his Ph.D. and post-doc, he worked on image databases for effective and efficient image retrieval based on color, shape attributes, and spatial relationships. He also investigated the problem of retrieval from repositories distributed on the net using resource selection and results fusion. He provided several contributions on 3D object retrieval and partitioning, face biometrics (from 2D and 3D data), facial expression and emotion recognition (from 3D and 3D dynamic data), human action recognition from depth data, and 3D surface descriptors for relief patterns classification.

He recently extended his interests to deep learning methods for face recognition and to their generalization to non-Euclidean domains (i.e., graphs, meshes, manifolds, etc.). He is a member of the Italian Association for "Computer Vision, Pattern Recognition and Machine Learning" (CVPL), previously known as "Group of Italian Researchers on Pattern Recognition" (GIRPR), affiliated to the International Association on Pattern Recognition (IAPR) of the Computer Vision Foundation (CVF) of ACM, Eurographics, and a senior member of the IEEE. He has been the Information Director of the ACM Transactions on Multimedia Computing, Communications, and Applications (ACM TOMM) and is now an Associate Editor for ACM TOMM, IEEE TCSVT, the IET Computer Vision journal, and the MDPI Sensors journal. He has also organized special issues of highly ranked journals (ACM TOMM, IEEE J-BHI, CAG Elsevier, IEEE TII) and served as editor of several books. He has been general chair, program chair, and area chair of several conferences and workshops.

Ashima Anand is an Assistant Professor in the Computer Science and Engineering Department, Thapar Institute of Engineering and Technology, Thaper University, Patiala, Punjab. She earned a Ph.D. from the National Institute of Technology, Patna, in 2021 and a B.Tech from the National Institute of Technology, Hamirpur, in 2017. She has authored many peer-reviewed journals and conferences in repute. Her areas of specialization are Data Hiding methods, Digital Image Processing, Information Security, and Cryptography.

Amrit Kumar Agrawal is an Associate Professor in the Department of Computer Science and Engineering, Sharda University, Greater Noida. He earned his Ph.D. in Computer Science & Engineering from Dr. APJ Abdul Kalam Technical University, Lucknow, Uttar Pradesh, India, in June 2020; M.Tech. (Gold Medalist) in Computer Science and Engineering from Jaypee University of Information Technology (JUIT), Waknaghat, Solan, Himachal Pradesh, in 2010; and B.Tech. in Computer Science and Engineering from UNS, Institute of Engineering and Technology, Veer Bahadur Singh Purvanchal University, Jaunpur, Uttar Pradesh, in 2005. He has authored many peer-reviewed journals and conferences in repute. His research interests include Biometrics, Image Analysis, and Image Security.

List of contributors

F. Adedoyin
Department of Computing,
 Bournemouth University
Poole, UK

Amrit Kumar Agrawal
Department of CSE, School of
 Engineering & Technology,
 Sharda University
Greater Noida, UP, India

Ashima Anand
Department of CSE, Thapar
 Institute of Engineering and
 Technology
Patiala, Punjab, India

Ashish Arya
Indian Institute of Information
 Technology, Sonepat, India

Divyanshu Awasthi
Department of ECE, MNNIT
 Allahabad, Prayagraj, India

Vivek Singh Baghel
Department of Computer Science
 & Engineering, Indian Institute of
 Technology Indore, India

Shrish Bajpai
Integral University
Lucknow, Uttar Pradesh, India

Vandana Bharti
Department of Computer Science
 and Engineering, Indian Institute
 of Technology (BHU)
Varanasi, Uttar Pradesh, India

A. Bruno
IULM AI Lab, IULM Libera
 Universit`a di Lingue e
 Comunicazione
Milan, Italy

A. Chetouani
Orleans University
Orleans, France

Mou Dasgupta
Department of Computer
 Application, National Institute of
 Technology Raipur
Raipur, Chhattisgarh, India

M. Gao
Shandong University of Technology
Shandong, China

M.A. Kerkouri
Orleans University
Orleans, France

Priyank Khare
Department of ECE, IIIT Ranchi
Ranchi, Jharkhand, India

C. Mala
Computer Science and Engineering
   Department, National Institute of
   Technology
Tiruchirappalli, India

S. Neelakandan
R.M.K. Engineering College
Chennai, India

P. Oza
Institute of Technology, Nirma
   University
Ahmedabad, India

Nivedita Palia
Vivekananda School of
   Engineering & Technology,
   Vivekananda Institute of
   Professional Studies-Technical
   Campus
Delhi, India

Shetanshu Parmar
Computer Science and Engineering
   Department, National Institute of
   Technology
Tiruchirappalli, India

D. Paulraj
R.M.K. Engineering College
Chennai, India

M. Prakash
VIT University
Vellore, India

Surya Prakash
Department of Computer Science
   & Engineering, Indian Institute of
   Technology Indore
Indore, India

Nishita Priyadarshini
AIIMS Bibinagar
Hyderabad, Telangana, India

Arti Ranjan
Department of CSE, IGDTUW
New Delhi, India

M. Ravinder
Department of CSE, IGDTUW
New Delhi, India

Sangram Ray
Department of Computer Science
   and Engineering, National
   Institute of Technology Sikkim
Ravangla, Sikkim, India

Dipanwita Sadhukhan
Department of Computer Science
   and Engineering, National
   Institute of Technology Sikkim
Ravangla, Sikkim, India

Sima Sahu
Department of ECE, Malla
   Reddy Engineering College
   (Autonomous)
Maisammaguda, Hyderabad,
   Telengana, India

A. Sekhri
Orleans University
Orleans, France

Anshul Sharma
Department of Computer Science
   and Engineering, National
   Institute of Technology
Patna, Bihar, India

Divya Sharma
Institute of Engineering &
   Technology Lucknow
Lucknow, Uttar Pradesh, India

Amit Kumar Singh
Department of Computer Science
   and Engineering, National
   Institute of Technology
Patna, Bihar, India

Kedar Nath Singh
Jaypee Institute of Information
  Technology
Noida, UP, India

Om Prakash Singh
Indian Institute of Information
  Technology
Bhagalpur, India

Jaya Sinha
Department of Computer Science
  and Engineering, Galgotias
  College of Engineering and
  Technology
Greater Noida, UP, India

Vinay Kumar Srivastava
Department of ECE, MNNIT
  Allahabad
Prayagraj, India

M. Tliba
Orleans University
Orleans, France

S. Velmurugan
R.M.D. Engineering College
Chennai, India

Huiyu Zhou
School of Computing and
  Mathematical Sciences, University
  of Leicester
Leicester, United Kingdom

Chapter 1

COVID-19 electronic health data security for smart hospitals

Ashima Anand
Thapar Institute of Engineering and Technology, Patiala, India

Amit Kumar Singh
NIT Patna, Patna, India

Huiyu Zhou
University of Leicester, Leicester, United Kingdom

1.1 INTRODUCTION

COVID-19 was a devastating pandemic, and its variants infected millions worldwide within only a few days [1]. Large volumes of medical data, called electronic health data (EHD), were collected and transmitted among healthcare professionals and hospitals to combat the pandemic by ensuring accurate diagnosis. According to the report [2], the size of the digital healthcare market was USD 96.5 billion in 2020. It is expected to reach USD 295.4 billion in 2028, with a compound annual growth rate of about 15%. Also, post-COVID, a remarkable growth of 14.2% in digital healthcare market was seen in 2021, owing to the increase in demand of digital healthcare solutions [2]. However, the exchange of data, specifically digital medical records, led to a significant increase in the unauthorized access and illegal distribution of such confidential data [3].

Therefore, it is important to study the authenticity and the copy-protection of the electronic version of patient data.

Watermarking algorithms are recommended cost-effective solutions to guarantee the security of EHD. In watermarking, different kinds of secret mark(s) are imperceptibly inserted into media to maintain their security [3, 4]. In addition, save bandwidth and storage demands, efficient archiving, and fast retrieval are other advantages of watermarking in medical domain. Researchers have developed various watermarking algorithms based on image fusion to manage security with high diagnostic accuracy [5–7]. There are still certain issues related to maintaining a proper balance between robustness and invisibility; however, security analyses of some algorithms are inadequate.

Recently, image fusion-based watermarking has been developed for better diagnostic accuracy with high security of the digital records in the healthcare domain [5–7].

DOI: 10.1201/9781003468974-1

1

By using the COVID-19 patient image as a mark carrier, this paper develops a secure watermarking algorithm using encryption and medical image fusion that can offer an excellent balance among the watermark robustness and invisibility. In our proposed algorithm, we first obtain the fused image as watermark by applying NSCT on the CT scan and MRI image. Then, the combination of NSCT, HD, and MSVD is employed to conceal the fused mark image into the carrier media. Finally, an encryption scheme is utilized to encrypt the final marked image before being circulated online. The major contributions of this work include:

1. The proposed algorithm uses NSCT to fuse the CT scan and MRI images. The fused image is considered as mark image, which is useful for better clinical experience.
2. The combination of NSCT, HD, and MSVD is employed to conceal the fused image within the carrier image. The combination of these transforms enhances the watermark robustness and invisibility at low cost [8, 9].
3. The marked image is further encrypted using modernized stereo image encryption, which is useful for enhancing the security of the media data [10].

The rest of the chapter is divided into the following segments: Section 1.2 discusses the recent advances in watermarking-encryption-fusion-based methods, followed by a detailed explanation of the preliminary concepts in Section 1.3. The proposed methodology is presented in Section 1.4. Section 1.5 is a detailed discussion of the experimental results, and the chapter is summarized in Section 1.6.

1.2 LITERATURE SURVEY

A review of several related watermarking methods using fusion and encryption is presented in this section.

Hemdan developed a robust watermarking approach using the fused image as the watermark [5]. The fused image is scrambled using the Arnold and chaotic methods and then concealed via the discrete wavelet transform (DWT)-singular value decomposition (SVD)-based marking technique. Further, a robust and secure fusion-based watermarking method for medical images is developed by the authors of Ref. [6]. It implemented a hybrid of transform and spatial domain to improve the robustness, along with increasing the message payload. Finally, an advanced encryption using DNA, chaotic map, and hash function is used to secure the marked image. Another fusion-based watermarking framework is proposed by the authors of Ref. [7] to secure the digital healthcare records. It applies NSST-based fusion on a CT scan and MRI image. The fused image is then concealed with the MAC address of the sender's system and image mark using a combination of DWT, Fisher-Yates permutation, firefly optimization, and dual tree complex wavelet transform (DTCWT)-SVD. Also, the patient's report is hidden in the marked image for better embedding payload, maintaining high visual quality. Finally, the marked image is secured using a low-cost encryption method. Compared with other schemes [11–13], this framework provides a better solution to ensure higher security for privacy preservation.

Singh et al. developed a secure watermarking model for copyright protection of digital images [14]. Initially, a series of transforms including lifting wavelet transform (LWT), Hessenberg decomposition (HD), and randomized SVD (RSVD) is applied on the carrier image. Further, the mark is concealed inside the singular values of the carrier image using a suitable embedding factor. Finally, the marked image is encrypted and then compressed for secure transmission with reduced bandwidth demand. During extraction, a convolutional neural network (CNN)-based denoising model is applied on the extracted mark for improved robustness. Anand et al. proposed a secure watermarking method to authenticate the digital healthcare records [15]. The proposed work implemented wavelet-based watermarking to generate a dual watermark by hiding the encoded MAC address into the mark image. The generated mark is hidden in the IWT-Schur-RSVD coefficients of the carrier image using an optimized scaling factor. Fuzzy inference system is used to maintain a balance between robustness and visual quality by computing the optimal value of the scaling factor. In the final stage, chaotic encryption is used to cipher the marked image to improve security while transmitting over the open network. A blind watermarking method based on Diffie-Hellman and Number Theoretic Transform (NTT) is proposed by Soualmi et al. for protection of medical records [16]. Initially, the mark is encrypted using Diffie-Hellman for better security of this scheme. In the embedding phase, the host image is transformed using NTT, and the resultant coefficients are altered to embed the encrypted mark. The performance of this scheme offers better computational complexity and visual quality in comparison to many existing methods.

Yan et al. developed a multiple watermarking technique to verify the integrity and authenticity of the digital medical content [17]. The proposed work blended watermarking with encryption and compression for better security and compression performance. An encrypted image mark is hidden in the ROI of the carrier image using fragile watermarking. Further, a compressed text mark is placed in the RONI using DWT-SVD and brain storm optimization (BSO) to improve invisibility and robustness. The robustness analysis of this work inferred better results when compared with similar techniques [15, 18, 19]. A blind and robust watermarking method for medical applications is presented by Nguyen-Thanh and Le-Tien [20]. The authors transformed the cover image using Scale Invariant Feature Transform

(SIFT) and applied even-odd quantization to conceal the secret information. Further, the security is improved by using a key-based embedding and extraction process. Another robust watermarking-encryption-based framework for e-health applications is presented by Soualmi et al. [21]. In the pre-processing stage, both the cover and image mark are ciphered by XORing with chaotic sequence. Further, the cyphered mark is hidden in the Schur coefficient of the encrypted host image. At the receiver end, the mark is blindly extracted from the received image. The proposed work focused on high security; however, the embedding capacity can be further improved.

Vaidya proposed a robust watermarking solution for healthcare records in wavelet domain [22]. Initially, two-level decomposition using LWT and DWT is applied on the host image. Further, the high frequency coefficient of the host image is altered using adaptive scaling factors to conceal the fingerprint image. The adaptive scaling factors are computed using Local Binary Pattern, which ensures high robustness with minimum visual distortion. The author also enhanced the security by encrypting the marked image using Arnold transform.

1.3 PRELIMINARY CONCEPTS

1.3.1 Non-Subsampled Contourlet Transform (NSCT)

Although wavelet transforms offer multiresolution and spatio-frequency properties, these transforms suffer from the issues of poor directionality, shift variance, and poor capturing of edge information [23]. To overcome these issues, contourlet transform (CT) is used, having multiresolution and multidirectional properties. However, it uses up- and down-sampling processes, which cause a shift variant problem [23].

Based on CT, NSCT is capable of efficient representation of any image with better directionality, with edge and smooth contour information. It holds shift invariant property, along with all the advantages of CT. The construction of NSCT includes the use of non-subsampled pyramid filter bank (NSPFB) and non-subsampled directional filter bank (NSDFB). NSPFB ensures multi-scalability, and NSDFB provides better directional information. Both filter banks eliminate the operation of up- and down-sampling, confirming shift invariant property [23].

Initially, the input image is decomposed with NSPFB, which results in high- and low-pass sub-bands, with the same size of the input image. Further, NSPFB is applied on a low-pass coefficient to achieve multi-scalability. The result has 'l+1' count of sub-images, where 'l' represents the decomposition level. Here, 'l' is the count of high-pass coefficients, and the rest is the low-pass coefficient. The condition for perfect reconstruction is given as [24],

$$Z_L(l) \times R_L(l) + Z_H(l) \times R_H(l) = 1 \tag{1.1}$$

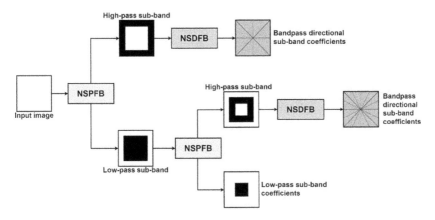

Figure 1.1 Non-subsampled contourlet transform.

Here, $Z_L(l)$ and $R_L(l)$ denote the decomposed and reconstructed low-pass filters, respectively. Also, decomposed and reconstructed high-pass filters are denoted by $Z_H(l)$ and $R_H(l)$.

In the next stage, NSDFB is implemented on a high-pass sub-band with 'd' level directionality. It results in total 2^d directional sub-bands whose size is the same as that of the input image; it provides more precise directional information. The procedure of NSCT decomposition of an input image is shown in Figure 1.1 [23].

1.3.2 Hessenberg Decomposition (HD)

In linear algebra, the matrix decompositions of square matrix are done with the help of HD [25]. It decomposes the square matrix, 'A' of size '$m \times m$' into the product of three matrices, which is mentioned in Eq. (1.2).

$$PHP^T = HD(A) \tag{1.2}$$

Where, 'P' is indicated as orthogonal matrix and 'H' is an upper Hessenberg matrix, and $h_{i,\,j}=0$, where i > j + 1.

The mathematical computation of HD is obtained with the help of Householder matrices. The mathematical equation of Householder matrix, 'Q' is described below.

$$Q = \left(I_n - 2\mu\mu^T\right)\!/\mu^T\mu \tag{1.3}$$

Where, 'I_n' is denoted as identity matrix with dimension '$m \times m$', and 'R' is an orthogonal matrix. 'μ' is termed as non-zero vector.

For example, pixel value of matrix, 'A' with size of 4 × 4 is obtained from input image, is presented below.

$$A = \begin{bmatrix} 104.6010 & 42.2519 & 56.5573 & 106.6036 \\ 100.1120 & 43.6523 & 63.5101 & 141.4542 \\ 83.2060 & 81.4629 & 45.2070 & 118.1840 \\ 24.4301 & 56.1044 & 83.4849 & 93.2716 \end{bmatrix} \tag{1.4}$$

Where, HD decomposed the matrix, 'A' into two matrices such as 'P' and 'H', which are mentioned below.

$$P = \begin{bmatrix} 1 & 0 & 0 & 0 \\ 0 & -0.7559 & 0.3109 & 0.5762 \\ 0 & -0.6282 & -0.0964 & -0.7720 \\ 0 & -0.1845 & -0.9455 & 0.2682 \end{bmatrix} \tag{1.5}$$

$$H = \begin{bmatrix} 104.6010 & -89.5251 & -91.7719 & 12.3475 \\ -132.4481 & 167.6635 & 164.2178 & -36.9402 \\ 0 & 86.3894 & 43.9222 & 6.9409 \\ 0 & 0 & -23.9644 & -27.4539 \end{bmatrix} \tag{1.6}$$

We have observed that 167.6635 is the highest energy element of Hessenberg matrix, 'H', which can be used to insert the mark data.

1.3.3 Multiresolution Singular Value Decomposition (MSVD)

MSVD is a linear complexity transform that uses SVD in place of low- and high-pass filters in wavelet transform [26]. The procedure of calculating MSVD coefficients of the input image, 'E' of size p × q, as discussed in Figure 1.2, includes the following processes [26]:

a. Initially, the input image, E, is segmented into non-overlapping blocks. Size of each block is m × n.
b. Rearrange each block into separate vector of size mn × 1. Further, the resultant vectors are stacked as new columns to generate a matrix, $\bar{E}$, of size mn × pq.
c. Furthermore, corresponding centered matrix, $\bar{E}_1$, is calculated.
d. In the next step, the scatter matrix, S, is computed using the following equation:

$$S = \bar{E}_1 \times \bar{E}_1^{\mathrm{T}} \tag{1.7}$$

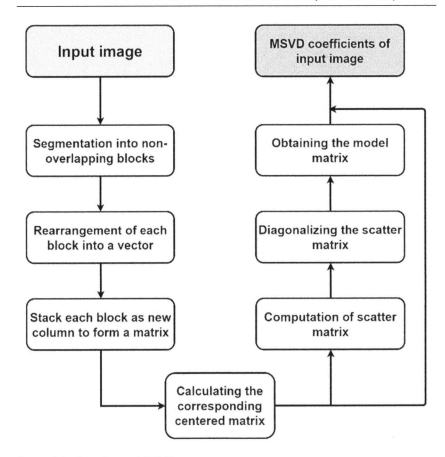

Figure 1.2 Flowchart of MSVD.

  e. Further, a modal matrix, *M*, comprising the eigenvector, is computed
     by diagonalizing *S*.

$$M^T \times S \times M = A^2 \tag{1.8}$$

  Here, A^2 = diagonal $(a(1)^2, a(2)^2 \ldots \ldots a(mn)^2)$ have the square of singular values of *S*.
  f. Finally, compute the matrix $\bar{I}$ using Eq. (1.9).

$$\bar{I} = M^T \times \bar{E} \tag{1.9}$$

  Since the first row of $\bar{I}$ contains the largest singular values, it is considered
as the approximation sub-band, Φ. The remaining rows are treated as the
detailed part of the input image, Ψ [26].

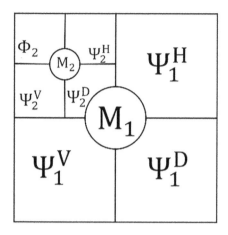

Figure 1.3 Two-level MSVD structure.

$$E = \left\{ \Phi_L, \left\{ \Psi_i^V, \Psi_i^H, \Psi_i^D \right\}_{i=1}^L, \left\{ M_i \right\}_{i=1}^L \right\} \tag{1.10}$$

Here, 'L' denotes the decomposition level.

The MSVD coefficients of an input image with two decomposition levels are shown in Figure 1.3 [27].

1.4 PROPOSED METHOD

The suggested fusion-based watermarking method is implemented in three segments: a) Fusion of medical images, b) Transform-based embedding and recovery of fused image, and c) Security of marked image using encryption (see Figure 1.4). Each segment is elaborated in Algorithms 1–3. Table 1.1 describes the notations used in our algorithms.

In the pre-processing segment, the CT scan image '*in_CT*' and MRI image, '*in_MRI*' are fused using the NSCT-based fusing method. It uses phase congruency and local Laplacian fusion rules to fuse the high-pass and low-pass NSCT components of the input images, respectively. The detailed process of generating the fused image is provided in Algorithm 1.

For embedding of the fused image, '*out_Fus*', the sub-component of the cover image with highest entropy value is decomposed using hybrid of NSCT, HD, and MSVD. Further, MSVD is applied on '*out_*Fus', resulting in the following coefficients: '*wLL*', '*wHL*', '*wLH*', and '*wHH*'. Further, singular matrix of cover image, '*in_Cov*', is altered using gain factor and '*wHL*'. Finally, inverse MSVD, inverse HD, and inverse NSCT are applied to generate

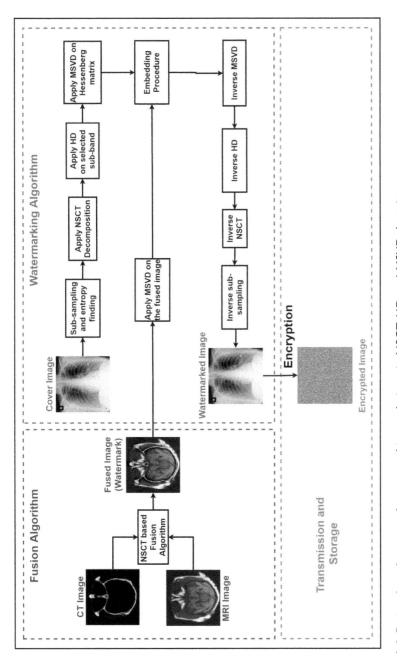

Figure 1.4 Fusion-based proposed watermarking technique in NSCT, HD, and MSVD domain.

Table 1.1 Notations used in our algorithms with descriptions

Notation	Explanation	Notation	Explanation
in_MRI, in_CT	MRI and CT scan as input	wat_HL	Watermarked cHL
out_Fus	Fused image	wat_H	Watermarked cH
ML, MH, CL, CH	Low-pass and high-pass NSCT coefficients of input images	wat_NSCT	Watermarked c_nsct
MW, CW	Weighted local energy of ML and CL	wat_c	Watermarked c_max
MWS, CWS	Weighted sum of eight-neighborhood-based modified Laplacian of ML and CL	enc_img	Encrypted image
out_FL, out_FH	Fused low-pass and high-pass coefficient	[r c]	Number of rows and columns in $\bar{F}$
in_Cov	Cover image	v_img	Vector form of wat_img
A	Scaling factor	L	Length of v_img
out_Cov	Watermarked image	S'	Identity permutation matrix of length L
c1, c2, c3, c4	Sub-sampling coefficients of fused_img	R_s	Random sequence
e1, e2, e3, e4	Entropy of sub-sampling coefficients	R_p	Random permutation
c_max	Sub-sampling coefficient with maximum entropy	v_Sh	Shuffled image vector
c_nsct	NSCT coefficient of c_max	a_Sh	Shuffled image array
P, H	Unitary and Hessenberg matrix of HL sub-band (256×256)	c_seq	Random sequence of length $r \times c$ using non-linear Chaotic map
cLL, cLH, cHL, cHH	Sub-bands obtained on applying MSVD on c_NSCT (256×256)	[sU, sS, sV]	Left, middle, and right singular matrices of c_seq
wLL, wLH, wHL, wHH	Sub-bands obtained on applying MSVD on out_Fus (256×256)	Key	Final key

the watermarked image, '*out_Cov*'. Algorithm 2 provides a detailed explanation of the NSCT-HD-MSVD-based embedding process.

Finally, we utilized updated stereo image encryption (SIE) to encrypt '*out_Cov*'. SIE encryption is based on Step Space Filling Curve (SSFC), SVD, and chaotic maps [10]. Its encryption process is explained in Algorithm 3.

ALGORITHM 1: Image Fusion Using NSCT

Input: in_MRI, in_CT
Output: out_Fus
  Begin
    Step 1: Apply NSCT on in_CT and in_MRI
        1. [ML, MH] ← NSCT (MRI);
        2. [CL, CH] ← NSCT (CT);
    Step 2: Fusion of high- and low-pass NSCT sub-bands
        3. (MW, CW) ← WLE (ML, CL);
        4. (MWS, CWS) ← WSEML (ML, CL);
        5. out_FL ← $\begin{cases} ML, \text{if } MW \times MWS \geq CW \times CWS \\ CL, \text{otherwise} \end{cases}$;

        6. out_FH ← $\begin{cases} MH, \text{if } L\_mapl = 1 \\ CH, \text{otherwise} \end{cases}$;
    Step 3: Apply inverse NSCT
        7. out_Fus ← Inverse_NSCT (out_FL, out_FH);
  return out_Fus

ALGORITHM 2: NSCT-HD-MSVD-based Embedding Procedure

Input: in_Cov, out_Fus, α
Output: out_Cov
  Begin
    Step 1: Subsampling of fused image and calculating
            entropy of each component
        1. [c1, c2, c3, c4] ← Subsampling (in_Cov);
        2. [e1, e2, e3, e4] ← Entropy (c1, c2, c3, c4);
        3. c_max ← Maximum (e1, e2, e3, e4);
    Step 2: Apply NSCT, HD, and MSVD on c_max
        4. c_nsct ← NSCT (c_max);
        5. [cP, cH] ← HD (c_nsct {1,4} {1,2});
        6. [cLL, cLH, cHL, cHH] ← MSVD (cH);
    Step 3: Apply MSVD on out_Fus
        7. [wLL, wLH, wHL, wHH] ← MSVD (out_Fus);
    Step 4: Embedding using α
        8. wat_HL ← cHL + α × wHL;
    Step 5: Apply inverse MSVD, HD, and NSCT
        9. wat_H ← iMSVD (cLL, cLH, wat_HL, cHH);
        10. wat_nsct {1,4} {1,2} ← cP × wat_H × cP^T;
        11. wat_c ← Inverse_NSCT (wat_nsct);
    Step 6: Inverse Subsampling procedure
        12. out_Cov ← Inverse_Subsampling (c1, c2, c3,
            wat_c);
  return out_Cov

ALGORITHM 3:   Updated SIE Encryption

```
Input: out_Cov
Output: out_Enc
  Begin
   Step 1: Scrambling wat_img
          1. [r c] ← Size (out_Cov);
          2. v_img ← Vector (out_Cov);
          3. L ← Length (v_img);
```

$$4.\ S' \leftarrow \begin{pmatrix} 12......L \\ 12.......L \end{pmatrix};$$

```
          5. R_s ← Random (s), such that R_s ∈ [1, s];
          6. R_p ← (S'[n], S'[R_pₙ]) (S'[n-1], S'[R_
             pₙ₋₁]) ....... (S'[p], S'[R_pₚ]) ......(S'[2],
             S'[R_p₂])
          7. v_Sh ← Shuffle (v_img, R_p);
          8. a_Sh ← Vector2Array (v_Sh);
   Step 2: Key generation
          9. c_seq ← Chaotic Map (r × c);
          10. [sU, sS, sV] ← SVD (c_seq);
          11. Key ← sU × sVT;
   Step 3: Final Encryption
          12. out_Enc ← Key × a_Sh × Keyᵀ;
     return out_Enc
```

1.5 RESULTS AND ANALYSIS

We utilized a CT scan and MRI image, Source: Ref. [28], to form a fused image of size 256×256 and conceal it within a COVID-19 patient's data (Dimension: 512×512) [29]. We evaluate the performance of our proposed solution with peak signal-to-noise-ratio (PSNR), structural similarity index measure (SSIM), and normalized coefficient (NC) [30]. Meanwhile, the performance of the encryption used is evaluated with number of changing pixel rate (NPCR) and unified averaged changed intensity (UACI). The gain factor (α) is used to maintain an excellent balance among the watermark robustness and invisibility.

The proposed technique is tested for different 'α' values from 0.005 to 1, and the results are summarized in Table 1.2, with the highest PSNR and SSIM score of 94.7683 dB and 1, respectively, with 'α' of 0.005, while highest NC = 0.9954 is achieved at 'α' = 1.0. Notably, higher values of gain factor result in better robustness at the cost of visual quality. Moreover, NPCR and UACI scores are always greater than 0.9927 and 0.3202, respectively, indicating that the selected encryption can achieve high security. Further, we evaluated the impact of invisibility and robustness on various non-medical images and 300 CT scan images of COVID-19 patients [29]. The results are

Table 1.2 Evaluation of proposed work with varying value of gain factor

Gain Factor	PSNR (in dB)	SSIM	NC	NPCR	UACI
0.005	94.7683	1	0.6969	0.9928	0.3202
0.01	88.7477	1	0.5654	0.9929	0.3218
0.05	74.7683	1	0.9094	0.9926	0.3217
0.07	71.8457	1	0.9425	0.9931	0.3219
0.3	59.2053	1	0.9919	0.9928	0.3217
0.5	54.7683	1	0.9943	0.993	0.3216
0.7	51.8457	0.9999	0.995	0.9927	0.3217
1	48.7477	0.9998	0.9954	0.9927	0.3221

Table 1.3 Objective evaluation of the proposed work on different images

Cover Image	PSNR (in dB)	SSIM	NC	NPCR	UACI
MRI	54.7683	1	0.9943	0.993	0.3216
Barbara	60.0697	1	0.9925	0.9949	0.3451
Cameraman	57.4668	1	0.9915	0.9957	0.3778
Cell	57.1606	0.9997	0.9957	0.9962	0.3589
Chest X-Ray	57.282	1	0.9949	0.9998	0.3605
Colon MRI	57.1079	1	0.9944	0.9923	0.1595
Head CT scan	57.2301	1	0.9878	1	0.3721
Kidney Stone	56.9985	1	0.9986	0.9964	0.3341
Rice	56.963	1	0.9936	0.9935	0.3899
Zelda	57.255	1	0.9945	0.9933	0.3182
Average of 300 COVID-19 images [29]	**54.3941**	**1**	**0.9903**	**0.9986**	**0.3598**

presented in Table 1.3. Notably, the average results of PSNR, SSIM, and NC are 54.3941 dB, 1.0, and 0.9903, respectively.

Further, the proposed work is subjectively quantified by various related professionals, and Table 1.4 summarizes the obtained results. The results indicate acceptable visual quality of the marked host image with value of gain factor below 1.5. Based on the results, the quality degrades as the value of gain factor is incremented. Figure 1.5 shows the histogram analysis of the original cover image and the marked image. Low variations between the two histogram plots confirm high visual quality with minimized distortion. The histogram of any image gives the details of frequency distribution in its pixels [31]. The evaluation of the encryption method is done based on the histogram analysis.

Another histogram-based analysis is shown in Figure 1.6. It provides the frequency distribution of marked image and encrypted image. The histogram

Table 1.4 Subjective analysis of the proposed watermarking method

Gain factor	Visual Quality
0.005	Excellent
0.01	Excellent
0.05	Excellent
0.09	Very Good
0.3	Very Good
0.5	Very Good
1	Above Average
1.5	Acceptable
1.7	Less than Acceptable
2	Weak

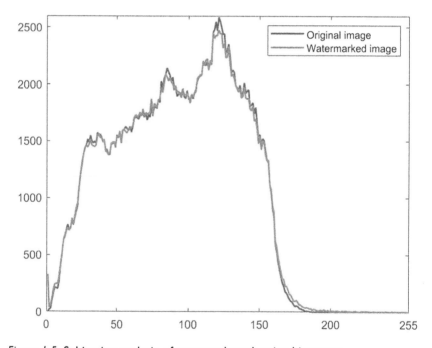

Figure 1.5 Subjective analysis of proposed work using histogram.

of marked image shows stiff peaks, providing statistical information. On the contrary, the histogram of cyphered image is uniform, which makes it robust against statistical attacks. Table 1.5 shows the impact of attacks on the NC score. The NC score against different considered attacks is usually greater than 0.9409, which shows high resistance. Finally, Figure 1.7 confirms high robustness of the proposed work in comparison to the existing work [13], [32], [33]. The result shows 99% more robustness in best case over the traditional schemes, indicating its potential for secure healthcare applications.

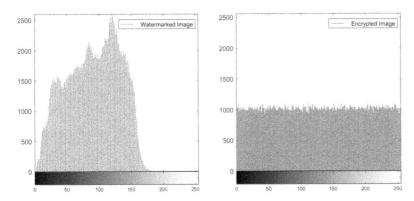

Figure 1.6 Security analysis of the encryption technique using histogram comparison.

Table 1.5 Robustness evaluation of the proposed work

Attack	NC
Salt and pepper noise (0.0001, 0.001, 0.01, 0.1)	0.9943, 0.9936, 0.9889, 0.9514
Gaussian noise (0.0001, 0.001, 0.01, 0.1)	0.9942, 0.9929, 0.9853, 0.9409
Rotation (1°, 45°, 90°)	0.9944, 0.9943, 0.9941
JPEG compression (10, 50, 90)	0.9932, 0.9937, 0.9948
Gaussian low-pass filter (0.4, 0.6)	0.9943, 0.9943
Speckle noise (0.001, 0.05, 0.5)	0.9942, 0.9903, 0.9685
Cropping [20 20 400 480]	0.9928
Median filter ([3 3], [2 2])	0.9946, 0.9945
Sharpening mask (0.01, 0.1)	0.9905, 0.9906
Histogram equalization	0.9847
Image scaling (0.5, 2)	0.9949, 0.9921

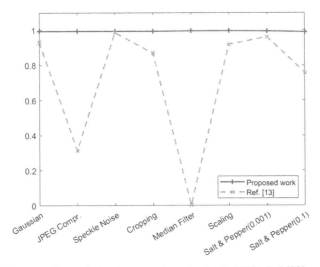

Figure 1.7 Comparative analysis of proposed work with Ref. [13], Ref. [32], and Ref. [33].

(Continued)

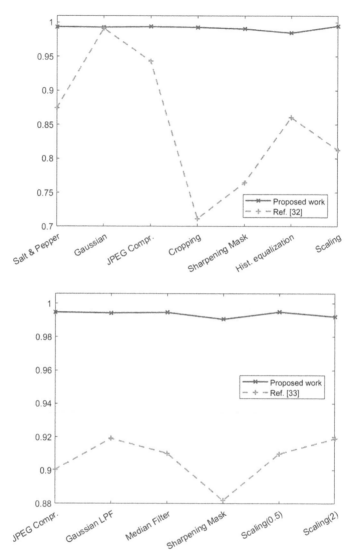

Figure 1.7 (Continued) Comparative analysis of proposed work with Ref. [13], Ref. [32], and Ref. [33].

1.6 CONCLUSION

In this chapter, a robust and secure watermarking technique using NSCT-based image fusion is proposed for healthcare applications. Initially, NSCT-based fusion is applied on CT scan and MRI images to generate a fused image, used as watermark. Further, the fused mark is concealed in the NSCT-HD-MSVD coefficients of the carrier image. The marked image is encrypted with updated stereo image encryption for better security. Also, average PSNR and

NC scores of 54.3941 dB and 0.9903 confirm high visual quality and ability to extract high quality mark. Better robustness is observed in comparison to traditional work with maximum improvement of 99%. The aforementioned outcomes indicate that the suggested solution is useful for the authenticity and copy-protection of the electronic version of COVID-19 patient data.

ACKNOWLEDGEMENTS

This work is supported by Thapar Institute of Engineering & Technology, Patiala, India, under SEED Research Grant, and research project order no. IES212111 - International Exchanges 2021 Round 2, dt. 28 February 2022, under Royal Society, UK.

REFERENCES

[1] S. Salehi, A. Abedi, S. Balakrishnan, and A. Gholamrezanezhad, "Coronavirus disease 2019 (COVID-19): A systematic review of imaging findings in 919 patients," *Am. J. Roentgenol.*, vol. 215, no. 1, pp. 87–93, 2020, doi: https://www.ajronline.org/doi/10.2214/AJR.20.23034

[2] "Digital Health Market Size & Growth Report, 2021–2028," 2021.

[3] A. Anand and A. K. Singh, "Watermarking techniques for medical data authentication: A survey," *Multimed. Tools Appl.*, vol. 80, no. 4, pp. 30165–30197, 2021, doi: 10.1007/s11042-020-08801-0

[4] A. K. Singh, B. Kumar, G. Singh, and A. Mohan, *Medical Image Watermarking: Techniques and Applications*. Springer International Publishing USA, 2017.

[5] E. E-D. Hemdan, "An efficient and robust watermarking approach based on single value decompression, multi-level DWT, and wavelet fusion with scrambled medical images," *Multimed. Tools Appl.*, vol. 80, no. 19, pp. 1–29, 2021, doi: 10.1007/s11042-020-09769-7

[6] A. Anand and A. K. Singh, "SDH: Secure data hiding in fused medical image for smart healthcare," *IEEE Trans. Comput. Soc. Syst.*, vol. 9, no. 4, pp. 1265–1273, 2022.

[7] A. Anand and A. K. Singh, "Health record security through multiple watermarking on fused medical images," *IEEE Trans. Comput. Soc. Syst.*, vol. 9, no. 6, pp. 1594–1603, 2021.

[8] J.-Y. Li and C.-Z. Zhang, "Blind watermarking scheme based on Schur decomposition and non-subsampled contourlet transform," *Multimed. Tools Appl.*, vol. 79, pp. 30007–30021, 2020, doi: 10.1007/s11042-020-09389-1

[9] B. Akhbari and S. Ghaemmaghami, "Watermarking of still images using multi-resolution singular value decomposition," in *Intelligent Signal Processing and Communication Systems, ISPACS*, 2005, pp. 325–328.

[10] S. Kumar and G. Bhatnagar, "SIE: An application to secure stereo images using encryption," in *Handbook of Multimedia Information Security: Techniques and Applications*, Springer, Cham, 2019, pp. 37–61.

[11] C. Kumar, A. K. Singh, and P. Kumar, "Improved wavelet-based image watermarking through SPIHT," *Multimed. Tools Appl.*, vol. 79, no. 15–16, pp. 11069–11082, 2020, doi: 10.1007/s11042-018-6177-0

[12] F. N. Thakkar and V. K. Srivastava, "A blind medical image watermarking: DWT-SVD based robust and secure approach for telemedicine applications," *Multimed. Tools Appl.*, vol. 76, no. 3, pp. 3669–3697, 2017, doi: 10.1007/s11042-016-3928-7

[13] H. S. Alshanbari, "Medical image watermarking for ownership & tamper detection," *Multimed. Tools Appl.*, vol. 80, pp. 16549–16564, 2021, doi: 10.1007/s11042-020-08814-9

[14] O. P. Singh and A. K. Singh, "Data hiding in encryption-compression domain," *Complex Intell. Syst.*, vol. 9, pp. 2759–2772, 2023, doi: 10.1007/s40747-021-00309-w

[15] A. Anand and A. K. Singh, "Cloud based secure watermarking using IWT-Schur-RSVD with fuzzy inference system for smart healthcare applications," *Sustain. Cities Soc.*, vol. 75, no. 1, pp. 103398, 2021, doi: 10.1016/j.scs.2021.103398

[16] A. Soualmi, A. Alti, and L. Laouamer, "Medical data protection using blind watermarking technique," in *Enabling AI Applications in Data Science*, Studies in., A.-E. Hassanien et al. (eds.), Springer Nature Switzerland, 2021, pp. 557–576.

[17] F. Yan, H. Huang, and X. Yu, "A multiwatermarking scheme for verifying medical image integrity and authenticity in the Internet of Medical Things," *IEEE Trans. Ind. Informatics*, vol. 18, no. 12, pp. 8885–8894, 2022, doi: 10.1109/TII.2022.3159863

[18] A. Anand and A. K. Singh, "Joint watermarking-encryption-ECC for patient record security in wavelet domain," *IEEE Multimed.*, vol. 27, no. 3, pp. 66–75, 2020, doi: 10.1109/MMUL.2020.2985973

[19] S. Thakur, A. K. Singh, B. Kumar, and S. P. Ghrera, "Improved DWT-SVD-based medical image watermarking through hamming code and chaotic encryption," in D. Dutta, H. Kar, C. Kumar, V. Bhadauria (eds.), *Advances in VLSI, Communication, and Signal Processing. Lecture Notes in Electrical Engineering*, vol. 587, Springer Singapore, 2020, pp. 897–905.

[20] T. Nguyen-Thanh and T. Le-Tien, "Robust blind medical image watermarking using quantization and SIFT with enhanced security," *J. Adv. Inf. Technol.*, vol. 13, no. 1, pp. 45–52, 2022, doi: 10.12720/jait.13.1.45-52

[21] A. Soualmi, A. Alti, and L. Laouamer, "A novel blind medical image watermarking scheme based on Schur triangulation and chaotic sequence," *Concurr. Comput. Pract. Exp.*, vol. 34, no. 1, pp. 1–21, 2022, doi: 10.1002/cpe.6480

[22] S. P. Vaidya, "Fingerprint-based robust medical image watermarking in hybrid transform," *Vis. Comput.*, vol. 39, no. 3, pp. 1–16, 2022, doi: 10.1007/s00371-022-02406-4

[23] J. Ravi and R. Narmadha, "Image fusion based on nonsubsampled shearlet transform," *Int. J. Eng. Adv. Technol.*, vol. 9, no. 3, pp. 4177–4180, 2020, doi: 10.35940/ijeat.C5452.029320

[24] Z. Zhao, "The nonsubsampled contourlet transform for image fusion," in *Proceedings of the 2007 International Conference on Wavelet Analysis and Pattern Recognition*, 2007, pp. 305–310.

[25] J. Liu et al., "An optimized image watermarking method based on HD and SVD in DWT domain," *IEEE Access*, vol. 7, pp. 80849–80860, 2019, doi: 10.1109/ACCESS.2019.2915596

[26] G. Bhatnagar, A. Saha, Q. M. J. Wu, and P. K. Atrey, "Analysis and extension of multiresolution singular value decomposition," *Inf. Sci. (Ny).*, vol. 277, pp. 247–262, 2014, doi: 10.1016/j.ins.2014.02.018

[27] V. P. S. Naidu, "Image fusion technique using multi-resolution singular value decomposition," *Def. Sci. J.*, vol. 61, no. 5, pp. 479–484, 2011, doi: 10.14429/dsj.61.705

[28] K. A. Johnson and J. A. Becker, *The Whole Brain Atlas*. http://www.med.harvard.edu/aanlib/home.html (accessed Jan. 17, 2021).

[29] "COVID-19 image data collection." https://github.com/ieee8023/covid-chestxray-dataset (accessed Aug. 12, 2021).

[30] A. Anand and A. K. Singh, "An improved DWT-SVD domain watermarking for medical information security," *Comput. Commun.*, vol. 152, pp. 72–80, 2020, doi: 10.1016/j.comcom.2020.01.038

[31] M. T. Elkandoz and W. Alexan, "Image encryption based on a combination of multiple chaotic maps," *Multimed. Tools Appl.*, vol. 81, no. 18, pp. 25497–25518, 2022, doi: 10.1007/s11042-022-12595-8

[32] A. Zear, A. K. Singh, and P. Kumar, "A proposed secure multiple watermarking technique based on DWT, DCT and SVD for application in medicine," *Multimed. Tools Appl.*, vol. 77, no. 5, pp. 4863–4882, 2018, doi: 10.1007/s11042-016-3862-8

[33] F. Kahlessenane, A. Khaldi, R. Kafi, and S. Euschi, "A robust blind medical image watermarking approach for telemedicine applications," *Cluster Comput.*, vol. 24, no. 3, pp. 2069–2082, 2021, doi: 10.1007/s10586-020-03215-x

Chapter 2

Image security using quantum hash functions

Arti Ranjan and M. Ravinder
IGDTUW, New Delhi, India

2.1 INTRODUCTION

Images serve as crucial data carriers since they are densely packed with digital information. This issue makes it more challenging to securely transmit or retain images than text data. Therefore, image security has emerged as a significant concern for researchers. Images can be shielded from dangers like eavesdropping and unauthorized copying and manipulation with security. Many picture encryption techniques have their roots in the traditional ideas of encryption. These plans render the original graphics incomprehensible. Due to the internet's recent rapid development, the database needed to store images like fingerprints gathered by Internet of Things (IOT) networks around the world is growing, necessitating more storage capacity and speed. In 1982, Feynman was the first to propose the idea of a quantum computer. Since then, advances in quantum computing have continued. Shor and Grover, respectively, proposed quantum factorization and quantum search algorithms in the 1990s [1–3].

Various studies on image processing have been conducted from classical image processing (CIP) to quantum image processing (QIP), which has aroused interest among academics due to the rapid growth of quantum calculations [3]. Because of the quantum properties of coherence, entanglement, superposition, and parallelism, quantum information processing (QIP) is a growing topic and a great tool for real-time processing. Additionally, QIP allows for the storage of n bits of classical information using just $\log_2 n$ quantum bits [3, 4]. Because of the quantum properties of coherence, entanglement, superposition, and parallelism, quantum information processing (QIP) is a growing topic and a great tool for real-time processing. Additionally, QIP allows for the storage of n bits of classical information using just $\log_2 n$ quantum bits [3, 4]. It is a much more effective tool for processing, storing, and transmitting photos thanks to its exponential storage capacity [4, 5]. However, QIP as a young technology has only recently begun, and research on it is in its early stages. In comparison to classical image encryption, quantum image encryption is still in its infancy. Important QIP concerns include quantum image storage and representation. Venegas-Andraca first mentioned the idea

DOI: 10.1201/9781003468974-2

of a qubit lattice in [5, 6]. The Real Ket expression, which requires n qubits to represent a $2n \times 2n$ image, was then proposed by Latorre in [6].

Due to its simplicity, the Flexible Representation of Quantum Image (FRQI) model presented by the authors in [7] has become a popular paradigm for quantum image expressions. To represent the color visuals, a few systems have been put forth [8–10]. In [11], the authors presented the Novel Enhanced Quantum Representation (NEQR) model, which differs significantly from the FRQI model in that it allows for the representation of more colors than the maximum of 2q. The primary issue with quantum computing is how challenging it is to accomplish many sophisticated processes.

We will examine the following scheme for this chapter. We start with a brief explanation of the classical cryptographic system and classical image security covering transposition and substitution systems. This is followed by the emergence of quantum computing and quantum image processing. Representation of image in quantum computing will be covered in detail. Image security in the post quantum world has been discussed in reference to hash function. Classical hash functions, cryptographic hash functions, and quantum hash function are introduced and discussed. Thereafter, we discuss quantum key distribution and its specific and most recent implementation under T22 protocol. We end the chapter with the conclusion and future trends.

We will discuss the following in this chapter:

1. An introduction to Classical Cryptographic Systems.
2. A gentle introduction representation of images in quantum computing.
3. Exposition on various Quantum Image Formats.
4. Discussion on Classical and Quantum Hash Functions.
5. An introduction to Quantum Key Distribution (QKD).
6. An explanation and discussion on T22 QKD protocol.

2.2 CLASSICAL CRYPTOGRAPHIC SYSTEM

Information security is more crucial for data storage and transmission today. Images are employed in many procedures since they may convey a lot more info. As a result, picture encryption and decryption algorithms play a crucial role in the security of image data. Digital images are employed in a variety of industries, including the medical, military, and private sectors. In a public setting, when unauthorized users and hostile attackers are present, safe communication between two parties is accomplished using cryptography. Encryption and decryption are two operations carried out at the transmitter and receiver ends, respectively, in cryptography. A simple multimedia file is joined with some additional data (known as the key) during the encryption process to create an unintelligible encoded format known as a "Cipher." Decryption is the opposite of encryption, where the cypher is decoded and transformed into the actual multimedia data using the same or a different key (additional data) [12].

Image security can be approached in multiple ways. One method for securing an image is image encryption, which involves recreating the original image as an encrypted or cypher image that is difficult for unauthorized users to distinguish from the original [13]. Only the owner, authorized users, and intended users can decrypt an encrypted image. Numerous image encryption techniques have been developed and made usable by researchers from around the world. These algorithms can be divided into three major categories: position-permutation-based algorithms based on transposition, value-substitution-based algorithms based on transformation, and position-substitution-based strategies based on transposition [14].

A quintuple (K, P, C, E, D) represents a symmetric-key crypt-system, where,

K = finite set of possible keys, which must be shared with legitimate users.
P = finite set of possible plaintexts,
C = finite set of possible ciphertexts,
E and D = encryption algorithm and decryption algorithm.

The simplest case is two people wishing to interact with one another via an unsafe route. Typically, these people are referred to as Alice and Bob. Due to the channel's vulnerability, an eavesdropper under the name of Eve may intercept all messages sent over it [15]. By agreeing on a secret key k via another secure communication channel, Alice and Bob can utilize a crypt-system to keep their information private even in the presence of the eavesdropper [16].

Alice computes the ciphertext $c = e_k(m)$ using the key k and sends it to Bob across the insecure channel in order to send her secret message m.

Bob can use the decryption technique and uses $d_k(c) = d_k, e_k(m) = m$ to decrypt the ciphertext because he also has access to the key k. But there is no simple method to get the original message m because Eve wiretaps the ciphertext c but is unaware of the key k.

The symmetric-key crypt-system that achieves perfect secrecy is the one-time pad. Let us assume that $P = C = K = \{0, 1\}^n$, $e_k(m) = m \otimes k$ and $d_k(c) = c \otimes k$, where $\otimes$ is a bitwise XOR operation [17].

2.2.1 Transposition-based algorithm

Rearranging the components of the simple image is known as transposition. This element rearrangement must be done bit-level, pixel-by-pixel, and/or block-by-block. While the permutation of pixels and blocks results in higher level security, the permutation of bits results in a reduction in perceptual information. In the bit permutation method, each pixel's bits are permuted using permutation keys with an 8-bit key length. The pixel permutation involves taking a collection of 8 pixels and permuting them using a key of the same size. Block, bit, and pixel permutations are employed, respectively, in this inquiry [18].

2.2.2 Value-substitution-based algorithm

A technique known as a value-substitution-based algorithm converts each pixel's value to a different value. Applying a sophisticated computational algorithm to the pixel results in the computation of its new value. Digital Signatures, Lossless Image Compression and Encryption using SCAN, Image Cryptosystems, Color Image Encryption using Double Random Phase Encoding, Image Encryption using Block-Based Transformation Algorithmic function, etc., are examples of value-transformation-based methods [19].

2.2.3 Position-substitution-based algorithm

Position permutation and value transformation are both used in this method. In this method, pixels are first rearranged before their values are substituted using a key generator. A fascinating area of research is the integration of signal and image processing with encryption. Combining cryptography and image processing is what is referred to as picture encryption. Methods for encrypted images are used to implement privacy, identity verification, and content access control [20].

2.3 QUANTUM COMPUTING

A quantum computer is a device that uses quantum bits or qubits instead of bits as with classical computers. The qubits are realized physically in multiple ways such as using the quantum state of fundamental particles such as electrons or light particles (photons). These particles have the quantum state that exhibits the properties of like spin that can be used to define a two-state quantum system with one and zero, very much in the same way as in classical computers. Thus, qubits are the quantum analogue of the classical bits. However, quantum computing differs significantly from conventional computing on a basic level [21].

Quantum properties such as the Entanglement and Superposition play a fundamental role in the quantum computer. Under Superposition, two states can coexist at the same time for a quantum system [22]. In superposition, a linear combination of basis states with normalized coefficients exists, which is a probability distribution of the pure states. The superposition is an inherent property of a quantum system [23].

Under Entanglement, if two qubits are under entanglement, then the two qubits have no individual description of state. They can't be described individually. In fact, measuring one qubit will give the state of the other one as well.

The first stage of the speed increase offered by quantum computers is driven by the two quantum effects of entanglement and superposition [24].

A major problem with quantum computers is that a limited number of qubits are currently used in small-scale quantum computers. Quantum computers have to scale up to compete with traditional systems. Although the situation has significantly improved over the past few decades, solving other technological problems like quantum error correction is still necessary to further the development of quantum computers [25]. Because quantum information cannot be duplicated and because subsystems cannot function independently, scaling quantum computer chips is inherently challenging. As a result, global design trade-offs are inevitable. Superconducting qubits, however, are beginning to emerge as commercially viable in quantum computers and increasingly demonstrate the capacity to overcome these challenges [26].

2.3.1 Quantum image processing

A subfield of research in quantum information and quantum computing is quantum image processing (QIP). It investigates how to use the advantages of quantum mechanics to store images in a quantum computer and then perform various image operations depending on that image format. QIP has inherent advantages over traditional image processing because it uses quantum parallel computing, which is derived from quantum state superposition and entanglement.

Quantum image processing is a rapidly emerging field that uses the principles of quantum mechanics to process digital images. It has been used to solve problems such as facial recognition and object detection. Using the principles of quantum computing, it is capable of analyzing large amounts of data more quickly and accurately than traditional methods.

Quantum image processing works by using qubits, which are particles with two states—on or off—to represent information. This allows for complex calculations to be done in a small number of steps. It can also be used to analyze large datasets in parallel, reducing the amount of time needed for analysis. By harnessing the power of superposition, quantum computing can extract more information from an image than traditional methods alone [27].

The main advantage of quantum image processing is its ability to handle large datasets quickly and accurately. It can also provide better accuracy when dealing with noisy data sets due to its improved error correction capabilities.

Additionally, quantum computing is not limited by memory or computational constraints as traditional methods are, allowing it to tackle computation-intensive tasks such as feature extraction from images more efficiently [28].

In addition to its advantages in speed and accuracy, quantum image processing has some unique capabilities not available with standard methods.

For example, it can perform non-linear operations on images not possible with traditional algorithms such as applying high-pass filters or edge detection operations at a single step. Furthermore, comparing two images side by side using quantum computing can provide insights into their similarities and differences that would otherwise be difficult or impossible to detect through conventional means [29].

The potential applications for quantum image processing are wide-ranging; from medical-imaging technologies to computer vision systems for autonomous vehicles, quantum computing could revolutionize how we interact with digital imagery and enable new possibilities for machine learning applications in various fields. As research continues into this burgeoning field, the future holds great promise for those interested in exploiting the power of quantum computing for their own projects or businesses [30].

Quantum image processing can generally be classified into two main categories: quantum-enhanced image processing and quantum computing-assisted image processing. Quantum-enhanced image processing techniques make use of the principles of quantum mechanics to improve the performance of existing digital imaging techniques. These techniques typically involve applying an algorithm to process an image using a quantum computer.

The idea is to exploit the advantages offered by quantum computing such as increased speed and precision in computations as well as enhanced security due to entanglement or other properties of superposition. Examples include finding patterns, identifying objects in images, or analyzing data from sensors [31].

On the other hand, quantum computing-assisted image processing relies on developing new algorithms specifically tailored for use on a quantum computer platform. Typically, these algorithms combine aspects from traditional digital imaging techniques such as filtering and histogram preparation with the capabilities offered by a quantum computer system such as parallelism or entanglement.

Examples include neural networks implemented using qubits, Grover's algorithm for searching databases efficiently, or HHL algorithm for solving linear systems quickly and accurately.

Finally, there has been increasing interest in combining both approaches into hybrid frameworks that make use of both classical and quantum components simultaneously for tackling different tasks within an imaging pipeline more efficiently than either could do independently. Examples include utilizing a classical component for inputting data from sensors while employing a quantum component to perform certain tasks faster than what would be possible with classical methods alone. Additionally, such hybrid approaches allow us to take advantage of both types of resources found within modern computing systems, namely high performance CPUs and GPUs alongside emerging technologies such as neuromorphic chips that can provide specialized hardware acceleration capabilities for certain processes like neural networks or machine learning algorithms.

We are currently witnessing a rapid development in the field of quantum image processing with many exciting opportunities arising from combining classical digital imaging techniques with those enabled by today's emerging technologies like superconducting qubits, analog signal processors, and neuromorphic microchips. As this technology matures further, it will open up new pathways towards more efficient solutions in terms of speed accuracy and security when tackling complex problems involving large amounts/types of data such as those encountered in fields like medical imaging or facial recognition, among others [32].

2.4 REPRESENTATION OF IMAGES IN QUANTUM COMPUTING

The fundamental difference between classical and quantum computers necessitates different formats for representation of images on a quantum computer. There are multiple such formats, namely Flexible Representation of Quantum Images (FRQI) [7], Real Ket image format [6], and Qubit Lattice format [33].

2.4.1 Flexible Representation of Quantum Images (FRQI)

Le et al. [7] proposed a more sophisticated qubit utilizing the lattice's quantum state superposition. While adding a second qubit to represent each pixel's position in space, the approach continues to convert each pixel's greyscale value to amplitude. The entire image then enters a significant quantum superposition state. Each image is a combination of pixel, and each pixel is a qubit state in superposition, as shown in the Equations 2.1 and 2.2.

$$|pixel_i\rangle = \cos\theta_i|0\rangle + \sin\theta_i|1\rangle$$
$$\theta_i \in [0, \pi/2], i = 0, 1, \ldots, 2^{2n} - 1 \tag{2.1}$$

$$|image\rangle = \frac{1}{2^n}\sum_{i=0}^{2^{2n}-1}(\cos\theta_i|0\rangle + \sin\theta_i|1\rangle) \otimes |i\rangle \tag{2.2}$$

i = pixels encoding in terms of qubit state

As an example, a 2 × 2 image can be represented as in Table. 2.1 [34].

Table 2.1 FRQI image representation

$\theta_0, |00\rangle$	$\theta_1, |01\rangle$
$\theta_2, |10\rangle$	$\theta_3, |11\rangle$

Flexible Representation of Quantum Images (FRQI) is a method for representing and manipulating quantum images, which are images encoded in a quantum state rather than classical bits. Quantum images have the potential to offer advantages in certain applications, such as in secure communication, where they can be used to transmit information in a way that is resistant to interception and tampering.

The FRQI method represents quantum images as a combination of quantum states and classical information. This allows for a flexible representation that can be easily manipulated and processed, while still retaining the benefits of quantum information. The method has been applied in various contexts, including in the analysis of quantum noise and the compression of quantum images.

Overall, the development of methods for representing and manipulating quantum images is an active area of research, with the goal of finding ways to harness the unique properties of quantum information for practical applications.

2.4.2 Real Ket image format

This format was proposed by Latorre [35]. In this image format, the coordinates of the pixel and the intensity of the pixels are separated. As a first step, the given image is divided into four quadrants of equal size. In the next step, each quadrant is divided into four quadrants again. This process is continued until each quadrant contains only one pixel. Now a pair of qubits is used to represent the pixel coordinate in the grid square, and an additional qubit describes the intensity as its amplitude 2.1 [36].

$$\left|\psi_{2^l \times 2^l}\right\rangle = \sum_{i_i=1}^{4} C_{i_1}\left|i_1\right\rangle,$$

$$\text{such that} \sum_{i_i=1}^{4} \left|C_{i_1}\right|^2 = 1$$

(2.3)

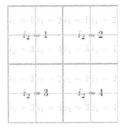

Figure 2.1 A 2 × 2 Real Ket image encoding.

2.4.3 Qubit lattice format

A qubit lattice is a way of organizing qubits (quantum bits) in a quantum computer. In a qubit lattice, qubits are arranged in a grid or lattice structure, with each qubit connected to its neighbors in the lattice [33].

There are several different ways that qubit lattices can be represented, depending on the specific needs and goals of the quantum computing system. One common way to represent a qubit lattice is as a graph, where the qubits are represented as vertices and the connections between qubits are represented as edges. This can be done using a variety of graph formats, such as adjacency matrices or adjacency lists.

Other methods for representing qubit lattices include using arrays or matrices to represent the positions and connections of the qubits, or using specialized file formats or data structures specifically designed for storing and manipulating qubit lattices.

2.5 DATA SECURITY IN POST QUANTUM CRYPTOGRAPHY

Post quantum data security is the study and development of technologies to protect data in the event that quantum computing becomes widespread. With advancements in technology, it is becoming more likely that quantum computers will become available and powerful enough to break current encryption algorithms. This means that the confidentiality of information held by organizations and individuals is at risk, as any sensitive data stored using traditional methods could be exposed [37].

The main challenge for post quantum data security lies in developing new types of cryptography that can resist being broken by a quantum computer. This requires crypto-systems tailored to take advantage of the unique properties of quantum mechanics, such as entanglement and superposition. One type of system being studied is called Quantum Key Distribution (QKD). QKD uses single photons to generate cryptographic keys between two parties. These keys are highly secure since any attempt to intercept them causes detectable changes in their state, meaning that any malicious attempts to access them can be detected easily [38].

Another form of post-quantum cryptography being investigated is lattice-based cryptography, which leverages various mathematical structures such as lattices and error correcting codes [39]. This form of cryptography provides a high level of security while also requiring less computation power than other forms such as elliptic curve cryptography (ECC), making it suitable for low-power devices such as smartphones or IoT devices [40] as in [41].

In addition to these solutions, various post quantum algorithms are being developed that use different techniques like multivariate polynomials [42], supersingular elliptic curve Isogenies (SECI) [43], or hash-based signatures (HBS) [44]. By applying these techniques with specific parameters, greater levels of security can be achieved compared to traditional approaches used

Algorithm	Problem Addressed	Block Size	Key Size	Rounds	Methodology	Output	Inference
PRINCE	Throughput and Efficiency in hardware	64	128	12	Implemented in FPGA-Vertex 6, Vertex 4	Throughput=4.18Gbps,Efficiency= 8.681 Mbps/Slice	Better than ICEBERG and SEA
HIGHT	Efficiency in software or Hardware	64	128	32	Implemented in FPGA, Altera Quartus II, Version 13	Transfer rate = 157 Mbps, Delay=9.8ns, F=11.35 MHZ	Hardware is better than software
AES	Area and throughput in Hardware	128	128	10	Parallelism for third Stage Mix column	Throughput=25.54,Area=30% reduced	Pipelined Concept-Reduced the Area and increase the Speed
SIMON	Number of Gates in Hardware	32,48, 64,96, 128	Vari able	32,36, 42,44, 52,54	Implemented In FPGA	32 slices in SPARTAN 3 and 6 FPGA	Better than X-TEA and Humming bird
BLOWFISH	Throughput in Hardware	64	32-448	16	Implemented in Spartan 3E XC35-500E-5FG 320	Throughput=6.3 Gbps, F=295.63 MHZ	Better than AES and DES
ECC-RSD	Processing speed	NA	NPK C	NA	RSD, Pipeline KATATUSUBE OFFMAN	LUT=34612, F=160MHZ Time= 2.26 ms	Pipelined architecture increase the Speed
ECC	Health care Monitoring	NA	NPK C	NA	Light weight Scheme	Light weight ECC suitable for IoT	Less RAM size
HUMMING BIRD	Low power and Low Memory size	16	256	NA	Different S-box method	Less power and Area	Asynchronous better than Synchronous Design
PRESENT	Number of Gates in Hardware	64	128	32	GRP-COMPRESSED	Reduced from 3200 to 2980 GE	Better than CLEFIA and ICEBERG

Figure 2.2 Comparison of several image security algorithms, credit D. J. Rani et. al. [56].

today such as RSA or ECC. As the need for stronger encryption increases due to the potential threat posed by quantum computers, research into post quantum data security will become ever more important to ensure confidential information remains safe from malicious attackers.

Companies and organizations should consider investing in research into this field to benefit from the increased levels of protection offered by these solutions when they become available. A trillion-item list may be searched through by a quantum computer in approximately one second. The identical task would take a traditional computer about a week to complete. Data privacy is seriously impacted by quantum computers' ability to consider so many possibilities quickly; even the most sophisticated encryption techniques could soon be broken by brute force attacks.

Since quantum technologies are developing quickly, privacy leaders must make responding to this a top priority. Organizations need to re-evaluate their privacy strategies, develop flexibility so they can adjust to a changing market, and inform everyone about the potential of quantum technology [45].

2.6 IMAGE SECURITY IN POST QUANTUM CRYPTOGRAPHY

Encryption is seen as the practice of hiding information to render it unintelligible to those lacking specialized knowledge as a practical application of the discipline of cryptography. This is frequently done for secret discussions

Table 2.2 Qubit pairings

Pair 1	Pair 2	Label
(q_0, q_1)	(q_0, q_1)	A
(q_0, q_1)	(q_0, q_1)	B
(q_0, q_1)	(q_0, q_1)	C

and secrecy. Information hiding focuses on hiding the presence of messages, whereas cryptography protects the substance of messages. Using techniques like steganography and watermarking to conceal data seems more secure because attackers are less likely to spot them. The high need for the quantity of information that may be concealed inside a cover image without causing distortions to its visible imperceptibility, however, is one of its key limitations. Despite their similarities, steganography and watermarking serve different goals and/or have different applications, and they have different needs for those purposes.

The Figure 2.2 summarizes the application of several image security algorithms in post quantum scenario [56].

2.7 CLASSICAL HASH FUNCTIONS

A classical hash function is a type of cryptographic function used for data encryption and authentication. It is a mathematical algorithm that takes an input of any arbitrary length and produces a fixed-length output. The output is known as the hash value, which is unique for any given input. A traditional hash function generally has three main properties: it must be fast to compute, it must be one-way (i.e., it should not be possible to derive the original message from the computed hash), and it should produce different output values for different inputs. The most common type of classical hashing functions are Message Digest algorithms (MD). MD take messages of arbitrary length and generate a fixed-length output known as a digest or a checksum. The resulting digest can then be used to verify the integrity of the initial message, since if any change is made to the message, then its digest will no longer match that originally provided by a secure source. Examples of popular Message Digest algorithms include MD5 (Message Digest 5) and SHA (Secure Hash Algorithm) [46].

Another type of classical hashing functions is based on block cipher operations, such as DES or AES. Block ciphers require an input that consists of a sequence of blocks with identical size, so these types of algorithms may not always provide the best performance when dealing with messages that have variable lengths. Furthermore, block ciphers may require more storage space due to their larger input sizes when compared to other hashing functions such as MD or cyclic redundancy check (CRC) algorithms [47].

The security provided by classical hash functions depends on various factors including their ability to resist malicious attacks and collisions. Collisions occur when two different messages have the same computed hash value; this can lead to potential security issues since an attacker could use this information to substitute another malicious message for the original without being detected by the recipient. To help mitigate this problem, some hashing functions utilize salt values, which help prevent two different messages from having similar outputs even if they share some common characters [48].

In addition, most classical hashing functions also make use of iterative processes to increase their resistance towards cryptanalysis—which simply involve analyzing a cryptographic system to find weaknesses or vulnerabilities within its design structure. By increasing its computational complexity through iterations, an attacker would need to spend significantly more time and resources to break into the cryptographic system successfully, thereby making it much harder to gain access without authorization or permission from legitimate users or sources such as administrators or owners [49].

Mathematically, a hash function can be defined as a function that converts input data of any length into output encrypted text of a specific length. A message digest, hash value, hash code, or just a hash are all terms used to describe this result. A hash function, in more formal terms, is a mathematical function $H: D \otimes R$ where $D = 0, 1$ and $R = 0, 1^n$ for some $n > = 1$, and it transforms a numerical input value m of any length into a compacted numerical output h of a specific length. Therefore, $h = H(m)$.

2.7.1 Cryptographic hash function

We can define a cryptographic hash function as a hash function that satisfies additional conditions to be utilized for cryptographic purposes. These are fundamental building blocks with many applications. Their primary areas of use include certificate-based digital signatures, authentications, password storage security, and digital signatures in general. Cryptographic hash functions can generally be classified as Manipulation Detection Code (MDC) or Message Authentication Code (MAC) with a single parameter—an input message—and keyed hash functions with two distinct inputs—an input message and a secret key—are the two main categories for cryptographic hash functions. Hash functions often refer to unkeyed hash functions.

2.8 QUANTUM HASH FUNCTIONS

A quantum hash function is a cryptographic technique used to protect data against malicious tampering. It utilizes properties of quantum computing and an algorithm designed to ensure that the integrity of the data is maintained even if an attacker attempts to modify it.

The most important property of a quantum hash function is its ability to create unique "fingerprints" for each piece of data. These fingerprints are created by applying a mathematical algorithm based on the principles of quantum physics to the data being hashed. This process creates a unique hash value that serves as a signature for the original piece of data, allowing its integrity to be verified even if it is edited or modified. In this way, quantum hash functions can be used to detect changes to sensitive information that might otherwise go undetected by other security measures [50].

In addition to providing strong protection against malicious tampering with data, quantum hashing also offers improved performance over traditional methods. The calculations involved in creating the fingerprint are incredibly fast and efficient, allowing for shorter processing times and higher throughput rates than conventional hashing algorithms. This makes them ideal for applications where time-sensitive decisions are required or where large volumes of data need to be processed quickly and securely.

Quantum hashing also offers enhanced scalability compared with other approaches due to its reliance on mathematical algorithms rather than hardware or physical components like memory chips. This allows it to easily keep up with high-volume environments where large amounts of data must be protected quickly without any noticeable delay or interruption in service delivery.

Finally, one significant advantage provided by quantum hashes is their resistance against brute force attacks—attempts by hackers or malicious code writers to guess their respective keys through trial and error—that would otherwise render traditional hashes vulnerable over time. By relying on complex mathematical equations that cannot be solved through brute force techniques, quantum hashing algorithms offer superior protection against these types of attacks, making them an attractive choice for protecting valuable digital assets and sensitive information from unauthorized access and manipulation.

Mathematically, quantum hash functions are functions that can act as a hash function for privacy amplification of the quantum key distribution process. Quantum hash function (QHF) can also be used for multiple other purposes such as pseudo random number generation, image encryptions, etc. There are various ways of generating quantum hash functions. One of the principal ways of generating QHF is using Quantum Walk (QW).

2.8.1 Generation of QHF

Generation of QHF can achieved by using Quantum Walk. QW can be slightly altered to create QHF. The generation model uses two quantum systems, that is, first, the Walker (W) and second, the Coin (C). If H_t is a vector in the Hilbert space, then if it is taken as $H_t = H_p \otimes H_c$, with the subscripts p and c standing for the W and the C, then Ht will denote the combined state of the W and C quantum system [51].

Through the use of a conditional shift operator, the coin state conditions in the walk's motion can be given as:

$$\hat{S} = \sum_{x} |x+1,0\rangle\langle x,0| + |x-1,1\rangle|x,1\rangle \tag{2.4}$$

Where the sum over all conceivable places is represented by the summation symbol. Repeating the global unitary operator allows for the dynamical evolution of the combined system.

$$\hat{U} = \hat{S}\left(\hat{I} \otimes \hat{C}\right) \tag{2.5}$$

Where C = *coin* operator used on the coin state and i = identity operator. As a result, the final state of the combined system after t steps is represented as:

$$|\psi_t\rangle = \hat{U}^t|\psi_t\rangle = \sum_{x}\sum_{v} \lambda_{x,v}|x,v\rangle \tag{2.6}$$

and after t steps, the probability of finding the W at position X is,

$$P(x,t) = \sum_{v=0,1} \left|\langle x,v|\hat{U}^t\|\psi\rangle\right|^2 \tag{2.7}$$

Where $\psi_{initial}$ initial state combined W-C system.

This is a discrete state quantum system, and the original coin state and step number are used to determine the probability distribution that results. Imagine that each step's coin operator is dependent on a binary values string or the message, and that a QHF is afterwards built. A binary text, or message, serves as the constructed QHF's input, and the probability distribution that results serves as the output hash value. The built QHF is keyed since the coin state serves as the control factors. The nth step of the walk is controlled by the nth bit of the message.

Two coin operators will be as in Figure 2.3:

1. Choose a quantum hash function: There are several different quantum hash functions that have been proposed and implemented, such as Sha-256 and Sha-3. The choice of quantum hash function will depend on the specific security requirements and constraints of the system in which it is being used.

$$\hat{C}_0 = \frac{1}{2} \begin{pmatrix} -1 & 1 & 1 & 1 \\ 1 & -1 & 1 & 1 \\ 1 & 1 & -1 & 1 \\ 1 & 1 & 1 & -1 \end{pmatrix},$$

$$\hat{C}_1 = \frac{1}{2} \begin{pmatrix} 1 & 1 & 1 & 1 \\ 1 & -1 & -1 & 1 \\ -1 & 1 & -1 & 1 \\ -1 & -1 & 1 & 1 \end{pmatrix}.$$

Figure 2.3 Coin operators $\hat{C}_0, \hat{C}_1$.

2. Prepare the input data: The input data to be hashed can be any type of data, such as a message, a file, or a password. The input data should be prepared in a format compatible with the chosen quantum hash function.

3. Initialize the quantum hash function: Some quantum hash functions require the use of additional data, such as a secret key or a seed value, to initialize the hash function. This data should be prepared and provided to the quantum hash function as needed.

4. Run the quantum hash function: The quantum hash function is then run on the input data using a quantum algorithm to perform the hashing process. This will produce a fixed-size output, known as the hash value or digest.

5. Output the hash value: The hash value is then output and can be used for a variety of purposes, such as verifying the integrity of data, authenticating messages, or storing passwords.

Main application of the QHF is in connection with Quantum Key Distribution (QKD). We will have a quick discussion of QKD so as to appreciate the importance of QHF.

2.9 QUANTUM KEY DISTRIBUTION

A perfect secure key between two communicating parties is what QKD aims to achieve. The QKD process typically consists of three steps: privacy amplification, error reconciliation, and raw key filtering. Using universal hash functions to implement the privacy amplification process is a crucial component of QKD. These hash functions are secure in terms of computation because they are often built based on mathematical complexity. Numerous quantum cryptographic protocol are guaranteed to be unconditionally secure by the underlying principles of quantum mechanics, which prompts us to think about the security as in terms of quantum information with the goal of finding a more reliable method to the privacy amplification process [52].

It is clarified that QKD is a method used only for producing and distributing a "key." QKD is not used to send or receive the message; however, the key is used to encrypt the message and send it or receive it over a channel.

2.9.1 Types of QKD

The whole process of quantum key distribution is carried out using qubits. Mostly photons are used as qubits, and standard protocols have been discovered to implement QKD. This QKD class of protocols can be divided into following categories [53]:

1. Preparation and Measurement-based protocols,
2. Entanglement-based protocols.

BB84 protocol and E91 protocols are the most famous implementations of QKD, where the first corresponds to the Preparation and Measurement-based category and the second is based on Entanglement. T22 is the most recent protocol based on Entanglement proposed in 2022.

As BB84 protocol has been widely discussed in the literature and in order to appreciate and understand the QKD using Entanglement, we shall discuss the T22 protocol in the next section [54].

2.10 T22 PROTOCOL

T22 is a quantum-resistant key exchange algorithm designed to protect data from quantum computing attacks. It is based on post-quantum cryptography and is believed to be secure against quantum computing attacks. It allows two parties to securely exchange a secret key over an unsecured channel without the risk of an eavesdropper intercepting it [54].

T22 has a close relationship with Quantum Key Distribution (QKD); the T22 protocol can be used to implement QKD systems, as it provides a secure way to generate and exchange keys without the use of a trusted third party. Additionally, T22 can be used to securely transmit messages between two parties using the generated secret key.

2.10.1 Two qubit entangled states

A general two-qubit state can be written as the Eq. 2.8.

$$|\psi\rangle = c_{00}|00\rangle + c_{01}|01\rangle + c_{10}|10\rangle + c_{11}|11\rangle \tag{2.8}$$

A two-qubit state will be an entangled state if the state cannot be represented as a product of states of the two individual qubits, as in the state in Eq. 2.9.

$$|\psi\rangle = \frac{1}{2}\left[|00\rangle + |01\rangle + |10\rangle - |11\rangle\right] \tag{2.9}$$

Another example of an entangled state is in Eq. 2.10,

$$|\psi\rangle = \frac{1}{\sqrt{(2)}}\left[|00\rangle + |11\rangle\right] \tag{2.10}$$

2.10.2 Bell states

The bell state is a maximally entangled state, meaning that the two qubits are in a state of perfect entanglement. This means that if one qubit is measured to be 0, then the other qubit will also be 0, and vice versa. This property makes the bell state useful for quantum computing tasks such as teleportation and quantum computing algorithms. For a system of two qubits, different bell states are shown in the Eqs. 2.11, 2.12, 2.13, and 2.14.

$$|\Phi_+\rangle = \frac{1}{\sqrt{(2)}}\left[|00\rangle + |11\rangle\right] \tag{2.11}$$

$$|\Phi_-\rangle = \frac{1}{\sqrt{(2)}}\left[|00\rangle + |11\rangle\right] \tag{2.12}$$

$$|\Psi_+\rangle = \frac{1}{\sqrt{(2)}}\left[|01\rangle + |10\rangle\right] \tag{2.13}$$

$$|\Psi_-\rangle = \frac{1}{\sqrt{(2)}}\left[|01\rangle + |10\rangle\right] \tag{2.14}$$

2.10.3 T22 methodology

T22 protocol utilizes the Bell states as described in the section above. It is inspired by the approach given by Song and Chen [55].

Since the Bell state when measured can be used to decisively distinguish between the Bell states in Eq. 2.11, 2.12, 2.13, and 2.14, the encoding is based on this property. The steps of the T22 protocols are as follows:

1. Let Alice and Bob both have 4 qubits each. They need to choose between pairings of qubits and groupings of '00', '01', '10', and '11' for key transfer.

Table 2.3 Pairing and grouping

Pair 1	Pair 2	Grouping
Φ_+	Φ_-	00
Φ_-	Φ_+	01
Ψ_+	Ψ_-	10
Ψ_-	Ψ_+	11

Table 2.4 Pairing/grouping with measurement

Step	Circuit 1	Circuit 2	Circuit 3	Circuit 4	Circuit 5	Circuit 6	Circuit 7
Alice's pairing	A	B	C	A	B	C	A
Alice's grouping	11	10	01	00	11	10	01
Bob's pairing	B	B	C	A	B	C	A
Bob's grouping	11	10	01	00	00	10	01
Eve detection		Verified				Verified	
Final key			01	00			01

2. Possible pairings of qubits can be as per Table 2.2.
3. Alice and Bob are required to choose groupings on the qubits based on what string of '0' or '1' they want to send/receive as a part of the key. This is denoted in Table 2.3.
4. Alice is going to choose the Bell states for encryption based on Table 2.3 randomly.
5. Bob also chooses his own grouping based on Table 2.3 randomly.
6. If Alice and Bob both happen to choose the same pairing and same grouping, then both will measure the same code; otherwise, Bob will measure '00'. All possible pairings/groupings and their corresponding measurement by Bob is listed in Table 2.4.
7. The circuits of different pairing are set up as per Bell state in Table 2.5.

2.10.4 Probability of getting the correct measurement

As per the analysis given by the inventor of T22 [54] in Eq. 2.10.4.

$$P_{correct} = P_{Alice's-pairing} P_{Alice's-grouping} P_{Bob-same-pairing} P_{Bob-same-grouping} \qquad (2.15)$$

Table 2.5 Bell state circuits

State	Circuit
Φ_+	q_0 —[H]—•— q_1 —————⊕—
Φ_-	0 —[X]—[H]—•— 1 —————————⊕—
Ψ_+	q_0 —[H]—•— q_1 —[X]—⊕—
Ψ_-	q_0 —[H]—[Z]—•— q_1 —[X]—[Z]—⊕—

2.11 CONCLUSION

In this chapter we have discussed the problem of image security in the post quantum world. We began with the basics of classical image security and its main terms and the asymmetric key encryption. A comparison of a few well known asymmetric key algorithms was tabulated.

To have a complete picture of the bouquet of techniques/algorithms available in the post quantum cryptography era, we first introduced the basics of theory and key terminology of the quantum computing and its various models. Qubits, single-qubit gates, two-qubit gates, multi-qubit gates, and measurement basis were introduced. These were required to formally introduce the crux of this chapter that is the QKD and BB84 protocol. Thereafter, several new upcoming and recently introduced methods such as Lattice-based cryptography, Multivariate cryptography, Hash-based cryptography, Code-based cryptography, Supersingular elliptic curve isogeny cryptography, and Symmetric key quantum resistance were discussed, along with their specific importance and useability for image data. We have restricted our discussion to qualitative only, as these topics each deserve a chapter of their own.

After going through a plethora of algorithms and techniques for post quantum cryptography, it is certain we will have a rich theory of new cryptography protocols, as well as dexterous implementation of them. As we move toward a more connected world with more connected devices, image and multimedia data will only increase—and so will be the demand for security and privacy of such data. We are hopeful the scientific community can provide a sufficiently safe alternative until the quantum computer progresses to a level that will break existing standard cryptography protocols.

REFERENCES

1. S. Gill, A. Kumar, and H. Singh, et al. "Quantum computing: A taxonomy, systematic review and future directions," *Softw: Pract Exper*. vol. 52, no. 1, pp. 66–114, 2022.
2. R. Arti, A. K. Arya, and M. Ravinder, "Quantum techniques for image processing," *2nd International Conference on Advances in Computing, Communication Control and Networking (ICACCCN)*, IEEE.
3. L. Wang, "QRCI: A new quantum representation model of color digital images," *Opt. Commun*, vol. 438, pp. 147–158, 2019.
4. F. Yan, A. Iliyasu, and S. Venegas-Andraca, *Quantum Image Processing*. Berlin, Germany: Springer.
5. R. Abdelfatah, "Secure image transmission using chaotic-enhanced elliptic curve cryptography," *IEEE Access*, vol. 8, pp. 3875–3890, 2020.
6. R.-G. Zhou and D.-Q. Liu, "Quantum image edge extraction based on improved sobel operator," *Int. J. Theor. Phys*, vol. 58, no. 9, pp. 2969–2985, 2019.
7. P. Le, F. Dong, and K. Hirota, "A flexible representation of quantum images for polynomial preparation, image compression, and processing operations," *Quantum Inf. Process*, vol. 10, no. 1, pp. 63–84, 2011.
8. A. El-Latif, B. Abd-El-Atty, and M. Talha, "Robust encryption of quantum medical images," *IEEE Access*, vol. 6, pp. 1073–1081, 2017.
9. X. Liu, D. Xiao, W. Huang, and C. Liu, "Quantum block image encryption based on Arnold transform and sine chaotification model," *IEEE Access*, vol. 7, pp. 57188–57199, 2019.
10. M. Khan and A. Rasheed, "Permutation-based special linear transforms with application in quantum image encryption algorithm," *Quantum Inf. Process*, vol. 18, no. 10, pp. 1–21, 2019.
11. Y. Zhang, K. Lu, Y. Gao, and M. Wang, "NEQR: A novel enhanced quantum representation of digital images," *Quantum Inf. Process*, vol. 12, pp. 2833–2860, 2013.
12. V. Rajasekar, J. Premalatha, R. K. Dhanaraj, and O. Geman, "Introduction to classical cryptography," *Quantum Blockchain: An Emerging Cryptographic Paradigm*, pp. 1–29, 2022.
13. K. N. Singh and A. K. Singh, "Towards integrating image encryption with compression: A survey," *ACM Transactions on Multimedia Computing, Communications, and Applications (TOMM)*, vol. 18, no. 3, pp. 1–21, 2022.
14. M. Abu-Faraj, A. Al-Hyari, and Z. Alqadi, "A complex matrix private key to enhance the security level of image cryptography," *Symmetry*, vol. 14, no. 4, p. 664, 2022.
15. M. K. Ibrahim and F. T. Mohammed, "Image cryptography based on image processing technique and classification algorithm," *Journal of Algebraic Statistics*, vol. 13, no. 2, pp. 989–1001, 2022.

16. L. Teng, X. Wang, and Y. Xian, "Image encryption algorithm based on a 2D-CLSS hyperchaotic map using simultaneous permutation and diffusion," *Information Sciences*, vol. 605, pp. 71–85, 2022.

17. L. Huang, W. Li, X. Xiong, R. Yu, Q. Wang, and S. Cai, "Designing a double-way spread permutation framework utilizing chaos and S-box for symmetric image encryption," *Optics Communications*, vol. 517, p. 128365, 2022.

18. S. Sharma, A. Kumar, N. S. Hada, G. Choudhary, and S. M. Kashif, "Image encryption algorithm based on timeout, pixel transposition and modified Fisher-Yates shuffling," in *Advancements in Smart Computing and Information Security: First International Conference, ASCIS 2022, Rajkot, India, November 24–26, 2022, Revised Selected Papers, Part II*, pp. 24–43, Springer, 2023.

19. I. Ahmad and S. Shin, "A pixel-based encryption method for privacy-preserving deep learning models," *arXiv preprint arXiv:2203.16780*, 2022.

20. S. W. Kang, U. S. Choi, and S. J. Cho, "Fast image encryption algorithm based on (n, m, k)-PCMLCA," *Multimedia Tools and Applications*, vol. 81, no. 7, pp. 1–27, 2022.

21. J. Vos, *Quantum Computing in Action*. Simon and Schuster, 2022.

22. R. Rietsche, C. Dremel, S. Bosch, L. Steinacker, M. Meckel, and J.-M. Leimeister, "Quantum computing," *Electronic Markets*, vol. 32, no. 4, pp. 1–12, 2022.

23. H. Bez and T. Croft, *Quantum Computation*. CRC Press, 2023.

24. K. P. Gnatenko and N. A. Susulovska, "Geometric measure of entanglement of multi-qubit graph states and its detection on a quantum computer," *Europhysics Letters*, vol. 136, no. 4, p. 40003, 2022.

25. B. Mohan, S. Das, and A. K. Pati, "Quantum speed limits for information and coherence," *New Journal of Physics*, vol. 24, no. 6, p. 065003, 2022.

26. U. Awan, L. Hannola, A. Tandon, R. K. Goyal, and A. Dhir, "Quantum computing challenges in the software industry. A fuzzy AHP-based approach," *Information and Software Technology*, vol. 147, p. 106896, 2022.

27. F. Yan, A. M. Iliyasu, and P. Q. Le, "Quantum image processing: A review of advances in its security technologies," *International Journal of Quantum Information*, vol. 15, no. 3, p. 1730001, 2017.

28. Z. Wang, M. Xu, and Y. Zhang, "Review of quantum image processing," *Archives of Computational Methods in Engineering*, vol. 29, no. 2, pp. 737–761, 2022.

29. F. Yan and S. E. Venegas-Andraca, *Quantum Image Processing*. Springer Nature, 2020.

30. X.-W. Yao, H. Wang, Z. Liao, M.-C. Chen, J. Pan, J. Li, K. Zhang, X. Lin, Z. Wang, Z. Luo, et al., "Quantum image processing and its application to edge detection: Theory and experiment," *Physical Review X*, vol. 7, no. 3, p. 031041, 2017.

31. S. Chakraborty, S. B. Mandal, and S. H. Shaikh, "Quantum image processing: Challenges and future research issues," *International Journal of Information Technology*, vol. 10, no. 3, pp. 1–15, 2018.

32. J. J. Ranjani, "Quantum image processing and its applications," *Handbook of Multimedia Information Security: Techniques and Applications*, pp. 395–411, 2019.

33. S. E. Venegas-Andraca and S. Bose, "Storing, processing, and retrieving an image using quantum mechanics," in *Quantum Information and Computation*, vol. 5105, pp. 137–147, SPIE, 2003.

34. "Quantum image processing - FRQI and NEQR image representations." https://qiskit.org/textbook/ch-applications/image-processing-frqi-neqr.html. (Accessed on 12/18/2022).

35. J. I. Latorre, "Image compression and entanglement," *arXiv preprint quant-ph/0510031*, 2005.

36. O. F. Mohammad, M. Shafry, M. Rahim, S. Rafeeq, M. Zeebaree, and F. Ahmed, "A survey and analysis of the image encryption methods," *International Journal of Applied Engineering Research*, vol. 12, no. 23, pp. 13265–13280, 2017.

37. A. Kumar, C. Ottaviani, S. S. Gill, and R. Buyya, "Securing the future Internet of Things with post-quantum cryptography," *Security and Privacy*, vol. 5, no. 2, p. e200, 2022.

38. Y. Cao, Y. Zhao, Q. Wang, J. Zhang, S. X. Ng, and L. Hanzo, "The evolution of quantum key distribution networks: On the road to the qinternet," *IEEE Communications Surveys & Tutorials*, vol. 24, no. 2, pp. 839–894, 2022.

39. H. Bandara, Y. Herath, T. Weerasundara, and J. Alawatugoda, "On advances of lattice-based cryptographic schemes and their implementations," *Cryptography*, vol. 6, no. 4, p. 56, 2022.

40. S. Ullah, J. Zheng, N. Din, M. T. Hussain, F. Ullah, and M. Yousaf, "Elliptic curve cryptography; applications, challenges, recent advances, and future trends: A comprehensive survey," *Computer Science Review*, vol. 47, p. 100530, 2023.

41. B. S. Alhayani, N. Hamid, F. H. Almukhtar, O. A. Alkawak, H. B. Mahajan, A. S. Kwekha-Rashid, H. İlhan, H. A. Marhoon, H. J. Mohammed, I. Z. Chaloob, et al., "Optimized Video Internet of Things using elliptic curve cryptography based encryption and decryption," *Computers and Electrical Engineering*, vol. 101, p. 108022, 2022.

42. J. Dey and R. Dutta, "Progress in multivariate cryptography: Systematic review, challenges and research directions," *ACM Computing Surveys*, vol. 55, no. 12, pp. 1–34, 2022.

43. P. Longa, "Efficient algorithms for large prime characteristic fields and their application to bilinear pairings and supersingular isogeny-based protocols.," *IACR Cryptol. ePrint Arch.*, vol. 2022, p. 367, 2022.

44. P. Thanalakshmi, R. Anitha, N. Anbazhagan, C. Park, G. P. Joshi, and C. Seo, "A hash-based quantum-resistant designated verifier signature scheme," *Mathematics*, vol. 10, no. 10, p. 1642, 2022.

45. D. Joseph, R. Misoczki, M. Manzano, J. Tricot, F. D. Pinuaga, O. Lacombe, S. Leichenauer, J. Hidary, P. Venables, and R. Hansen, "Transitioning organizations to post-quantum cryptography," *Nature*, vol. 605, no. 7909, pp. 237–243, 2022.

46. S. Windarta, S. Suryadi, K. Ramli, B. Pranggono, and T. S. Gunawan, "Lightweight cryptographic hash functions: Design trends, comparative study, and future directions," *IEEE Access*, vol. 10, pp. 82272–82294, 2022.

47. K. Sakan, S. Nyssanbayeva, N. Kapalova, K. Algazy, A. Khompysh, and D. Dyusenbayev, "Development and analysis of the new hashing algorithm based on block cipher," *Eastern-European Journal of Enterprise Technologies*, vol. 2, no. 9, p. 116, 2022.

48. S. P. Cohen and M. Naor, "Low communication complexity protocols, collision resistant hash functions and secret key-agreement protocols," in *Advances in Cryptology–CRYPTO 2022: 42nd Annual International Cryptology Conference, CRYPTO 2022, Santa Barbara, CA, USA, August 15–18, 2022, Proceedings, Part III*, pp. 252–281, Springer, 2022.

49. Q. Yuan, M. Tibouchi, and M. Abe, "On subset-resilient hash function families," *Designs, Codes and Cryptography*, vol. 90, no. 3, pp. 719–758, 2022.

50. Y.-G. Yang, J.-L. Bi, X.-B. Chen, Z. Yuan, Y.-H. Zhou, and W.-M. Shi, "Simple hash function using discrete-time quantum walks," *Quantum Information Processing*, vol. 17, no. 8, pp. 1–19, 2018.

51. Y.-G. Yang, J.-R. Dong, Y.-L. Yang, Y.-H. Zhou, and W.-M. Shi, "Usefulness of decoherence in quantum-walk-based hash function," *International Journal of Theoretical Physics*, vol. 60, pp. 1025–1037, 2021.

52. R. Renner, "Security of quantum key distribution," *International Journal of Quantum Information*, vol. 6, no. 01, pp. 1–127, 2008.

53. R. Wolf, *Quantum Key Distribution*. Springer, 2021.

54. N. Tiwari, "Quantum key distribution simulation using entangled bell states," 2022.

55. D. Song and D. Chen, "Quantum key distribution based on random grouping bell state measurement," *IEEE Communications Letters*, vol. 24, no. 7, pp. 1496–1499, 2020.

56. D. J. Rani and S. E. Roslin, "Light weight cryptographic algorithms for medical internet of things (iot)-a review," in *2016 Online International Conference On Green Engineering and Technologies (IC-GET)*, pp. 1–6, IEEE, 2016.

Chapter 3

Post-quantum image security

Challenges and opportunities

Ashish Arya
Indian Institute of Information Technology, Sonepat, India

Arti Ranjan
IGDTUW, New Delhi, India

Amrit Kumar Agrawal
Sharda University, Greater Noida, India

3.1 INTRODUCTION

The security of communication has been a field of science and technology since the advent of electronic communications. The traditional methods of ensuring the security of communications were incapable of capturing the various aspects of electronic communications as both the message and encryption key were out in the open once it left the transmitter. Frequency hopping, channel encoding, etc., were standard techniques of electronic communications [1, 2], but the invention of asymmetric key protocols added a new level of complexity to the paradigm [3]. A rich theory developed after the rise of multimedia transfer through the internet, such as for image [4] and video data [5]. Now, as the revolution of Quantum Computing redefines the contours of communications security, especially image security, we are experiencing this emerging field as the next level of abstraction and complexity in the well-established field of communications security, which is eager to demolish existing notions and boundaries of what is possible and what is not.

We begin this chapter with a discussion about classical data security, with special reference to image security. A brief introduction to symmetric and asymmetric key cryptography follows. Thereafter, we introduce basics of quantum computing—qubit/gate model of quantum computing. We describe quantum cryptography methods and connect them with the overall problem of image security. In this context, a few image representation models in the quantum computing system are also discussed. Subsequent to this, the emerging paradigm of post-quantum cryptography is discussed, along with its opportunities and challenges. The chapter concludes with a summary of the topics discussed and a comment on the current state and future trends of post-quantum image security.

DOI: 10.1201/9781003468974-3

The main points of this chapter are:

1. An introduction to classical data security protocols for image security with comparison based on existing literature.
2. An introduction to the basics of quantum computing.
3. A friendly introduction to quantum cryptography protocols; may serve as a reference for the research community engaged in classical methods.
4. A detailed survey of multiple methods that may be suitable to take on challenges offered by the quantum computing field, dispelling many myths and unfounded notions.
5. The novelty over the existing literature is the collection of comments on each of these methods from the perspective of image security in a post-quantum setting.
6. The most significant topic of this chapter is presenting a comprehensive survey, as well as an evaluation of multiple methods relevant in a post-quantum setting—along with a comprehensive straightforward discussion of the basics of quantum computing and classical security methods for the practitioner of classical image security.

3.2 CLASSICAL IMAGE SECURITY

Before embarking on the description of image security methods, we begin with the classical data security paradigm. The term/techniques/methods of image security are not fundamentally different from standard data security techniques; however, we should not forget that the 2-dimensional data (image) presents its own structures and peculiarities for the purposes of security.

Classical data security can be divided into two parts: physical security and encryption. Physical security is simply keeping the information under lock and key and hoping that no one can find where the information is kept—or even if they do, they won't be able to locate the key. This was quite cumbersome, as it was often required to transmit the information from place to place. A better and more reliable scheme of data security was required, and thus ciphers were invented.

Ciphers are akin to lock and key in motion [6]. Ciphers were produced simply by applying a transformation, denoted by a crossed circle in Figure 3.1, to the alphabets of the message (in literature, a message required to be secured has been called plaintext) using a "key" turning the message into cipher or cipher code (*cipher means zero in Arabic*). The sender would have the key in advance and apply the inverse transformation on the message to recover its true contents. It is said Roman emperor Julius Caesar was a pioneer of ciphers. The army maintained by Caeser used ciphers extensively.

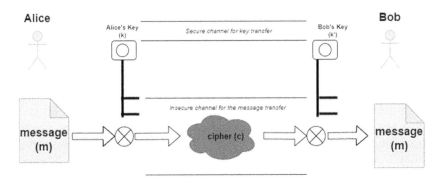

Figure 3.1 A general message transfer schematics using key and cipher.

The above process as summarized in Figure 3.1 requires the following assumptions:

- plaintext/message m
- key k for the sender Alice and key k' for the receiver Bob
- presence of a secure channel for key transfer
- key k' has be to be present with the receiver Bob prior to decryption of the message
- keys k and k' need not be same in general

Traditional cipher-based systems come with multiple variations, the main type being the substitution cipher and transpositional ciphers.

The substitution cipher simply substitutes the units of the plaintext with other characters. The transpositional cipher is a technique where the location of the units of plaintext are changed based on certain rules, i.e., transposition. This transposition can be based on another message.

The key can be just a function to be applied to the alphabet of the plaintext/message, or the key itself can be another plaintext/message to be used in the transformation from message m to cipher c. If the key is a another plaintext/message used to transform the original message to cipher using transposition, it is called a key-based transposition; if the key is a mathematical operation used to achieve the transformation of plaintext/message m to cipher c, it is called a keyless transposition cipher.

3.2.1 Asymmetric key encryption

Most of the later advancements in the area of secure message transfer emerge from the diagram in Figure 3.1. Consider the keys k and k'; traditionally these two keys used to be the same. However, they need not be. Asymmetric Key Encryption uses two (or multiple different) keys. If the keys k and k' are the same, the encryption algorithm is known as symmetric key encryption algorithm.

In fact, if there are multiple receivers, then each can have a different key, while the sender's key can be unique. This is the most basic fundamental behind asymmetric key encryption [7].

3.2.1.1 RSA algorithm

RSA algorithm, named after Rivest-Shamir-Adlemann, its inventors, is a widely used encryption algorithm based on the mathematical properties of large prime numbers [8]. It is commonly used to secure sensitive information, such as credit card numbers and passwords, during online transactions. RSA is an asymmetric algorithm, which means that it uses a pair of keys for encryption and decryption: a public key, which can be distributed to anyone, and a private key, which is known only to the owner of the data. Data encrypted with the public key can only be decrypted with the corresponding private key. Despite being in use for approximately three decades, RSA algorithms are still some of the most celebrated and used algorithms [9].

3.2.2 Image security

One way to enhance image security is to consider it as data and encrypt the same as a substitution/transpositional cipher.

The next step would be to use asymmetric key encryption. This is useful when the image is required to be accessed by multiple receivers simultaneously, and we have a method of transmitting the receivers their key in advance through a secure channel [3]. The most popular algorithms used for asymmetric key encryption are again the RSA as introduced above [8] [10], Digital Signature Algorithm (DSA) [11, 12], YAK [13], Diffie Hellman algorithm and its variations [14], El Gamal [15] and its variations [16], Merkle's Puzzles [17], Elliptic Curve Cryptography (ECC) [18, 19], Chaotic map [20], and Hyper-chaotic map [21]. These general classes of algorithms have multiple specific implementation techniques that perform differently on various evaluation parameters. Table 3.1 compares different image encryption techniques on a set of parameters [6].

A comparison of the computation time for these image encryption techniques is shown in Table 3.2.

3.2.3 Discussion and analysis

Classical image encryption techniques unfortunately include the following fundamental issues:

Drawbacks of classical image security algorithms

1. The assumption of a secure channel for the key exchange.
2. There is a no way to detect if an attempt has been made to intercept and decode the transmitted message.

Table 3.1 Comparison of various techniques for image encryption [6]

Techniques	Key space	Histogram analysis	Correlation analysis	Pixel sensitivity	Entropy	PSNR
Vigenère	Poor	Very poor	Very poor	Very poor	Moderate	Moderate
RC4	Good	Good	Good	Excellent	Good	Good
DES	Very poor	Moderate	Moderate	Very poor	Good	Good
-DES	Poor	Moderate	Moderate	Very poor	Good	Good
AES	Poor	Good	Moderate	Very poor	Good	Good
ECC	Poor	Moderate	Moderate	Good	Poor	Excellent
Chaotic map	Poor	Excellent	Excellent	Excellent	Excellent	Good
Hyper-chaotic map	Good	Excellent	Excellent	Excellent	Excellent	Good

Table 3.2 Computational time for various image encryption techniques [6]

Techniques	Encryption time
Vigenère	0.01634
RC4	0.23275
DES	49.1286
DES	143.7368
AES	169.4769
ECC	202.1892
Chaotic map	0.37168
Hyper-chaotic map	0.45343

3. High Computational Cost: Classical image security algorithms are usually computationally expensive, which can be a hindrance when processing large images.

4. Insecurity due to Advanced Attack Techniques: Classical image security algorithms can be vulnerable to advanced attack techniques such as differential cryptanalysis and linear cryptanalysis.

5. Prone to Key Exhaustion: Classical image security algorithms are prone to key exhaustion, which means that the same key is used for encrypting multiple images, which can lead to security issues.

6. Limited Security Capabilities: Classical techniques are generally based on the assumption that it is computationally difficult to generate the key, i.e., a brute force attack is difficult. Classical image security algorithms usually provide limited security capabilities and can be cracked using simple/specialized attack techniques.

7. Limited Encryption Algorithms: Classical image security algorithms usually employ limited encryption algorithms that can easily be broken.

We will revisit these issues later in this chapter; but now let's discuss—an introduction to Quantum Computing.

3.3 QUANTUM COMPUTING PRIMER

3.3.1 Emergence of quantum computing

In 1955, physicist Richard Feynman proposed the idea of a quantum computer, a machine that could harness the quirks of quantum mechanics to solve certain problems faster than any traditional computer. For decades, physicists have worked on building such a device, but the challenges have been daunting. In recent years, however, several groups finally succeeded in constructing working prototypes. This has led to renewed interest in quantum computing from business and scientific communities alike [22].

Quantum computing models are a relatively new development in the world of computing. Unlike classical computers, which rely on transistors to store information, quantum computers use qubits, loosely a quantum variation of bits, which can represent a 0, a 1, or any combination of the two. This allows quantum computers to solve certain problems much faster than classical computers. Three main defining features of quantum mechanics make quantum computing a different paradigm of computing.

3.3.2 Quantum mechanics and quantum computing

Quantum mechanics is the most accurate theory for understanding and predicting properties about the physical universe. Quantum interactions are quite unlike those experienced by people every day, but some defining principles can be described below:

3.3.2.1 Wave-particle duality

A quantum object generally has both wave like or particle status during its evolution; while measurements may give rise to one result depending on what is being measured (a measurement will either indicate *particlesness* or *waveness*). In a more succinct way, we need to invoke both the wave property and particle property of the system in a single experiment. Any single property of the object doesn't exist until we observe it!

3.3.2.2 Superposition

Superposition is a quantum mechanical phenomenon that describes the state of an atom or particle that exists in more than one place simultaneously.

In other words, it is a state of being in two or more places at the same time. The wave function for such superposed states is described by linear combinations with a complex coefficient of the "basis" states.

3.3.2.3 Coherence

Quantum coherence is a quantum phenomenon in which two or more quantum systems remain correlated even when they are separated by a distance. This correlation is maintained despite any noise or disturbances that may be present. In other words, the state of one system can influence the state of the other, even if they are not physically connected.

Quantum coherence is thought to play a role in many quantum phenomena, including superpositions and entanglement. It is also considered to be an important resource for developing quantum computing and communication technologies.

3.3.2.4 Entanglement

Quantum entanglement is a phenomenon that occurs when two or more particles are closely linked in such a way that the state of one particle can instantaneously affect the state of the other, no matter how far apart they are. This strange connection seems to defy the laws of physics and has puzzled scientists for years. However, recent research has shown that quantum entanglement may help us unlock some of the mysteries of the universe, as well as perform faster using quantum computing.

3.3.2.5 Measurement

Quantum measurement is one of the most fundamental and mysterious aspects of quantum mechanics. In classical mechanics, a particle's position, momentum, and energy are all well-defined quantities that can be measured with complete accuracy. In quantum mechanics, however, the act of measuring a particle changes its properties. This phenomenon is known as quantum uncertainty or indeterminacy as encapsulated in the Heisenberg Uncertainty Principle. However, once measurement of the quantum system is performed, the system, which might have been in *superposition* of multiple states, will collapse into one single state. The probability of the collapse of the quantum system into a particular state is given by the Born rule [23].

There are a number of interpretations of quantum mechanics, and scientists still don't agree on exactly what it all means; all the phenomena mentioned above are still an open and active area of research in terms of their applications as well as interpretation.

There are several different quantum computing models currently in use, each with its own advantages and disadvantages.

3.3.3 Continuous Variable Quantum Computing (CVQC)

CVQCs are different from classical quantum computers in that they use a continuous range of qubits, called *Qumodes* instead of discrete qubits. This makes the system smaller and more efficient, and allows for more accurate simulation of physical systems. CVQCs have already been used to model molecules and simulate optical processes, and there is potential for further application in areas like drug discovery, machine learning, and data security.

The development of CVQCs is still in its early stages, but it holds much promise for the future of quantum computing.

3.3.4 Gate-based quantum computing

This is the usual and most heard of model of quantum computing, i.e., the discrete valued qubit-based model. It is called the gate-based model, as the inputs to the quantum system, also called "quantum circuits," are generally (not always) modeled as the qubit states, and then these qubit states are transformed using different "gates," as we describe later, so as to reach the solution to the problem we want the quantum circuit to solve [24].

3.3.4.1 Qubits

A qubit (or quantum bit) is the fundamental unit of quantum information. A qubit is the quantum mechanical analogue of a classical bit. In classical computing the information is encoded in bits, where each bit can have the value zero or one. Qubit can represent a zero or a one or a linear combination of the two simultaneously. A qubit is a two-level quantum system where the two basis qubit states are usually written as $|0\rangle$ and $|1\rangle$. Here, the right-angled bracket is *ket*, and it represents a column vector. This is unlike a classical bit, which can exist in only one state at a time. As already explained, this is known as superposition.

A multi-qubit system is denoted by the tensor product of each individual qubit state.

3.3.4.2 Bloch sphere representation

As noted in the previous subsection, the qubit can be in a state of superposition of $|0\rangle$ and $|1\rangle$. This state of the qubit, known as statevector and conventionally represented as $|\psi\rangle$, can be written as Eq. 3.1:

$$|\psi\rangle\rangle = c_0|0\rangle + c_1|1\rangle, \tag{3.1}$$

where,

$$|0\rangle = \begin{bmatrix} 1 \\ 0 \end{bmatrix}, |1\rangle = \begin{bmatrix} 0 \\ 1 \end{bmatrix},$$

$$\|c_0\|^2 + \|c_1\|^2 = 1, \text{and } c_0, c_1 \in \mathbb{C} \tag{3.2}$$

Now, the c_0 and c_1 are complex numbers; therefore, they can be represented as equivalent polar representations:

$$c_0 := r_0 e^{j\phi_0},$$
$$c_1 := r_1 e^{j\phi_1}, \tag{3.3}$$

or,

$$|\psi\rangle = \cos\theta|0\rangle + e^{j\phi}\sin\theta|1\rangle,$$
$$\phi := \phi_1 - \phi_0, r_0 = \cos\theta, r_1 = \sin\theta \tag{3.4}$$

where r_i is amplitude and ϕ_i are phases. In this way the complex coefficients can be represented as points on a unit sphere. The logic behind choosing a sphere instead of a circle is that we have four variables from two complex coefficients. However, due to Eq. 3.2, only three variables are independent. Thus, a sphere with three dimensions will be required to truly represent the arbitrary qubit states.

Traditionally, under the Bloch sphere representation of qubit, and the $|0\rangle$ state, i.e., the statevector with $c_0 = 1$ and $c_1 = 0$, is represented at the north pole of a unit sphere. The $|1\rangle$ state, i.e., the statevector with $c_0 = 0$ and $c_1 = 1$, is represented at the south pole of a unit sphere. See Figure 3.2.

3.3.4.3 Measurement

It is important to note the concept of basis in quantum computing at this juncture, as this is required to understand some of the material that will come up later. According to the Born rule, the probability $P(x)$ of measuring a state of a qubit $|\psi\rangle$ in the state $|x\rangle$ will be given by Eq. 3.5:

$$P(x) := |\langle x | \psi \rangle|^2 \tag{3.5}$$

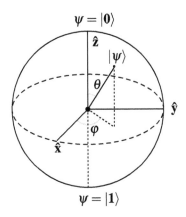

Figure 3.2 Bloch sphere representation of a qubit.

Where the left angle bracket is called the *bra*, which is shorthand for row vector, $\langle Bra \mid ket \rangle$ is the inner product of the element of row vector and complex conjugate of the column vector representing the *ket*.

Therefore, measuring $|0\rangle$ in the state $|0\rangle$, i.e., $|\langle 0|0\rangle|^2$, will give us probability 1. Similarly, measuring $|0\rangle$ in the state $|1\rangle$, i.e., $|\langle 1|0\rangle|^2$, will give us probability 0 (orthogonal).

If $|\psi\rangle = \dfrac{1}{\sqrt{2}}|0\rangle + \dfrac{1}{\sqrt{2}}|1\rangle$:

$$\left|\langle 0|\psi\rangle\right|^2 = \left|\langle 0|\dfrac{1}{\sqrt{2}}|0\rangle + \dfrac{1}{\sqrt{2}}|1\rangle\right|^2 \tag{3.6}$$

On simplification,

$$|\langle 0|\psi\rangle|^2 = \dfrac{1}{2}\left|\langle 0|0\rangle + \langle 0|1\rangle\right|^2$$
$$= \dfrac{1}{2} \tag{3.7}$$

The measurement can be either in the qubits state $|0\rangle$ or $|1\rangle$ or in any other orthogonal state. Such an orthogonal set of states is called basis. If the basis states are $|0\rangle$ and $|1\rangle$, then it is called *computation basis* or z-basis. Another alternative set of orthogonal state is $|+\rangle = \dfrac{1}{\sqrt{2}}|0\rangle + \dfrac{1}{\sqrt{2}}|1\rangle$ and $|-\rangle = \dfrac{1}{\sqrt{2}}|0\rangle - \dfrac{1}{\sqrt{2}}|1\rangle$. It is called as the x-basis.

3.3.4.4 Single qubit gates

Now, in order to let the qubit perform certain computation, we must have the methods to transform them. There, transformation methods are called "gates" [25].

Due to the Born rule, the state vector $|\psi\rangle$ always remains on the surface of the Bloch sphere as $\|\psi\| = 1$; however, the statevector is free to rotate on the sphere. The single qubit gates are nothing but rotations of the statevector on the Bloch sphere. Standard single qubit gates are following:

1. X-gate: Rotates $|\psi\rangle$ to $|1\rangle$ and vice versa. It is rotation by π around the x-axis.
2. Y-gate and Z-gate: perform rotations by π radians around y and z-axis of the Bloch sphere, respectively.
3. H-gate: This makes a rotation around the line between the x and z-axis.

   If applied to $|0\rangle$, generates equal superposition, i.e., $\dfrac{1}{\sqrt{2}}|0\rangle + \dfrac{1}{\sqrt{2}}|1\rangle$ state.

   If applied to $|1\rangle$, generates equal superposition, i.e., $\dfrac{1}{\sqrt{2}}|0\rangle - \dfrac{1}{\sqrt{2}}|1\rangle$ state.

4. I-gate: Identity gate; does not change the state. X applied twice becomes I gate.
5. S-gate: It does a quarter-turn around the Bloch sphere. S applied twice become Z gate.
6. *Rx*-gate: Rotation around x-axis by a specified angle.
7. *Ry*-gate: Rotation around y-axis by a specified angle.
8. *Rz*-gate: Rotation around y-axis by a specified angle.

3.3.4.5 Two qubit gates

Now, here is a brief discussion on the two qubit gates. Since a single qubit has only two basis states, i.e., $|0\rangle$ or $|1\rangle$, two qubits can have four basis states, i.e., $|00\rangle, |01\rangle, |10\rangle$, and $|11\rangle$. In general:

$$|\psi\rangle = c_{00}|00\rangle + c_{01}|01\rangle + c_{10}|10\rangle + c_{11}|11\rangle, \tag{3.8}$$

where,

$$\|c_{00}\|^2 + \|c_{01}\|^2 + \|c_{10}\|^2 + \|c_{11}\|^2 = 1, \tag{3.9}$$
$$c_{00}, c_{01}, c_{10} \text{ and } c_{11} \in \mathbb{C}$$

The two qubit gates are generally controlled versions of single qubit gates. It will be clearer with an example. A standard two-qubit gate is C-NOT or CX gate. The truth table for CX gate is given in the Table 3.3, where q_0 is control qubit and q_1 is output qubit and q'_1 is the state of output after application of CX gate. The CX in combination with H gate can build an entangled qubit pair for us. The state of the two-qubit system under entanglement will be $\frac{1}{\sqrt{2}}|00\rangle + \frac{1}{\sqrt{2}}|11\rangle$. Refer to Figure 3.3.

Table 3.3 Truth table for the CX gate

q_0	q_1	q'_1
0	0	0
0	1	1
1	0	1
1	1	0

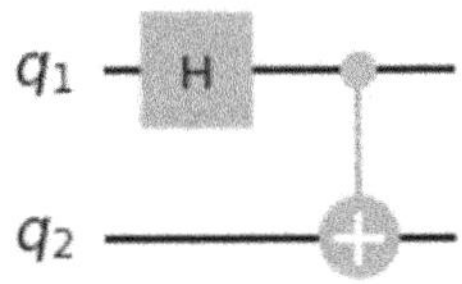

Figure 3.3 Generation of entangled qubit pair.

3.3.4.6 Multi-qubit gates

Multi-qubit gates are an extension of two-qubit gates. For example, a two-qubit C-NOT gate can be defined to have two control-qubits and one output qubit. Thus, the state of the output qubit will change only if the two control qubits are in $|1\rangle$ state.

3.3.5 Quantum circuit

So far, we have used the term *quantum circuit* without properly introducing it, so we will do so here.

According to IBM Quantum:

> A quantum circuit is an ordered sequence of quantum gates, measurements, and resets, all of which may be conditioned on and use data from real-time classical computation [26].

A good example of a quantum circuit, which is also relevant to this chapter, is a Quantum teleportation circuit. A quantum teleportation circuit is the method by which a state of a qubit can be transferred from a sender (Alice) to a receiver (Bob) without violating the fundamentals of quantum mechanics.

3.3.6 Quantum teleportation circuit

First created in 1993 [27], the quantum teleportation circuit is one of the most important components of quantum cryptography. In order to implement quantum teleportation, the sender (Alice) and the receiver (Bob) need a third person (often called as Telamon) so as to enable them to have one qubit each from a entangled qubit pair. Both the sender (Alice) and the receiver (Bob) are required to do certain gate operations on their qubits and exchange certain information over a classical channel to receive the state of Alice's qubit at Bob.

Step 1: Suppose Alice is trying to send the state $|\psi\rangle$ of her qubit q_0 to Bob.
Step 2: The third party (telemon) creates an entangled pair of qubits and gives one qubit (q_a) to Alice and one qubit (q_b) to Bob.
Step 3: Alice is required to apply a CX gate to q_a with q_0 as the control qubit.
Step 4: Alice is required to apply an H gate to q_0.
Step 5: Alice is required to perform measurement of both her qubits and save the result in two classical bits, then send the two classical bits to Bob through a classical channel.
Step 6: Now the receiver, Bob, who is receiving the qubits q_b, applies the gates as per Table 3.4.
Step 7: After Step 6, Bob will have the state of his qubit same as $|\psi_0\rangle$.

Table 3.4 Action by Bob

Bits	Action
00	Nothing
01	X
10	Z
11	ZX

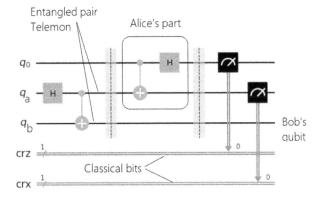

Figure 3.4 Quantum teleportation circuit.

The quantum circuit for quantum teleportation is shown in Figure 3.4. The given figure demonstrates the quantum teleportation circuit for the case of classical bits being 00, hence no action by Bob. In the figure the *crz* and *crx* channels are for keeping the measurments after applying Z, X gates, respectively.

3.4 QUANTUM COMMUNICATION

Quantum communication is the natural and necessary extension of quantum teleportation discussed in the previous section. Quantum communication basically utilizes the laws of quantum physics as enumerated in Subsec. 3.3.2. Quantum communication has been predicted to evolve as quantum internet in the future. Such a network would be analogous to the classical network; however, the end nodes of such network would be a quantum processor inhabited by qubits, and the information exchanged would be the quantum information [28].

3.5 SECURITY IN POST-QUANTUM ERA

We have covered thorough ground in introducing the basic ingredients of the subject starting from the basics of quantum mechanics, quantum computing, gate-model of quantum computing, standard gates, and quantum teleportation circuit and also mentioned a general concept about quantum communication.

Now, let us consider all these developments and analyze what it means for classical cryptography methods, including those which are in use for images.

3.5.1 Challenges for classical cryptographic methods

As already stated, the classical cryptography methods are dependent on the difficulty of mainly the following two problems: 1) Factorization Problem – this is crux to the public-key cryptography as proposed by the RSA algorithm; and 2) Discrete Logarithm Problem (DLP) – The Diffie-Hellman scheme and the Elliptic Curve Cryptography algorithms are based on the difficulty of the Discrete Logarithm problem.

As per a report from 2015, the 2048-bit RSA algorithm can be broken by a quantum computer with a billion qubits. However, later in 2017, Gidney and Ekerå demonstrated that the 2048-bit RSA algorithms can be broken by only a 20-million qubit quantum computer in under eight hours [29]. Thus, there is a reduction of two orders of magnitude in the requirement of the number of qubits for breaking the 2048-bit RSA security encryption within a few years [30].

The current capacity of quantum computers is far below the required number of qubits to break the RSA algorithm. Existing quantum computers are marred with the problem of rapid decoherence and noise. However, industry giants like Google and IBM are continuously working on improving quantum hardware. Figure 3.5 [31] shows the growth of the number of qubits achieved by major players across the world in the last 20 years. As we see in the figure, the number of qubits are increasing at an almost exponential speed.

Organization	Year	Qubits	Progress
IBM, MIT, Oxford, Berkeley, Stanford	1998	2	
TU Munich	2000	5	
Las Almos National Lab.	2000	7	
Institute of Quantum Computing, Perimeter Institute, MIT	2006	12	
D-Wave Systems	2008	28	
MIT, Stanford, Berkeley	2017	50	
Intel	2018	49	
Google	2018	72	
Rigetti	2019	128	
IBM	2021	127	
IBM	2022	433	

Figure 3.5 Growth of number of qubits, 1998–2022.

The current state of development of quantum computing offers a maximum of 433 qubits, as announced by IBM on 9 November 2022 [32]. It is pertinent to mention the plans of industry giants like IBM to achieve scaled-up quantum computing. The quantum roadmap issued by IBM in 2022 demonstrates the past and future plans of IBM to develop and sustain the quantum computing technology between 2019 to 2026 and beyond. As shown in Figure 3.6, the IBM roadmap exhibits an ambitious plan for achieving a state of quantum computing technology where up to 10k to 100k qubits are deployed by 2026 with the capacity of classical and quantum communication [33]. The Figure 3.7 gives the broad usage and applications for Post-Quantum Cryptography.

It has been estimated in a report published by the National Institute of Standard and Technology [34] that most if not all classical cryptography methods are vulnerable to a sufficient sized quantum computer. We can see a world where quantum computing will become ubiquitous is just around the corner. We have a lead time of only a few decades to update and revise classical cryptography protocols [35].

3.5.2 Benefits of post-quantum cryptography

Given the analysis above, the major technology companies today are bracing for the next quantum revolution. The term Post-Quantum Cryptography is used to refer to the technology, concepts, algorithms, and methods that will be used in an era where quantum computing is widely available [36].

3.5.2.1 Intrusion detection

This feature is a fundamental and defining feature of post-quantum cryptography methods. Post-quantum cryptography methods are based on the laws of physics as enshrined in the theory of quantum mechanics. Any attempt by an eavesdropper to read or record the signal being transmitted from the sender to receiver alters the information in a fundamental way. The receiver immediately knows that the signal has been altered, and thus, an attempt was made to eavesdrop.

3.5.2.2 Homomorphic cryptography

It is believed that post-quantum cryptography will enable us to develop a viable *homomorphic cryptography*, which refers to the state of cryptography where data sets are shared between multiple users for processing in encrypted form. Thus, there will be no need for the user to *see* the data in an unencrypted form; however, he will be able to perform the processing of the same set. Homomorphic cryptography will allow large data sets to be shared among organizations without any concern for the leakage of sensitive information. This will also enable organizations to proactively share

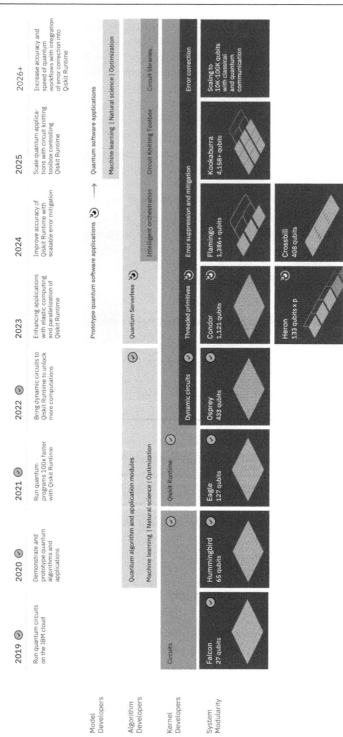

Figure 3.6 IBM roadmap for quantum computing 2019–2026 and beyond. (Image credit: IBM [33]).

data that are so far not shared for privacy concerns. Personal data safety shall reach new heights with this kind of technology [37].

3.6 A SURVEY OF POST-QUANTUM CRYPTOGRAPHY TECHNIQUES

We will now discuss a few recently developed techniques for post-quantum cryptography. Post-quantum cryptography is a large emerging field with its adjunct areas. Figure 3.7 shows the landscape covered by the field of post-quantum cryptography with the algorithmic as well as the physical side identified.

3.6.1 Quantum key distribution

Quantum key distribution (QKD) is a technique used to generate an encryption key between two parties in the most secure way possible. It is a type of cryptography in which the security of the key exchange is guaranteed by the laws of quantum mechanics. QKD works by using single photons, or individual quanta of light, to send information between two parties. This information can then generate a cryptographic key that securely encrypts and decrypts data.

QKD has become increasingly attractive and one of the backbones of the quantum cryptographic toolkit because it is virtually unbreakable, as any attempt to intercept or manipulate the transmission will be detected due to the laws of quantum mechanics. In addition, due to its reliance on single

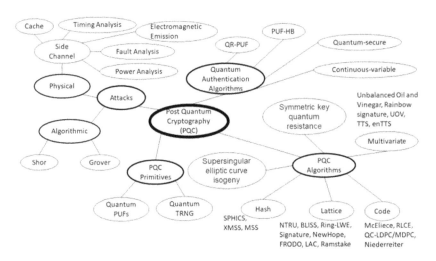

Figure 3.7 Post-Quantum Cryptography and its related fields. (Image credit: IBM [33].)

photons for communication, it offers greater security than traditional methods such as one-time pads or public-key cryptography. As such, QKD can provide a secure means for sharing secrets between people over long distances, making it particularly useful for applications that require secure communications across large geographic areas [38].

The first experiments in quantum key distribution were conducted in 1989 by Bennett and Brassard, who developed the now-famous BB84 protocol, which is still widely used today. The protocol involves sending random bits encoded onto single photons over an optical channel from one party (Alice) to another (Bob). Each bit is represented by either a vertical or horizontal polarization state of a single photon, and Alice randomly selects each polarization state using a device called a quantum random number generator (QRNG). Bob then measures each incoming photon with his own QRNG and compares his results with those sent by Alice. If they match up, he keeps them; otherwise he discards them as errors and resends the bits until he receives an exact match. Once all bits are successfully exchanged, both parties have established their cryptographic keys with high confidence that they have not been intercepted or manipulated in transit.

From there they can use this secret key for symmetric encryption via an algorithm such as AES or 3DES; this encryption method offers much greater security than other methods since it relies on keeping the same secret key throughout all communications, which makes interception significantly more difficult, if not impossible. Additionally, due to its nature as an unbreakable encryption method, even if someone does obtain access to the transmitted data, they cannot decrypt it without knowing that exact same secret key used during transmission; thus providing unprecedented levels of security for sensitive data transmissions even over large distances.

3.6.2 BB84 protocol

QKD is a class or rather a concept for use in post-quantum cryptography. The BB84 protocol is its very first practical implementation. We will now go through the technical details of the BB84 protocols [39].

3.6.2.1 Overview

Let use assume Alice wants to send her private key to Bob. Alice decides to have two binary strings a and b each of n bit length. In this setting Alice and Bob communicate over a two-way classical channel and a one-way quantum channel, as shown in Figure 3.8. The quantum channel usually uses polarized photons as qubits. A single photon in its polarization state will represent state $|\psi\rangle$ of the qubit. The classical channel is the usual telephone or internet line, where Eve (the eavesdropper) has access.

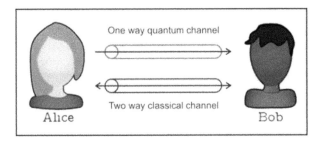

Figure 3.8 BB84 setting. (Image credit: Lahiru Madushanka [40].)

3.6.2.2 Basic principle

The basic principle behind BB84 is the fact that measuring a qubit alters its state. In the quantum channel, the act of measuring the photon will alter its polarization state. Therefore, if Eve tries to snoop on the communication through the quantum channel, Bob will know someone has tried to look at his communication and may decide to alter the key.

If Alice encodes 0 as $|+\rangle$ and Bob measures it in x-basis, he will measure the 0 with 100% probability, but if Bob measures it in z-basis, he will measure the 0 with 50% probability and 1 with 50% probability.

The BB84 is basically making sure that the eavesdropper has negligible probability of getting the true value of the qubit state being sent.

Step 1: Alice to choose a random binary string '00 11 10 11 00 10'.

Step 2: Alice to choose a random sequence of basis 'XZ XX ZX ZX XZ XX'.

Step 3: Alice to encode the binary string on the basis of random sequence of basis. The output of this string would be:
$|-\rangle|0\rangle|-\rangle|+\rangle|+\rangle|1\rangle|-\rangle|1\rangle|+\rangle|-\rangle|-\rangle|0\rangle|+\rangle|1\rangle$.
This is the sequence Alice sent to Bob.

Step 4: Bob measures the sequence of qubits received in a random choice of basis such as 'ZX XZ XZ XX ZZ ZX'.

Step 5: Alice shares in the classical channel, which basis she used to encode and measure the qubits respectively.

Step 6: Bob compares his result with the basis shared by Alice and keeps only those bits that match with the basis shared by Alice. This becomes part of the secret key with Bob.

Step 7: Bob and Alice share a sample from the sequence they have. If both match, it means the key exchange has taken place.

3.6.3 Analysis

Despite its numerous advantages, however, quantum key distribution isn't without its challenges when it comes to practical implementation; namely its extremely low speed compared to conventional methods and its relatively high cost associated with generating single photons needed for successful communication due to their rarity in nature compared to other forms of light sources (such as lasers). Nevertheless, these issues are now being actively researched by scientists and engineers around the world who are working hard to find new ways to make QKD more practical and cost-effective so that everyone can benefit from its unparalleled security potential—while also enjoying lightning-fast speeds expected from modern-day networks like 5G technology, etc. [41].

Now we will discuss a few techniques that are supposed to be relevant for cryptography in the post-quantum era. These methods combined with quantum methods such as the QKD/BB84 may be able to provide us with quantum-safe cryptography.

3.6.4 Lattice-based cryptography

3.6.4.1 Overview

Lattice-based cryptography is a type of public-key cryptography that utilizes multivariate polynomials to generate and manipulate cryptographic keys. This type of cryptography offers increased security compared to traditional public-key systems like RSA and Diffie–Hellman by using a lattice structure to solve the discrete logarithm problem [42].

In lattice-based cryptography, cryptographic keys are represented as points (or vectors) on a lattice. A lattice $\mathbb{L}$ is an n-dimensional space comprised of parallel planes that form an array of points that can be used for computations as denoted in Eq. 3.10 and Figure 3.9.

$$
\mathbb{L} \subset \mathbb{R}^n,
$$
$$
\{b_1, b_2, ..., b_n\} \text{ basis of } \mathbb{R}^n, \tag{3.10}
$$
$$
\mathbb{L} = \left\{ \sum_{i=1}^{n} a_i b_i, a_i \in \mathbb{Z} \right\}
$$

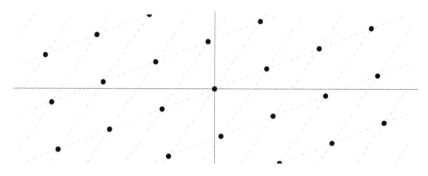

Figure 3.9 Lattice points on a grid. (Credit [43].)

3.6.4.2 Short Integer Solutions (SIS)

We know from Linear Algebra that the basis is not unique, so is Lattice. This structure allows us to find mathematical relationships between points by connecting them in different ways on the lattice, allowing for more efficient encryption and decryption processes than other types of public key crypto-systems.

In order to create a difficult enough problem to achieve the objective of cryptography, we may consider the following problem.

Let's say we are given a random matrix $\mathbf{A}$ with elements ranging from 0 to q. The challenge is to identify a "short" vector x that solves Eq. 3.11.

$$\mathbf{A} \equiv 0 \ (\mathrm{mod}\, q) \tag{3.11}$$

The collection of vectors (of any length) that satisfy Eq. 3.11 can be plotted as a lattice or in a grid-like form. Finding a solution x that is near the origin but not exactly equal to it is the goal of the SIS issue. The lattice diagram in Figure 3.10 is an illustration. Finding a place inside the red circle that isn't the blue point is the difficult part.

In order to generate a secure key in lattice-based cryptography, multiple layers of polynomials are used to create the lattice structure. The polynomials are chosen such that they have no common factors that make them difficult to factorize, making it extremely difficult for attackers to deduce the underlying key values. Furthermore, these polynomials are typically chosen so that they include large prime numbers that further increase the difficulty of finding the underlying keys.

One advantage of lattice-based cryptography is its ability to create almost perfect secrecy, meaning that an attacker would need unlimited computing power to even come close to cracking the encryption algorithm or decoding messages encrypted with it. Additionally, because this type of cryptosystem relies on mathematics rather than hard coding specific values into algorithms, it can be made highly resistant against side channel attacks where

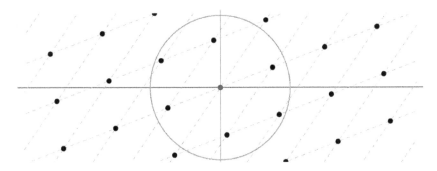

Figure 3.10 Solution for the SIS problem on the Lattice points on a grid. (Credit [43].)

attackers attempt to get information about cryptographic keys through timing or power analysis techniques [44].

Since its inception over 20 years ago, lattice algorithms have been included in numerous security protocols such as IBE (Identity-Based Encryption), FHE (Fully Homomorphic Encryption), ABE (Attribute-Based Encryption), and PKE (Public Key Encryption). These types of encryption schemes use complex mathematical models based on hard problems from number theory such as integer factorization and discrete logarithms to provide secure communication over untrusted networks or shared areas where adversaries could potentially intercept or modify data transmitted between two parties. Recently, quantum-classical hybrid algorithms for lattice-based cryptography have been proposed [45].

3.6.4.3 Image security perspective

While there are some drawbacks associated with this type of encryption—such as its high computational demand—these challenges can be overcome with advances in hardware technology enabling faster and more powerful computers while also reducing energy consumption costs associated with running these algorithms at scale. As far as image data is concerned, it would require further computational load due to two-dimensional data. As such, it is likely that we will continue seeing advances in this field and applications thereof become increasingly widespread over time as we strive toward greater data security across all industries [46]. It is worth metioning that research on faster hardware implementation of the lattice-based cryptography is an active area [47].

3.6.5 Multivariate cryptography

3.6.5.1 Overview

Multivariate cryptography is a type of encryption technology that uses multiple variables instead of a single key to secure data. It is based on mathematical algorithms that use multiple parameters, such as points, lines, and curves, to generate an extremely complex code. This code can then be used to lock and unlock data in a secure manner by providing the right combination of variables. Multivariate cryptography is considered more secure than traditional methods due to its higher level of complexity.

Multivariate cryptography was first developed in the early 2000s by researchers at IBM who sought to create a more robust form of encryption than those available at the time. Since then, it has become increasingly popular with both businesses and individuals, as its security capabilities offer greater protection against hacking attempts and other malicious activities [48]. The main benefit of multivariate cryptography is that it does not require users to remember complex passwords or pass phrases; instead, all that is needed are combinations of parameters that can be easily memorized or written down for safekeeping [49].

3.6.5.2 Methodology

The process for generating codes using multivariate cryptography requires the use of mathematical polynomials over finite fields. These polynomials are then used to create an extremely complex code, which can only be decrypted when the correct combination of variables is provided. This makes it highly resistant to brute force attacks since even if hackers have access to the underlying equations, they would still need to correctly guess the right combinations to decrypt any encrypted data. In a sense, multivariate cryptography is also a kind of public key cryptography [50].

Systems of nonlinear polynomial equations in multiple variables, often quadratic equations over a finite field F = Fq with q elements, are the fundamental building blocks of multivariate cryptography. Refer to Eq. 3.12.

$$p^{(1)}\left(x_1,\ldots,x_n\right) = \sum_{i=1}^{n}\sum_{j=1}^{m}p_{ij}^{(1)} \cdot x_i x_j + \sum_{i=1}^{n}p_i^{(1)} \cdot x_i + p_0^{(1)},$$

$$p^{(2)}\left(x_1,\ldots,x_n\right) = \sum_{i=1}^{n}\sum_{j=1}^{n}p_{ij}^{(2)} \cdot x_i x_j + \sum_{i=1}^{n}p_i^{(2)} \cdot x_i + p_0^{(2)} \qquad (3.12)$$

$$\vdots$$

$$p^{(n)}\left(x_1,\ldots,x_n\right) = \sum_{i=1}^{n}\sum_{j=1}^{n}p_{ij}^{(n)} \cdot x_i x_j + \sum_{i=1}^{n}p_i^{(n)} \cdot x_i + p_0^{(n)}$$

The security of the multivariate cryptographic system lies in the difficulty of the following problem:

Problem: Given $p^{(1)}, p^{(2)}, \ldots, p^{(n)}$ as in Eq. 3.12 in the variable $x = (x_1, x_2, \ldots, x_n)$, find x such that $p^{(1)} = 0, p^{(2)} = 0, \ldots, p^{(n)} = 0$ [50].

To further enhance security measures, multivariate cryptography also utilizes elements from chaos theory and random number generation techniques. By introducing randomness into the equation through these methods, hackers cannot predict what combination will yield a successful result even if they possess knowledge about the underlying mathematics behind it. This ensures that any attempt at breaking into multivariately encrypted data will prove futile in most cases due to the sheer complexity involved in guessing all possible combinations correctly before successfully unlocking any encrypted data files.

Due to its many advantages over traditional forms of encryption, multivariate cryptography has been adopted for use in many different industries ranging from banking and finance to telecommunications and government applications where heightened security measures are required. It is also increasingly being incorporated into everyday applications such as online shopping websites that seek an extra layer of protection against cybercriminals to provide their customers with peace of mind when making purchases online.

3.6.5.3 Image security perspective

The multivariate cryptography has been recognized as one of the main candidates for post-quantum cryptographic algorithms [51]. The multivariate cryptography will be specifically applicable for image data. The inherent multivariate property of this method makes it suitable for 2D image data, which can be encoded with the multivariate key. Another benefit of multivariate cryptography is that it can provide the same security with shorter keys [52].

3.6.6 Hash-based cryptography

3.6.6.1 Overview

Hash-based cryptography is a type of encryption that uses cryptographic hash functions to secure data. It is a form of symmetric cryptography, which means that the same key is used to both encrypt and decrypt data. Hash-based cryptography was developed in the late 1970s and has since become an increasingly popular choice for securing digital data.

Hash-based encryption works by taking a piece of input data such as a message or file, running it through a one-way cryptographic hash function, and then using the resulting output (called the digest) as an encryption key. By using this technique, the same message can be encrypted multiple times but each time with a different key, making it virtually impossible to reverse engineer the original message. The hash function also ensures that any changes made to the input will produce drastically different outputs, making it equally difficult to attempt to tamper with or alter the original file without detection [53].

3.6.6.2 Methodology

One-time signature techniques are the foundation of hash-based signature systems. Only one message can be safely signed with a given one-time signing key. The security of an underlying hash function is the only factor affecting the security of (hash-based) one-time signature methods. The hash-based systems have been found useful for the verifier signature scheme [54].

The Lamport-Diffie scheme [55], the Winternitz scheme [56], and its upgrades, such as the W-OTS+ scheme [57], are all frequently used one-time signature schemes. The Winternitz system and its variations may sign multiple bits simultaneously, unlike the groundbreaking Lamport-Diffie technique. The Winternitz parameter's value determines how many bits will be signed simultaneously. There is a trade-off between size and speed because of the existence of this parameter. Short signatures result from large values of the Winternitz parameter.

One of the primary advantages of hash-based cryptography is that it can provide stronger security than traditional encryption methods due to its ability to detect even small changes in data. Additionally, modern implementations of hash functions are typically much faster than more traditional forms of encryption such as RSA and DES, meaning that these algorithms are more suitable for applications where speed is essential [58].

Another benefit of this type of algorithm is that it does not require public/private keys, which makes it much easier and cheaper to implement than other types of encryption. Furthermore, unlike most other types of encryption, hashing does not need expensive hardware or software components so it can be implemented in virtually any environment quickly and easily. This makes it ideal for applications like mobile device authentication where resources are limited and speed is paramount [34].

3.6.6.3 Image security perspective

The development of quantum hash functions has given hash-based cryptography another leap toward making it quantum safe. This technique is one of the prime candidates for post-quantum cryptography due to this development including for image data.

3.6.7 Code-based cryptography

3.6.7.1 Overview

Code-based cryptography is a type of encryption technique that combines the use of both traditional algorithms and error-correcting codes. It is based on the idea that data can be sent securely between two or more parties, even when an adversary has full access to the transmitted message. It relies on encoding the data with a code that is both secure and easily decoded by authorized persons [59].

The main advantage of code-based cryptography compared to other cryptographic techniques is its ability to correct errors in transmission without requiring any additional data. This makes it far more resilient against manipulation or interception by malicious actors than traditional cryptography alone [60]. Code-based cryptography provides not just confidentiality but also authentication, meaning it can be used to verify that two parties are communicating with each other and that no third party has been able to intercept or tamper with the data. This enhances security and trust between those making transactions online. This is the reason why code-based cryptography has been found to be attractive for digital signatures [61].

The most widely used form of code-based cryptography is Reed-Solomon coding, which was first developed in 1960 by Irving Reed and Gustave Solomon [62].

3.6.7.2 Methodology

The basic idea behind this technique is to break a message into smaller pieces called 'codewords,' then add redundant information (i.e., check digits), which allows errors in transmission to be detected and corrected without resending the entire message. Other popular forms include Low Density Parity Check (LDPC) codes, Convolutional codes, and Turbo codes, all of which provide varying levels of resilience against malicious attacks while still allowing for efficient transmission of data across networks [63].

3.6.7.3 Image security perspective

As technology advances, so does code-based cryptography, making it an ever more useful tool for protecting sensitive communications from prying eyes online. More sophisticated forms are being developed all the time as researchers aim to find ways to make their systems more secure and resistant to attack, while still providing low latency for real-time applications such as streaming images/media over networks like the internet or mobile phones. Furthermore, with computers becoming increasingly powerful and faster than ever before, code-based cryptography can now be used at much larger scales than was previously possible—potentially allowing for greater security on a global scale than ever before. Distributed computing can be effectuvely utilized for implementation of code-based cryptography [64].

3.6.8 Supersingular elliptic curve isogeny cryptography

3.6.8.1 Overview

Supersingular elliptic curve isogeny cryptography, also known as SIDH (Supersingular Isogeny Diffie-Hellman), is a type of public key cryptography that utilizes different types of mathematical objects called supersingular isogenies. It was first introduced by Jean-Francois Biasse, Nicolas Costello, and Michael Naehrig in 2015 as an alternative to the traditional Diffie-Hellman key exchange protocol. Since then, it has been extensively studied and developed by cryptographers for its potential applications in post-quantum cryptography [65].

SIDH works by generating two elliptic curves that are related through an isogeny; the underlying mathematics of these curves then allow for secure communication between two parties. Each party generates a secret key from the shared curve parameters and their own private input—this secret key can be used to encrypt messages between the two parties without having to worry about decryption or tampering with the message during transit. This makes SIDH particularly resilient against quantum attacks as compared to traditional algorithms such as AES or RSA [66].

3.6.8.2 Methodology

A prime of the form $p = l_A^{e_A} \cdot l_B^{e_B} \cdot f \mp 1$ serves as the setup for SIDH, where l_A and l_B are small primes with e_A, e_B as large exponents, f is called a small cofactor with an elliptic curve E over field $\mathbf{F}_{p}^{2}$.

Two significant torsion subgroups exist in such a curve, denoted by $E[l_A]$ and $E[l_B]$, which are allocated to Alice and Bob, respectively, as hinted by the subscripts. The protocol begins with each party computing the relevant (secret) isogeny and choosing a (secret) random cyclic subgroup of their respective torsion subgroup. The equation for the target curve of their model is then published or otherwise made available to the other party.

In addition to its superior security, SIDH also offers several advantages over classical cryptosystems such as better performance and efficiency due to its scalability and reduced storage requirements. Furthermore, while all traditional cryptographic protocols require some type of trusted third party to provide a secure channel for communication, SIDH does not rely on any such third party—instead it provides a completely decentralized solution that allows any two parties to communicate securely without requiring a centralized authority. Finally, since SIDH does not require any large precomputed tables or other complex data structures for its operation, it can be implemented easily on resource-constrained devices such as embedded systems or mobile phones [67].

3.6.8.3 Image security perspective

All these features make SIDH an attractive potential candidate for use in post-quantum cryptography applications; however, further research needs to be done before it can be adopted widely across different platforms and applications. As more cryptanalysts continue to study SIDH's security properties and develop tools that further enhance its usefulness in real-world situations, we will hopefully see it become more commonplace in years to come. Its applicability for image-based data is subject to further research.

3.6.9 Symmetric key quantum resistance

3.6.9.1 Overview

Symmetric key quantum resistance is a form of cryptography that protects against the potential threat posed by quantum computing to existing encryption algorithms. This type of encryption is important for organizations and individuals who want to protect their information from attack by malicious actors using quantum computers.

Unlike traditional encryption algorithms, symmetric key quantum-resistant cryptography uses a particularly secure algorithm known as a Hash-Based Message Authentication Code (HMAC) to ensure the integrity of encrypted data. HMACs use two different keys: one used to encrypt data and the other to decrypt it. These keys are never stored on the same machine or transmitted together; this ensures that if one key is compromised, the other will remain safe. Additionally, a HMAC can be configured so that even if an attacker knows both keys, they still won't be able to access the encrypted data [68].

In addition to providing protection from attacks via quantum computing, symmetric key quantum-resistant cryptography also provides better security against traditional attacks like brute force attacks as well as side channel attacks such as timing attacks and fault injection attacks. This makes these types of crypto algorithms especially attractive for organizations who need an extra layer of security on top of traditional encryption methods. As an added bonus, symmetric key quantum-resistant cryptography does not require complex mathematical operations for it to remain effective; this means that it has much lower computational overhead than other types of cryptographic techniques. In the latest cutting-edge research, it has been shown that symmetric key quantum resistance has potential applications in the field of block-chain technology [69].

3.6.9.2 Image security perspective

Symmetric key quantum-resistant cryptography is an important tool for ensuring that sensitive data remains secure in today's digital world. By its design, this type of crypto algorithm greatly reduces the chances that any malicious actor will be able to break through its defenses and gain access to confidential information. Additionally, because it requires lower computational overhead compared to other crypto techniques, it's ideal for those who may not have access to powerful computing resources but still need reliable protection against cyber threats. The low computational requirement makes this method suitable for image/2D data.

3.7 CONCLUSION

In this chapter we have discussed the problem of image security in the post-quantum world. We began with the basics of classical image security and its main terms and asymmetric key encryption. A comparison of a few well-known asymmetric key algorithms was tabulated.

In order to have a complete picture of the bouquet of techniques/algorithms available in the post-quantum cryptography era, we introduced the basics of theory and key terminology of quantum computing and its various models. Qubits, single-qubit gates, two-qubit gates, multi-qubit gates, and measurement basis were introduced. These were required to formally introduce the crux of this chapter that is the QKD and BB84 protocol. Thereafter, several new upcoming and recently introduced methods such as Lattice-based cryptography, Multivariate cryptography, Hash-based cryptography, Code-based cryptography, Supersingular elliptic curve isogeny cryptography, and Symmetric key quantum resistance were discussed, along with their specific importance and useability for image data. We restricted our discussion to qualitative only, as these topics each deserve a chapter of their own.

After going through a plethora of algorithms and techniques for post-quantum cryptography, we discovered a rich theory of new cryptography protocols as well as a dexterous implementation of them. As we will soon have a more connected world with more connected devices, image and multimedia data is only going to increase, and so will be the demand for security and privacy of such data. We are hopeful the current scientific community can provide us a sufficiently safe alternative until the quantum computer evolves to a level to where it can break existing standard cryptography protocols.

REFERENCES

1. A. Ephremides, J. E. Wieselthier, and D. J. Baker, "A design concept for reliable mobile radio networks with frequency hopping signaling," *Proceedings of the IEEE*, vol. 75, no. 1, pp. 56–73, 1987.
2. J. L. Massey, "Foundation and methods of channel encoding," in *Proc. Int. Conf. Information Theory and Systems*, vol. 65, pp. 148–157, NTG-Fachberichte, 1978.
3. S. Chandra, S. Paira, S. S. Alam, and G. Sanyal, "A comparative survey of symmetric and asymmetric key cryptography," in *2014 International Conference on Electronics, Communication and Computational Engineering (ICECCE)*, pp. 83–93, IEEE, 2014.
4. B. Furht and D. Kirovski, *Multimedia Security Handbook*. CRC Press, 2004.
5. L. Guan, *Multimedia Image and Video Processing*. CRC Press, 2017.
6. O. F. Mohammad, M. Shafry, M. Rahim, S. Rafeeq, M. Zeebaree, and F. Ahmed, "A survey and analysis of the image encryption methods," *International Journal of Applied Engineering Research*, vol. 12, no. 23, pp. 13265–13280, 2017.
7. M. B. Yassein, S. Aljawarneh, E. Qawasmeh, W. Mardini, and Y. Khamayseh, "Comprehensive study of symmetric key and asymmetric key encryption algorithms," in *2017 International Conference on Engineering and Technology (ICET)*, pp. 1–7, 2017.
8. E. Milanov, "The RSA algorithm," *RSA Laboratories*, pp. 1–11, 2009.
9. F. O. Mojisola, S. Misra, C. F. Febisola, O. Abayomi-Alli, and G. Sengul, "An improved random bit-stuffing technique with a modified RSA algorithm for resisting attacks in information security (RBMRSA)," *Egyptian Informatics Journal*, vol. 23, no. 2, pp. 291–301, 2022.

10. A. Sahoo, P. Mohanty, and P. C. Sethi, "Image encryption using RSA algorithm," in *Intelligent Systems*, pp. 641–652, Springer, 2022.

11. V. Jain, "A review on different types of cryptography techniques," *ACADEMICIA: An International Multidisciplinary Research Journal*, vol. 11, no. 11, pp. 1087–1094, 2021.

12. H. Xu, K. Thakur, A. S. Kamruzzaman, and M. L. Ali, "Applications of cryptography in database: A review," in *2021 IEEE International IOT, Electronics and Mechatronics Conference (IEMTRONICS)*, pp. 1–6, IEEE, 2021.

13. C. Easttom, "Asymmetric algorithms," in *Modern Cryptography*, pp. 233–252, Springer, 2022.

14. Z. Bashir, M. Malik, M. Hussain, and N. Iqbal, "Multiple RGB images encryption algorithm based on elliptic curve, improved Diffie Hellman protocol," *Multimedia Tools and Applications*, vol. 81, no. 3, pp. 3867–3897, 2022.

15. D. Kumar, A. B. Joshi, S. Singh, and V. N. Mishra, "Digital color-image encryption scheme based on elliptic curve cryptography ElGamal encryption and 3D Lorenz map," in M. Seenivasan, K. Pattabiraman, A. Vadivel (eds.), *AIP Conference Proceedings*, vol. 2364, p. 020026, AIP Publishing LLC, 2021.

16. S. Thomas and A. Krishna, "Securing grayscale image using improved Arnold transform and ElGamal encryption," *Journal of Electronic Imaging*, vol. 31, no. 6, p. 063012, 2022.

17. I. Dinur and B. Hasson, "Distributed Merkle's puzzles," in *Theory of Cryptography Conference*, pp. 310–332, Springer, 2021.

18. L. D. Singh and K. M. Singh, "Image encryption using elliptic curve cryptography," *Procedia Computer Science*, vol. 54, pp. 472–481, 2015.

19. P. Parida, C. Pradhan, X.-Z. Gao, D. S. Roy, and R. K. Barik, "Image encryption and authentication with elliptic curve cryptography and multidimensional chaotic maps," *IEEE Access*, vol. 9, pp. 76191–76204, 2021.

20. N. K. Pareek, V. Patidar, and K. K. Sud, "Image encryption using chaotic logistic map," *Image and Vision Computing*, vol. 24, no. 9, pp. 926–934, 2006.

21. X. Gao, "Image encryption algorithm based on 2D hyperchaotic map," *Optics & Laser Technology*, vol. 142, p. 107252, 2021.

22. "Quantum computing history - Azure Quantum|Microsoft learn." https://learn.microsoft.com/en-us/azure/quantum/concepts-overview. (Accessed on 11/26/2022).

23. N. P. Landsman, "Born rule and its interpretation," in D. Greenberger, K. Hentschel, F. Weinert (eds.), *Compendium of Quantum Physics*, pp. 64–70, Springer, 2009.

24. L. Gyongyosi and S. Imre, "A survey on quantum computing technology," *Computer Science Review*, vol. 31, pp. 51–71, 2019.

25. "Single qubit gates." https://qiskit.org/textbook/ch-states/single-qubit-gates.html. (Accessed on 11/26/2022).

26. "Quantum circuits." https://learn.qiskit.org/course/ch-algorithms/quantum-circuits. (Accessed on 11/29/2022).

27. C. H. Bennett, G. Brassard, C. Crépeau, R. Jozsa, A. Peres, and W. K. Wootters, "Teleporting an unknown quantum state via dual classical and Einstein-Podolsky-Rosen channels," *Physical Review Letters*, vol. 70, no. 13, pp. 1895–1899, 1993.

28. O. Alshehri, Z.-H. Li, and M. Al-Amri, "Basics of quantum communication," in M. D. Al-Amri, D. L. Andrews, M. Babiker (eds.), *Structured Light for Optical Communication*, pp. 1–36, Elsevier, 2021.

29. "How a quantum computer could break 2048-bit RSA encryption in 8 hours," *MIT Technology Review*, 2019. https://www.technologyreview.com/2019/05/30/65724/how-a-quantum-computer-could-break-2048-bit-rsa-encryption-in-8-hours/. (Accessed on 11/29/2022).

30. C. Gidney and M. Ekerå, "How to factor 2048 bit RSA integers in 8 hours using 20 million noisy qubits," *Quantum*, vol. 5, p. 433, 2021.

31. "The realities of quantum computing: Promises vs facts," LITSLINK blog, 2021. https://litslink.com/blog/the-realities-of-quantum-computing-promises-vs-facts. (Accessed on 12/01/2022).

32. "IBM unveils 400 qubit-plus quantum processor and next-generation IBM Quantum System Two." https://newsroom.ibm.com/2022-11-09-IBM-Unveils-400-Qubit-Plus-Quantum-Processor-and-Next-Generation-IBM-Quantum--System-Two#::text='IBM (Accessed on 11/30/2022).

33. "IBM quantum computing|roadmap." https://www.ibm.com/quantum/roadmap. (Accessed on 12/01/2022.

34. L. Chen, L. Chen, S. Jordan, Y.-K. Liu, D. Moody, R. Peralta, R. Perlner, and D. Smith-Tone, *Report on post-quantum cryptography*, vol. 12. US Department of Commerce, National Institute of Standards and Technology …, 2016.

35. V. Mavroeidis, K. Vishi, M. D. Zych, and A. Jøsang, "The impact of quantum computing on present cryptography," *arXiv preprint arXiv:1804.00200*, 2018.

36. A. Kumar, C. Ottaviani, S. S. Gill, and R. Buyya, "Securing the future Internet of Things with post-quantum cryptography," *Security and Privacy*, vol. 5, no. 2, p. e200, 2022.

37. "Prepare yourself for post-quantum security," Thales Group, 2021. https://www.thalesgroup.com/en/worldwide-digital-identity-and-security/enterprise-cybersecurity/magazine/prepare-yourself-post. (Accessed on 12/01/2022).

38. A. Sharma and A. Kumar, "A survey on quantum key distribution," in *2019 International Conference on Issues and Challenges in Intelligent Computing Techniques (ICICT)*, vol. 1, pp. 1–4, IEEE, 2019.

39. A. Ruiz Alba Gaya, D. Calvo Daz-Aldagalán, V. Garca Muñoz, A. Martnez Garca, W. A. Amaya Ocampo, J. G. Rozo Chicue, J. Mora Almerich, and J. Capmany Francoy, "Practical quantum key distribution based on the BB84 protocol," in *Waves*, vol. 1, pp. 4–14, Instituto de Telecomunicaciones y Aplicaciones Multimedia (iTEAM), 2011.

40. "BB84 explained – lahiru madushanka." https://lahirumadushankablog.wordpress.com/2019/05/01/bb84-explained/. (Accessed on 12/01/2022).

41. S. Sun and A. Huang, "A review of security evaluation of practical quantum key distribution system," *Entropy*, vol. 24, no. 2, p. 260, 2022.

42. H. Nejatollahi, N. Dutt, S. Ray, F. Regazzoni, I. Banerjee, and R. Cammarota, "Post-quantum lattice-based cryptography implementations: A survey," *ACM Computing Surveys (CSUR)*, vol. 51, no. 6, pp. 1–41, 2019.

43. "Lattice-based cryptography," ISARA Corporation. https://www.isara.com/blog-posts/lattice-based-cryptography.html. (Accessed on 12/02/2022).

44. J. van de Pol, "Lattice-based cryptography," *Eindhoven University of Technology, Department of Mathematics and Computer Science*, 2011.

45. M. Kachurova, T. Shuminoski, and M. Bogdanoski, "Lattice-based cryptography: A quantum approach to secure the iot technology," in M. Bogdanoski (ed.), *Building Cyber Resilience Against Hybrid Threats*, pp. 122–133, IOS Press, 2022.

46. R. Chaudhary, G. S. Aujla, N. Kumar, and S. Zeadally, "Lattice-based public key cryptosystem for Internet of Things environment: Challenges and solutions," *IEEE Internet of Things Journal*, vol. 6, no. 3, pp. 4897–4909, 2018.

47. D. Kundi, Y. Zhang, C. Wang, A. Khalid, M. O'Neill, W. Liu, et al., "Ultra high-speed polynomial multiplications for lattice-based cryptography on FPGAs," *IEEE Transactions on Emerging Topics in Computing*, vol. 10, no. 4, 1993–2005, 2022.

48. J. Dey and R. Dutta, "Progress in multivariate cryptography: Systematic review, challenges and research directions," *ACM Computing Surveys*, vol. 55, no. 12, 1–34, 2022.

49. J. Ding and A. Petzoldt, "Current state of multivariate cryptography," *IEEE Security & Privacy*, vol. 15, no. 4, pp. 28–36, 2017.

50. "978-3-540-88702-7_6.pdf." https://link.springer.com/content/pdf/10.1007/978-3-540-88702-7_6.pdf?pdf=inline (Accessed on 12/02/2022).

51. C. Easttom, "More approaches to quantum-resistant cryptography," in C. Easttom (ed.), *Modern Cryptography: Applied Mathematics for Encryption and Information Security*, pp. 427–449, Springer, 2022.

52. X. Arnal Clemente, "Shorter secret keys in multivariate cryptography through optimal subspace representations," Master's thesis, Universitat Politècnica de Catalunya, 2022.

53. D. J. Bernstein, "Introduction to post-quantum cryptography," in D. J. Bernstein, J. Buchmann, E. Dahmen (eds.), *Post-Quantum Cryptography*, pp. 1–14, Springer, 2009.

54. P. Thanalakshmi, R. Anitha, N. Anbazhagan, C. Park, G. P. Joshi, and C. Seo, "A hash-based quantum-resistant designated verifier signature scheme," *Mathematics*, vol. 10, no. 10, p. 1642, 2022.

55. M. Iavich, G. Iashvili, S. Gnatyuk, A. Tolbatov, and L. Mirtskhulava, "Efficient and secure digital signature scheme for post quantum epoch," in *International Conference on Information and Software Technologies*, pp. 185–193, Springer, 2021.

56. C. Dods, N. P. Smart, and M. Stam, "Hash based digital signature schemes," in *IMA International Conference on Cryptography and Coding*, pp. 96–115, Springer, 2005.

57. A. Hülsing, "W-ots+–shorter signatures for hash-based signature schemes," in *International Conference on Cryptology in Africa*, pp. 173–188, Springer, 2013.

58. J. H. Cheon and T. Johansson, *Post-Quantum Cryptography: 13th International Workshop, PQCrypto 2022, Virtual Event, September 28–30, 2022, Proceedings*, vol. 13512. Springer Nature, 2022.

59. "Code-based cryptography," Springer Link. https://link.springer.com/reference workentry/10.1007/978-1-4419-5906-5_378#: (Accessed on 12/02/2022).

60. A. Wachter-Zeh, H. Bartz, and G. Liva, "Code-based cryptography," 2022.

61. M. Baldi, F. Chiaraluce, and P. Santini, "SPANSE: Combining sparsity with density for efficient one-time code-based digital signatures," *arXiv preprint arXiv:2205.12887*, 2022.

62. S. B. Wicker and V. K. Bhargava, *Reed-Solomon Codes and Their Applications*. John Wiley & Sons, 1999.

63. V. Weger, N. Gassner, and J. Rosenthal, "A survey on code-based cryptography," *arXiv preprint arXiv:2201.07119*, 2022.

64. Z. Fu, L. Fang, H. Huang, and B. Yu, "Distributed three-level QR codes based on visual cryptography scheme," *Journal of Visual Communication and Image Representation*, vol. 87, no. 10, p. 103567, 2022.

65. J. Oupický, "Theoretical foundations of cryptosystems based on isogenies of supersingular elliptic curves," 2022.

66. R. Nieminen et al., "Supersingular elliptic curve isogeny cryptography," 2016.

67. S. Kim, "Complete analysis of implementing isogeny-based cryptography using Huff form of elliptic curves," *IEEE Access*, vol. 9, pp. 154500–154512, 2021.

68. M. Campagna, T. Hardjono, L. Pintsov, B. Romansky, and T. Yu, "Kerberos revisited quantum-safe authentication," in *ETSI Quantum-Safe-Crypto Workshop, Sophia Antipolis, France*, 2013.

69. O. J. Unogwu, R. Doshi, K. K. Hiran, and M. M. Mijwil, "Introduction to quantum-resistant blockchain," in M. K. Shrivas, K. K. Hiran, A. Bhansali, R. Doshi (eds.), *Advancements in Quantum Blockchain with Real-Time Applications*, pp. 36–55, IGI Global, 2022.

Chapter 4

Moving towards 3D-biometric

Shrish Bajpai
Integral University, Lucknow, India

Divya Sharma
Institute of Engineering & Technology, Lucknow, India

4.1 INTRODUCTION

Biometrics is a Greek term that generally refers to the biological, physical, and behavioral traits of people [1]. Biological biometric features are DNA, ECG, etc.; physical biometric features include face, ear, iris, fingerprint, and hand geometry; and behavioral biometrics features include signatures and gait pattern [2]. For the last two decades, personal identification was based on the knowledge-based (password, pin, etc.) or physical token-based (ID card, passport, etc.). The physical token may be stolen, lost, or exchanged while lengthy passwords/pins are hard to remember. Hence, personal biometric (human identity from his unique anatomical features) is used to overcome the issues stated above. Initially, the 2D biometric system, such as fingerprint and images, is used for personal identification. These 2D biometrics have simple processing with less requirement of the hardware and a unimodal biometric framework (information obtained from the single source). Thus, 2D biometric systems have issues of commotion with sensitive information, intraclass varieties, etc. To solve the above-mentioned issues, multimodal biometrics are required.

On the other hand, biometrics can be classified based on the touch-based and touchless. One of the most widely utilized touch-based biometrics today is the fingerprint. But, due to the advancement of technologies, hackers can imitate fingerprints to access crucial data. Furthermore, the fingerprint-based security system may experience issues whether it is raining, snowing, or humid outside. In addition, hardware quality deteriorates over time. Alongside touch-based, facial recognition is considered the leading contactless biometric. Although it has advantages over fingerprinting, it faces many challenges including lighting, change, and age [3–4].

3D biometric systems have the following advantages over 1D and 2D biometric systems [5]:

- Compared to 2D biometrics, 3D biometrics is far more resistant to changes in lighting and position.
- For feature extraction, 3D data range may present a more comprehensive information source. Additionally, it may typically be integrated with 2D biometrics to improve system accuracy.

DOI: 10.1201/9781003468974-4

- Biometric systems using 3D biometrics are more resistant to attacks because 3D data is more difficult to forge or replicate.

The functioning of the 3D biometric system is the same as 2D biometric, which has four modules: User Interface Module, Acquisition Module, Recognition Module, and External Module [6]. An interface between the system and users is provided by the user interface module to provide efficient authentication. For people to enjoy using the device, a suitable user interface must be created. The route through which biometric features are obtained for further processing is the acquisition module. The crucial component of our system that decides if a user has been authenticated is called the Recognition Module. Pre-processing of the images, feature extraction, template generation, database updating, and matching are all included. The result of identification and verification is then displayed. The signal from the recognition module is received by the external module, which decides whether to approve or disapprove the requested operations. In reality, this module is an interface that can be attached to either other hardware or software components [7].

Any biometric system works in the three modes of operation: enrollment, identification, and verification [8]. In the first step, the user needs to enroll itself to a biometric system. The user's biometric data is recorded, processed accordingly, and features are extracted from the recorded data. This is completed in the first three modules. After this, captured user data is saved in the concern database. In the identification stage, a person whose information is saved in the biometric database is identified by the biometric system without any prior knowledge. The first three stages of one-to-many matching are completed to produce the identification template. For the feature matching procedure, the biometric system will use the entire database of existing templates. The result (fail or pass) will turn up after that. The verification procedure requires that the person's identification be claimed before the verification template is compared to the database in use to validate the person's claim of identity [9].

The 3D biometric can be divided into the three major categories named as Face, Hand, and Gait [10]. Again, 3D face biometric is sub classified into facial, ear, iris, and skull biometrics. In a similar way, 3D hand biometrics is sub classified into fingerprint, finger vein, and palm. The gait biometric has no further sub classifications. 3D biometric methods can be classified on the basis of the light source. These methods can be split into the active method and passive method. The light source of the active method directly hits the surface to create the 3D reconstruction, while the passive method uses ambient light conditions to capture the 3D image [11].

The false acceptance rate, also known as FAR, is a measure that may be used to assess the likelihood that an unauthorized user's attempt to enter the personal detail would be wrongly acquired by the biometric security system. The false recognition rate, often known as FRR, is a measurement used to determine the likelihood that a biometric security system may incorrectly refuse access to a valid user [12–14]. Mathematically, FAR and FRR are calculated as follows:

$$FAR = \frac{The\ total\ number\ of\ erroneous\ acceptances\ made\ during\ the\ procedure.}{The\ total\ number\ of\ identifications\ made\ throughout\ the\ procedure}$$

$$FRR = \frac{The\ total\ number\ of\ erroneous\ rejections\ made\ during\ the\ procedure.}{The\ total\ number\ of\ identifications\ made\ throughout\ the\ procedure}$$

Table 4.1 provides a short analysis (advantage and limitations) of 3D biometric methods, while Table 4.2 gives a brief analysis of 3D biometric

Table 4.1 Short analysis on advantage and disadvantage of different type 3D biometric methods

3D Biometric	Advantage	Limitation
3D Face Biometric		
Facial [15]	It is the most common biometric method used today. It is less expensive than other biometric methods.	It can be easily hacked. It has many data vulnerabilities.
Ear [16]	It has unique security advantages over other biometrics. It supports acoustic recognition.	It has high FAR with ears having hairs. It requires a special hardware device for scanning the ear biometric.
Iris [17]	It is safe as unique surface in human iris made of two muscular fibers. It is easy to use as non-touch method.	The camera setup is very complex.
Skull [18]	It has very low FAR and FRR.	It has many obstacles with complex mechanism.
3D Hand Biometric		
Fingerprint [19]	It is easy to implement. It is very cost-effective.	It has a low accuracy. It has high rate of error or technical failures.
Finger Vein [20]	It is very safe, as vein pattern is not easy to replicate.	Not good for small data size.
Palm [21]	Large number of data points for the authorization process. It has very low FAR and FRR.	Human's consent is necessary. It suffers from human age, body fat, and physical activity on hand.
3D Gait Biometric [22]	Non-touch biometric identification method. Based on behavioral (walking style) biometric technology. Ability of distance recognition. Human's consent is not necessary.	Lot of camera required for capturing the human motion. Complex learning process.

Table 4.2 Brief Analysis of 3D biometric methods on the different conditions

3D Biometric	Piracy	Weather Condition	Health Issue	Cost	Authentication Process	Authentication Complexity	Hardware Setup
Facial [15]	High	No	No	Low	Non-Touch	Low	Easy
Ear [16]	Medium	No	No	Low	Non-Touch	Low	Easy
Iris [17]	Low	No	Yes	Medium	Non-Touch	Medium	Medium
Skull [18]	Low	No	No	Medium	Non-Touch	High	Complex
Fingerprint [19]	High	Yes	Yes	Low	Touch/Non-Touch	Low	Easy
Finger Vein [20]	Low	No	Yes	Medium	Touch/Non-Touch	Low	Easy
Palm [21]	Low	No	Yes	Low	Touch/Non-Touch	Low	Easy
Gait [22]	Low	No	No	High	Non-Touch	High	Complex

Table 4.3 Major datasets related to the 3D biometrics

3D Biometric	Major Biometric Dataset
Facial [15]	Labeled faces database [23] 3D Facial Expression Database (606) [24] The Photoface Database [25]
Ear [16]	IIT-Kanpur, India (465) [26] Mathematical Analysis of Images (AMI) Ear Database, Spain (700) [27] University of California (UCR) dataset, U.S.A. [28]
Iris [17]	IIT Delhi, India Iris Database (1120) [29]
Skull [18]	XM2VTSDB dataset, University of Surrey, United Kingdom (2360 mug shots) [30]
Fingerprint [19]	Hong Kong Polytechnic dataset, Hong Kong (1560) [31]
Finger Vein [20]	3D Pose Varied Finger Vein (SCUT LFMB-3DPVFV) dataset (16848) [32]
Palm [21]	Rendered Hand Pose (RHD) dataset (41258) [33]
Gait [22]	AVAMVG dataset (200 video) [34] Multicamera Human Action Video (MuHAVi) dataset (136 video) [35]

Table 4.4 Perception of 3D Biometric systems (LOW is Low, MED is medium, and HIGH is High)

	3D Face Biometric [15–18]				3D Hand Biometric [19–21]			3D Gait Biometric [22]
	Facial	Ear	Iris	Skull	Finger print	Finger Vein	Palm	Gait
Universality	HIGH	MED	HIGH	HIGH	MED	HIGH	MED	MED
Uniqueness	LOW	LOW	HIGH	MED	HIGH	HIGH	HIGH	MED
Permanence	MED	MED	HIGH	MED	HIGH	HIGH	HIGH	LOW
Collectability	HIGH	HIGH	MED	MED	MED	MED	MED	MED
Circumvention	HIGH	HIGH	LOW	MED	MED	LOW	MED	HIGH

methods on physical conditions. Table 4.3 provides the information regarding the state of art datasets for 3D biometric algorithms, while Table 4.4 throws light on the perceptions of 3D biometric systems. Table 4.5 covers the classification of 3D biometric methods on the basis of 3D image reconstruction. The operational prevalence and major technological challenges in the context of 3D biometric systems are covered in Table 4.6.

There are two primary tenets of biometric recognition: the first is that physical characteristics are unique, and the second is that they remain constant throughout time. Whether these two assumptions hold true for the target population is a major factor in the biometric trait's viability and identification accuracy. Popular biometric features used in commercial systems include fingerprints, faces, and irises, with fingerprints alone accounting for

Table 4.5 Classification of 3D biometric methods on the basis of the 3D image reconstruction

3D Biometric on basis of 3D image reconstruction	Active Method	Projection of Structuring Light
		Tomography
		Time of Flight and Dwell Time
		Photometric Stereo Approach
	Passive Method	Structure from Silhouette Approach
		Structure from Texture Approach
		Structure from Motion Approach
		Stereo Vision Approach

Table 4.6 Characteristics and usability of 3D biometric systems

			Application Area			
3D Biometric	Biometric Data Capture Hardware	Operational Popularity	Handheld Devices	Access Control	Surveillance Devices	Forensics
Facial [15]	Commodity HW	Wide	✓	✓	✓	✓
Ear [16]	Commodity HW	Low	✓	✓	×	×
Iris [17]	Special Sensor	Wide	✓	✓	×	×
Skull [18]	Commodity HW	Low	✓	✓	×	×
Fingerprint [19]	Special Sensor	Wide	✓	✓	×	✓
Finger Vein [20]	Special Sensor	Average	✓	✓	×	✓
Palm [21]	Commodity HW	Wide	✓	✓	×	×
Gait [22]	Commodity HW	Low	✓	✓	×	×

Table 4.7 Major applications of 3D biometric systems

3D Biometric	Major Applications
Facial [15]	Commercial, security, and medical applications
Ear [16]	Forensic analysis and commercial
Iris [17]	Commercial, security, and medical applications
Skull [18]	Forensic analysis
Fingerprint [19]	Commercial
Finger Vein [20]	Commercial
Palm [21]	Commercial
Gait [22]	Surveillance, virtual and augmented

more than half of the civilian market share in 2010. Several of the behavioral features proposed in the literature are not very distinctive, and there is little evidence that they are stable over time.

Some functioning biometric systems based on these characteristics have been implemented thus far. While selecting a biometric modality, it is important to keep in mind the specifics of the application used for identification. Since a sensor for capturing voice (microphone) is already built into the phone, voice biometric is a good choice for authentication applications involving mobile phones.

A practical biometric system must also address a number of other issues, though (i.e., a system that uses biometrics for personal recognition), such as:

- The effectiveness of biometric systems banks on multiple aspects, such as the precision and speed with which recognition can be done, the resources available to accomplish this, and the operational and environmental factors that influence these metrics.
- The degree to which individuals are willing to make use of a particular biometric characteristic (identifier) in their day-to-day activities is a measurement of the acceptability of the biometric system.
- Circumvention is a term used to describe how quickly a system may be made to function improperly.

A viable 3D biometric system should be able to recognize individuals with the required precision, speed, and resource efficiency; it should also be safe for users, well-liked by the target audience, and resistant to various fraud schemes and systemic attacks. Figure 4.1 represents the process flow of a 3D biometric system.

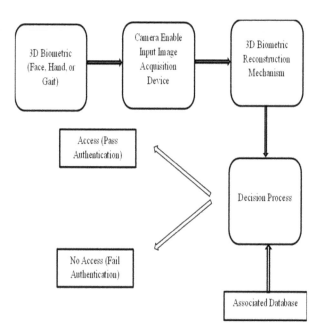

Figure 4.1 Flow chart of the 3D biometric system.

Because biometric recognition systems are by nature probabilistic, it is important to evaluate their performance in light of this fundamental quality. Within a certain tolerance of approximation, biometric recognition entails comparing a subject's observable biometric features to previously gathered data. It is vital to use approximate matching because of the disparities in biological traits and behaviors that exist both within individuals and across groups of people. As a result, biometric systems provide probabilistic outputs rather than the largely binary outputs typical of traditional information technology systems. This chapter gives a short and constructive review of the different 3D biometric systems.

4.2 3D FACE BIOMETRIC

Face is the most common and popular 3D biometric category. It is sub divided into facial, ear, iris, and skull [10]. 3D face biometric systems have the highest penetration in the total 3D biometric system, as their working mechanism is simple with the least requirement of hardware and software.

4.2.1 Facial biometric

This is the most common 3D biometric method used by most 3D biometric systems. It solves the problems of 2D face biometrics, which have many issues identifying facial images in low light or not proper posture, and it also recognizes the target with different angles rather than capturing the straight-on appearance. It is helpful to indicate straight borders in 3D spacing, and 3D face images contain a handful of focal points that correspond to 2D facial images. The location of the surface of the three-dimensional face is determined by hidden aspects of the physical anatomy. It is concerned with the development of technologies that (a) recognize faces and (b) scan 3D facial models to verify individuals [36, 37]. Many algorithms have been proposed for 3D facial biometric methods, which broadly splits into metric learning, geometric deep learning, biometric fusion, and face-to-DNA matching. Among them, deep learning-based algorithms have a high performance with low FAR and FRR [38].

4.2.2 Ear biometric

The development of the ear on a fetus begins between five weeks to seven weeks of pregnancy. In five weeks, a cluster of embryonic cells is connected to develop the ear. These develop cells in the lower part of the neck and are known as auricular hillocks. In the seventh week, the auricular hillocks widen and intertwine to form the shape of the ear. The hillocks move to the ear canal in the ninth week and become increasingly apparent as the ear develops [38]. After that, the ear will almost certainly develop in a linear fashion. Beginning at around four months of age and continuing until around eight years, the ear goes through a period of extended development.

Up to the age of seventy, neither the size nor the form of an individual's ear will change. Before the COVID-19 pandemic, the face-based biometric system was used, but because of extensive mask use, facial recognition has been unsuccessful. The fact that the human ear is visible makes it more suitable [39]. Ear biometric analysis has multiple advantages over other biometric methods such as face, iris, fingerprints, and palm prints. These advantages can be attributed to the fact that ear biometric analysis is easier to acquire, that facial expressions remain consistent over time, and that ear biometric analysis is more stable [10].

Utilizing 3D data, studies have been done to identify ears in profile images. By Chen et al., one of the pioneering works is provided. The scientists used a modified iterative closest point (ICP) approach to extract step edges from the 3D image and to detect the helix and antihelix of the ear. Their method is vulnerable to changes in scale and position, however. In order to identify ears from a 3D image, Zhou et al. suggested a technique called histograms of classified shapes (HCS), which integrated a 3D form model with an SVM classifier. However, when prior information about the given ear is not available, their method is unable to locate an ear. To identify ears from 3D images, Prakash et al. proposed an edge connection graph. As a result, they struggled on the UND J2 dataset and were unable to handle the impact of off-plain rotation. Pflug et al. introduced an approach based on a binarized mean curvature map for identifying edges in 3D profile photos [39].

4.2.3 Iris biometric

The 3D iris biometric has certain qualities due to a distinctive surface consisting of two muscle fibers of the human eye. Iris as a biometric has generally been the subject of extensive scientific study; however, this research is only two dimensional [17]. According to Bastia et al., this is the first attempt to model his 3D iris using near-infrared (NIR) images obtained from a Raspberry Pi v2.1 camera. In addition, four NIR LEDs produced infrared light. Two white LEDs were utilized in tandem to generate a bright atmosphere around the pupil while maintaining a relatively tiny pupil. [40]. This is significant because the pupil is eliminated prior to the 3D reconstruction, and information about the eye's depth perception is derived from the remainder of the eye.

The Raspberry Pi 3 Model B system was used to operate the camera and temporarily save the photographs in system memory. The VR glass set had all the aforementioned components installed. Additionally, a proposed attachment for the camera gave it the ability to move in a 40-degree arc. A total of 17 iris images were intended to be captured by the device, with a

2.5-degree angle between each image. The Python photogrammetry tool-box was also utilized by the authors to construct the 3D model. The model was built from a variety of photos taken from various angles by the open-source toolkit. It is also stated that the lack of information on measurements and results made it challenging to assess the work's outcomes and methodology [41].

Benalcazta et al. decided to use visible light as the source of illumination, as opposed to the earlier strategy. They created a unique device that shines lateral and frontal visible light onto the iris (LFVL). Six LEDs in the front and two more on the sides of each eye provide the light. The varying degrees of incidence from the light source are what produce the shadows and infor-mation about the depth of the iris. By filming each eye for three seconds, 120 different people made up the dataset.

According to the preceding research, facial recognition is the most com-mon method for 3D biometric applications. To be utilized as a biometric, a 3D model must initially be made, which is trailed by highlight extraction [42]. Computer vision methods can be used to finish this. The method of reconstruction is determined by how the images are captured. It can be split into the two group active method and passive method as mentioned in Table 4.5. Further examination of the passive methods reveals three subcategories connected to facial recognition: stereo vision, SfS, and SfM. Seven applica-tions made use of SfS, six applications made use of stereo vision, and five applications made use of SfM.

Only one of the active methods made use of transmissive computerized tomography, whereas the rest of the active methods relied on reflecting light from a source. The percentages were almost the same: six applications used SfM, seven used SfS, and five used SfM. The reflective methods can also be further broken down into two subcategories: time-of-flight and structured light. These proportions were also similar, with four using time-of-flight and five using structured light [43].

4.2.4 Skull biometric

The skull biometric is the least-used biometric system, as it has high com-plexity in the capturing of a 3D image of a human skull. Its scope is very dif-ferent than other biometric methods, as it usually involves a cadaver, which is very difficult to recognize by other human body features [10, 18].

4.3 3D HAND BIOMETRIC

The user's hand shape and vascular pattern are measured as part of a pro-posed hand biometric authentication system. The lengths and angles of the finger valleys, the lengths and profiles of the fingers, the thickness of the side view of the hand, the K-curvature with a hand-shaped chain code, and the direction-based vascular-pattern extraction method were all employed to obtain the hand geometry [10].

4.3.1 Fingerprint biometric

One of the most distinctive biometrics is the fingerprint. For human authentication, fingerprints are frequently employed because of their great accuracy and uniqueness. Traditional fingerprint scans usually produce fragmentary or poor-quality images since they require placing and pressing the fingers against a hard surface, such as glass or silicon. Typically, skin deformations, wetness, finger dirt residue, finger sweat, finger slips and smear, or sensor noise are to blame for this frequent deterioration in fingerprint picture quality. In addition to dealing with the leftovers of prior fingerprint impressions, which might constitute a security risk, contactless fingerprint systems can offer hygienic solutions to these problems [44]. In order to address the shortcomings of the contact-based 2D fingerprint identification system and increase recognition accuracy, contactless 3D fingerprint reconstruction and recognition techniques have been developed in response to the rapid development of 3D scanning and reconstruction technologies. In recent years, an increasing number of 3D fingerprint identification technologies have been created. The most accurate techniques for contactless 3D fingerprint recognition have been found to be minutiae-based fingerprint matching techniques. However, viewpoint distortion and reconstruction error during 3D fingerprint capture can greatly impair the performance of contactless 3D fingerprint matching and the accuracy of minutiae extraction [45].

4.3.2 Finger vein biometric

Finger vein biometric offers many advantages with reference to other biometric methods, as the vein pattern in the finger reveals the vast network of blood vessels. It uses ultrasound or optical scanning to record the vein pattern of the finger under observation. The vein pattern within a human's finger is unique and invisible from the outside; consequently, it is difficult to replicate [46]. Doppler ultrasound has been utilized to identify major blood vessels based on tissue blood flow. However, the system's sensitivity to small vascular structures is inadequate.

In contrast to pure optical modalities, photoacoustic tomography (PAT) can acquire highly detailed images of the vasculature with sufficient depth information. In PAT, a laser light pulse illuminates the skin's surface, causing thermoelastic expansion that converts into ultrasonic waves. However, even if quite accurate patterns were obtained, the acquisition time was too long for both technologies. Veins are utilized in multimodal systems alongside other characteristics, particularly the fingerprint. This technique, also known as biometric fusion, enhances the performance of the biometric system in terms of recognition accuracy, universality, and security [47].

4.3.3 Palm biometric

The palm biometric system also uses ultrasound waves to capture the image of a human palm. Any effective palm biometric system acquires the 3D image of a human palm (dimension for the system should be 50 mm by 30 mm with 15 mm height) for 5 seconds having the four 10 mW laser [48]. The 3D images are obtained by the single transducer performing the mechanical scan in two orthogonal directions. In this way, exact palm features (palm line's depth and curve, as well as creases on the surface of the hand) are extracted from the recoded image, and further identification or verification process is done. Filters and statistical tools and neural network- based algorithms are used for the identification and verification of the human palm [49].

4.4 3D GAIT BIOMETRIC

An application of biometrics known as gait recognition determines a person's identity based on their walking patterns. The fact that a person can be identified from a distance using gait as a biometric is its greatest advantage. To put it another way, gait can be used with low resolution. Human gait describes human motion's temporal dynamics and spatial statics. Compared to other biometrics, it typically takes up significantly more pixels [50].

Borelli pioneered the idea of step analysis. He provided a description of the various gait cycles and muscle movements when a person is walking. He was the first scientist to measure the center of gravity of the human body. He described when a person walks, how the body balances as the center of gravity moves forward outside the area of support. Step detection was first used in the fields of medicine and psychology [51]. The 3D method of human movement was introduced by Brown and Fisher. Images were generated using luminescent marks with built-in triangulation capabilities. Images are generated at a frequency of 26 frames per second. A 3D technique examines the angular displacement of the lower extremity joints [22, 52].

Yamauchi et al. captured the 3D data using an active vision sensor. Following that, he made an effort to include the 3D model into the data so that he could acquire information on kinematics. They collected subject poses with the use of a laser range sensor. These subject poses solely reflect the critical frames of a gait cycle. The standard of excellence of the 3D data is rather good in this particular situation. The complete gait sequence is generated by interpolating joint locations and motions using body models fitted to a computer. The results of the experiments indicate high recognition rates, despite the fact that there are currently only six participants [53].

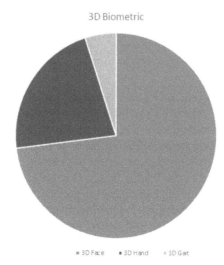

3D Biometric

■ 3D Face   ■ 3D Hand   ■ 3D Gait

Figure 4.2 Represents a pie chart of a 3D biometric system with several different applications.

Seely et al. developed the Soton 3D gait dataset, which was then used in a view-invariant gait identification experiment employing model-free analysis with great success. Simple approaches based on an average silhouette in two dimensions and viewpoint projection techniques were used to transform 3D data into 2D data that was unaffected by the viewer's point of view. Three different viewpoint projections were utilized: side-on, front-on, and top-down. The results demonstrated that using 3D gait data can result in a high degree of accuracy (99.6%), with the best performance achieved by combining projected views [54].

4.5 CONCLUSION

In this chapter, we described the different type of biometrics with their applications. After performing an in-depth investigation into the many papers, preliminary statistical data indicated that face recognition was the 3D biometric employed most of the time in this specific study field. The remaining seven categories were: palm, iris, gait, skull, ear, finger vein, and finger. Face, hand, and gait are the three basic categories that can be used to group them. Future research should be organized according to a framework that includes measurements for the related 2D photos for every new 3D biometric study. Devices should have 2D capabilities to achieve this. In order to facilitate future researchers' experimentation, more datasets for uncommon biometric traits should be produced. These issues must be resolved to demonstrate the need for 3D technology, and they will form the foundation for future advancements.

ACKNOWLEDGEMENTS

I am sincerely thankful to the anonymous reviewers for their critical comments and suggestions to improve the quality of this chapter. The authors want to express their gratitude to Integral University, Lucknow, Uttar Pradesh, India, for providing manuscript number IU/R&D/2023-MCN0001967 for the present research work.

REFERENCES

1. Prakash, A. J., Patro, K. K., Samantray, S., Pławiak, P., & Hammad, M. (2023). A deep learning technique for biometric authentication using ECG beat template matching. *Information*, 14(2), 65. doi:10.3390/info14020065
2. Goutham, V., Lakshmi, D. L., Hamsashree, M. K., Naveen, B., & Girijamba, D. L. (2023, January). A review on detection of vein pattern in human body for the biometric applications. In *Cognition and Recognition: 8th International Conference, ICCR 2021*, Mandya, India, December 30–31, 2021, *Revised Selected Papers* (pp. 1–17). Cham: Springer Nature Switzerland. doi:10.1007/978-3-031-22405-8_1
3. Nayar, G. R., & Thomas, T. (2023). Partial palm vein based biometric authentication. *Journal of Information Security and Applications*, 72, 103390. doi:10.1016/j.jisa.2022.103390
4. Singh, T., Zaka-Ur-Rab, S., & Arrin, S. (2023). Effect of pupil dilation on biometric iris recognition systems for personal authentication. *Indian Journal of Ophthalmology*, 71(1), 57–61. doi:10.4103/ijo.IJO_1417_22
5. Iula, A., & Micucci, M. (2022). Multimodal biometric recognition based on 3D ultrasound palmprint-hand geometry fusion. *IEEE Access*, 10, 7914–7925. doi:10.1109/ACCESS.2022.3143433
6. Prakash, S., & Gupta, P. (2015). *Ear Biometrics in 2D and 3D: Localization and Recognition* (Vol. 10). Springer, Singapore. ISBN: 78-981-287-374-3.
7. Zhang, D., & Lu, G. (2013). *3D Biometrics*. New York: Springer.
8. Boulgouris, N. V., Plataniotis, K. N., & Micheli-Tzanakou, E. (eds.). (2009). *Biometrics: Theory, Methods, and Applications*. John Wiley & Sons, Canada. ISBN: 9780470247822.
9. Zhang, D., Lu, G., & Zhang, L. (2018). *Advanced Biometrics*. Springer International Publishing, Switzerland. ISBN: 9783319615448.
10. Samatas, G. G., & Papakostas, G. A. (2022). Biometrics: Going 3D. *Sensors*, 22(17), 6364. doi:10.3390/s22176364
11. Bronstein, A. M., Bronstein, M. M., & Kimmel, R. (2003). Expression-invariant 3D face recognition. In *Audio-and Video-Based Biometric Person Authentication: 4th International Conference, AVBPA 2003* Guildford, UK, June 9–11, 2003 *Proceedings 4* (pp. 62–70). Berlin Heidelberg: Springer. doi:10.1007/3-540-44887-X
12. Rathod, V. J., Iyer, N. C., & Meena, S. M. (2015, October). A survey on fingerprint biometric recognition system. In *2015 International Conference on Green Computing and Internet of Things (ICGCIoT)*. (pp. 323–326). IEEE. doi:10.1109/ICGCIoT.2015.7380482

13. Chang, K. I., Bowyer, K. W., & Flynn, P. J. (2005). An evaluation of multimodal 2D+3D face biometrics. *IEEE Transactions on Pattern Analysis and Machine Intelligence*, 27(4), 619–624. doi:10.1109/TPAMI.2005.70

14. Yan, P., & Bowyer, K. W. (2007). Biometric recognition using 3D ear shape. *IEEE Transactions on Pattern Analysis and Machine Intelligence*, 29(8), 1297–1308. doi:10.1109/TPAMI.2007.1067

15. Hoskens, H., Liu, D., Naqvi, S., Lee, M. K., Eller, R. J., Indencleef, K., ... & Claes, P. (2021). 3D facial phenotyping by biometric sibling matching used in contemporary genomic methodologies. *PLoS Genetics*, 17(5), e1009528. doi:10.1371/journal.pgen.1009528

16. Ganapathi, I. I., Ali, S. S., Vu, N.-S., Prakash, S., & Werghi, N. (2022). A survey of 3D ear recognition techniques. *ACM Computing Surveys (CSUR)*, 55(10), 1–36. doi:10.1145/3560884

17. Benalcazar, D. P., Bastias, D., Perez, C. A., & Bowyer, K. W. (2019). A 3D iris scanner from multiple 2D visible light images. *IEEE Access*, 7, 61461–61472. doi:10.1109/ACCESS.2019.2915786

18. Hameed, S. A., Zaidan, B. B., Zaidan, A. A., Naji, A. W., & Tawfiq, O. F. (2010). An accurate method to obtain bio-metric measurements for three dimensional skull. *Journal of Applied Sciences*, 10(2), 145–150.

19. Cheng, K. H., & Kumar, A. (2019). Contactless biometric identification using 3D finger knuckle patterns. *IEEE Transactions on Pattern Analysis and Machine Intelligence*, 42(8), 1868–1883. doi:10.1109/TPAMI.2019.2904232

20. Zhan, Y., Rathore, A. S., Milione, G., Wang, Y., Zheng, W., Xu, W., & Xia, J. (2020). 3D finger vein biometric authentication with photoacoustic tomography. *Applied Optics*, 59(28), 8751–8758. doi:10.1364/AO.400550

21. De Santis, M., Agnelli, S., Nardiello, D., & Iula, A. (2017, September). 3D ultrasound palm vein recognition through the centroid method for biometric purposes. In *2017 IEEE International Ultrasonics Symposium (IUS)* (pp. 1–4). IEEE. doi:10.1109/ULTSYM.2017.8091946

22. Santos, G., Tavares, T., & Rocha, A. (2022). Reliability and generalization of gait biometrics using 3D inertial sensor data and 3D optical system trajectories. *Scientific Reports*, 12(1), 1–15. doi:10.1038/s41598-022-12452-6

23. Huang, G. B., & Learned-Miller, E. (2014). *Labeled faces in the wild: Updates and new reporting procedures*. Dept. Comput. Sci., Univ. Massachusetts Amherst, Amherst, MA, USA, Tech. Rep, 14(003).

24. Yin, L., Wei, X., Sun, Y., Wang, J., Rosato, M. A 3D facial expression database for facial behavior research. In *Proc. IEEE Int. Conf. on Automatic Face and Gesture Recognition, Southampton, UK*, pp. 211–216 (2006).

25. Zafeiriou, S., Hansen, M., Atkinson, G., Argyriou, V., Petrou, M., Smith, M., Smith, L. The photoface database. In *Proceedings of the CVPR 2011 WORKSHOPS, Colorado Springs, CO, USA*, 20–25 June 2011; pp. 132–139.

26. Kumar, A., & Wu, C. (2012). Automated human identification using ear imaging. *Pattern Recognition*, 45(3), 956–968. doi:10.1016/j.patcog.2011.06.005

27. AMI Ear Database. Available online: https://webctim.ulpgc.es/research_works/ami_ear_database/

28. Chen, H., & Bhanu, B. (2007). Human ear recognition in 3D. *IEEE Transactions on Pattern Analysis and Machine Intelligence*, 29(4), 718–737. doi:10.1109/TPAMI.2007.1005

29. IIT Delhi Iris Database. Available online: https://www4.comp.polyu.edu. hk/~csajaykr/IITD/Database_Iris.htm

30. Alanazi, H., Zaidan, B. B., & Zaidan, A. A. (2010). 3D skull recognition using 3D matching technique. arXiv preprint arXiv:1001.3502.

31. The Hong Kong Polytechnic University 3D Fingerprint Images Database. Available online: https://tinyurl.com/4nmb2keb

32. Xu, H., Yang, W., Wu, Q., & Kang, W. (2022). Endowing rotation invariance for 3D finger shape and vein verification. *Frontiers in Computer Science*, 16, 1–16.

33. Nicodemou, V. C., Oikonomidis, I., Tzimiropoulos, G., & Argyros, A. (2020, July). Learning to infer the depth map of a hand from its color image. In *2020 International Joint Conference on Neural Networks (IJCNN)* (pp. 1–8). IEEE.

34. López-Fernández, D., Madrid-Cuevas, F. J., Carmona-Poyato, Á., Marín-Jiménez, M. J., & Muñoz-Salinas, R. (2014). The AVA multi-view dataset for gait recognition. In *International Workshop on Activity Monitoring by Multiple Distributed Sensing*. Cham, Switzerland: Springer, pp. 26–39.

35. Singh, S., Velastin, S.A., & Ragheb, H. (2010). Muhavi: A multicamera human action video dataset for the evaluation of action recognition methods. In *Proceedings of the 2010 7th IEEE International Conference on Advanced Video and Signal Based Surveillance*, Boston, MA, USA, 29 August–1 September; pp. 48–55.

36. Smeets, D., Claes, P., Vandermeulen, D., & Clement, J. G. (2010). Objective 3D face recognition: Evolution, approaches and challenges. *Forensic Science International*, 201(1–3), 125–132. doi:10.1016/j.forsciint.2010.03.023

37. Kelkboom, E. J., Gökberk, B., Kevenaar, T. A., Akkermans, A. H., & van der Veen, M. (2007). "3D face": Biometric template protection for 3D face recognition. In *Advances in Biometrics: International Conference, ICB 2007*, Seoul, Korea, August 27–29, 2007. Proceedings (pp. 566–573). Springer Berlin Heidelberg. doi:10.1007/978-3-540-74549-5_60

38. Tharewal, S., Malche, T., Tiwari, P. K., Jabarulla, M. Y., Alnuaim, A. A., Mostafa, A. M., & Ullah, M. A. (2022). Score-level fusion of 3D face and 3D ear for multimodal biometric human recognition. *Computational Intelligence and Neuroscience*, 2022. doi:10.1155/2022/3019194

39. Kaur, G., & Verma, H. K. (2022, October). Existing approaches in ear biometrics. In *2022 IEEE 4th International Conference on Cybernetics, Cognition and Machine Learning Applications (ICCCMLA)* (pp. 490–496). IEEE. doi:10.1109/ICCCMLA56841.2022.9989290

40. Bastias, D., Perez, C. A., Benalcazar, D. P., & Bowyer, K. W. (2017). A method for 3D iris reconstruction from multiple 2D near-infrared images. In *Proceedings of the 2017 IEEE International Joint Conference on Biometrics (IJCB)*, Denver, CO, USA, 1–4 October, pp. 503–509. doi:10.1109/BTAS.2017.8272735

41. Moulon, P., & Bezzi, A. (2011). Python photogrammetry toolbox: A free solution for three-dimensional documentation; ArcheoFoss: Napoli, Italy, pp. 1–12.

42. Benalcazar, D. P., Zambrano, J. E., Bastias, D., Perez, C. A., & Bowyer, K. W. (2020). A 3D iris scanner from a single image using convolutional neural networks. *IEEE Access*, 8, 98584–98599.

43. Zheng, C., Cham, T. J., & Cai, J. (2018). T2net: Synthetic-to-realistic translation for solving single-image depth estimation tasks. In *Proceedings of the European Conference on Computer Vision (ECCV)*, Munich, Germany, 8–14 September, pp. 767–783.

44. Zhou, W., Hu, J., Wang, S., Petersen, I., & Bennamoun, M. (2014). Performance evaluation of large 3D fingerprint databases. *Electronics Letters*, 50(15), 1060–1061. doi:10.1049/el.2014.1927

45. Huang, S., Zhang, Z., Zhao, Y., Dai, J., Chen, C., Xu, Y., … & Xie, L. (2014). 3D fingerprint imaging system based on full-field fringe projection profilometry. *Optics and Lasers in Engineering*, 52, 123–130. doi:10.1016/j.optlaseng.2013.07.001

46. Xu, H., Yang, W., Wu, Q., & Kang, W. (2022). Endowing rotation invariance for 3D finger shape and vein verification. *Frontiers of Computer Science*, 16(5), 165332. doi:10.1007/s11704-021-0475-9

47. Jia, W., Xia, W., Zhao, Y., Min, H., & Chen, Y.-X. (2021). 2D and 3D palmprint and palm vein recognition based on neural architecture search. *International Journal of Automation and Computing*, 18, 377–409. doi:10.1007/s11633-021-1292-1

48. De Santis, M., Agnelli, S., Nardiello, D., & Iula, A. (2017, September). 3D ultrasound palm vein recognition through the centroid method for biometric purposes. In *2017 IEEE International Ultrasonics Symposium (IUS)* (pp. 1–4). IEEE. doi:10.1109/ULTSYM.2017.8091946

49. Dargan, S., & Kumar, M. (2020). A comprehensive survey on the biometric recognition systems based on physiological and behavioral modalities. *Expert Systems with Applications*, 143, 113114. doi:10.1016/j.eswa.2019.113114

50. Liu, Y., Jiang, X., Sun, T., & Xu, K. (2019, September). 3D gait recognition based on a CNN-LSTM network with the fusion of SkeGEI and DA features. In *2019 16th IEEE International Conference on Advanced Video and Signal Based Surveillance (AVSS)* (pp. 1–8). IEEE. doi:10.1109/AVSS.2019.8909881

51. Sethi, D., Bharti, S., & Prakash, C. (2022). A comprehensive survey on gait analysis: History, parameters, approaches, pose estimation, and future work. *Artificial Intelligence in Medicine*, 129, 102314. doi:10.1016/j.artmed.2022.102314

52. Zhao, G., Liu, G., Li, H., & Pietikainen, M. (2006, April). 3D gait recognition using multiple cameras. In *7th International Conference on Automatic Face and Gesture Recognition (FGR06)* (pp. 529–534). IEEE. doi:10.1109/FGR.2006.2

53. Yamauchi, K., Bhanu, B., & Saito, H. (2009, June). Recognition of walking humans in 3D: Initial results. In *2009 IEEE Computer Society Conference on Computer Vision and Pattern Recognition Workshops* (pp. 45–52). IEEE. doi:10.1109/CVPRW.2009.5204296

54. Seely, R. D., Samangooei, S., Lee, M., Carter, J. N., & Nixon, M. S. (2008, September). The University of Southampton Multi-Biometric Tunnel and introducing a novel 3D gait dataset. In *2008 IEEE Second International Conference on Biometrics: Theory, Applications and Systems* (pp. 1–6). IEEE. doi:10.1109/BTAS.2008.4699353

Chapter 5

A Secured Dual Image Watermarking technique using QR decomposition, Hénon map, and Chaotic encryption in wavelet domain and its authentication using BRISK

Divyanshu Awasthi
MNNIT Allahabad, Allahabad, India

Priyank Khare
IIIT Ranchi, Ranchi, India

Vinay Kumar Srivastava
MNNIT Allahabad, Allahabad, India

5.1 INTRODUCTION

The protection of multimedia data is a major problem because of the development of computer technology and 5G networking. Speech, video, and image data are all examples of multimedia data [1]. Medical data forgery or phishing is an alarming situation for researchers to provide higher security. The size of medical data is increasing day by day; therefore, the confidentiality and integrity of that data are also important. Due to numerous passive (the attacker's objective is to get information) and active (the attacker may change the data or harm the system) attacks, the authentication of medical data is also critically important. The details of active and passive attacks are shown in Figure 5.1.

A universal standard for the storage, exchange, and transmission of medical images is called DICOM, which stands for Digital Imaging and Communications in Medicine [2]. Watermarking systems can be divided into two primary categories based on the embedding process: transform domain and spatial domain. In the spatial domain, the watermark is embedded into certain host image pixels. Before a watermark is introduced to the frequency coefficients in the transform domain, the host picture is transformed in frequency domain [3]. According to the computer emergency response team (CERT), security breaching trends are increasing drastically. In 2020, the security breaching trends were as unauthorized network

DOI: 10.1201/9781003468974-5

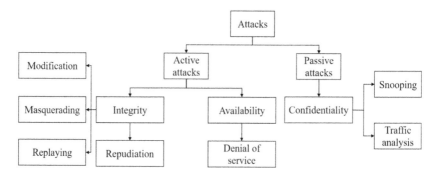

Figure 5.1 Details of active and passive attacks.

scanning (89%), virus or malicious codes (9%), website defacements (2%), phishing (<1%), website intrusion and malware propagation (<1%), others (<1%) [4]. Cybersecurity techniques have primarily been used in the e-banking, multimedia, social media, e-commerce, defense, and e-healthcare industries [5]. Numerous security objectives can be pursued, including authentication (which is a necessary part of nonrepudiation), integrity (because information must continually change), confidentiality (to safeguard our private information), and availability (the information created and stored by an organization needs to be available to authorized entities). The proposed watermarking method uses encryption techniques, a Hénon map, and a Chaotic logistic map. For authentication, BRISK feature matching is used.

The comparison of LWT with discrete wavelet transform (DWT) is shown in [1]. To obtain the ideal scaling factor, two different optimization techniques are used. The comparison of particle swarm (PSO) and JAYA optimization is also mentioned in [1]. But this technique lacks in security, as no extra security algorithm is used. The normalized correlation coefficient (NCC) can further be improved for shearing, thresholding, and histogram equalization attacks. In [2], Schur decomposition is used, along with singular value decomposition (SVD) for embedding. Speeded-up robust features (SURF) are utilized for feature matching to offer authentication. But this technique is also lacking in security, as no extra security algorithm is used. The NCC value is not up to the mark for histogram equalization. The input DICOM images are taken from the Cancer imaging archive (TCIA) [6]. In [3], a DWT-SVD-based robust watermarking technique is proposed. DWT is used to split the image into different sub-bands. SVD suffers from the false positive problem (FPP). The lack of security is also the primary concern of this work. Hurrah et al. [5] proposed a double watermarking-based digital multimedia validation and privacy protection method. The DWT, DCT, encryption, and Arnold transform are all used in this scheme. A detailed imperceptibility and robustness explanation is not discussed, whereas the complexity of the proposed technique is also very high. In [7], DWT is used to transform the image into different sub-bands, and SVD is used for the embedding procedure. Low-low sub-band is used for watermarking with a 20% increase in the efficiency [7] of results. But this technique is also lacking in security, as no extra security algorithm is used. Homomorphic transform-based watermarking technique is proposed in [8] by using the wavelet domain. SVD is used to add the dominant component of the input and watermark image. The results also suffer from a diagonal line problem. The technique is robust and imperceptible, but the security is compromised in [8]. In [9], QR decomposition-based image watermarking is proposed where Arnold transform is used for encryption. This method overcomes the problem of false-positive detection, and the NCC values are not good for JPEG (30) compression and Gaussian noise (0.6). The DWT-SVD-based watermarking scheme is proposed in [10]. The region of interest in the medical image is split into sub-bands. Hamming code is applied to electronic patient records to reduce the bit error rate. The FPP of SVD is also removed in this method. The NCC values are not good for JPEG compression (20), Shearing, and Dither. Separate security enhancing algorithm is missing in [10]. The PSO is used in [11] to get the optimized gain value. Block-SVD is used instead of normal SVD to overcome FPP. The healthcare application of watermarking is explored in [12]. DWT-DCT-SVD-based watermarking is proposed in [12]. The robustness is increased by using back propagation neural network (BPNN). In [13], a method for a low-complex, distortion-controlled, reliable, and secure color image watermarking for tele-health applications is proposed. This technique applied dual watermarks to the cover image (using LWT-DCT) for nonrepudiation, confidentiality, and authenticity. Hsu et al. [14] proposes a dual image watermarking technique to enhance the performance of algorithm against cropping attack, and QR decomposition is used in this proposed work. According to Koley et al. [15], a dual watermarking approach based on an attention and focus model has been suggested for concomitant image copyright protection and identification. Two watermarks are concurrently embedded in the host image using the suggested technique, and Hessenberg decomposition is used, which is slightly complex in comparison with other transforms. In [16], LWT- and SVD-based dual image watermarking is proposed, which suffers from a false positive problem, and this work is also not highly robust. For applications such as copyright protection, authentication, and recovery, a unique dual-color image watermarking is created by Al-Otum et al. [17], and this work is semi-fragile. The dual image watermarking offers better copyright protection over single image watermarking with the following merits: reduction in bandwidth, better authentication with improved security, and storage requirements are also reduced.

Using the dual image watermarking approach, two watermark logos are incorporated into a single host image. The dual image watermarking technique's main challenge is to offer great durability, imperceptibility, and capacity. Two logos could be utilized to offer strong copyright defense.

Processing cost, or the computational overheads involved in inserting and detecting the watermark, is another problem. The creation of a common strategy for all digital media that is resilient to different attacks is another issue. The proposed work overcomes all the above-mentioned problems. With the use of Hénon map, chaotic logistic encryption, and BRSIK feature authentication, an effective watermarking strategy to address the research gaps identified by the overview of the existing strategies stated above is presented.

The main features of the technique proposed in this chapter are listed below:

(1) The diagonal components of the upper triangular matrix resulting from the QR decomposed image have a better degree of significance because they are used for embedding.
(2) The security of the proposed watermarking approach is further strengthened by use of the dual watermark images, which offers better robustness against malicious attacks.
(3) A chaotic logistic map is used to transmit the watermarked image securely, which ensures better transmission.
(4) Hénon map is used to encrypt the sub-band, which is used for embedding dual watermark images, which enhance the security of details of the patient used as a watermark image providing better medical treatment.
(5) In this proposed work, we have achieved feature verification using BRISK, which facilitates copyright protection in a better way against unwanted attacks.

The remainder of the chapter is structured as follows: Section 5.2 provides a detail of preliminaries. The embedding and extraction process for watermarks is described in Section 5.3. In Section 5.4, the discussion and simulation findings are mentioned. Section 5.5 discusses BRISK feature matching. Section 5.6 contains the comparison of results, and the Conclusion is in Section 5.7.

5.2 PRELIMINARIES

5.2.1 Lifting wavelet transform

LWT is the second generation transform faster than DWT [1]. It has three main steps: Split, Predict, and Update [2, 18]. Split is used to bifurcate the signal into even and odd. Predict tries to foresee the odd signal with the help of even, and vice versa, and the last step is Updating. In 1998, Sweldens [19] developed the lifting wavelet transform. Figure 5.2 shows the schematic diagram of LWT.

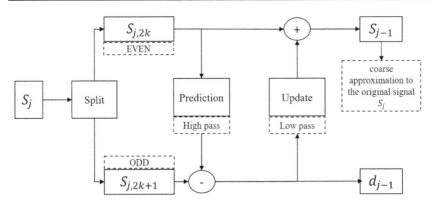

Figure 5.2 Block representation of LWT.

5.2.2 QR decomposition

For an input matrix '*M*' the QR decomposition [9] can be defined as:

$$[Q,R] = qr(M) \tag{5.1}$$

In Eq. (5.1), *R* is an *n*×*k* upper triangular matrix, and *Q* is an *n*×*n* orthogonal matrix [20]. Figure 5.3 shows the number of non-zero elements (32896) of matrix *R*.

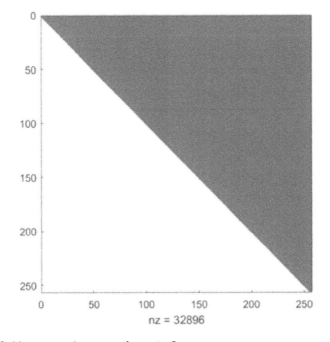

nz = 32896

Figure 5.3 Non-zero elements of matrix R.

5.2.3 Hénon map

In 1976, Michel Hénon, a French mathematician and astronomer, proposed the Hénon map, a two-dimensional map [21]. The following equations can be used to define the Hénon map mathematically [22]:

$$p(j+1) = 1 + q(j) - a_1 \times p(j)^2 \tag{5.2}$$

$$q(j+1) = a_2 \times p(j) \tag{5.3}$$

a_1 and a_2 are referred to as bifurcation parameters in Eqs. (5.2) and (5.3). The values of p and q have no bearing on the contraction in a 2D Hénon map. The Hénon attractor for $a_1 = 1.4$, and $a_2 = 0.3$ is shown in Figure 5.4.

5.2.4 Chaotic logistic map

The behavior of some nonlinear dynamic systems that, under certain circumstances, display dynamics that are sensitive to beginning conditions, is described by chaos theory [23]. The state evolution [23] can be described as shown in Eq. (5.4).

$$z(i+1) = r \times z(i) * (1 - z(i)) \tag{5.4}$$

where $r \in [0, 4]$ and Figure 5.5 shows the logistic encrypted watermarked image.

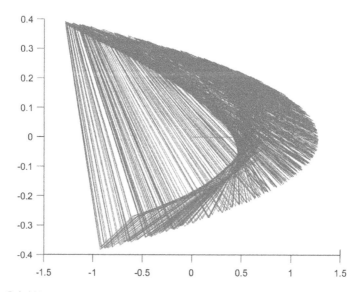

Figure 5.4 Hénon attractor.

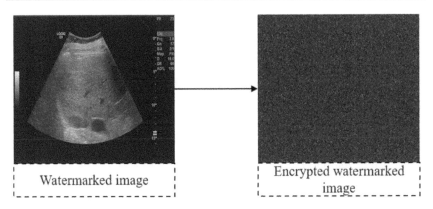

Figure 5.5 Encrypted watermarked image.

5.3 WATERMARKING PROCEDURE

The watermark embedding and extraction procedure is mentioned in sections 3.1 and 3.2. In the embedding procedure, the cover image is first divided into sub-bands (LL_1, HL_1, LH_1, HH_1) using one LWT. Apply QR decomposition to HL_1 and LH_1, and then extract the diagonal component of both the sub-bands of the input host image. Take the first watermark image as the cameraman and the second as details of the patient and apply LWT to both watermark images and apply Hénon scrambling to low-high sub-band of details of patient, and then extract the diagonal components of both watermark images. Add the diagonal components of both the watermark images and the cover image by taking suitable scaling factor. Apply inverse QR and LWT to get the watermarked image, then apply chaotic logistic map to scramble the image and send it to another end. In the extraction procedure, first receive the scrambled watermarked image and apply the decryption process to get the watermarked image. Apply LWT to get the watermarked sub-bands and get the watermarked diagonal components after applying QR decomposition. Apply inverse embedding, inverse QR decomposition, Hénon decryption, and inverse LWT to get both the watermark images back.

5.3.1 Embedding process

Step 1: To divide the input cover image into sub-bands as shown in Eq. (5.5), apply one level LWT.

$$[LL_1, HL_1, LH_1, HH_1] = lwt2(host\ image)$$ (5.5)

Step 2: Apply QR decomposition to HL_1 and LH_1 and then extract the diagonal component of both the sub-bands of the input host image. In Eq. (5.6), R_1 is the upper triangular matrix for HL_1 sub-band.

In Eq. (5.7), d_1 are the diagonal components of R_1, D_1 is the diagonal matrix corresponding to d_1 components, and s_1 is having components excluding diagonal components. In Eq. (5.8), R_2 is the upper triangular matrix for LH_1 sub-band. In Eq. (5.9), d_2 are the diagonal components of R_2, D_2 is the diagonal matrix corresponding to d_2 components, and s_2 is having components excluding diagonal components.

$$[Q_1, R_1] = qr(HL_1) \tag{5.6}$$

$$\begin{cases} d_1 = diag(R_1) \\ D_1 = diag(d_1) \\ s_1 = R_1 - D_1 \end{cases} \tag{5.7}$$

$$[Q_2, R_2] = qr(LH_1) \tag{5.8}$$

$$\begin{cases} d_2 = diag(R_2) \\ D_2 = diag(d_2) \\ s_2 = R_2 - D_2 \end{cases} \tag{5.9}$$

Step 3: Take the first watermark image, i.e., the cameraman image and apply first level LWT to it to split it into sub-bands, as shown in Eq. (5.10):

$$[LL_{1W}, HL_{1W}, LH_{1W}, HH_{1W}] = lwt2(cameraman) \tag{5.10}$$

Step 4: Apply QR decomposition to HL_{1W} sub-band and then extract the diagonal component from an upper triangular matrix. In Eq. (5.11), R_1_W is the upper triangular matrix for HL_{1W} sub-band. In Eq. (5.12), d_1_W is the diagonal components of R_1_W, D_1_W is the diagonal matrix corresponding to d_1_W components, and s_1_W is having components excluding diagonal components.

$$[Q_1\_W, R_1\_W] = qr(HL_{1W}) \tag{5.11}$$

$$\begin{cases} d_1\_W = diag(R_1\_W) \\ D_1\_W = diag(d_1\_W) \\ s_1\_W = R_1 - D_1\_W \end{cases} \tag{5.12}$$

Step 5: Take the second watermark image, i.e., details of patient image, and apply first level LWT to it to split it into sub-bands, as shown in Eq. (5.13):

$$[LL_{2W}, HL_{2W}, LH_{2W}, HH_{2W}] = lwt2(details \ of \ patient) \tag{5.13}$$

Step 6: Apply the Hénon map to LH_{2W} to get an encrypted sub-band, as shown in Eq. (5.14), and then apply QR decomposition to En and then extract the diagonal component from an upper triangular matrix.

$$En = henon\left(LH_{2W}\right) \tag{5.14}$$

In Eq. (5.15), R_2_W is the upper triangular matrix for LH_{2W} sub-band. In Eq. (5.16), d_2_W is the diagonal components of R_2_W, D_2_W is the diagonal matrix corresponding to d_2_W components, and s_2_W is having components excluding diagonal components.

$$\left[Q_2\_W, R_2\_W\right] = qr\left(En\right) \tag{5.15}$$

$$\begin{cases} d_2\_W = diag\left(R_2\_W\right) \\ D_2\_W = diag\left(d_2\_W\right) \\ s_2\_W = R_2 - D_2\_W \end{cases} \tag{5.16}$$

Step 7: Add the diagonal components of the input host image with watermark images of corresponding sub-bands, as shown in Eqs. (5.17) and (5.18).

$$SS_1 = D_1 + \alpha \times D_1\_W \tag{5.17}$$

$$SS_2 = D_2 + \alpha \times D_2\_W \tag{5.18}$$

where SS_1 and SS_2 are the modified diagonal components and α is the scaling factor.

Step 8: Modified diagonal components that are found above are added with excluded diagonal components. Apply inverse QR decomposition and LWT to get the watermarked image. Apply chaotic logistic map to the watermarked image, and transmit it to another end.

5.3.2 Extraction process

Step 1: Apply chaotic logistic decryption to get the watermarked image back at the receiver's end.

Step 2: Apply LWT to the watermarked image to split it into the sub-bands, as shown in Eq. (5.19):

$$\left[LL_1W, HL_1W, LH_1W, HH_1W\right] = lwt2\left(watermarked\ image\right) \tag{5.19}$$

Step 3: Apply QR decomposition to HL_1W and LH_1W, and then extract the diagonal component of both the sub-bands of the input host image. In Eq. (5.20), $R_1 W$ is the upper triangular matrix for $HL_1 W$ sub-band. In Eq. (5.21), $d_1 W$ is the diagonal component of $R_1 W$, and $D_1 W$ is the diagonal matrix corresponding to $d_1 W$. In Eq. (5.22), $R_2 W$ is the upper triangular matrix for $LH_1 W$ sub-band. In Eq. (5.23), $d_2 W$ is the diagonal component of $R_2 W$, and $D_2 W$ is the diagonal matrix corresponding to $d_2 W$.

$$[Q_1 W, R_1 W] = qr(HL_1 W) \tag{5.20}$$

$$\begin{cases} d_1 W = diag(R_1 W) \\ D_1 W = diag(d_1 W) \end{cases} \tag{5.21}$$

$$[Q_2 W, R_2 W] = qr(LH_1 W) \tag{5.22}$$

$$\begin{cases} d_2 W = diag(R_2 W) \\ D_2 W = diag(d_2 W) \end{cases} \tag{5.23}$$

Step 4: Apply inverse process as shown in Eqs. (5.24) and (5.25):

$$sw_1 = (D_1 W - D_1)/\alpha \tag{5.24}$$

$$sw_2 = (D_2 W - D_2)/\alpha \tag{5.25}$$

where sw_1 and sw_2 are the extracted diagonal components corresponding to their watermark images.

Step 5: Add the above extracted diagonal components corresponding to their components, excluding diagonals (s_1_W and s_2_W).

Step 6: Apply inverse QR decomposition and LWT to get the first watermark image back.

Step 7: Apply inverse QR decomposition, Hénon decryption, and inverse LWT to get the second watermark image back.

5.4 SIMULATION RESULTS AND DISCUSSION

The proposed algorithm is implemented with the help of MATLAB R2017a installed in the system with specifications as Lenovo 11th generation Intel(R) Core (TM) i5-1135G7 @ 2.40GHz - 2.42 GHz. The proposed watermarking method is tested on an ultrasound image of the liver of three different patients taken from the cancer imaging archive [6] shown in Figure 5.6, and two watermark images are used, shown in Figure 5.7. The cameraman image is the first watermark image, and the details of the patient are the

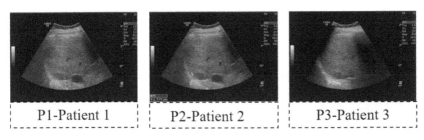

Figure 5.6 Host images.

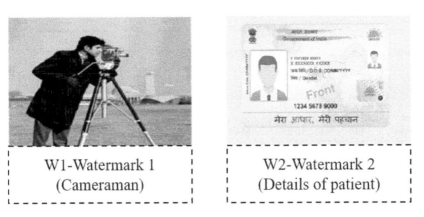

Figure 5.7 Watermark images.

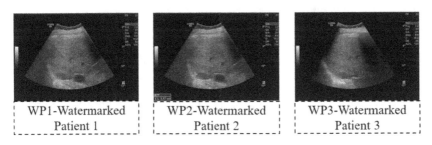

Figure 5.8 Watermarked images.

second image. The watermarked image is shown in Figure 5.8, and extracted watermark images are shown in Figure 5.9.

Table 5.1 shows the values of PSNR (dB), MSE (Mean square error), NCC1 (Cameraman), NCC2 (Detail of patient) [11], SSIM (Structural similarity index measurement) [10], and KL and JS distances for three different input images. The PSNR value is highest for P3 (49.9574). SSIM is higher for P2 (0.9958), and NCC1 values for P1 and P3 are 1.0000. NCC1 for P2

| EW1-Extracted Watermark 1 (Cameraman) | EW2-Extracted Watermark 2 (Details of patient) |

Figure 5.9 Extracted watermark images.

Table 5.1 Values of performance parameters (No attack)

Input Images	PSNR (dB)	MSE	SSIM	NCC1	NCC2	KL distance	JS distance
P1	49.7073	1.2259e-05	0.9951	1.0000	0.9998	0.8639	0.2071
P2	49.8335	1.2259e-05	0.9958	0.9999	0.9998	0.8389	0.1952
P3	49.9574	1.2259e-05	0.9945	1.0000	0.9998	0.8346	0.1977

is 0.9999, and NCC2 values are 0.9998 in all cases. KL and JS distances are used to test imperceptibility. Lesser values of both distances imply that the imperceptibility is high. The best value for KL distance is for P3 and JS distance is for P2.

Table 5.2 shows the values of PSNR, NCC1, and NCC2 for P1 under various attacks. The value of PSNR is highest for JPEG 2000, i.e., 48.6785 (P1). The values of NCC1 and NCC2 are highest for JPEG 2000 (10), i.e., 0.9998 (P1) and 0.9995 (P1), respectively. The least value for PSNR is for histogram equalization (9.2285-P2). The lowest value of NCC1 and NCC2 is for Gaussian noise (0.1), i.e., 0.9738 (P1) and 0.9871 (P1), respectively. In almost all the cases, the NCC value is greater than 0.9. Table 5.3 and Table 5.4 show the values of performance parameters for P2 and P3, respectively. Figure 5.10 shows the embedding procedure, and Figure 5.11 shows the extraction and authentication process. Figure 5.12 shows the comparison of PSNR (dB), NCC, and KL and JS distances.

In Table 5.5, the timing analysis is mentioned for different input images. The embedding, extraction, and total time elapsed is shown separately in which embedding time is less for input image P2 and extraction time is less for P1. The total time elapsed is less for input image P2.

Table 5.2 Values of performance parameters against various attacks (P1)

Attacks	Specifications	PSNR	NCC1	NCC2
Salt and Peppernoise	0.001	34.6261	0.9997	0.9994
	0.01	24.6409	0.9978	0.9987
	0.1	14.6913	0.9820	0.9914
Gaussian noise	0.001	30.4816	0.9993	0.9991
	0.01	21.5186	0.9958	0.9973
	0.1	12.7819	0.9738	0.9871
Speckle noise	0.001	42.9603	0.9998	0.9994
	0.01	33.9194	0.9996	0.9993
	0.1	24.0596	0.9977	0.9985
Gaussian low-pass filter	3×3	25.4936	0.9997	0.9992
	5×5	25.4827	0.9997	0.9992
	7×7	25.4827	0.9997	0.9992
Average filter	3×3	18.4186	0.9994	0.9990
	5×5	18.0725	0.9997	0.9993
	7×7	17.9743	0.9998	0.9993
Median filter	3×3	17.2098	0.9990	0.9988
	5×5	16.6957	0.9996	0.9992
	7×7	16.5164	0.9998	0.9994
Rotation (degrees)	1	15.0588	0.9926	0.9960
	2	14.9976	0.9924	0.9960
	3	14.9925	0.9921	0.9957
	180	17.0868	0.9920	0.9966
Histogram equalization		10.9962	0.9988	0.9968
Sharpening	4	20.8889	0.9976	0.9982
JPEG	25	20.4372	0.9968	0.9976
JPEG2000	10	48.6785	0.9998	0.9995
Motion blur	(5,5)	19.0599	0.9992	0.9988
Region of interest filtering	3	30.0597	0.9992	0.9992
	5	29.5072	0.9992	0.9991
	7	32.4440	0.9994	0.9992
Rescaling	0.5	14.9874	0.9916	0.9962
	5	14.9225	0.9913	0.9960
	10	14.9225	0.9913	0.9960

5.5 BRISK FEATURES MATCHING

The scale-space keypoint detection, keypoint description, and descriptor matching are the three essential components of the BRISK algorithm [24]. Table 5.6 shows the BRISK feature matching for different input images

Table 5.3 Values of performance parameters against various attacks (P2)

Attacks	Specifications	PSNR	NCC1	NCC2
Salt and Peppernoise	0.001	34.2870	0.9996	0.9993
	0.01	24.4842	0.9977	0.9983
	0.1	14.5339	0.9816	0.9907
Gaussian noise	0.001	30.3420	0.9992	0.9990
	0.01	21.3894	0.9958	0.9972
	0.1	12.6287	0.9742	0.9871
Speckle noise	0.001	41.9087	0.9997	0.9992
	0.01	32.8491	0.9993	0.9991
	0.1	22.9929	0.9970	0.9981
Gaussian low-pass filter	3×3	23.1812	0.9995	0.9991
	5×5	23.1703	0.9995	0.9991
	7×7	23.1703	0.9995	0.9991
Average filter	3×3	16.1114	0.9991	0.9982
	5×5	15.7755	0.9995	0.9985
	7×7	15.6853	0.9997	0.9985
Median filter	3×3	15.0547	0.9987	0.9980
	5×5	14.5907	0.9994	0.9985
	7×7	14.4113	0.9997	0.9986
Rotation (degrees)	1	13.0304	0.9878	0.9932
	2	12.9638	0.9876	0.9926
	3	12.9825	0.9870	0.9923
	180	14.8918	0.9868	0.9945
Histogram equalization		9.2285	0.9987	0.9969
Sharpening	4	18.7815	0.9968	0.9920
JPEG	25	19.3050	0.9951	0.9966
JPEG2000	10	48.2570	0.9998	0.9994
Motion blur	(5,5)	16.7715	0.9988	0.9981
Region of interest filtering	3	28.7203	0.9990	0.9989
	5	27.6803	0.9988	0.9989
	7	30.1160	0.9992	0.9992
Rescaling	0.5	13.2109	0.9881	0.9923
	5	12.7592	0.9872	0.9917
	10	12.7592	0.9872	0.9917

under various attacks. For P1, the highest number of matched points is for Speckle noise (0.001), i.e., 252. For P2, the highest number of matched points are for JPEG 2000, i.e., 198, and P3, Speckle noise (0.001), i.e., 195. The least matches are found for the gaussian low-pass filter. Figures 5.13, 5.14, and 5.15 show the matched features.

Table 5.4 Values of performance parameters against various attacks (P3)

Attacks	Specifications	PSNR	NCC1	NCC2
Salt and Peppernoise	0.001	34.5033	0.9996	0.9994
	0.01	24.4141	0.9978	0.9983
	0.1	14.5814	0.9816	0.9906
Gaussian noise	0.001	30.5143	0.9993	0.9989
	0.01	21.6880	0.9959	0.9975
	0.1	12.9458	0.9746	0.9878
Speckle noise	0.001	42.2552	0.9998	0.9992
	0.01	33.5430	0.9995	0.9991
	0.1	23.7748	0.9975	0.9983
Gaussian low-pass filter	3×3	23.1957	0.9997	0.9993
	5×5	23.1849	0.9997	0.9993
	7×7	23.1849	0.9997	0.9993
Average filter	3×3	16.1289	0.9991	0.9985
	5×5	15.8068	0.9995	0.9988
	7×7	15.7119	0.9997	0.9988
Median filter	3×3	15.0675	0.9995	0.9988
	5×5	14.7673	0.9999	0.9990
	7×7	14.6990	0.9999	0.9990
Rotation (degrees)	1	13.0252	0.9876	0.9934
	2	12.9615	0.9873	0.9937
	3	12.9870	0.9875	0.9927
	180	14.9947	0.9865	0.9947
Histogram equalization		9.8016	0.9987	0.9955
Sharpening	4	18.8475	0.9970	0.9921
JPEG	25	19.5427	0.9952	0.9968
JPEG 2000	10	47.7776	0.9998	0.9995
Motion blur	(5,5)	16.7913	0.9988	0.9985
Region of interest filtering	3	28.8629	0.9992	0.9990
	5	26.4156	0.9987	0.9989
	7	26.4529	0.9987	0.9988
Rescaling	0.5	13.0192	0.9884	0.9928
	5	12.7061	0.9875	0.9925
	10	12.7061	0.9875	0.9925

5.6 COMPARISON OF RESULTS

Table 5.7 shows the comparison of PSNR values of the proposed scheme with [2] for input images P1, P2, and P3. The PSNR values of proposed scheme is higher for the presented work. Table 5.8 shows the comparison

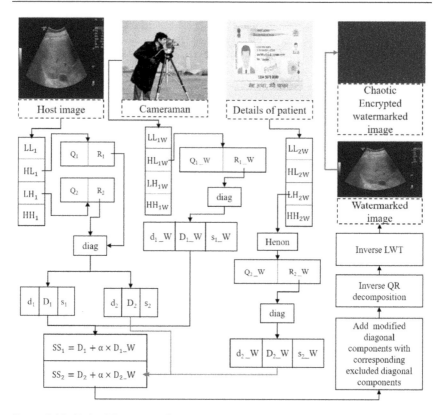

Figure 5.10 Embedding procedure.

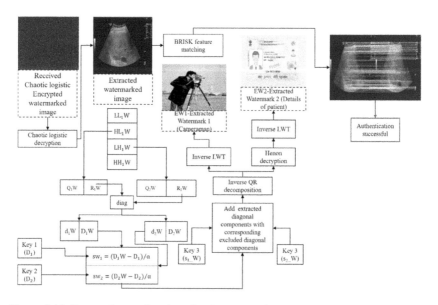

Figure 5.11 Extraction and authentication procedure.

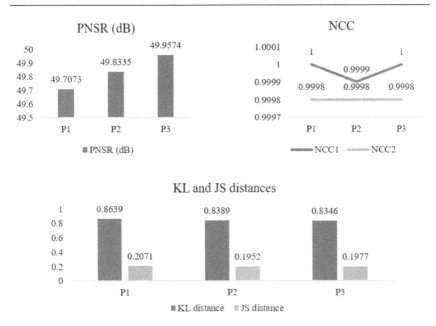

Figure 5.12 Comparison of PSNR (dB), NCC, and KL and JS distances.

Table 5.5 Timing analysis (in seconds)

Input Images	Embedding time	Extraction time	Total time elapsed
P1	1.7234	0.64001	2.3634
P2	1.6015	0.66406	2.2655
P3	1.6152	0.68780	2.3030

Table 5.6 BRISK feature matching for different input images under various attacks

Attacks	Specifications	Number of features matched (P1)	Number of features matched (P2)	Number of features matched (P3)
Salt and pepper noise	0.001	242	191	169
	0.002	211	181	156
Gaussian noise	0.001	164	147	126
	0.002	117	112	98
Speckle noise	0.001	252	161	195
	0.002	215	193	172
Gaussian low-pass filter	3×3	89	56	60
	5×5	99	59	59
JPEG 2000	10	229	198	186
Region of interest filtering	7×7	114	126	83

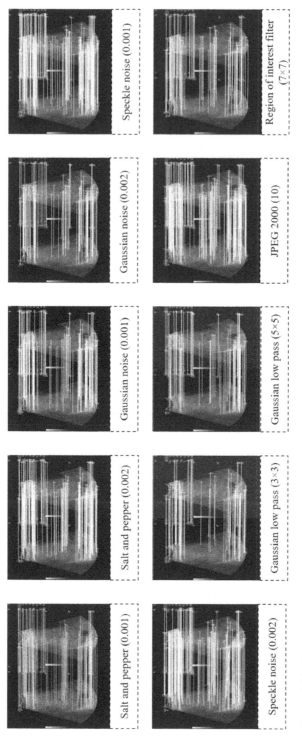

Figure 5.13 BRISK matched features (P1)

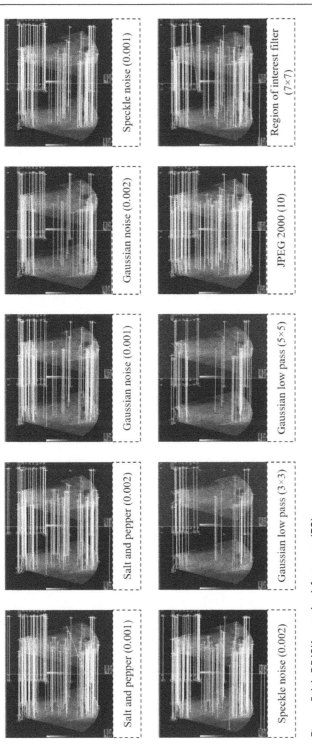

Figure 5.14 BRISK matched features (P2)

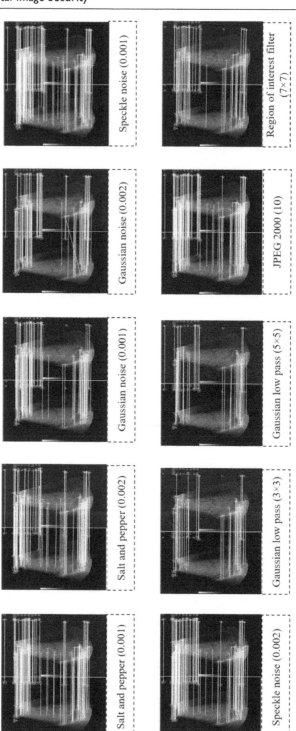

Figure 5.15 BRISK matched features (P3)

Table 5.7 Comparison of PSNR (dB) values

Input Images	[2]	Proposed scheme
P1	45.8168	49.7073
P2	45.7966	49.8335
P3	45.8186	49.9574

Table 5.8 Comparison of PSNR (dB) values with other schemes

Ref. No.	[1]	[3]	[5]	Proposed scheme
PSNR (dB)	44.9488	32.9505	40.12	49.7073

Table 5.9 Comparison of NCC against different attacks with [12]

	Zear et al. [12]				Proposed Method	
	Without BPNN		With BPNN			
Attacks	NCC1	NCC2	NCC1	NCC2	NCC1	NCC2
Gaussian noise (0, 0.001)	0.9901	0.8939	0.9908	0.9515	**0.9992**	**0.9990**
Salt and Pepper noise (0.05)	0.6596	0.6287	0.6828	0.8405	**0.9904**	**0.9950**
Median filter (3×3)	0.9833	0.8457	0.9861	0.8657	**0.9990**	**0.9988**
Average filter (3×3)	0.9809	0.6709	0.9863	0.7348	**0.9994**	**0.9990**
Rotation (5 degrees)	0.7843	0.5798	0.9806	0.7912	**0.9920**	**0.9958**

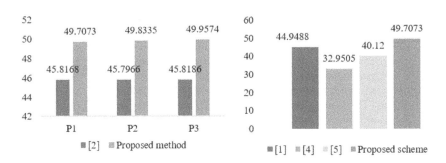

Figure 5.16 Comparison of PSNR (dB) values with [1–3, 5].

of PSNR values of the proposed work with [1–3, 5]. In Table 5.9, comparison of the normalized correlation coefficient for different attacks is shown. The proposed method has higher NCC values in comparison with [12]. Figure 5.16 shows the comparison of PSNR values with other schemes.

5.7 CONCLUSION

A consistent and undetectable image watermarking method is put forth in this chapter using the Hénon map, Chaotic logistic map, LWT, and QR decomposition. BRISK features are used for authentication. Dual watermark images are used to further enhance the security of the presented work. Both the watermark images are well retrieved. All performance parameter values fall well within the permitted range. The proposed watermarking method has higher robustness and imperceptibility in comparison with other techniques, as shown in Section 5.6. The proposed work can further be improved for geometric attacks. The scaling value is crucial to the watermarking process; therefore, optimization techniques can further be used to obtain the optimized scaling factor to balance between the performance parameters.

REFERENCES

[1] Awasthi, D., & Srivastava, V. K. (2022). LWT-DCT-SVD and DWT-DCT-SVD based watermarking schemes with their performance enhancement using Jaya and Particle swarm optimization and comparison of results under various attacks. *Multimedia Tools and Applications*, 81(18), 25075–25099.

[2] Awasthi, D., & Srivastava, V. K. (2022). Robust, imperceptible and optimized watermarking of DICOM image using Schur decomposition, LWT-DCT-SVD and its authentication using SURF. *Multimedia Tools and Applications*, 82(11), 16555–16589.

[3] Furqan, A., & Kumar, M. (2015, February). Study and analysis of robust DWT-SVD domain based digital image watermarking technique using MATLAB. In: *2015 IEEE International Conference on Computational Intelligence & Communication Technology*. IEEE. pp. 638–644.

[4] https://www.cert-in.org.in/s2cMainServlet?pageid=PUBANULREPRT

[5] Hurrah, N., Parah, S., Loan, N., Sheikh, J., Elhoseny, M., & Muhammad, K. (2018). Dual watermarking framework for privacy protection and content authentication of multimedia. *Future Generation Computer Systems 94*, 654–673. https://doi.org/10.1016/j.future.2018.12.036

[6] Clark, K., Vendt, B., Smith, K., Freymann, J., Kirby, J., Koppel, P., … & Prior, F. (2013). The Cancer Imaging Archive (TCIA): Maintaining and operating a public information repository. *Journal of Digital Imaging*, 26, 1045–1057.

[7] Jane, O., & Elbaşi, E. (2014). Hybrid non-blind watermarking based on DWT and SVD. *Journal of Applied Research and Technology*, 12(4), 750–761.

[8] Khare, P., & Srivastava, V. K. (2018, November). Image watermarking scheme using homomorphic transform in wavelet domain. In *2018 5th IEEE Uttar Pradesh Section International Conference on Electrical, Electronics and Computer Engineering (UPCON)* (pp. 1–6). IEEE.

[9] Su, Q., Wang, G., Zhang, X., et al. (2017). An improved color image watermarking algorithm based on QR decomposition. *Multimedia Tools and Applications*, 76, 707–729. https://doi.org/10.1007/s11042-015-3071-x

[10] Thakkar, F. N., & Srivastava, V. K. (2017). A blind medical image watermarking: DWT-SVD based robust and secure approach for telemedicine applications. *Multimedia Tools and Applications, 76*, 3669–3697.

[11] Thakkar, F., & Srivastava, V. K. (2017). A particle swarm optimization and block-SVD-based watermarking for digital images. *Turkish Journal of Electrical Engineering and Computer Sciences, 25*(4), 3273–3288.

[12] Zear, A., Singh, A. K., & Kumar, P. (2018). Multiple watermarking for healthcare applications. *Journal of Intelligent Systems, 27*(1), 5–18.

[13] Singh, A. K. (2019). Robust and distortion control dual watermarking in LWT domain using DCT and error correction code for color medical image. *Multimedia Tools and Applications, 78*, 30523–30533.

[14] Hsu, C. S., & Tu, S. F. (2020). Enhancing the robustness of image watermarking against cropping attacks with dual watermarks. *Multimedia Tools and Applications, 79*(17–18), 11297–11323.

[15] Koley, S. (2021). Visual attention model based dual watermarking for simultaneous image copyright protection and authentication. *Multimedia Tools and Applications, 80*(5), 6755–6783.

[16] Zear, A., & Singh, P. K. (2022). Secure and robust color image dual watermarking based on LWT-DCT-SVD. *Multimedia Tools and Applications, 81*(19), 26721–26738.

[17] Al-Otum, H. M. (2022). Dual image watermarking using a multi-level thresholding and selective zone-quantization for copyright protection, authentication and recovery applications. *Multimedia Tools and Applications, 81*(18), 25787–25828.

[18] Sweldens, W. (1996). The lifting scheme: A custom-design construction of biorthogonal wavelets. *Applied and Computational Harmonic Analysis, 3*(2), 186–200.

[19] Sweldens, W. (1998). The lifting scheme: A construction of second-generation wavelets. *SIAM Journal on Mathematical Analysis, 29*(2), 511–546.

[20] Wang, H., & Su, Q. (2022). A color image watermarking method combined QR decomposition and spatial domain. *Multimedia Tools and Applications, 81*(26), 37895–37916.

[21] Sheela, S. J., Suresh, K. V., & Tandur, D. (2018). Image encryption based on modified Henon map using hybrid chaotic shift transform. *Multimedia Tools and Applications, 77*, 25223–25251. https://doi.org/10.1007/s11042-018-5782-2

[22] Rathore, V., Bagan, K. B., & Pal, A. K. (2021). An image encryption scheme in bit plane content using Henon map based generated edge map. *Multimedia Tools and Applications, 80*, 22275–22300.

[23] Sathishkumar, G. A., & Sriraam, N. (2011). Image encryption based on diffusion and multiple chaotic maps. *arXiv preprint arXiv:1103.3792*.

[24] Leutenegger, S., Chli, M., & Siegwart, R. Y. (2011, November). BRISK: Binary robust invariant scalable keypoints. In *2011 International Conference on Computer Vision* (pp. 2548–2555). Ieee.

Chapter 6

Securing digital images using HT-MSVD in wavelet domain

Priyank Khare
IIIT Ranchi, Ranchi, India

Divyanshu Awasthi and Vinay Kumar Srivastava
MNNIT Allahabad, Prayagraj, India

6.1 INTRODUCTION

Radical progress in technologies has made accessibility of multimedia data very convenient. The mutual exchange of confidential data becomes easy due to this process. So, confidentiality and protection from intruders is a prime goal, especially in images where manipulation is easily possible. This problem is rapidly increasing at an alarming rate, so researchers have focused their attention on providing secure information exchange.

The remedy for resolving this severe concern is image watermarking in which confidential images are concealed in a cover image so that they become perceptually invisible to the human visual system [1, 2]. Visually watermarked and cover images should be similar. Further, this concealed watermark is retrieved by the legitimate user to ensure copyright protection. Visual similarity among images is signified with the aid of imperceptibility, whereas resilience of the scheme against attacks is highlighted through robustness. The main challenge is to concurrently maintain a trade-off between these two attributes while designing an effectual image watermarking technique [3, 4]. Typically, image watermarking is performed in either the spatial or transform domain. Transform domain watermarking proves to be better in robustness and imperceptibility. In contrast, hybrid image transforms watermarking is generally employed efficiently so that the features of different image transforms can be utilized.

This chapter presents HT-RDWT-MSVD-based image watermarking for protecting digital images. This proposed technique efficiently uses attributes of each transform so that a proper balance is maintained among different characteristics of watermarking. Vital aspects of the proposed technique are presented below:

- The reflectance component attained from HT [5, 6] of the cover image is preferred for watermark embedding, as it provides better robustness and perceptual invisibility to the technique.

DOI: 10.1201/9781003468974-6

- RDWT [7–9] provides excellent robustness in comparison to discrete wavelet transform (DWT), as it has shift invariance property, whereas capacity also increases with its usage.
- MSVD [10, 11] offers better robustness to the scheme against geometric attacks compared to singular value decomposition (SVD), and thus, combining it with RDWT results in a robust watermarking technique.
- Salient features of these transforms motivate us to propose an effective watermarking technique that aims to maximize the various features of watermarking. Hence, confidentiality of digital images is retained.

The structure of the rest of the chapter is as follows: Section 6.2 comprises related works, Section 6.3 deals with the proposed watermarking scheme, and simulation results are investigated in Section 6.4. Section 6.5 states the Conclusion of this chapter.

6.2 RELATED WORKS

In [10], a multiple image watermarking (MIW) is reported in which non-subsampled contourlet transform (NSCT), discrete cosine transform (DCT), and MSVD are employed together. But this technique fails to deliver sufficient robustness and imperceptibility due to the non-directional property of DCT. An extended version of [10] is developed in [12], where robustness is slightly improved due to the usage of RDWT, but this scheme still does not provide satisfactory robustness against noise attacks. In [13], fusion of DCT-DWT is applied for watermark embedding. In this approach, the authors have chosen high-high (HH) subband as the embedding location due to which robustness yield is not up to the mark. Analysis against affine and image enhancement attacks is also missing.

A neural network-based image watermarking is developed in [14], in which a watermark is embedded into the edges of the color host image. Contourlet transform is used for electing directions in which embedding can be performed. However, this scheme lacks security. A fragile watermarking using particle swarm bacterial foraging optimization (PSBFO) is investigated in [15], where RDWT-QR transforms are applied concurrently. This technique provides authenticity against tamper detection for vital medical images.

A DWT-SVD watermarking scheme [16] is proposed in which encryption-compression is concurrently applied to the watermarked image. In this methodology, the watermark image, along with the text watermark, is concurrently embedded in the desired subbands of host image. Encryption is performed using chaotic and hyper-chaotic mapping. The proposed scheme seems to be effective, but it appears to offer weak robustness against affine transformations. Non-subsampled shearlet transform (NSST)–MSVD [17] watermarking algorithm is developed in which embedding of the watermark is done using the permutation-based scrambling technique for providing better security. Simultaneously, the authors used optimization-based encryption technique for authenticating the watermarked image. However, the time complexity of the developed method can be reduced.

In [18], chaotic encryption-based watermarking is reported. In this method, text and image watermarks are embedded into the desired subbands of the host image using DWT-SVD. It seems that values of the peak signal-to-noise ratio (PSNR) are quite low, which accounts for poor perceptual invisibility. HT-RDWT-SVD-based watermarking is described in [5]. In this methodology, a cover image is transformed using HT-RDWT-SVD, while a watermark image is transformed using RDWT-SVD. Results clearly show that this scheme provides better security and authenticity to the watermarked image by encryption. Using fuzzy logic, authors in [19] have utilized NSCT-RDWT-SVD combination to embed watermark images into the cover image. Fuzzy logic is used to determine the optimal scaling factor in this method. This scheme depicts poor robustness toward filtering attacks.

De-noising convolutional neural network (DnCNN)-based watermarking technique is developed in [20] where lifting wavelet transform (LWT), along with Hessenberg decomposition and redundant singular value decomposition (RSVD), is employed for embedding the watermark. DnCNN is applied to strengthen robustness against attacks, whereas encryption succeeded by compression is also done on the watermarked image to achieve better results. However, robustness against geometric attacks is not reported. Curvelet transform, along with RDWT, is used in [21] to embed the watermark. In this methodology the scrambled watermark is embedded along with Pseudo Noise (PN) sequences in subbands of the host image. Robustness against filtering and scaling attacks is the main shortcoming of the developed method.

Error correction codes (ECC) and DWT are used for watermark embedding [22]. Dual embedding of the watermark is performed to protect sensitive medical information, while a comparative analysis among various ECC is also conducted. Embedding of the watermark using Walsh Hadamard transform (WHT) is investigated in [23]. In this approach, WHT is applied over a segmented block cover image, while shuffling of bit information is done to achieve security. However, robustness is weak against median filter attack.

The concept of deep learning is utilized in [24], where robustness is significantly improved. The concatenation principle is used for the embedding process, while the block-level transposed convolution technique is employed in the extraction process. However, the imperceptibility attained is lesser in this technique. Fusion-based image watermarking using NSCT is briefed in [25], where two medical images are fused. A fused cover image is used for the embedding process in which image and text watermarks are concurrently embedded for smart healthcare applications.

A similar technique that uses principal component analysis (PCA) and RDWT is reported in [26], where principal components are used for embedding and extraction processes. A review of various image watermarking techniques for smart healthcare system is discussed in [27]. In this article, open issues and challenges are elaborated on telemedicine applications. The presented review regarding different techniques inspires us to contribute a new watermarking technique that meets research gaps. There are numerous potential research issues that need to be focused, such as better robustness and perceptual invisibility, capacity, etc. Thus, by developing this novel technique, digital image copyright protection can be attained effectively with better attributes.

6.3 PROPOSED WATERMARKING TECHNIQUE

Watermark embedding and extraction techniques are presented in this section. Initially, HT decomposes a cover image into reflectance and illumination components. Further multiresolution analysis is attained by decomposing the reflectance component using RDWT. Low high (LH) subband is chosen to maintain an adequate balance between robustness and perceptual invisibility. MSVD is applied to this LH subband to attain better imperceptibility. Similarly, RDWT-MSVD transforms are applied over the watermark image. The selection of the optimal scaling factor yields the watermarked image. Embedding and extraction watermark procedures are depicted in Figure 6.1(a, b).

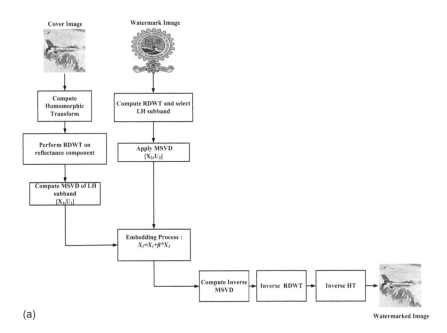

(a)

Figure 6.1 Watermarking technique procedure (a) embedding.

(Continued)

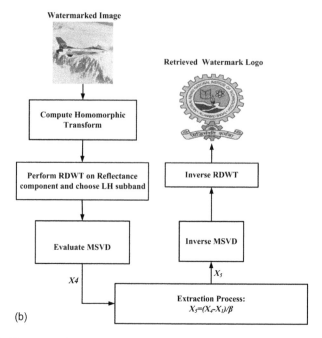

Figure 6.1 (Continued) Watermarking technique procedure (b) extraction.

6.3.1 Embedding technique

- HT of the cover image 'C' is computed, yielding 'C_R' as the reflectance component whereas 'C_I' as an illumination component.
- 'C_R' is decomposed using RDWT resulting in four subbands.

$$C_R \xrightarrow{RDWT} [C_{RLL}, C_{RHL}, C_{RLH}, C_{RHH}] \qquad (6.1)$$

- MSVD of 'C_{RLH}' subband is computed as:

$$C_{RLH} \xrightarrow{MSVD} [X_1, U_1] \qquad (6.2)$$

- RDWT is performed over the watermark image 'W_{mk}'.

$$W_{mk} \xrightarrow{RDWT} [W_{mkLL}, W_{mkHL}, W_{mkLH}, W_{mkHH}] \qquad (6.3)$$

- MSVD for 'W_{mkLH}' is computed, which results in $[X_2, U_2]$.

$$W_{mkLH} \xrightarrow{MSVD} [X_2, U_2] \qquad (6.4)$$

- Watermark is embedded in accordance with Eq. (6.5):

$$X_3 = X_1 + \beta^* X_2 \qquad (6.5)$$

where 'β' is the scaling factor.

- Inverse MSVD, RDWT, HT transformation results in watermarked image 'W_I'.

6.3.2 Extraction technique

- HT of 'W_I' watermarked image is evaluated, which results in 'W_{IR}' as the reflectance component, whereas 'W_{II}' as an illumination component.
- RDWT is applied over 'W_{IR}' as:

$$W_{IR} \xrightarrow{RDWT} [W_{IRLL}, W_{IRHL}, W_{IRLH}, W_{IRHH}] \qquad (6.6)$$

- MSVD coefficients of 'W_{IRLH}' are evaluated according to Eq. (6.7):

$$W_{IRLH} \xrightarrow{MSVD} [X_4, U_4] \qquad (6.7)$$

- Extraction process is done in accordance with Eq. (6.8):

$$X_5 = (X_4 - X_1)/\beta \qquad (6.8)$$

- Inverse MSVD and RDWT of 'X_5' is computed to retrieve the watermark image 'W_{mk}'.

6.4 SIMULATION RESULTS

The proposed watermarking technique in this chapter is implemented using 'MATLAB'. Several cover images, which comprise standard and medical images [28, 29] of size 512×512, are taken, while a watermark image of size 512×512 is chosen. Cover images are represented in Figure 6.2(a), and a watermark image in Figure 6.2(b). The value of 'β' is selected as 0.1 for experimental analysis. Weighted peak signal-to-noise ratio (WPSNR) [30, 31], PSNR, structural similarity index (SSIM), and normalized correlation (NC) [31] metrics are evaluated for analyzing the proposed technique imperceptibility and robustness. The values of these metrics are tabulated in Table 6.1, which clearly emphasizes performance of the proposed technique under no attacks. 53.22179 dB and 66.17175 dB are the mean values of PSNR and WPSNR, respectively, while NC and SSIM values are near to unity.

Proposed technique robustness is analyzed under several attacks such as sharpening, affine, compression, etc. Figure 6.3 illustrates the 'Airplane' watermarked image subjected to different attacks and corresponding retrieved watermark images. Proposed technique is robust toward attacks, as the visual quality of extracted watermark images is better. In Tables 6.2, 6.3, 6.4, and 6.5 NC values are computed for the proposed technique under different attacks.

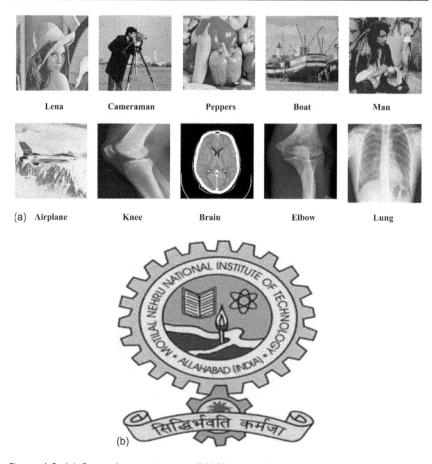

Figure 6.2 (a) Several cover images (b) Watermark image.

Table 6.1 Performance metric values for the proposed scheme

Image	SSIM	PSNR (dB)	WPSNR (dB)	NC
Lena	0.9986	55.5431	64.9250	0.9996
Cameraman	0.9943	50.6895	66.5252	0.9989
Peppers	0.9961	51.6619	67.1621	0.9994
Boat	0.9961	51.4885	66.9485	0.9994
Man	0.9972	52.5542	67.9080	0.9994
Airplane	0.9980	54.7573	63.5201	0.9996
Lung	0.9924	50.1003	66.9217	0.9958
Knee	0.9959	52.9325	66.0630	0.9991
Elbow	0.9987	57.2672	66.0620	0.9996
Brain	0.9980	55.2234	65.6819	0.9985

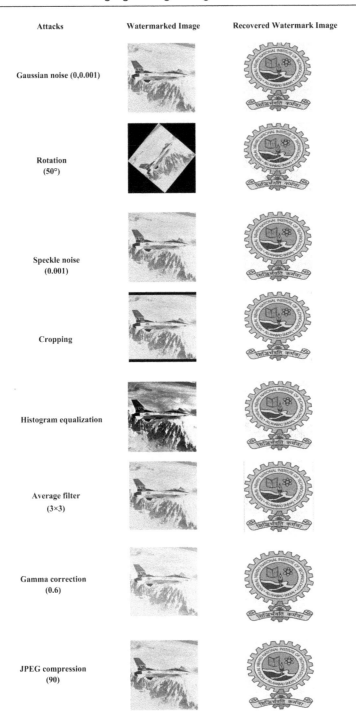

Figure 6.3 Retrieved watermark images from distinct attacks.

Table 6.2 NC values under different noise attacks

Attack		Lena	Cameraman	Airplane	Elbow	Brain
Salt & Pepper	0.001	0.9753	0.9883	0.9760	0.9754	0.9810
	0.005	0.8704	0.9441	0.8481	0.9431	0.9174
	0.0001	0.9985	0.9982	0.9978	0.9990	0.9963
Gaussian	0.001	0.9453	0.9607	0.9611	0.9526	0.9657
	0.0001	0.9798	0.9947	0.9962	0.9923	0.9938
	0.010.0001	0.9941	0.9949	0.9962	0.9920	0.9923
Speckle	0.001	0.9786	0.9905	0.9773	0.9943	0.9934
Poisson		0.9996	0.9989	0.9996	0.9996	0.9987

Table 6.3 NC values under different filtering attacks

Attack		Lena	Cameraman	Airplane	Elbow	Brain
Average Filter	2×2	0.9688	0.8247	0.9438	0.9970	0.8479
	3×3	0.9471	0.8869	0.9433	0.9970	0.8776
Median Filter	1×1	0.9996	0.9989	0.9996	0.9996	0.9985
	2×2	0.9678	0.8076	0.9433	0.9968	0.8968
Wiener Filter	2×2	0.9938	0.7897	0.9955	0.9988	0.9870
	3×3	0.9906	0.8010	0.8861	0.9985	0.9866
Gaussian Filter	3×3	0.9184	0.8147	0.8944	0.9992	0.9639

Table 6.4 NC values under different image enhancement attacks

Attack		Lena	Cameraman	Airplane	Elbow	Brain
Histogram Equalization		0.9802	0.9625	0.9222	0.9959	0.9461
Sharpening		0.9981	0.9943	0.9981	0.9995	0.9911
Gamma Correction (0.6)		0.9972	0.9921	0.9939	0.9983	0.9774
JPEG Compression	80	0.9984	0.9991	0.9964	0.9979	0.9894
	90	0.9989	0.9987	0.9991	0.9986	0.9987

Table 6.5 NC values under different geometric attacks

Attack	Lena	Cameraman	Airplane	Elbow	Brain
Rotation (50°)	0.9315	0.8866	0.9117	0.9879	0.8450
Scaling	0.9970	0.8037	0.8906	0.9994	0.9629
Cropping	0.9970	0.9944	0.9963	0.9978	0.9552

Table 6.2 tabulates the robustness of the proposed technique under various noise attacks, while Table 6.3 illustrates filtering attacks. Upon investigating Table 6.2, it can be determined that the presented work offers good resilience against noise attacks, especially towards Gaussian and speckle

noise attacks. Similarly, the proposed method is robust toward filtering attacks as the 'Elbow' cover image results in better NC values with highest value of 0.9996 toward a median filter attack.

Robustness toward image enhancement attacks are specified in Table 6.4, whereas Table 6.5 details the NC values for geometric attacks. 'Elbow' host image offers better robustness against sharpening attack, while 'Cameraman' yields highest NC values for compression attacks. 'Elbow' host image yields highest NC value of 0.9994 for scaling attack.

Figures 6.4 and 6.5 graphically demonstrate the SSIM and PSNR values for the proposed technique subjected to numerous attacks such as noise, filtering, enhancement, and geometric. In Figure 6.4(c), 'Brain' cover image attains 0.3684 for histogram equalization attack, while 'Cameraman' host image has 0.1362 as SSIM value under rotation attack as the lowest value in Figure 6.4(d). For most attacks, SSIM values lie close to unity, which signifies better perceptual invisibility. From Figure 6.5, it can be clearly observed that the proposed scheme has good imperceptibility, as PSNR values are well above 30 dB, except for a few attacks, such as histogram equalization and rotation attacks.

Computational time complexity is tabulated in Table 6.6 for different cover images with an average total time of 3.4973 sec. Proposed technique is computationally time efficient with a lesser value of embedding and

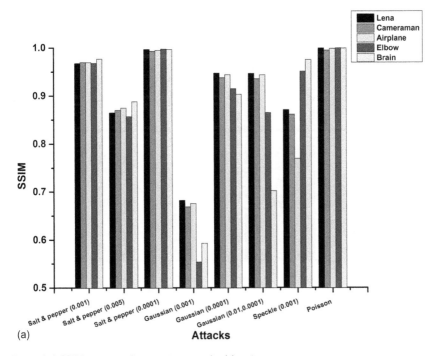

(a)

Figure 6.4 SSIM metric values against attacks (a) noise.

(*Continued*)

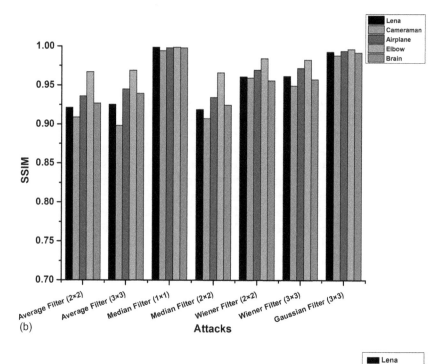

(b)

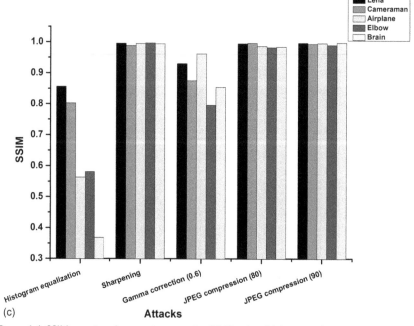

(c)

Figure 6.4 SSIM metric values against attacks (b) filtering (c) image enhancement.

(*Continued*)

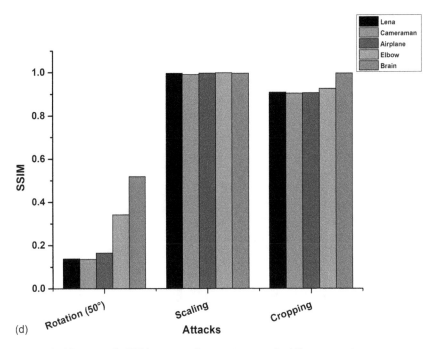

Figure 6.4 (Continued) SSIM metric values against attacks (d) geometric.

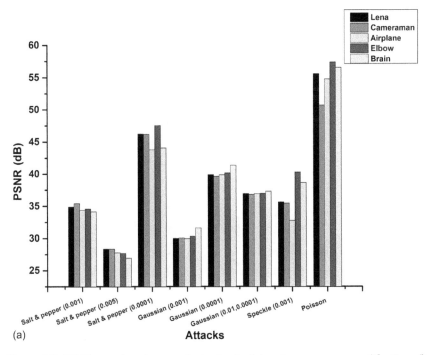

Figure 6.5 PSNR metric values against attacks (a) noise. (Continued)

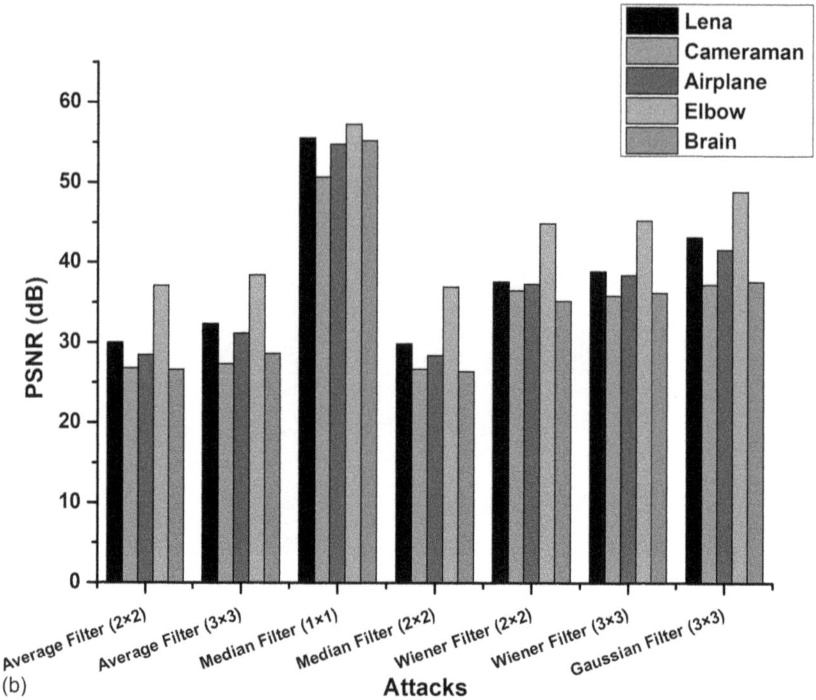

(b)

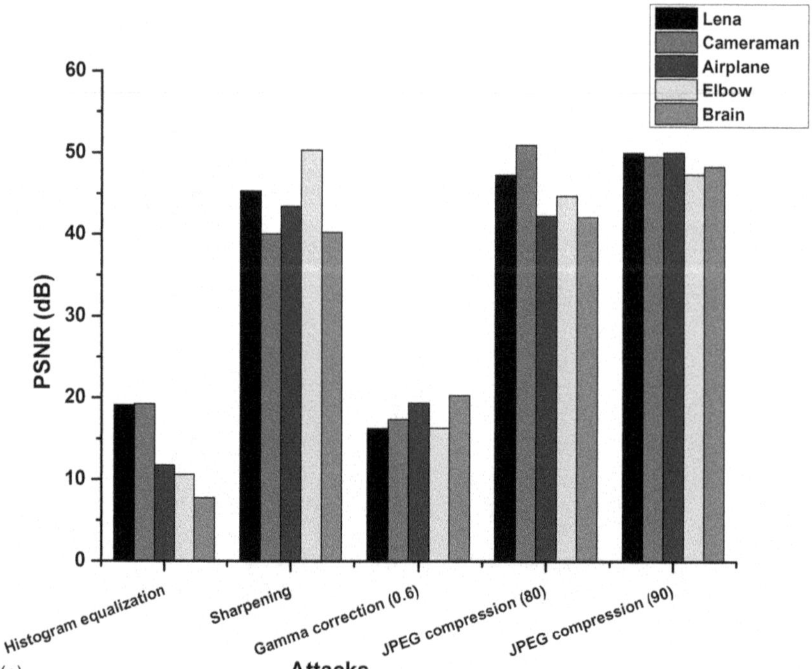

(c)

Figure 6.5 (Continued) PSNR metric values against attacks (b) filtering (c) image
enhancement.

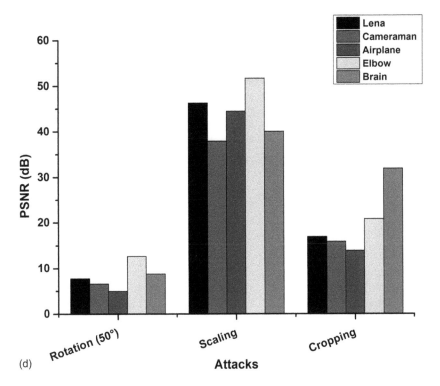

(d)

Figure 6.5 (Continued) PSNR metric values against attacks (d) geometric.

extraction time. Table 6.7 demonstrates a comparative analysis of proposed work done with other persisting techniques [14, 16, 21]. '*' represents that NC values are not reported. Proposed scheme is found to be better in terms of NC values, except for the median filter attack where technique [14] has a higher NC value. Similarly, for histogram equalization, attack [21] has a higher NC. For the rest of the attacks, proposed scheme proves to be better in terms of robustness. Further, graphical comparison of proposed scheme and reported technique [22] is depicted in Figure 6.6, in which the proposed technique outperforms.

Table 6.6 Computational time analysis for the proposed scheme

Image	Embedding time (sec)	Extraction time (sec)	Total computational time (sec)
Lena	2.0511	1.4323	3.4834
Cameraman	2.0014	1.4612	3.4626
Airplane	2.0317	1.5638	3.5955
Elbow	2.0226	1.3962	3.4188
Brain	2.0599	1.4663	3.5262

Table 6.7 Proposed scheme comparison with other persisting techniques

Attacks	[16]	[14]	[21]	Proposed scheme
Salt & Pepper Noise (0.0001)	0.9879	*	*	0.9985
Average Filter	*	0.8984	0.2258	0.9471
Median Filter [3 3]	*	0.9609	0.4576	0.9274
Sharpening	0.6763	*	0.9916	0.9981
Scaling	0.7075	0.9004	0.5051	0.9970
Histogram Equalization	0.7223	0.5039	0.9904	0.9802
JPEG Compression (90)	0.9796	*	0.9910	0.9989

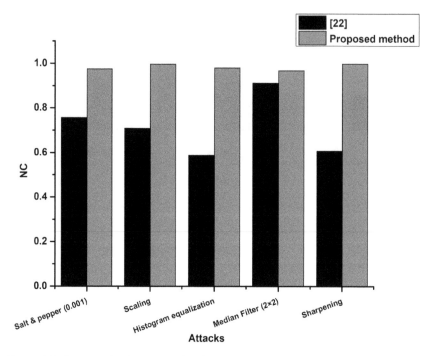

Figure 6.6 Proposed scheme graphically compared with [22].

6.5 CONCLUSIONS

This chapter presents a novel image watermarking technique that easily facilitates copyright protection of digital images. Fusion of HT-RDWT-MSVD transforms produces a better robust and imperceptible watermarking technique. Better imperceptibility is ensured by embedding the watermark in the reflectance component, whereas the usage of RDWT strengthens robustness. MSVD also provides indispensable aid in making the proposed scheme more imperceptible so that confidential information remains intact. Results demonstrate the presented work efficacy with other existing comparison methods. In the future, we would like to enhance the security of the presented watermarking technique by employing various authentication techniques to become more robust and secure against attacks.

REFERENCES

[1] Anand, A., Singh, A. K., Lv, Z., & Bhatnagar, G. (2020). Compression-then-encryption-based secure watermarking technique for smart healthcare system. *IEEE MultiMedia*, 27(4), 133–143.

[2] Kumar, S., Singh, B. K., & Yadav, M. (2020). A recent survey on multimedia and database watermarking. *Multimedia Tools and Applications*, 79(27), 20149–20197.

[3] Mazurczyk, W., & Wendzel, S. (2017). Information hiding: Challenges for forensic experts. *Communications of the ACM*, 61(1), 86–94.

[4] Anand, A., & Singh, A. K. (2021). Watermarking techniques for medical data authentication: A survey. *Multimedia Tools and Applications*, 80(20), 30165–30197.

[5] Khare, P., & Srivastava, V. K. (2021). A secured and robust medical image watermarking approach for protecting integrity of medical images. *Transactions on Emerging Telecommunications Technologies*, 32(2), e3918.

[6] Khare, P., & Srivastava, V. K. (2021). A reliable and secure image watermarking algorithm using homomorphic transform in DWT domain. *Multidimensional Systems and Signal Processing*, 32(1), 131–160.

[7] Sharma, S., Sharma, H., & Sharma, J. B. (2019). An adaptive color image watermarking using RDWT-SVD and artificial bee colony based quality metric strength factor optimization. *Applied Soft Computing*, 84, 105696.

[8] Anand, A., & Singh, A. K. (2020, September). RDWT-SVD-firefly based dual watermarking technique for medical images (workshop paper). In *2020 IEEE Sixth International Conference on Multimedia Big Data (BigMM)*, New Delhi, India (pp. 366–372). IEEE.

[9] Khare, P., & Srivastava, V. K. (2019). Secure and robust image watermarking scheme using homomorphic transform, SVD and Arnold transform in RDWT domain. *Advances in Electrical and Electronic Engineering*, 17(3), 343–351.

[10] Singh, S., Rathore, V. S., & Singh, R. (2017). Hybrid NSCT domain multiple watermarking for medical images. *Multimedia Tools and Applications*, 76(3), 3557–3575.

[11] Kakarala, R., & Ogunbona, P. O. (2001). Signal analysis using a multiresolution form of the singular value decomposition. *IEEE Transactions on Image Processing*, 10(5), 724–735.

[12] Singh, S., Rathore, V. S., Singh, R., & Singh, M. K. (2017). Hybrid semi-blind image watermarking in redundant wavelet domain. *Multimedia Tools and Applications*, 76(18), 19113–19137.

[13] Begum, M., Ferdush, J., & Uddin, M. S. (2022). A hybrid robust watermarking system based on discrete cosine transform, discrete wavelet transform, and singular value decomposition. *Journal of King Saud University-Computer and Information Sciences*, 34(8), 5856–5867.

[14] Kazemi, M. F., Pourmina, M. A., & Mazinan, A. H. (2020). Analysis of watermarking framework for color image through a neural network-based approach. *Complex & Intelligent Systems*, 6(1), 213–220.

[15] Swaraja, K., Meenakshi, K., & Kora, P. (2021). Hierarchical multilevel framework using RDWT-QR optimized watermarking in telemedicine. *Biomedical Signal Processing and Control*, 68, 102688.

[16] Anand, A., & Singh, A. K. (2020). An improved DWT-SVD domain watermarking for medical information security. *Computer Communications*, 152, 72–80.

[17] Anand, A., & Singh, A. K. (2022). A hybrid optimization-based medical data hiding scheme for industrial Internet of Things security. *IEEE Transactions on Industrial Informatics*, 19(1), 1051–1058

[18] Thakur, S., Singh, A. K., Kumar, B., & Ghrera, S. P. (2020). Improved DWT-SVD-based medical image watermarking through hamming code and chaotic encryption. In *Advances in VLSI, Communication, and Signal Processing* (pp. 897–905). Springer, Singapore.

[19] Singh, O. P., Kumar, C., Singh, A. K., Singh, M. P., & Ko, H. (2021). Fuzzy-based secure exchange of digital data using watermarking in NSCT-RDWT-SVD domain. *Concurrency and Computation: Practice and Experience*, 35(16), e6251.

[20] Singh, O. P., & Singh, A. K. (2021). Data hiding in encryption–compression domain. *Complex & Intelligent Systems*, 9(11), 1–14.

[21] Thanki, R., Kothari, A., & Trivedi, D. (2019). Hybrid and blind watermarking scheme in DCuT–RDWT domain. *Journal of Information Security and Applications*, 46, 231–249.

[22] Singh, A. K., Kumar, B., Dave, M., & Mohan, A. (2015). Robust and imperceptible dual watermarking for telemedicine applications. *Wireless Personal Communications*, 80(4), 1415–1433.

[23] Prabha, K., & Sam, I. S. (2022). An effective robust and imperceptible blind color image watermarking using WHT. *Journal of King Saud University–Computer and Information Sciences*, 34(6, Part A), 2982–2992.

[24] Mahapatra, D., Amrit, P., Singh, O. P., Singh, A. K., & Agrawal, A. K. (2022). Autoencoder-convolutional neural network-based embedding and extraction model for image watermarking. *Journal of Electronic Imaging*, 32(2), 021604.

[25] Anand, A., & Singh, A. K. (2021). SDH: Secure data hiding in fused medical image for smart healthcare. *IEEE Transactions on Computational Social Systems*, 9(4), 1265–1273.

[26] Singh, O. P., Singh, A. K., Agrawal, A. K., & Zhou, H. (2022). SecDH: Security of COVID-19 images based on data hiding with PCA. *Computer Communications*, 191, 368–377.

[27] Singh, O. P., Anand, A., Agrawal, A. K., & Singh, A. K. (2022). Electronic health data security in the Internet of Things through watermarking: An introduction. *IEEE Internet of Things Magazine*, 5(2), 55–58.

[28] https://medpix.nlm.nih.gov/home

[29] https://commons.wikimedia.org/wiki

[30] Navas, K. A., Thampy, S. A., & Sasikumar, M. (2008). EPR hiding in medical images for telemedicine. *International Journal of Biomedical Sciences*, 3(1), 44–47.

[31] Khare, P., & Srivastava, V. K. (2021). A novel dual image watermarking technique using homomorphic transform and DWT. *Journal of Intelligent Systems*, 30(1), 297–311.

Chapter 7

Scalable edge computing architecture for multimedia data management

Challenges and research avenues

Jaya Sinha

Galgotias College of Engineering and Technology, Greater Noida, India

Nivedita Palia

Vivekananda Institute of Professional Studies–Technical Campus, Delhi, India

7.1 INTRODUCTION TO THE EDGE COMPUTING ECOSYSTEM

Expansion and development in the domain of Internet of things and achievement of cloud services have seen the rise of the innovative computing archi-type known as Edge Computing. Edge computing means processing data nearer to the edge of the network, where it is generated. It enables the user to process a large amount of the data at high speed with a faster response time. Currently, Internet of things connects a wide variety of electronic and electrical devices that generate a huge volume of data. Data volumes will increase substantially as a result of technologies like 5G.

Today, digitalization is sweeping the globe, and an abundance of data is generated in various arenas. In most cases, processing of data needs to be done quickly to support real-time applications. Cloud computing technologies gradually reduce the requirement for small-scale and medium-scale industry to own their own system to perform computation tasks. Still, the end user requires transmitting and acquiring data to and from where the machine is located. Cloud computing is not always efficient to process data produced at the edge of the network, so micro data center [1, 2], fog computing [3], and Cloudlet [4] have been introduced. In the following paragraphs, we will present several reasons for the emergence of edge computing, along with a comparative study between them.

7.1.1 Dig into edge computing: drive from cloud computing, wrench from Internet of Things, data consumer to data producer

In terms of computation, cloud computing has proven to be efficient, but in some cases due to the large volume of data generated at the edge, cloud-based computing experiences a bottleneck in the speed of data transmission. For example, a Boeing 787 will generate 5 Gigabytes (GBs) data per second, and transmitting this data between the airplane to a satellite or a base station on the ground is inefficient for data processing [5]. Consider another example of autonomous vehicles—it will generate 1 GB data every second and requires data processing in real time for the vehicle to make the right decisions [6]. Also, as per reports by Data Age 2025, approximately more than 5 billion customers are presently interacting with data owing to extensive usage of social media services, among others, which is expected to increase up to 6 billion, i.e., about 75% of the global populace in 2025. An enormous rise in worldwide data is again expected in 2025 from 33 zettabytes in 2018 to 175 zettabytes with a very significant contribution by IoT instruments in terms of data produced globally [7]. It is, therefore, not feasible to send all the data to the cloud for processing, as the network bandwidth is a bottleneck. Moreover, edge computing processes data efficiently at the edge for shorter response time by consuming less energy as compared to cloud technology.

Currently, all electronic devices like LEDs, voice controllers, cameras, activity trackers, etc., are parts of the IoT, and they will act as data producers as well as consumers. Even more electronic gadgets will be linked to the IoT in the future. It is impractical for cloud computing to process lots of data efficiently due to bandwidth and latency. This indicates most of the data produced by IoT needs to be processed at the edge of devices.

Figures 7.1 and 7.2 show the roadmap of cloud and edge computing concepts respectively. In a cloud computing paradigm, raw data is generated and transmitted to the cloud, and the consumer accesses the data from the cloud by sending a request. This structure is not optimal for IoT devices functioning in the cloud environment due to the aforementioned reasons. Firstly, a large amount of data needs to be transmitted. Secondly, data privacy, and thirdly, energy consumption. To overcome these drawbacks, edge

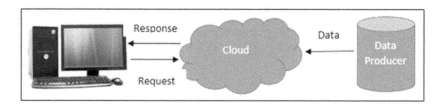

Figure 7.1 Cloud computing concept.

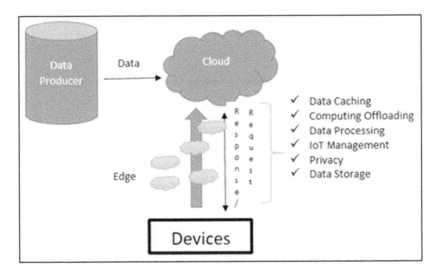

Figure 7.2 Edge computing concept.

computing is the solution, as it maintains data privacy by processing data at edges, which could be further energy efficient [8], as shown in Figure 7.2.

Previously, in the cloud computing paradigm, devices at the edge usually act as a data consumer, such as watching a YouTube video on a smart phone. Today, end users act as data producers by creating and uploading a reel to YouTube by a smart phone. This change of role from data consumer to data producer, and vice versa, forces more functions to the edge. When the edge user tries to upload images or videos clips, it could be reasonably large due to high resolution and occupy more bandwidth for the uploading. In that case, images and video clips need to be resized and transformed to the appropriate resolution at the edge before being uploaded to the cloud. Consider one example of wearable health devices where data is collected at the edge of network that is private. Therefore, it needs to process the data at edges to protect the user's privacy rather than uploading it to the cloud [8]. An exemplar layered infrastructure in this regard for edge computing has been presented in Figure 7.3.

The differences between cloud computing and edge computing are presented in Table 7.1. The distinctive features of edge computing include its widespread geographic distribution, mobility support, and closeness to the end users. Edge computing aims to provide low latency and quick response time for real-time application as compared to cloud computing [1–4, 9, 10].

7.1.2 Contribution and novelty of the work

A voluminous rise in multimedia content over the internet has become clearly evident in recent years; with this comes challenges to handle and

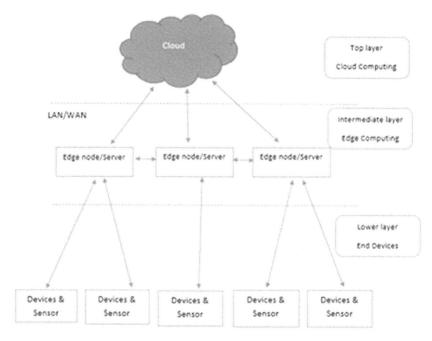

Figure 7.3 Exemplar layered infrastructure for edge computing.

Table 7.1 Comparative attributes of edge computing and cloud computing

Parameters	Cloud computing	Edge computing
Service Location	Lies in the internet	Lies at edge network
Distance	Multiple hops	Single hop
Latency	High	Low
Jitter	High	Very low
Location Awareness	No	Yes
Geo-distribution	Centralized	Distributed
Mobility Support	Limited	Supported
Data En Route Attacks	High probability	Very low probability
Target User	General internet users	Mobile users
Service Scope	Global	Limited
Hardware	Scalable competences	Limited competences

process such data. In this work, multimedia goes by its definition of being a wide variety of data representation including texts, audio, and video content; visual representation using images; animation that presents a vast range of services as audio and video streaming; and interactive gaming at real time, which has been visually presented in Figure 7.4. As an example,

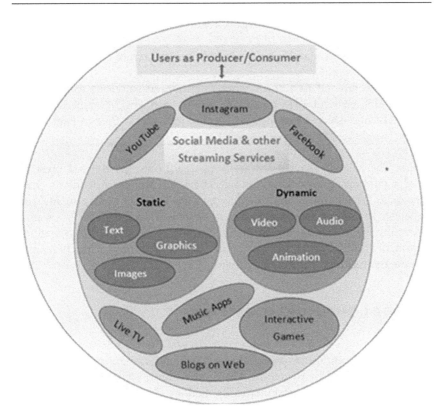

Figure 7.4 Real-time multimedia sources.

we can refer to multimedia content as data streaming from a variety of real-world web and social media applications such as YouTube, Instagram, Twitter, Facebook, Graphic Novels, Live TV, Animated TV, Interactive Games, Music Applications, Blogs, and many others.

There are some observable and unforeseen challenges in designing and developing a scalable edge computing infrastructure capable of handling a large variety of devices including IoT devices; capturing, storing, caching, and managing evolving heterogeneous data from different multimedia services; privacy and protection of user data flowing over the internet; coping with increasing user demands; and handling computational constraints.

Our research thus primarily concentrates on examining aspects of edge computing toward managing, processing, and consumption of multimedia content at network edges. The novelty of this work lies in presenting a generalized approach toward designing a scalable edge computing architecture capable of offering management and processing multimedia data at reduced cost, fast reaction time, consuming less bandwidth, and efficient energy consumption.

Primary contributions of the research work are as below:

- We examine studies on edge computing architecture and related work in this domain.
- We recommend two approaches as proposed solutions to designing scalable generalized edge architecture by applying Machine Learning (ML) and Deep Learning (DL) techniques and a Peer-to-Peer (P2P) networking approach.

Further, the current chapter is organized as follows: Section 7.2 presents the edge computing ecosystem, followed by MEC architecture and its characteristics. Detail about multimedia data processing, management, and challenges in edge architecture is discussed in Section 7.3. Section 7.4 proposes solutions for designing an Intelligent Edge Computing Ecosystem for Multimedia (MM) Data Processing, and Analysis. Section 7.5 concludes and presents the future scope in this domain.

7.2 EDGE COMPUTING ECOSYSTEM

Edge computing refers to an innovative decentralized approach that aims to bring cloud computing toward the network edges to improve the quality of services provided by the cloud. The decentralized approach used in edge computing concept is diagrammatically demonstrated in Figure 7.5. As we concentrate on the concept of multimedia (MM) data, this chapter will have a sharp focus on improving the quality of multimedia services by delegating cloud services to edges. Fog Computing, Cloudlets, and Mobile Edge

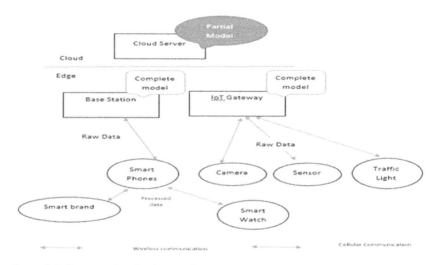

Figure 7.5 Decentralized edge intelligence concept.

Computing or Multi-access Edge Computing (MEC) are the major archetypes under the edge computing ecosystem. The above-mentioned technological advances share the same features and goal, which basically aims to reduce the proximity among service delivery locations and customers by trying to transfer cloud resources from remote, enormous cloud data centers to smaller, edges at the network end to provide low latency. Therefore, these are termed under the umbrella of Edge Computing mechanisms [11, 12].

Briefly, fog computing refers to a scenario where numerous heterogeneous, decentralized base stations and access points serve as fog nodes used to communicate, collaborate, process, and store data without the assistance of a third party. MEC refers to a model that facilitates smooth management of various time-sensitive applications with the help of mobile base stations serving as sensor nodes. Cloudlets are another facility that contains strong CPU and abundant storage spaces, in contrast to routers, gateways, set-top boxes, and other devices with limited resource availability [12]. Although fog and edge computing are substitutable environments, a different frame of reference exists. Fog computing views the entire ecosystem with reference to the cloud aspect, whereas edge computing refers to a networking viewpoint. The uniqueness of edge computing lies in the concept where it involves extending storage, computation, and processing resources to the edges of a network, which can be a mobile network also [13].

7.2.1 Edge computing architecture and characteristics

7.2.1.1 General architecture

OpenFog Reference Architecture is an open and unified architectural framework provided by the OpenFog Consortium for fog computing that enables combining edge and/or fog environment under defined standards. This reference architecture was accepted as an official standard by IEEE Standards Association in 2018 under IEEE 1934 [14].

Figure 7.6 displays a general layered architecture for edge computing that is simple to understand. The topmost layer shown in Figure 7.6 is made up of various sensing pieces of equipment, covering many mobile and cellular sensing devices. These devices can be wearables such as smartwatches, smart bands, and other sensing devices used in the healthcare industry or we can say the Internet of Medical Things (IofMT), transportation, agriculture, weather forecasting, supply chain industry, and in many other domains. Here, original data can be produced or sampled, which is then sent to the middle layer for subsequent operations. The edge layer, which has many edge nodes with computation and storage capabilities, is the middle layer. It exists to provide customers with temporary data storage and processing offloading, while at the same time lessening the pressure on the cloud. Edge servers, which could include mini data centers, routers, and IoT gateways, in mobile network base stations, on automobiles, among other places, that

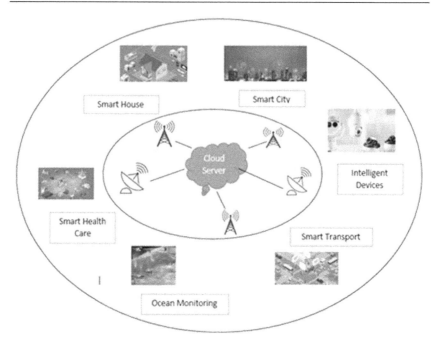

Figure 7.6 **A generalized edge computing architecture.**

provide services for end devices. In addition to this, edge devices are those end devices that make service requests to edge servers, such as mobile phones, embedded devices, and various Internet of Things devices [15]. The cloud server that supports additional large data processing and storage is the primary layer, as presented in Figure 7.6 [12].

7.2.1.2 Characteristic features

This section of the chapter presents characteristic features leading to popularize the edge computing ecosystem for multimedia data processing and management. Following are some of the major key characteristics among others of edge infrastructure.

1. **Proximity toward end users:** The fundamental goal of edge technologies is to expand cloud services closer to the end users and provide computing and storage facilities close to their devices to support real-time services and quick responses [11].
2. **Minimal latency:** In an edge computing ecosystem, computation typically takes place close to the data source, saving a significant amount of time during data transfer. Such a network is useful to process huge volumes of multimedia data with very less latency. Responses from edge servers to end devices are almost instantaneous [15].

3. **Content delivery from edge:** The backbone load and latency requirement can be significantly reduced by using edge infrastructure by caching user-requested content at edge. If the edge caches are placed closest
to the users, user requests can be handled with substantially lower
latency, thereby facilitating caching and delivering content at edges [11].

4. **Improved computation processing and storage:** As in edge computing ecosystem servers as well as storage units with strong CPUs have
been placed at the network edge, thus facilitating increased processing
capabilities and storage functionality. It allows increased processing
and storage power at the router and network equipment levels, which
causes delivery of processing power closer to users in addition to their
standard functions, as suggested by fog computing. As memory and
processor operate simultaneously thereby improving sensor capacities, it is now possible to provide processing capabilities that are as
close to the sensors as possible to clean, verify, encrypt or compress,
and gently preprocess data to be able to reduce the quantity of data
transferred to the cloud [11, 16].

5. **Energy saver ecosystem:** As we have seen, delegating computing duties
to edge servers and end devices' energy usage would drastically decrease.
The result would be an increase in the battery life of the devices.

Apart from these characteristic features, the edge computing ecosystem also
has the capability to unify and handle heterogeneous devices and data, and
support from Machine Learning tools for data analysis at edges.

7.2.2 Edge computing processing archetypes

This part of the chapter gives an overview of some of the archetypes for
local processing of data near to the end users or sensors at the edges with
respect to edge computing. Elaboration of each such technique is beyond the
scope of this chapter.

Mist Computing (MC): Edge computing in the form of Mist Computing
(MC) is simple and light (EC). With this model, networking, storage, and
elastic compute services are extended from the edge to the absolute edge/
endpoints. Modern smart endpoints can execute analyses and applications independently with real-time query and NoSQL-like files system
support because of improved networking stacks, greater memory, and
more effective CPUs. The mist encompasses smart devices and sensory
networks, and the paradigm has the advantage of keeping sensor data
near to its source and avoiding network exchange unless absolutely necessary. To limit the power ingestion of the IoT device, it is only employed
in the event of a cloud-to-IoT device communication failure [16].

Osmotic Computing (OC): Micro virtual machines (MVMs), which
Osmotic Computing (OC) employs, can be shifted between the local

level and the cloud, depending on the resources available. Osmotic pressure serves as the inspiration for this paradigm's task distribution between edge and cloud levels. Still, some security considerations related to maintaining data privacy remain an ongoing challenge [16].

Mobile Edge Computing (MEC): Mobile devices, namely smartphones and tablets, have rapidly increased in processing power and storage capacity, necessitating the development of MEC. It later developed to include Wi-Fi access and is now known as multi-access edge computing [16]. MEC is further explored in Section 2.3.

Dew Computing (DC): An additional component of cloud computing is DC. It is primarily built on on-premises computers, which are made up of a variety of heterogeneous devices and tools—such as smart sensors and smartphones—and moves computing programs and data, as well as services from the cloud, near to consumers, enabling low latency. The concept is to save data locally on the end user's device so they can have a local copy and easily examine them [16].

Jungle Computing (JC): Jungle Computing uses computing resources near to users to process data with improved Quality of Experience (QoE). The goal of JC is to utilize all such resources in their full capacity, which varies in terms of CPU architecture or GPUs, operating costs, memory capacity, and processing speed but still not very commonly used framework [16].

7.2.3 MEC architecture and characteristics

MEC's primary objective is to offer a lower latency mobile computing platform to mobile subscribers, including users of smartphones, drivers of cars, and even manufacturers of sensor devices to enable low-latency connectivity, resourceful computing, and coverage of a greater geographical part. In MEC, along with fog computing, as depicted in the picture, computing resources are located physically close to mobile devices (i.e., at the edge of networks), such as along wireless base stations, routers at edge, and mobile devices that have access to the cloud for MEC subscribers. Proud to being a low latency provider edge architecture, it is an evolving paradigm, as there are still some challenges to be overcome in current research scenarios of maintaining secure data access, providing scalability, handling data storage, and resource management [16, 17].

We list three MEC feature capabilities in terms of standard services it provides for processing multimedia and video streaming data, i.e., Content distribution and Cashing, Computational Offloading, and Data Analysis, which are demonstrated in Figure 7.7 [17]:

1. **Content distribution and Caching:** This feature enables an edge server to serve as a content server and has a content caching capability when it comes to content distribution and caching, which is shown in Figure 7.7.

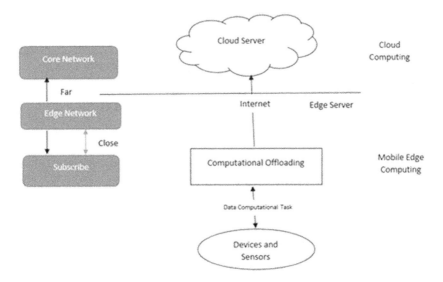

Figure 7.7 MEC feature capabilities.

2. **Computational Offloading**: MEC in this instance gathers a wide range of heterogeneous data from a variety of sensors and performs data fusions. To address the issue of task offloading, Y. Chen, F. Zhao, Y. Lu, and X. Chen examined the process of task scheduling in a dynamic mobile edge computing environment. The authors developed an algorithm for task offloading of a dynamic nature known as DTOME for MEC based on the theory of stochastic optimization with a hybrid energy supply on the basis of theory. An energy supply model that is hybrid in nature is used in the algorithm with the goal of minimizing offloading cost [18].

3. **Data Analysis**: MEC environment uses Machine Learning techniques and big data analytics to process heterogeneous and voluminous data, including audio, video, text in real time and draws inference.

7.3 MULTIMEDIA DATA PROCESSING AND MANAGEMENT IN EDGE ARCHITECTURE

This section of the chapter deals with the reasons why the edge computing scenario plays a more significant role in transferring, processing, and managing multimedia and IoT data rather than the cloud scenario, in addition to general standard services provided by the cloud.

It is anticipated that by 2030, globally the number of IoT devices connected over the entire network is expected to nearly treble around 29 billion from 9.7 billion in 2020. These devices range from sensor nodes that record and submit data at edge nodes that can be processed and analyzed for further appropriate actions [19]. So, there are many requirements to handle such enormous and heterogeneous multimedia data via edge services. In this process, several challenges are mentioned, along with requirements to design an edge/fog architecture to handle huge volumes of multimedia data.

7.3.1 Why edge processing for multimedia data?

The concept of cloud computing has evolved to address management, control, coordination, storage, computing, and processing limitations of the Internet of Things, but, due to the following issues, cloud computing does not effectively support massive multimedia data storage in remote IoT and other systems [12].

- The cloud environment cannot meet the real-time responsiveness of data processing, as it is located at a greater distance from the sensory devices placed locally. Therefore, processing enormous multimedia and other streaming data through cloud computing inevitably causes service delays.
- The cloud system lacks in precisely identifying location and mobility requirements of mobile sensor applications, again due to being far from local sensory devices.
- As there has been exponential growth in multimedia data that users access, secure transmission is also a significant and unimaginable hurdle for cloud services.
- Due to the lack of processing a huge volume of multimedia data in real time, presenting satisfying QoS to the end user is another constraint of the cloud environment.
- Cloud data centers are most frequently employed to process IoT data, and many IoT applications, such as demand prediction for smart power grids and voice response in Apple Siri, are latency sensitive. Carvalho et al. (2019) identified a significant issue with cloud architecture that is basically round trip latency time (RTT) ranging from edge to cloud is O(100) msec. In light of this, hosting analytics and decision-making in the cloud can result in degradation of execution [20].

The above discussion supports that edge processing is an aspect that can either supplement or completely replace cloud computing [20].

7.3.2 Challenges and requirements for managing multimedia data in edge computing

Edge computing has become a design paradigm that has an added advantage to a cloud environment that can empower the system in managing and processing multimedia data at the edge of the network. Following are the requirements with some proposed related work that is needed to design such

Figure 7.8 Challenges and requirements in edge computing.

an edge ecosystem. All these requirements are consolidated and presented in Figure 7.8 for easy representation.

- **Handling a variety of streaming multimedia data and real-time processing:** Today, due to a variety of multimedia applications such as virtual reality, augmented reality, 4K streaming, and others, voluminous and heterogeneous data is being generated that interests users. This data may be accessed from smartphones through wireless networks. In addition, real-time data can also be captured from many sensory devices, smart cams, and others for different applications such as weather forecasting, street light monitoring, traffic control, etc., and each data may be in a different format, as these devices are placed everywhere as IoT services. Computational Offloading is a mechanism in MEC to perform data fusion of heterogeneous data, and Big Data analytics could be a very important player here in edge/fog ecosystem to analyze such heterogeneous data at the edge [17].

- **Processing and computing at the edge:** The prime objective of the edge ecosystem is to move compute, networking, and storage to the edge of the network/mobile network for those operations that require high computation, latency, and are bandwidth prone such as voluminous multimedia data that require real-time processing to provide a sufficient Quality of Service (QoS) [21].

  An inquisitive content pushing system was proposed by Han et al. that anticipates a user's route of travel and propagates the enquired data to an edge server situated at a Wi-Fi hotspot [22]. Tran proposed a collaborative caching system to optimize adaptive rate control. Authors have used the edge server as a platform for content caching and transcoding. By taking into account cache storage and processing power constraints, they propose that it can increase the backbone network traffic [23].

  A game theory-based offloading technique was put out by Chen et al. based on Edge Accelerated Web Browsing technology, cloud, and edge server hybrids. By outsourcing the retrieval of web content and the rendering of web pages to the edge server, the suggested system can shorten the duration of a web-based application's execution [24]. For the delivery and transcoding of video/audio, Islam et al. have proposed a Void edge cloud system [25].

- **Low latency and bandwidth requirement:** The extraordinary rise in multimedia data due to applications and services such as live streaming, online video conferencing, YouTube, Instagram, and others has led to a huge increase in demand and requirement for QoS that requires data accessing and retrieval with low latency, utilizes less bandwidth, and allows fast data rate, thereby reducing reaction time. Low latency and consistent packet flow are required for these multimedia services. Fog and Edge Computing (EC) pitch themselves as a team-up to handle these latency-sensitive services, where all resources are managed in concert and in tiers, from the cloud to the end devices. The administration of all resources takes place in a coordinated and tiered way. The major objective is to physically place cloud resources closer to consumers. Similar advantages to CC are shared by these systems, such as a decrease in latency to milliseconds, lessened network congestion, and real-time user position detection [26].

- **Resource sharing and allocation:** The edge/fog environment presents a distributed way for sharing resources for processing data so an appropriate resource allocation strategy must be decided for proper utilization of resources. This can be achieved by enabling the service providers to allocate the resources uniformly for each subsystem. If we talk about industrial applications, Lin and Yang contend that clouds are typically located and handled centrally in smart logistics centers. However, if the industrial area is too big, it realizes larger response time from the centralized cloud to the massive IoT sensors [27]. Tremendous load and significant latency caused by the real-time processing of many IoT devices still remain a challenge in centralized cloud computing systems and that had been addressed via distributed fog/edge computing. Resources used in this computing environment handle a portion of the computer duties for logistical operations that can be completed based exclusively on local information, thereby reducing response time and improving the adaptability of the system [20].

- **Secure data transfer:** Possible dangers to cloud storage have long included many security concerns. Because each user has personal data that can be anywhere between Gigabyte (GB) and Terabyte TB in size, this massive demand is too great for local storage to handle. Deploying a low-complexity, highly secure cloud storage service is currently a common practice. In other words, more people will choose the cloud provider that enables IoT applications built on smart edge computing and has stronger security levels [12].
- **Intelligent infrastructure:** According to Varshney and Simmhan, in recent edge scenarios, network edge sensing is accelerating at a high pace. It is well known that a significant portion of the data streaming from the edge can be attributed to multimedia data streaming and the Internet of Things, where the convergence of low-cost sensors, open communications, and intelligent infrastructure management is required for managing the exponential growth of such streaming data [28].
- **Need for centralized cloud component:** Edge computing, also known as Mobile Cloud, incorporates certain processing and analytics at the edges of the devices or network for applications, whereas the cloud component is required to provide standard services of data archiving and supervision [12] for efficient functioning of the system. Also, L. F. Bittencourt et al. have proposed that although moving computing and data storage at network edges makes better use of newly available mobile device capabilities to coordinate all edge activity, a central cloud component is still required [29].
- **Energy efficiency:** Establishing an energy-efficient infrastructure for edge computing is still a daunting task and a foremost requirement. Because of the constrained energy budgets and poor computation capacities, edge devices have a resource-constrained environment that makes it difficult to install needed data analytics, especially in real-time applications [30]. As far as deep learning is concerned as an option to data analytics at edge, according to a function that considers consumption of battery power in addition to latency and present condition of network, Ran et al. established a system that determines whether to run a deep neural network model favoring the edge side or the cloud side [31].
- **Quality of Service (QoS) and/or Quality of Experience (QoE):** QoE is another important aspect of edge/fog computing environment, as the ultimate objective of such system is to provide the user the utmost

satisfaction when browsing multimedia content. The extraordinary rise in multimedia data due to applications and services such as live streaming, online video conferencing, YouTube, Instagram, and others has led to a huge increase in demand for QoS that requires data accessing and retrieval with low latency, utilizes less bandwidth, and allows fast data rate, thereby reducing reaction time. Low latency and consistent packet flow are required for these multimedia services.

There are many stringent QoS requirements because of continuous evolving voluminous and heterogeneous data from many sensors or devices, yet research in this area is to be seen with great priority [32]. In such an effort, a QoE model was put forth by Floris et al. for multimodal IoT applications. The authors assessed the performance for vehicular multimedia apps to verify and authenticate the proposed QoE model, and the results showed that the suggested QoE model had a high association with opinions of quality that are subjective [33].

Apart from the above challenges, edge computing still faces some challenges, even though it shows promising results. These problems are defined below:

- **Naming Schema:** There is no standard format available to name the edge computing mechanism. It creates difficulty for the programmer to understand which network and communication protocol is used.
- **Programmability:** Edge computing architecture is heterogeneous in nature. Programmers use different languages at different levels as compared to cloud computing, which is known for its transparency. Therefore, it is difficult to implement and understand code for it.
- **Managing edge devices:** Managing devices at the edge is a complex task. It involves factors such as mobility (shifting and gathering data from different location), scalability, security and privacy, heterogeneity, etc.

7.4 SOLUTIONS TO DESIGNING AN INTELLIGENT EDGE COMPUTING ECOSYSTEM FOR MULTIMEDIA (MM) DATA PROCESSING AND ANALYSIS

As per statistics by Data Age 2025, approximately 30% of global content will require processing in real time, so the importance of edge processing definitely arises [7]. Machine Learning (ML) and Deep Learning (DL) techniques have been applied in much research work, but practical implementation of each requirement for edge analytics is still an area that has to be improved upon. Machine Learning and Deep Learning are thereby striking paradigms to apply data analytics at edges of the network in real time, which has been explored in this section as a solution to edge processing. Another approach using Peer-to-Peer (P2P) networking is also discussed in this section as an innovative solution of load balancing and reducing download time in a distributive manner, as limited work has been done in this area to analyze the applicability of P2P networking in the edge computing paradigm.

7.4.1 Applying Machine Learning (ML) and Deep Learning (DL) techniques for MM data analysis

In this section, we will present a brief review of Machine Learning, as well as Deep Learning methods applied in many works as a means to design an appropriate Edge Ecosystem based on achieving the objective of low latency, less bandwidth, improved QoE, and QoS and others mentioned in Section 3.2 to process multimedia data incoming at edges. We briefly focus on aspects of data analysis, computational offloading, and content caching in this chapter for simplicity so that readers can understand this complex concept in simple terms in order to design the proposed system. These three major concerns have been prioritized, but the content is so complex and vast that it cannot be fully covered in one chapter.

Because of constrained energy budgets and poor computation capacities, edge devices have a resource-constrained environment that makes it difficult to install needed data analytics, especially in real-time applications, so the main contribution here consists of solution provided as services, learning, and inferencing at edges using multiple DL techniques for real-time analytics.

7.4.1.1 Services at edge

Several processes provide various multimedia services carried out at the edge network, thanks to multimedia edge computing. These services include sensing or identifying data, synthesizing data, and employing Machine Learning techniques for training and inferencing at edges, as shown in Figure 7.9.

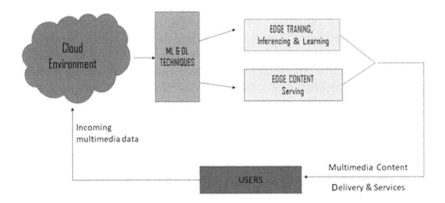

Figure 7.9 Machine and Deep Learning in cloud and edge environment services.

Also, caching, distributing, and delivering content is an important process provided as a service at the network edge [34].

1. **Sensing at Edge:** This facility enables multimedia users to submit data to edge devices that are close by. Multimedia material is produced through crowdsourced apps or live streaming, such as Facebook, TikTok, Instagram, Twitter, and others. In addition, the use of large-scale edge devices may also enable the detection of crowd behavior, especially identifying geographical preferences to improve the ability of multimedia services accordingly [34].
2. **Edge Computing with MM Data Analysis using ML and DL:** Machine Learning and Deep Learning are revolutionary technologies that empower data inferencing, learning, and data analysis at edges.
   a) **Inferencing at Edge using ML and DL Techniques**
      Due to the improvement in processing power of edge devices, researchers can investigate the performance of different Machine Learning and Deep Learning methods employed at network edges. Optimizing the inference accuracy and latency is a research challenge for deciding on edge and cloud architecture.

      In order to improve the accuracy and speed of inference over deep learning models, we propose that amalgamation of edge computing and deep learning offers a potential option for edge learning. Edge inference does the task of processing and analyzing the data—or a portion of the personal data—locally, successfully preserving the privacy of users while speeding up response times and conserving bandwidth. Machine Learning and Deep Learning methods as transfer learning, federated learning, along with meta learning, have also been functional in multimedia tasks supporting evolving inference requirements, such as low latency, heterogeneous data distributions, etc., deploying on various edge devices [34, 35].

      P. Joshi, M. Hasanuzzaman, C. Thapa, H. Afli, and T. Scully examined the state of the art for DL model training and inference at edges of the network. Training and inferencing at edges is still very difficult, so authors have discussed several DL possible architectures to achieve this. It was proposed that federated learning along with split were more successful than others since they improved privacy while training and giving inference by applying in DL model. The processing of DL models has been pushed to edge servers in a significant effort to offset the limitations of high latency and cost of reliable communication. In addition, there are some important indicators to measure performance of the models at edges. Open research challenges were also discussed in this paper [36].

b) **Learning at Edge using ML and DL Techniques for Real-Time Analysis**
   Using a deep neural network (DNN), a cutting-edge Machine Learning
   technique model that outperforms the traditional approaches has
   lately been used for a variety of multimedia data processing problems. Therefore, the edge computing system must analyze gathered
   multimedia data effectively to deploy unique multimedia data analysis
   methods with DNNs. Different compression and acceleration techniques have been created and developed to address this issue using
   DNNs [34, 35, 37].

   - DNNs are a perfect solution to accelerate computations by opti-
     mizing various DMM operators and Artificial Neural Network
     (ANN) Architecture [34].
   - In addition, another advantage of DNN is that it facilitates
     Computational Offloading by permitting inferencing and training
     of data by partially offloading content to remote computing servers
     that fasten computations and reduce the load on the local devices.
     Distributed DNNs provide a way to group edge devices based on
     the computational tasks performed on them and accordingly dis-
     tribute the load between these groups [34].
   - Federated Learning is another technique that helps to reduce con-
     cerns over data security and privacy problems [34, 35].
   - Deep Q-Learning and Reinforcement Learning (RL) accelerates
     smooth streaming of MM Data facilitating offloading and data com-
     pression [37]. Chang et al. proposed a Deep Q-Learning based model
     with a bandwidth sharing policy that optimizes data allocation so
     that users achieve satisfactory QoE while video streaming [38].
     Zhou et al. proposed MM segmentation using Deep Q-Learning.
     Park et al. also employed and tested Deep Q-Learning and achieved
     sufficiently smooth streaming of video data in moving vehicles [39].
     Ban et al. strived apply deep RL with Long Short Term Memory
     (LSTM) for predicting and allocating streaming resources to achieve
     360° streaming of video [40].
   - In order to achieve the objective of content caching and delivery
     from edge in the context of edge computing, Zang et al. presented
     the Recurrent Neural Network to optimize and improve video
     caching prediction and to update content [41].
   - When deploying Deep Learning systems, Jiang et al. suggested
     using devices at edge to excerpt global data that is inaccessible to a
     single client to lessen the redundant processing of each stream [42].
   - M. N. H. Nguyen, N. H. Tran, Y. K. Tun, Z. Han, and C. S. Hong
     have investigated the applicability of federated learning at MEC
     servers. Authors have put forth the MS-FEDL problem, which
     refers to resource allocation and adjusting hyper parameters and
     proposed a solution for this problem with relation to mobile device

energy usage with CPU allocation in a distributed manner to learning service at every mobile device and also minimizing overall learning time at MEC servers. The simulation that was conducted supports the efficiency of the proposed method over a heuristic approach and suggests that it protects privacy of learning services from each other [43].

7.4.2 Simulation of edge computing with scalable peer-to-peer (P2P) networking

In this section, we propose another solution with an objective to reduce download time of video streaming using the P2P networking concept in edge infrastructure. Edge infrastructure can capture the capabilities of P2P networking by integrating Content distribution networks (CDN) caching abilities with P2P system collaboration principles to deliver video streaming in real time, even in the case of momentary detachment from the cloud or edge structure [44].

Individual peers' end devices, such as mobile devices, servers, or other computing systems like laptops make up peer-to-peer (P2P) networks. The peers work together by sharing resources to fulfill one another's requests and allows the client to download from the source as well as making other people also download the same file. P2P systems are frequently used for file sharing and downloading. This concept is pictorially presented in Figure 7.10 below.

The simulation consists of downloading a video of about 208 MB using both normal and P2P download to demonstrate reduced download time using P2P in edge infrastructure. BitTorrent protocol has been used for P2P file sharing. The input source file is retrieved from https://www.youtube.com/watch?v=CSSKNCYaQUA.

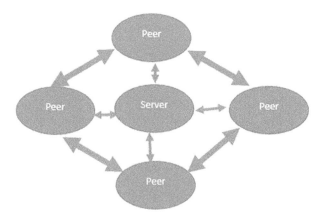

Figure 7.10 Peer-to-peer networking feature.

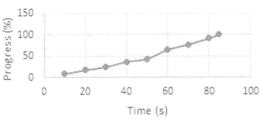

Figure 7.11 Download progress w.r.t. time for Instance 1: normal downloading.

Figure 7.12 Download progress w.r.t. time for Instance 1: P2P downloading.

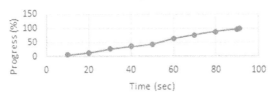

Figure 7.13 Progress of download w.r.t. time for Instance 2: normal downloading.

Two instances of simulation were conducted on different machines to ensure the efficiency of proposed results. Figure 7.11 shows the download progress with time in seconds in the case of normal download for instance 1, and Figure 7.12 shows the download progress with time in seconds in the case of P2P download using 4 peers for instance 1.

For Instance 2, Figure 7.13 shows the download progress with time in seconds in the case of normal download, and Figure 7.14 shows the download progress with time in seconds in the case of P2P download using 4 peers.

7.4.2.1 Simulation result of edge computing with peer-to-peer (P2P) networking

The result of the simulation is presented in Table 7.2 and Table 7.3 for Instances 1 and 2, respectively. Table 7.2 shows that total download time

Figure 7.14 Progress of download w.r.t. time for Instance 2: P2P downloading.

Table 7.2 Download progress with Time for normal and P2P download for Instance 1

Instance 1: Normal Download									
Time (s)	10	20	30	40	50	60	70	80	85
Progress (%)	9	18	25	37	44	65	77	91	100
Instance 1: P2P Download (Peers: 4)									
Time (s)	10	20	30	40	50	60	70	73	
Progress (%)	11	23	31	45	59	78	89	100	

Table 7.3 Download progress with Time for normal and P2P download for Instance 2

Instance 2: Normal Download										
Time (s)	10	20	30	40	50	60	70	80	90	91
Progress (%)	7	14	27	36	44	63	77	89	97	100
Instance 2: P2P Download (Peers: 4)										
Time (s)	10	20	30	40	50	60	70	80	81	
Progress (%)	12	23	35	43	54	71	82	95	100	

of source file (video) of size 208 MB for Instance 1. It takes 85 seconds using normal download, whereas it takes 73 seconds using P2P download, thereby download time is reduced to 14.12% using P2P file sharing.

Also, for Instance 2, Table 7.3 shows that total download time of source file (video) of size 208 MB takes 91 seconds using normal download, whereas it takes 81 seconds using P2P download, thereby reducing download time to 11% using P2P file sharing. Thus, the result shows that download time is significantly reduced for both instances on source input.

Due to its independence from a centralized system, peer-to-peer networking is a reliable and dependable solution. This implies that the interconnected and linked machines will be able to operate separately from one another. The network will not be disrupted even if one component fails. The issue that still persists is that only the corresponding user will have access to those files. P2P networking has best scalability qualities, which is an additional benefit. The network's performance won't suffer even if more clients are added. A single file may occasionally be shared by several users, in which case the network will make additional bandwidth available.

7.5 CONCLUSION AND FUTURE SCOPE

The rapid development in the field of communication provides abundant availability of real-time multimedia data and other streaming services 24/7. This calls for innovative approaches to guarantee handling heterogeneous voluminous data, maintaining low latency, less bandwidth requirement, and secure transmission with ensuring good quality of service (QoS) in real time, which are some of the major problems associated with storing, processing, and delivering multimedia data in real time. This chapter discusses edge computing technologies, mainly MEC, Fog technology, and Cloudlets. These technologies offer promising and workable solutions to handle various requirements and overcome challenges mentioned in the chapter by designing scalable edge computing infrastructure. The chapter also presents a review of work done in this area where edge computing provides a way to reduce transmission cost, less latency, low bandwidth utilization, energy-efficient usage, and other challenges.

This chapter also proposes applying Machine Learning and Deep Learning techniques for performing data analytics at edges for smooth availability of multimedia services to users. DNNs, Reinforcement Learning, and Deep-Q-Learning are some of the commonly used cutting-edge solutions to perform data training, inferencing, learning at edges, and managing computational offloading, among other challenges to designing a scalable edge ecosystem. It also promises another solution using P2P networking with edge computing by mixing Content distribution networks (CDN) caching with P2P structure to distribute video streaming in real time by lowering download time. Analysis based on the result of the simulation reveals that edge computing architecture that is distributive in nature with P2P offers a sustainable scalable environment to deliver trustworthy services and meets the requirement of low transmission rate and network latency. Thus, it may provide high user satisfaction by extending unfazed video and multimedia streaming services at a lower cost than conventional streaming methods.

Future chapters will focus more on precisely designing edge infrastructure for a specific challenge with some real-world data analysis.

REFERENCES

[1] Greenberg, A., Hamilton, J., Maltz, D. A., & Patel, P. (2008). The cost of a cloud: Research problems in data center networks. *ACM SIGCOMM Computer Communication Review*, 39(1), 68–73.

[2] Cuervo, E., Balasubramanian, A., Cho, D.-K., Wolman, A., Saroiu, S., Chandra, R., & Bahl, P. (2010, June). MAUI: Making smartphones last longer with code offload. In *Proceedings of the 8th International Conference on Mobile Systems, Applications, and Services* (pp. 49–62).

[3] Bonomi, F., Milito, R., Zhu, J., & Addepalli, S. (2012, August). Fog computing and its role in the internet of things. In *Proceedings of the First Edition of the MCC Workshop on Mobile Cloud Computing* (pp. 13–16).

[4] Satyanarayanan, M., Bahl, P., Caceres, R., & Davies, N. (2009). The case for VM-based cloudlets in mobile computing. *IEEE Pervasive Computing*, 8(4), 14–23.

[5] Boeing 787s to create half a terabyte of data per flight, says Virgin Atlantic, https://datafloq.com/read/self-driving-cars-create-2-petabytes-data-annually/ 172. Accessed 6/10/2022.

[6] Self-driving cars will create 2 petabytes of data. What are the big data opportunities for the car industry? https://datafloq.com/read/self-driving-cars-create-2-petabytes-data-annually/. Accessed 6/10/2022.

[7] Big data and analytics: Definitions, value, trends and applications, https://www.i-scoop.eu/big-data-action-value-context/. Accessed 10/1/2023.

[8] Cao, J., Zhang, Q., & Shi, W. (2018). *Edge computing: A primer*. Berlin/ Heidelberg, Germany: Springer International Publishing.

[9] Dolui, K., & Datta, S. K. (2017, June). Comparison of edge computing implementations: Fog computing, cloudlet and mobile edge computing. In *2017 Global Internet of Things Summit (GIoTS)* (pp. 1–6). IEEE.

[10] Ahmed, E., Ahmed, A., Yaqoob, I., Shuja, J., Gani, A., Imran, M., & Shoaib, M. (2017). Bringing computation closer toward the user network: Is edge computing the solution? *IEEE Communications Magazine*, 55(11), 138–144.

[11] Bilal, K., & Erbad, A. (2017, May). Edge computing for interactive media and video streaming. In *2017 Second International Conference on Fog and Mobile Edge Computing (FMEC)* (pp. 68–73). IEEE.

[12] Xiao, D., Li, M., & Zheng, H. (2020). Smart privacy protection for big video data storage based on hierarchical edge computing. *Sensors*, 20(5), 1517.

[13] Mahmood, Z., & Ramachandran, M. (2018). Fog computing: Concepts, principles and related paradigms. In Z. Mahmood (ed.), *Fog Computing* (pp. 3–21). Cham: Springer.

[14] OpenFog Reference Architecture for Fog Computing, Produced by the OpenFog Consortium Architecture Working Group. www.OpenFogConsortium.org, Feb 2017. https://www.iiconsortium.org/pdf/OpenFog_Reference_Architecture_2_09_17.pdf

[15] Xu, D., Li, T., Li, Y., Su, X., Tarkoma, S., Jiang, T., ... & Hui, P. (2020). Edge intelligence: Architectures, challenges, and applications. *arXiv preprint arXiv:2003.12172*.

[16] Debauche, O., Mahmoudi, S., & Guttadauria, A. (2022). A new edge computing architecture for IoT and multimedia data management. *Information*, 13(2), 89.

[17] Kanai, K., Imagane, K., & Katto, J. (2018). Overview of multimedia mobile edge computing. *ITE Transactions on Media Technology and Applications*, 6(1), 46–52.

[18] Chen, Y., Zhao, F., Lu, Y. & Chen, X. (2023). Dynamic task offloading for mobile edge computing with hybrid energy supply. *Tsinghua Science and Technology*, 28(3), 421–432. doi: 10.26599/TST.2021.9010050

[19] https://www.statista.com/statistics/1183457/iot-connected-devices-worldwide/. Accessed 12/12/2023.

[20] Carvalho, A., O'Mahony, N., Krpalkova, L., Campbell, S., Walsh, J., & Doody, P. (2019). Edge computing applied to industrial machines. *Procedia Manufacturing*, 38, 178–185.

[21] Abbas, N., Zhang, Y., Taherkordi, A., & Skeie, T., (2018). Mobile edge computing: A survey. *IEEE Internet of Things Journal*, 5(1), 450–465.

[22] Han, T., & Ansari, N. (2012, September). Opportunistic content pushing via WiFi hotspots. In *2012 3rd IEEE International Conference on Network Infrastructure and Digital Content* (pp. 680–684). IEEE.

[23] Tran, T. X., Pandey, P., Hajisami, A., & Pompili, D. (2017, February). Collaborative multi-bitrate video caching and processing in Mobile-Edge Computing networks. In *2017 13th Annual Conference on Wireless On-Demand Network Systems and Services (WONS)* (pp. 165–172). IEEE.

[24] Chen, X., Jiao, L., Li, W., & Fu, X. (2015). Efficient multi-user computation offloading for mobile-edge cloud computing. *IEEE/ACM Transactions on Networking, 24*(5), 2795–2808.

[25] Islam, S., & Grégoire, J. C. (2012). Giving users an edge: A flexible cloud model and its application for multimedia. *Future Generation Computer Systems, 28*(6), 823–832.

[26] Santos, F., Immich, R., & Madeira, E. R. (2022). Multimedia services placement algorithm for cloud-fog hierarchical environments. *Computer Communications, 191,* 78–91.

[27] Lin, C. C., & Yang, J. W. (2018). Cost-efficient deployment of fog computing systems at logistics centers in industry 4.0. *IEEE Transactions on Industrial Informatics, 14*(10), 4603–4611.

[28] Varshney, P., & Simmhan, Y. (2017, May). Demystifying fog computing: Characterizing architectures, applications and abstractions. In *2017 IEEE 1st International Conference on Fog and Edge Computing (ICFEC)* (pp. 115–124). IEEE.

[29] Bittencourt, L. F., Lopes, M. M., Petri, I., & Rana, O. F. (2015, November). Towards virtual machine migration in fog computing. In *2015 10th International Conference on P2P, Parallel, Grid, Cloud and Internet Computing (3PGCIC)* (pp. 1–8). IEEE.

[30] Plastiras, G., Terzi, M., Kyrkou, C., & Theocharidcs, T. (2018, July). Edge intelligence: Challenges and opportunities of near-sensor machine learning applications. In *2018 IEEE 29th International Conference on Application-Specific Systems, Architectures and Processors (ASAP)* (pp. 1–7). IEEE.

[31] Ran, X., Chen, H., Zhu, X., Liu, Z., & Chen, J. (2018, April). DeepDecision: A mobile deep learning framework for edge video analytics. In *IEEE INFOCOM 2018-IEEE Conference on Computer Communications* (pp. 1421–1429). IEEE.

[32] Bouraqia, K., Sabir, E., Sadik, M., & Ladid, L. (2020). Quality of experience for streaming services: Measurements, challenges and insights. *IEEE Access, 8,* 13341–13361.

[33] Floris, A., & Atzori, L. (2015, June). Quality of Experience in the Multimedia Internet of Things: Definition and practical use-cases. In *2015 IEEE International Conference on Communication Workshop (ICCW)* (pp. 1747–1752). IEEE.

[34] Wang, Z., Zhu, W., Sun, L., Hu, H., Ma, G., Ma, M., Pang, H., Ye, J., & Li, H. (2021). Multimedia edge computing. *arXiv preprint arXiv:2105.02409.*

[35] Ghosh, A. M., & Grolinger, K. (2021). Edge-cloud computing for Internet of Things data analytics: Embedding intelligence in the edge with deep learning. *IEEE Transactions on Industrial Informatics, 17*(3), 2191–2200.

[36] Joshi, P., Hasanuzzaman, M., Thapa, C., Afli, H., & Scully, T. (2023). Enabling all in-edge deep learning: A literature review. *IEEE Access.* doi: 10.1109/ACCESS.2023.3234761

[37] Seng, J. K. P., Ang, K. L.-M., Peter, E., & Mmonyi, A. (2022). Artificial Intelligence (AI) and machine learning for multimedia and edge information processing. *Electronics*, *11*(14), 2239.

[38] Chang, Z., Zhou, X., Wang, Z., Li, H., & Zhang, X. (2019, April). Edge-assisted adaptive video streaming with deep learning in mobile edge networks. In *2019 IEEE Wireless Communications and Networking Conference (WCNC)* (pp. 1–6). IEEE.

[39] Zhou, P., Xie, Y., Niu, B., Pu, L., Xu, Z., Jiang, H., & Huang, H. (2021). QoE-aware 3D video streaming via deep reinforcement learning in software defined networking enabled mobile edge computing. *IEEE Transactions on Network Science and Engineering*, *8*(1), 419–433.

[40] Ban, Y., Zhang, Y., Zhang, H., Zhang, X., & Guo, Z. (2020, July). MA360: Multi-agent deep reinforcement learning based live 360-degree video streaming on edge. In *2020 IEEE International Conference on Multimedia and Expo (ICME)* (pp. 1–6). IEEE.

[41] Zhang, C., Pang, H., Liu, J., Tang, S., Zhang, R., Wang, D., & Sun, L. (2019). Toward edge-assisted video content intelligent caching with long short-term memory learning. *IEEE Access*, *7*, 152832–152846.

[42] Jiang, J., Ananthanarayanan, G., Bodik, P., Sen, S., & Stoica, I. (2018). Chameleon: Scalable adaptation of video analytics. In *Proceedings of the 2018 Conference of the ACM Special Interest Group on Data Communication*, pp. 253–266.

[43] Nguyen, M. N., Tran, N. H., Tun, Y. K., Han, Z., & Hong, C. S. (2023). Toward multiple federated learning services resource sharing in mobile edge networks. *IEEE Transactions on Mobile Computing*, *22*(1), 541–555. doi: 10.1109/TMC.2021.3085979

[44] Karagiannis, V., Venito, A., Coelho, R., Borkowski, M., & Fohler, G. (2019, April). Edge computing with peer to peer interactions: Use cases and impact. In *Proceedings of the Workshop on Fog Computing and the IoT* (pp. 46–50).

Chapter 8

Trustworthiness in deepfake detection using explainability

Shetanshu Parmar and C. Mala

National Institute of Technology, Tiruchirappalli, India

8.1 INTRODUCTION

Deepfakes are a type of synthetic media that use deep learning to manipulate or generate images, videos or audio. They have become a hot topic in recent years due to their potential to be used for malicious purposes such as spreading fake news, propaganda and misinformation. The ability to generate realistic fake content presents a significant challenge for multimedia forensics, as it becomes increasingly difficult to determine the authenticity of digital media. It is important to discuss deepfakes from the perspective of multimedia forensics to understand the potential impact on society and to develop methods for detecting and combating the spread of false information [1]. Deepfakes are generally created by using Generative Adversarial Networks (GANs) and Autoencoders (AEs). There are various open-source tools available to create deepfakes. Some examples of deepfakes are shown in Figure 8.1, which are screenshots from an app used to create deepfakes. This shows the ease with which anyone with limited technical knowledge can also make deepfakes.

The increasing prevalence of deepfakes and their potential to spread misinformation has prompted the need for effective deepfake detection techniques. Various deepfake detection techniques can be classified into categories based on either the type of media involved or the methods used, such as conventional or machine learning and deep learning based. They can also be classified based on explainability from a forensics perspective. These categories are shown in Figure 8.2.

Detection can be based on the type of deepfake, whether audio, image, video, or both audio and video, or all three together. Generally, such combination is also called multimodal deepfake detection, which takes into account different media types. Videos can have frame-level detection where individual frames are processed [2] or entire video-level detection [3] is done.

Another way to distinguish is based on the techniques used, which can be conventional approaches or machine learning and deep learning-based

(a)

(b)

Figure 8.1 a) Ways to create deepfake media by using revoice, swap, face animation, and b) an example of deepfake created using swap face.

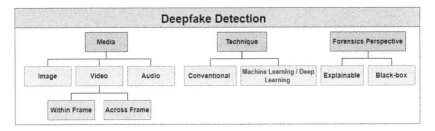

Figure 8.2 Categorization of deepfake detection.

approaches. Conventional approaches include methods that rely exclusively on the media asset under analysis and try to reveal anomalies, which may suggest the presence of a manipulation like lens distortion, noise patterns, compression artifacts. Whereas in machine learning and deep learning-based detection, features are extracted from the media such as facial landmarks [4], optical flow [5, 6], and texture analysis [7]. These features are then used to train a classifier to distinguish between real and fake videos. The benefit of approaches based on machine learning and deep learning is that there is a better grasp of the data and processes. Moreover, it is considerably easier to change model designs and tune hyperparameters.

From a forensics perspective, deepfake detection techniques can be classi-fied as explainable or black-box. Nowadays, the use of deep learning algo-rithms for deepfake detection has become a popular area of research, but the lack of transparency in these models has raised concerns about their reliability and accountability. Therefore, it is important to develop deepfake detection techniques that are not only effective but also explainable, so that the underlying decision-making process can be transparently understood by human experts. Explainability in deepfake detection refers to the ability to understand and interpret the reasoning behind a deepfake detection system's decisions. It is a crucial aspect of deepfake detection as it helps establish trust and transparency in the system and enables human users to verify the accuracy of its outputs. Explainability also helps to identify any biases or errors in the deepfake detection system, which is important for ensuring that the system is reliable and trustworthy [8].

Many deep learning solutions to detect deepfakes have been proposed before but with less focus on the explainability perspective. So, to address this issue in this chapter, an Explainable Artificial Intelligence (XAI) tool, Local Interpretable Model-Agnostic Explanations (LIME), has been used. To demonstrate the effectiveness of the use of XAI approaches in deepfake detection, various experiments are done on a sample taken from a popular dataset in this field, i.e., the Deepfake Detection Challenge (DFDC). Authors in [23] have also used LIME, but they worked on Face Forensics dataset and also did not use any pre-trained model comparisons for accuracy. Our proposed framework mentioned in Section 8.4 is quite different from that.

Also, graphs have been presented in form of accuracy and loss curves during model training and validation.

The main points of this chapter are as follows:

- Insights on the importance of explainable deepfake detection approaches that place an emphasis on the trustworthiness of the results in addition to accuracy.
- A focus on individual frames of the videos taken from the DFDC dataset.
- Various pre-trained deep learning models are used for training, and evaluation is done using accuracy metric.
- When models achieve a reasonable level of accuracy, the results are confirmed by visualizing them using the LIME tool—which draws boundaries around the super pixels that were focused on—for classification as either real or fake in deepfake detection.

In this chapter Section 8.2 is an overview of deepfake detection techniques in existing literature, and Section 8.3 covers explainability, its importance, types, and methods. Section 8.4 is about methodology, which includes a proposed framework in which data-preprocessing, deep learning models and LIME model use is explained. Section 8.5 is about metrics and an experimental setup used is mentioned as software and hardware specifications. Section 8.6 shows results in forms of graphs and table. Section 8.7 concludes the chapter.

8.2 LITERATURE SURVEY

As stated above, a way to categorize deepfake detection techniques is on the basis of the type of media. Most of the methods discussed below are for visual deepfakes. But similarly, Explainable Artificial Intelligence (XAI) methods can be applied to audio deepfakes such as [9] which is about post-hoc XAI methods for deepfake audio detection by analyzing the attribution score patterns. Techniques similar to visual explanations were used for audio-related tasks. In [5] authors show inter-frame dissimilarities in form of optical flow fields to detect deepfakes. Authors in [10] presented a framework that is helpful for deepfake detection not just based on one frame but also temporal information among frames. The work in [11] is about both audio and visual deepfakes. Such detection approaches are called multimodal approaches.

Sometimes deepfake detection is approached in sense of media forensics. Just like in media forensics, source identification is of concern; similarly, in the sense of deepfakes, it is about the model used to generate deepfakes. This type of approach has been followed in [12] where the objective was finding the model used to generate deepfakes by seeing fingerprints of the models.

Even though some researchers have given interpretable solutions to the deepfake problem, they have avoided the use of deep learning-based feature extraction and stressed on handcrafted features and fusion strategies [4]. However, deep learning-based deepfake detection approaches to extract features have proved to be more accurate and efficient than conventional approaches [13]. But deep learning approaches are black-box in nature and to improve the trustworthiness of deepfake detectors by visualizing the results rather than solely focusing on accuracy, some form of interpretability is needed. Some approaches have achieved good results but lack in explainability, as can be seen in [14], where a deepfake detection based on layer aggregation is proposed. The pipeline used by supervised approaches typically starts with the extraction of visual features from a deep backbone and ends with a binary classification head. The authors fine-tuned the backbone network and used a layer importance parameter but didn't incorporate explainability.

Recent works have focused on explainable deepfake detection and there are various ways to incorporate explainability, some of which are LIME, SHapley Additive exPlanations (SHAP), Gradient-weighted Class Activation Mapping (Grad CAM) and other techniques. Some authors have used not-so popular techniques such as a CNN-based localization method to generate heatmaps [15]. But such an approach will be limited to just CNN models, whereas LIME can be used on different types of datasets and is a model-agnostic method. The authors in [16] suggested the use of Grad CAM and LIME, among other methods for XAI in terms of interpretability.

Grad CAM is used in [17] for visualizing the predictions of the models: Xception, Capsule Network and one more network for deepfake detection in inter-and intra-database scenarios. Similarly, an attention-based explainable deepfake detection algorithm using Grad-CAM to focus on attention maps is presented in [18] where the authors worked on DFDC dataset and got good accuracy value. Also, new explainable methods are being developed by researchers, one of which is Score Class Activation Mapping (CAM), which has been used in [11]. Authors in [19] present a set of hypotheses based on fake, source, and target images and prove them by using Shapley value. A deepfake detection algorithm was proposed, which performed well for compressed images. However, authors in [20] observed that Shapley values are time-consuming, and since LIME is comparatively quicker, that's why this chapter shows the use of LIME in visualizing deepfake detection. There is a need to explore more explainable AI approaches from a deepfake forensics perspective and this chapter is an attempt towards that.

8.3 EXPLAINABILITY IN DEEPFAKE DETECTION

This section discusses preliminaries required to understand explainability in deepfake detection such as its importance, types and methods, and the LIME tool.

8.3.1 Importance of explainability in deepfake detection

Many deepfake detectors only provide a binary output, indicating whether the analyzed media is real or fake. However, this prediction, even if accurate, does not provide any further insight into the reasoning behind it. The absence of explainability may hinder the practical use of deepfake detectors, as it makes it difficult for users to trust their results [21].

Despite the ability of deep learning systems to produce reliable predictions, their "black-box" nature makes them less trustworthy. Explainability is crucial for creating transparency, but the lack of ability for deep learning to explain its decisions to humans restricts their effectiveness. Explainable Artificial Intelligence (XAI) can address this issue by providing interpretation of the predictions made by these systems [22].

8.3.2 Types and methods of explainability in deepfake detection

There are various types of explainability such as model-level, which provides insight into the internal workings of deep learning models; instance level, which provides explanations for specific deepfake detection decisions; and feature level, which provides explanation based on the most important features for decision. The types and various methods used for each type of explainability with respect to deepfake detection are given below:

Model-level Explainability
This type of explainability focuses on understanding how the deepfake detection model works and what factors it considers in making its predictions through methods such as Layer-wise Relevance Propagation (LRP) [23] or gradient-based methods [24, 25], which provide insights into how the deepfake detection model is making its predictions by highlighting the most important features in the input video.

Instance-level Explainability
This type of explainability focuses on explaining the decisions made by the deepfake detection model for a specific instance or video through methods such as saliency maps [26], which highlight the regions of the video that are most important for the deepfake detection model's prediction. Attention maps and activation maps [14] can also be used to show the regions of the video that the model is focusing on when making its predictions.

Feature-level Explainability
This type of explainability focuses on identifying the features or characteristics of the video that the deepfake detection model considers most important in making its predictions through methods such as feature

importance scores or decision trees, which provide insights into the specific features of the video that the deepfake detection model is considering in its predictions. Additionally, methods such as occlusion experiments can be used to show the impact of specific features on the deepfake detection model's predictions [27].

These methods can be used individually or in combination to provide a comprehensive view of how the deepfake detection model is making its predictions, and to build trust and credibility in the results produced by deepfake detection systems. These techniques can be implemented using open-source libraries and tools such as Matplotlib, TensorFlow, PyTorch, LIME and Shapley Additive Explanations (SHAP). LIME is quicker than SHAP in terms of cost and calculation time. Shapley values are time-consuming to calculate, however, SHAP enables the computation of a large number of Shapley values required for global model interpretations [20].

8.3.3 Local Interpretable Model-Agnostic Explanations (LIME)

In this chapter LIME tool is used. LIME is a type of instance-level explainability method used to provide local explanations for the predictions of any machine learning model, including deepfake detection models. LIME works by approximating the deepfake detection model's behavior locally around a specific instance or video by generating a simplified linear model. This linear model is then used to explain the deepfake detection model's prediction for that instance by highlighting the features that had the largest impact on the prediction [28]. LIME can be used with any machine learning model, regardless of the specific algorithm or architecture used. It does not require access to the underlying model's internal workings, which makes it model-agnostic. The tool works by generating perturbations of the input data and observing how the output changes. It then constructs a simpler model around the specific instance of interest to explain the behavior of the original model.

See Figure 8.3, where an example instance marked as the bold red cross is being explained. Let's say, a decision function f shown as pink vs. blue is not known to LIME which is the function of a black-box model. This function cannot be approximated adequately by a linear model, so the dashed line is used to show local explanation rather than global. That's how LIME tool samples instances, applies f to get predictions, and weighs them by nearness to the instance considered for explanation.

LIME relies on the assumption that every complex model is linear on a local scale because a simple model may not be able to approximate the black-box model globally. LIME provides explanations in the form of 'local feature importance' scores, which indicate how much each input feature contributed to the prediction for the specific instance being explained. These

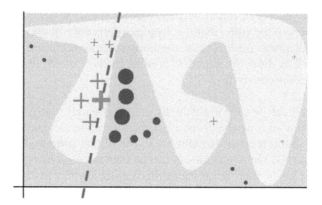

Figure 8.3 Local Interpretable Model-Agnostic Explanations (LIME) [28].

scores can be visualized in various ways, such as bar charts or heatmaps, to provide insights into how the model is making predictions. In the context of deepfake detection, LIME can be used to provide instance-level explanations for why a specific video was classified as a deepfake or not. This information can be useful for building trust and credibility in the deepfake detection system's results and for identifying potential areas for improvement.

8.4 METHODOLOGY

The methodology consists of various stages like data pre-processing, using classification models for getting results and finally using LIME to validate those results visually. The proposed framework is depicted in Figure 8.4. This section depicts all these stages of methodology in detail.

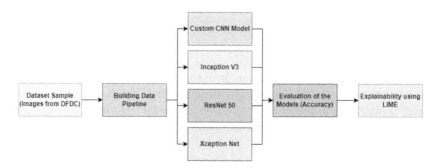

Figure 8.4 Overall architecture of the proposed framework.

8.4.1 Data pre-processing

This sub-section discusses the dataset, its splitting into train, validation and test sets and finally the process of building a data pipeline for the models.

8.4.1.1 Dataset

The dataset used contains face images sized at 224x224 pixels extracted from Deepfake-Detection-Challenge (DFDC) [29] taken from Kaggle which is one of the benchmark datasets in this field for performance analysis of models on deepfake detection. A sample of the entire dataset consisting of 20,000 images was taken for prediction consisting of an equal proportion of fake and real images, a few of which are shown in Figure 8.5.

8.4.1.2 Splitting

The dataset was divided into train, test and validation sets. Out of 20,000 images, 20% were kept as test set images and from the remaining 80% it was further split to train set and validation set in a ratio of 70% and 30%, respectively, as shown in Figure 8.6.

8.4.1.3 Building a data pipeline

Since the implementation was in Tensorflow, the common steps of building a data pipeline for Tensorflow were used, such as pre-process, shuffle, pre-fetch, taking batch size, i.e., 32 for the pre-trained models. API provided by Keras' applications includes functions to prepare data in a way that a given model may expect.

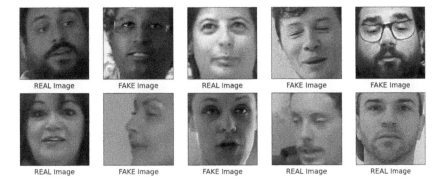

Figure 8.5 Sample data [29].

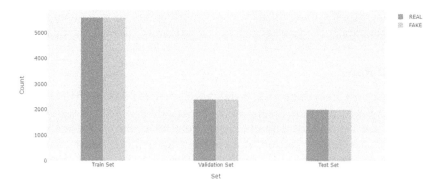

Figure 8.6 Class count in train, validation, and test sets.

8.4.2 Classification models

Various models were implemented, like a custom-built Convolutional Neural Network (CNN) model and some pre-trained models. The architecture of the custom CNN model is given in Figure 8.7. The other pre-trained models used were ResNet-50, Inception V3, and Xception Net, for which fine-tuning was done by freezing a few layers and training the rest. The evaluation was done by using accuracy metric for each of these models.

8.4.3 Explainability using LIME

Considering the implemented classification models of deep learning as black-box, finally the LIME model was used to incorporate explainability in our framework to show areas that the models focused on to classify an image as fake or real. As already discussed, in the context of deepfake detection, LIME can be used to provide instance-level explanations for why a specific video was classified as a deepfake or not. Since humans

Figure 8.7 Architecture of Custom CNN Model. Here Conv2D (m, n) means the number of filters are m and kernel size is n*n. And, for dropout layers, the number given in brackets is the dropout rate.

can interpret high-level features better than low-level ones, similarly, the LIME tool sees high-level features in the form of super pixels, which are collections of pixels of the image that cover a particular area in the image.

Evaluation of the results is done using metrics, which is discussed in the next section, along with the experimental setup for implementation of this whole framework.

8.5 METRICS AND EXPERIMENTAL SETUP

Metrics are used to evaluate the performance of models during training and testing, which is discussed in this section, along with the experimental setup, i.e., hardware and software used.

8.5.1 Evaluation metric

Accuracy is used as a metric to evaluate the results of the models on the test set after implementation and accuracy is also seen in graphs while training for train and validation sets. Accuracy stands for the number of correct predictions, i.e., real as real and fake as fake, out of the total number of predictions. Also, heatmaps and boundary maps from LIME are used to validate the results.

8.5.2 Experimental setup

This framework was implemented using Tensorflow version 2.10.1 and Keras API in Jupyter notebook and Anaconda GPU environment. For the explainability part, LIME was installed. The specifications for the GPU machine used were NVIDIA GeForce RTX 3060 GDDR6 @6GB.

Evaluation of the results obtained from this whole framework is given in Section 8.6 in the form of accuracy and loss curves, along with LIME visualization in the form of boundary maps for super pixels and heatmaps.

8.6 RESULTS AND DISCUSSION

This section shows the results of implementation in the form of graphs and visualization of classification using LIME. The accuracy and loss curves using the models given in Section 8.4 are shown here. The number of epochs is fixed as 10 for all the models since a reasonable accuracy rate was achieved with 10 epochs for some of the models. Figure 8.8 shows the loss and accuracy curve for the custom CNN model.

(a)

(b)

Figure 8.8 a) Accuracy curve and b) Loss curve for custom CNN.

As can be seen from the graphs in Figure 8.8, the accuracy values are gradually increasing and loss values are decreasing, which means learning was going well, but when testing was done on the test set, the accuracy value came out to be 0.6378, i.e., 63.78%. LIME results on the custom CNN are shown in Figure 8.9.

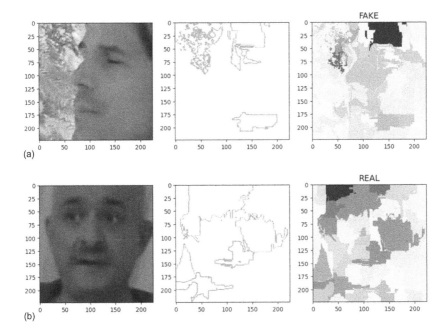

Figure 8.9 LIME Model results for custom CNN.

As can be seen from Figure 8.9, the marked boundary map for custom CNN is not so proper. Also, it shows different colors in heatmap to depict the super pixels it focused on during classification. Similarly, other pre-trained models were also implemented, and fine-tuning was done, for which the graphs of accuracy and loss are shown in Figures 8.10–8.12.

As can be seen from the graphs in Figure 8.10–8.12, the accuracy values are gradually increasing and loss values are decreasing, which means learning was going on, but when testing was done on the test set, the accuracy values came out as given in Table 8.1.

Figure 8.13 shows visualization of results using LIME tool. The most accurate model among the ones mentioned in Table 8.1 is Xception Net with an accuracy value of 81.35%, so it was taken and LIME was applied on that. The first column in the above figure shows the test images, and the second column shows highlighted positive and negative super pixels. Heatmaps are shown in the third column, which are obtained using LIME. These heatmaps show the importance of each super pixel to provide granular explainability. We can see the color changes in the displayed images with respect to the ones displayed by the custom CNN model. This is due to the pre-process input step included in the data pipeline for the pre-trained model Xception Net.

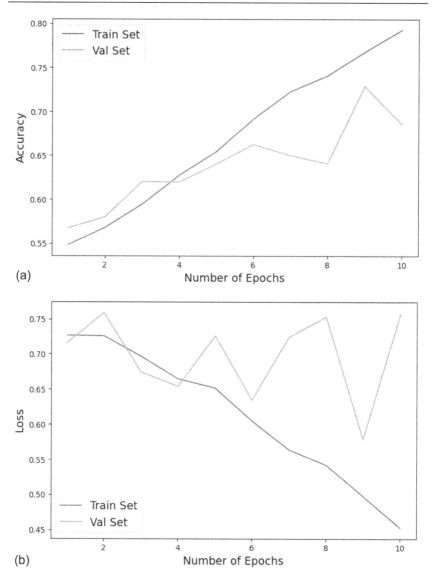

(a)

(b)

Figure 8.10 a) Accuracy curve and b) Loss curve for Inception V3.

From the results we can see that LIME provides super-pixel information, from which we can infer why the model has classified an image as
real or fake. This makes the classification results somewhat understandable to humans.

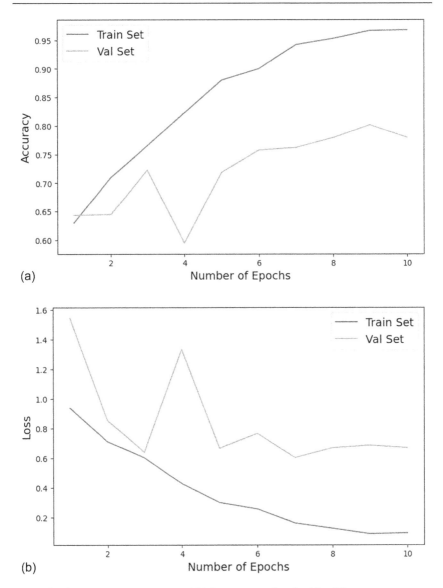

Figure 8.11 a) Accuracy curve and b) Loss curve for ResNet 50.

8.7 CONCLUSION

In conclusion, the development of explainable deepfake detection techniques is important for ensuring the reliability and accountability of deepfake detection systems. Various model-based and instance-based explanations have been proposed to provide insight into the workings of deepfake detection models and to provide human-interpretable explanations for deepfake

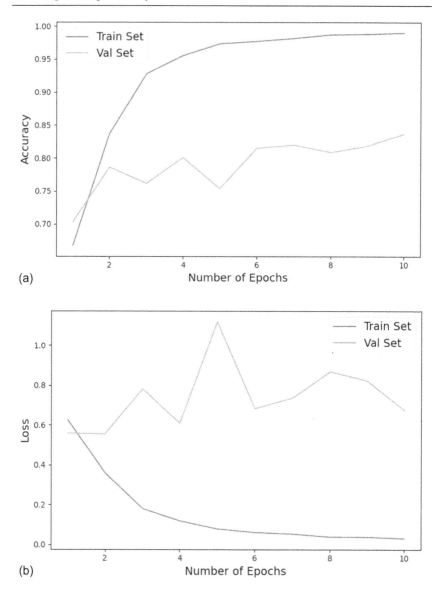

Figure 8.12 a) Accuracy curve and b) Loss curve for Xception Net.

Table 8.1 Accuracy values of the implemented classification models

S.No.	Model	Test accuracy (in %)
1	Custom CNN Model	63.78
2	Inception V3	69.02
3	ResNet 50	78.50
4	Xception Net	81.35

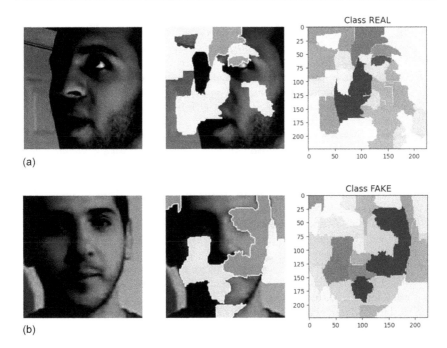

Figure 8.13 Visualization of results using LIME tool.

detection decisions. This chapter investigated the use of one such XAI technique known as LIME on various deep learning models and provided visual
results in the form of heatmaps and boundary maps for super pixels. Further
research is needed to investigate the effectiveness and efficiency of these
techniques, as well as to explore the trade-offs between explainability and
performance.

REFERENCES

1. Verdoliva, Luisa. "Media forensics and deepfakes: an overview." *IEEE Journal
of Selected Topics in Signal Processing* 14, no. 5 (2020): 910–932.
2. Güera, David, and Edward J. Delp. "Deepfake video detection using recurrent
neural networks." In *2018 15th IEEE International Conference on Advanced
Video and Signal Based Surveillance (AVSS)*, pp. 1–6. IEEE, 2018.
3. Tariq, Shahroz, Sangyup Lee, and Simon S. Woo. "A convolutional LSTM based
residual network for deepfake video detection." arXiv preprint arXiv:2009.
07480 (2020).
4. Siegel, Dennis, Christian Kraetzer, Stefan Seidlitz, and Jana Dittmann. "Media
forensics considerations on deepfake detection with hand-crafted features."
Journal of Imaging 7, no. 7 (2021): 108.

5. Amerini, Irene, Leonardo Galteri, Roberto Caldelli, and Alberto Del Bimbo. "Deepfake video detection through optical flow based cnn." In *Proceedings of the IEEE/CVF International Conference on Computer Vision Workshops*, pp. 1205–1207, 2019.

6. Chintha, Akash, Aishwarya Rao, Saniat Sohrawardi, Kartavya Bhatt, Matthew Wright, and Raymond Ptucha. "Leveraging edges and optical flow on faces for deepfake detection." In *2020 IEEE International Joint Conference on Biometrics (IJCB)*, pp. 1–10. IEEE, 2020.

7. Bonomi, Mattia, Cecilia Pasquini, and Giulia Boato. "Dynamic texture analysis for detecting fake faces in video sequences." *Journal of Visual Communication and Image Representation* 79 (2021): 103239.

8. Arrieta, Alejandro Barredo, Natalia Díaz-Rodríguez, Javier Del Ser, Adrien Bennetot, Siham Tabik, Alberto Barbado, Salvador García, Sergio Gil-Lopez, Daniel Molina, Richard Benjamins, Raja Chatila, Francisco Herrera. "Explainable Artificial Intelligence (XAI): Concepts, taxonomies, opportunities and challenges toward responsible AI." *Information Fusion* 58 (2020): 82–115.

9. Lim, Suk-Young, Dong-Kyu Chae, and Sang-Chul Lee. "Detecting Deepfake Voice Using Explainable Deep Learning Techniques." *Applied Sciences* 12, no. 8 (2022): 3926.

10. de Lima, Oscar, Sean Franklin, Shreshtha Basu, Blake Karwoski, and Annet George. "Deepfake detection using spatiotemporal convolutional networks." arXiv preprint arXiv:2006.14749 (2020).

11. Zhou, Yipin, and Ser-Nam Lim. "Joint audio-visual deepfake detection." In *Proceedings of the IEEE/CVF International Conference on Computer Vision*, pp. 14800–14809. 2021.

12. Guarnera, Luca, Oliver Giudice, Matthias Nießner, and Sebastiano Battiato. "On the exploitation of deepfake model recognition." In *Proceedings of the IEEE/CVF Conference on Computer Vision and Pattern Recognition*, pp. 61–70, 2022.

13. Rana, Md Shohel, Mohammad Nur Nobi, Beddhu Murali, and Andrew H. Sung. "Deepfake detection: A systematic literature review." *IEEE Access* 10 (2022): 25494–25513.

14. Jevnisek, Amir, and Shai Avidan. "Aggregating layers for deepfake detection." In *2022 26th International Conference on Pattern Recognition (ICPR)*, pp. 2027–2033. IEEE, 2022.

15. Verdoliva, Luisa. "Media forensics and deepfakes: An overview." *IEEE Journal of Selected Topics in Signal Processing* 14, no. 5 (2020): 910–932.

16. Kakogeorgiou, Ioannis, and Konstantinos Karantzalos. "Evaluating explainable artificial intelligence methods for multi-label deep learning classification tasks in remote sensing." *International Journal of Applied Earth Observation and Geoinformation* 103 (2021): 102520.

17. Tolosana, Ruben, Sergio Romero-Tapiador, Ruben Vera-Rodriguez, Ester Gonzalez-Sosa, and Julian Fierrez. "DeepFakes detection across generations: Analysis of facial regions, fusion, and performance evaluation." *Engineering Applications of Artificial Intelligence* 110 (2022): 104673.

18. Silva, Samuel Henrique, Mazal Bethany, Alexis Megan Votto, Ian Henry Scarff, Nicole Beebe, and Peyman Najafirad. "Deepfake forensics analysis:

An explainable hierarchical ensemble of weakly supervised models." *Forensic Science International: Synergy* 4 (2022): 100217.

19. Dong, Shichao, Jin Wang, Jiajun Liang, Haoqiang Fan, and Renhe Ji. "Explaining deepfake detection by analysing image matching." In *Computer Vision–ECCV 2022: 17th European Conference*, Tel Aviv, Israel, October 23–27, 2022, Proceedings, Part XIV, pp. 18–35. Cham: Springer Nature Switzerland, 2022.

20. Agarwal, Namita, and Saikat Das. "Interpretable machine learning tools: A survey." In *2020 IEEE Symposium Series on Computational Intelligence (SSCI)*, pp. 1528–1534. IEEE, 2020.

21. Pino, Samuele, Mark James Carman, and Paolo Bestagini. "What's wrong with this video? Comparing explainers for deepfake detection." arXiv preprint arXiv:2105.05902 (2021).

22. Abir, Wahidul Hasan, Faria Rahman Khanam, Kazi Nabiul Alam, Myriam Hadjouni, Hela Elmannai, Sami Bourouis, Rajesh Dey, and Mohammad Monirujjaman Khan. "Detecting deepfake images using deep learning techniques and explainable AI methods." *Intelligent Automation & Soft Computing* 35, no. 2 (2023): 2151–2169.

23. Malolan, Badhrinarayan, Ankit Parekh, and Faruk Kazi. "Explainable deepfake detection using visual interpretability methods." In *2020 3rd International Conference on Information and Computer Technologies (ICICT)*, pp. 289–293. IEEE, 2020.

24. Selvaraju, Ramprasaath R., Michael Cogswell, Abhishek Das, Ramakrishna Vedantam, Devi Parikh, and Dhruv Batra. "Grad-CAM: Visual explanations from deep networks via gradient-based localization." In *Proceedings of the IEEE International Conference on Computer Vision*, pp. 618–626. 2017.

25. Chattopadhay, Aditya, Anirban Sarkar, Prantik Howlader, and Vineeth N. Balasubramanian. "Grad-CAM++: Generalized gradient-based visual explanations for deep convolutional networks." In *2018 IEEE Winter Conference on Applications of Computer Vision (WACV)*, pp. 839–847. IEEE, 2018.

26. Ayhan, Murat Seçkin, Louis Benedikt Kümmerle, Laura Kühlewein, Werner Inhoffen, Gulnar Aliyeva, Focke Ziemssen, and Philipp Berens. "Clinical validation of saliency maps for understanding deep neural networks in ophthalmology." *Medical Image Analysis* 77 (2022): 102364.

27. Das, Sowmen, Selim Seferbekov, Arup Datta, Md Saiful Islam, and Md Ruhul Amin. "Towards solving the deepfake problem: An analysis on improving deepfake detection using dynamic face augmentation." In *Proceedings of the IEEE/ CVF International Conference on Computer Vision*, pp. 3776–3785. 2021.

28. Ribeiro, Marco Tulio, Sameer Singh, and Carlos Guestrin. "'Why should I trust you?': Explaining the predictions of any classifier." In *Proceedings of the 22nd ACM SIGKDD International Conference on Knowledge Discovery and Data Mining*, pp. 1135–1144. 2016.

29. Dolhansky, Brian, Joanna Bitton, Ben Pflaum, Jikuo Lu, Russ Howes, Menglin Wang, and Cristian Canton Ferrer. "The deepfake detection challenge (DFDC) dataset." arXiv preprint arXiv:2006.07397 (2020).

Chapter 9

Cyber threat intelligence
A standardized protective approach for industrial cyber defense

Dipanwita Sadhukhan
National Institute of Technology Sikkim, Ravangla, India

Mou Dasgupta
National Institute of Technology Raipur, Raipur, India

Sangram Ray
National Institute of Technology Sikkim, Ravangla, India

9.1 INTRODUCTION

The internet plays a vital role in global communications and has become firmly integrated into all aspects of human lives all around the world. The inexpensive but highly innovative nature of the internet has built a vast global network for communication and exponentially escalated its use and performance that has generated billions of dollars annually for the global economy [1]. Today, most of the commercial, economic, social, and cultural activities, and interactions among countries, including governmental, organizational, and institutional in any platform, are performed in cyberspace [2]—which fully controls and manages both vital and sensitive information exchange and financial transactions using the internet. While this landscape of enormous technological advancement in every domain of operations has helped organizations scale their business universally, it also left these organizations vulnerable to an emerging risk from cyberattacks through digital interfaces. Cyberattackers mostly target organizations' sensitive information and system resources, not only for financial gain but also for achieving geopolitical reasons. According to the annual report of Threat Horizon [3], the world's leading authority on cyber threats, information security and risk management reveals that cyberattackers constitute a huge likelihood for (i) Disruption – Over-reliance on fragile connectivity heightened risk that ransomware by hijacking Internet of things, (ii) Distortion – Compromise of automated sources causes trust and integrity issues of information, (iii) Deterioration – Negative impact of organizations' ability to control their own information [3–5].

The threat of cyberattacks brings with it the potential of an unpredictable impact due to the lack of a specific strategy to measure the extent of the

DOI: 10.1201/9781003468974-9

resulting digital destruction. The cyberattackers compromised various cyber systems and caused significant damage such as identity theft, sophisticated phishing, strategic ransomware, information leakage, DDOS, Social Engineering, Botnet, Cryptojacking, etc. [6]. The COVID-19 outbreak has further worsened, as no one in the world was prepared for the spread of the virus. The pandemic situation has illustrated that various popular digital platforms, interfaces, applications, and systems are vulnerable to severe cyber threats.

On top of that, in 2022 the war between Russia and Ukraine aggravated these troubles with an outbreak of politically inspired global cyber threats to business organizations. Examples of serious cyberattacks that occurred in the past two to three years are the DDos attack on the Finnish parliament's website during a parliament session, the ransomware operation of cyber-criminals to Greek national gas distributor (DESFA) by taking sensitive data hostage, a bot attack to the Ukrainian state nuclear power company that disrupted online services by making a flood of garbage web traffic and web-page requests, and a new remote access trojan (RAT) malware attack to Belgian public services and military defense forces, etc. [7–9].

Terminology such as advanced persistent threats (APTs) is currently inured to portray those actualities [10] that are deployed as exploiting military-related cyber weapons in high-precision attacks against specific victims. These APTs can easily evade traditional defense systems such as intrusion detection systems, conventional firewalls, security gateways, antimalware, antivirus, etc. These constantly changing threats make conventional defense approaches susceptible to zero-day vulnerabilities. This scenario illustrates the urgent need for a real-time, dynamic, and intelligent threat-sharing system to detect the agents of threats and possible targets. It has been observed that the adversaries of cyber domains frequently attack similar types of enterprises [11–13], which indicates that the distribution of any knowledge about possible threats to individual defenders may prevent any fatal incident. This scenario leads to a commonly known platform of Cyber Threat Intelligence (CTI). It is considered an actionable defense mechanism for eradicating sophisticated security attacks and showcasing defense standards. It has become an ever-increasing business priority [14], due to its immediate action and easier implementation.

The CTI paradigm yields a comprehensive platform for information security and threat sharing that provides evidence-based structured actionable knowledge about dynamic threats as shown in Figure 9.1. Thus, this information is treated as the core component by the decision makers of the organizations for knowing the present security measures and to point out essential security actions. It mainly checks the underlying threat information, observable artifacts, Indicators of Compromise (IoCs), or Tactics, Techniques, and Procedures (TTPs) that form the content structured by CTI formats. The artifacts can be extracted from the unstructured data analysis. The CTI frameworks enforce a standard format to support

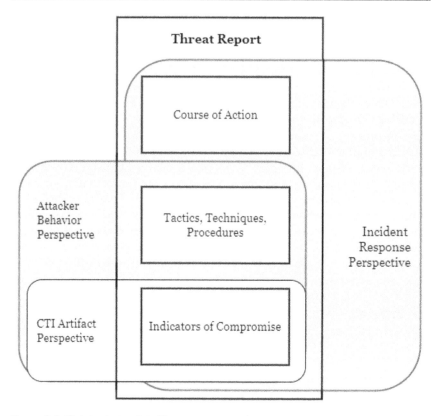

Figure 9.1 Cyber threat intelligence perspectives.

different essential activities like information exchange and incident response [15]. Organizations have their own CTI platform for information sharing and domain conceptualizations. The domain of incident response wraps the response procedures and various further Courses of Action (CoAs) as a defense against cyber threats. Correlated event exposure and traditional categorizations [16] are treated as the historic origin of CTI. Finally, the efficiency of CTI to protect against cyber threats may harm the quality of threat information caused by the deep impact of the substandard CTI. The relation between threat data, information, and intelligence is given in Figure 9.2.

To develop a successful defense approach, organizations can evade confusion and make effective use of time in case they precisely define the actual threat intelligence and how it can be used to diminish the inconveniences caused by diverse sub-categories. This chapter provides a comprehensive illustration of threat intelligence and its subdivisions made by the literature in terms of compound sources, various collective methods, the validity of the information, and the consumers of the produced intelligence. The findings help categorize and construct dissimilarity between the previously

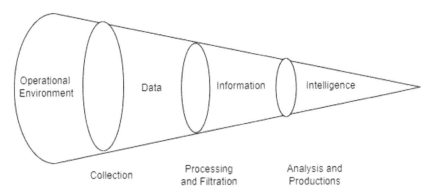

Figure 9.2 The relation between threat data information and CTI.

active threats and newly generated intelligence to exploit them in a better way. The CTI advantages and trends, CTI challenges, research, and standards to alleviate its consequences are particularly emphasized here. Through our analysis, we find that (i) in a different way than what is acknowledged, rapid deployment of CTI becomes inadequate to bypass security attacks, (ii) trust is a foremost requirement for a useful distribution of information about threats among various organizations, (iii) a universal standardized consistent format for sharing CTI to reduce the hazards of threat data loss and also minimizations of quality degradations of the same that gives automated methodological solutions over a huge quantity of CTI and (iv) selection of the most suited CTI tools must be determined by the objectives of the enterprise itself since some of them prioritize speedy identification while others go with standardized and automated analysis.

Compromise Indicators (CIs): CIs are usually defined as the artifacts that provide real evidence of a breach of system security of organizations with high assurance. The patterns that allow exposure of suspicious or malicious actions in cyber domains are mostly described as CIs and mostly include malicious IP addresses, domain names, email IDs, proxies, etc., with some derived indicators such as hash values. Finally, false and malicious activities are reported to detect alarming situations. However, taking any initiative in the detected CIs is questionable and depends on the use cases available. On the other hand, according to Tounsi et al. [17], it is important to take immediate action and automatically insert it into IDS. Moreover, CIs are more reactive than proactive, because if any CI is identified, it means the system is already infected. In another opinion by Rhoades [18], CIs are not dependable enough to rely on to detect any complicated suspicious adversarial activity. It is also stated that CIs are too simple to ensure any system attack by an adversary if does not have any previously existing CIs whose pattern can be matched for attack identification. According to

Chismon et al. [19], CIs and CTIs are fundamentally different from each other with little overlap. It is simple to match an attack pattern that has previously occurred and does not have any intelligent values. These observations diminish the actionabilities of Cis, and the importance of providing intelligence to the threat identification is required.

Chapter Contributions: The key contributions of this chapter are

i.   A brief description of the fundamental concepts of CTI is portrayed for a clear understanding of the basics of CTI. The data sources of CTI are also described.
ii.   We have identified the advanced and current-age cyber threats that can be fatal for organizations.
iii. A novel CTI model for automatic intelligent threat detection for actionable events for a use case of energy cloud environment is proposed here.
iv.   An assessment of the illustrated scenario is also described.

Chapter Outline: The outline of the chapter is given below: Section 9.2 expresses the primary concepts of CTI and its lifecycle and data sources, Section 9.3 illustrates the current threat vertical, Section 9.4 depicts how to model the threat intelligence, and Section 9.5 gives a basic idea about the sub domains of CTI. Section 9.6 illustrates the basic concept of incident response, Section 9.7 proposes CTI structure for energy cloud environments. Section 9.8 and Section 9.9 describe the benefits and challenges of CTI, and finally Section 9.10 concludes the chapter.

9.2 CTI LIFE CYCLE

CTI is primarily a data-driven procedure. Similar to the rest of the data analysis process, organizational intelligence need is first examined in view of the current threat scenario, supervising the cyber assets, and developing potential attack vectors. Threat intelligence modeling is complex since threats are constantly developing and require rapid adaptation and timely response from enterprises. The CTI cycle allows a typical guideline for the analysts to effectively employ their resources and acclimatize the current threat landscape. The CTI life cycle is depicted in Figure 9.3.

- **Phase 1: Intelligent Planning/Strategies**: In this phase of CTI life cycle, the roadmap for any specific threat intelligence operation is established. During this stage the stakeholders agree on the purpose, goals, targets, and the approach of their program associated with the enterprise policies. The approach is based on risk vertical, vulnerability estimation, identification of asset, demand simulation, etc.
- **Phase 2: Data Collection/Aggregation**: In this stage of the CTI life cycle, the analytics gather the essential data to accomplish the specified

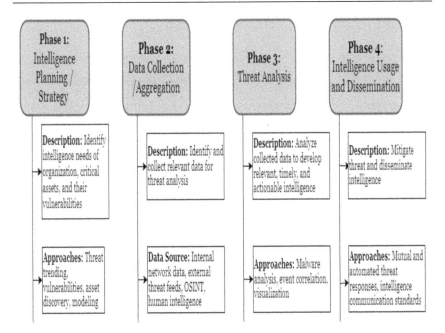

Figure 9.3 Life cycle of CTI.

goals depending on the previously established objectives. The data sources are internally received network records, externally received threat feeds, OSINT, human intellect, etc. It also organizes data points into spreadsheets, decrypts received files, interprets information accumulated from foreign sources, and assesses the trustworthiness of data.

- **Phase 3: Threat Analysis:** In this phase of the CTI life cycle, complete data analysis is performed to discover fundamental answers to the queries made during Phase 1. During this stage, the responsible team translates, transcripts, and interprets the information into final actionable data points and advises valuable propositions to the enterprise.
- **Phase 4: Intelligence Usage and Disseminations:** In this phase of the CTI life cycle, the team delivers a report to the stakeholders of the enterprise by conveying their findings of the research simply and conveniently. This report must be in simple language without any technological interpretation and understandable to the layman with brief pictorial representations.

The basic data sources of the CTI can generally be categorized in five different types [20]: (i) Open Source Intelligence (OSINT), (ii) Internal Intelligence, (iii) Human Intelligence (HUMINT), (iv) Counter Intelligence, and (v) Finished Intelligence (FINTEL). Each is described briefly below in a tabular format.

9.3 THREAT INTELLIGENCE MODELING

The fundamental concept of threat analysis by tracing cyberattacks basically depend on identification of the initial point of the attack, the path of progress, and discovering the attackers. This procedure sends a final proactive response to the cyberattack. Large-scale, high-quality security and event data are required for a comprehensive threat analysis. A distinctive digital environment includes multiple intricate interfaces that explicitly produce heterogonous and complex event data. Threat modeling methodology includes defining the characteristics of those data and formulation of technically expressing of same.

The Incident Object Description Exchange Format (IODEF) [21, 22] is the initial model that expresses the data associated with the cyberattacks. It is treated as the pioneer of this domain. Multiple researches have extended the results for interactive data sharing and for combining it with data expressing formats to form a further superior CTI system. The present de facto standard for advanced CTI and data sharing related to compromised cyberattacks are Structured Threat Information Expression (STIX)[23] and Trusted Automated Exchange of Intelligence Information (TAXII) [24, 25]. Several industrial data sharing and management are handled by these two CTI systems. Automated Threat Intelligence fuSion framework (ATIS) is another framework used for CTI implementations in terms of five different aspects that are analyzing, gathering, controlling, refining, and finally applying the refined data. Each aspect of ATIS peruses a precise role and simultaneously investigates heterogeneous data efficiently with the help of interacting among every adjacent aspect. Mantis is another platform proposed by Gascon et al. [27] that incorporates cyber threat data using diverse standards and recognizes the associations between threat data in terms of a correlation determination algorithm using an attributed-based graph. It showed on average approximately 80% accuracy in detecting single set threat intelligence data. CI Automatic Extractor (iACE) [27] is another platform proposed for data extraction utilizing natural language processing technology using a mining procedure for perfect analysis of the retrieved data. Patterns analysis and cyberattack identification by recognizing the grammatical links between the tokens are performed by iACE. This extracted data is then converted into the OpenIOC format. Nearly 75,000 articles and technical blogs were searched to find cyber threats, among which the accuracy rate of CTI identification is around 95%.

Threat modeling has also stepped forward in the direction of modeling the effectiveness and cost of the choices made by the defenders for identifying CTIs through game theory fusion. Moving Target Defenses (MTD) [27] procedures model the CTIs by the Markov game in a distributed network environment via the relations among the digital devices and attackers. In such cases, optimal behavior is determined in the zero-knowledge environment of IoT framework. Optimal MTD procedure implements the Markov game for investigating ATP in the cloud computing platform. These analyses are the outcome of determination of the best possible countermeasures in every condition by optimizing game theory regarding explicit problems and the network model to optimize the cost of security solutions.

9.4 NEXT-GENERATION THREATS

Next-generation cyberattacks are normally multi-directional and multi-folded. These threats are considered as multi-vectored because they use multiple means for propagating themselves like web applications, emails, chats, etc., whereas this is considered as multi-folded because it can penetrate networks and eventually exfiltrate the important information. Alternatively, next-generation cyber breach attackers are equipped with the newest zero-day vulnerabilities, as well as social engineering practice. Sophisticated strategies (polymorphic risks and complex risks) are applied that are modified in order to appear unknown to signature-based tools and yet genuine enough to avoid spam filters. A comprehensive taxonomy study of the advanced threat landscape in cyber was performed by European Union Agency for Network and Information (ENISA) in 2017. The below-mentioned threats are discussed in the ENISA report [17].

- Advanced Persistent Threats (APT): One perfect example of multi-vectored and multi-folded threats is APT, which is defined as sophisticated network attacks in which any attacker continues attempting breach until he gains access to the network and remains hidden for a long period of time. The primary intention of this attack is to steal crucial data instead of causing any harm to the system. The intended enterprises for ATP are those sectors that deal with a huge volume of sensitive information like government agencies and monetary organizations.
- Polymorphic Threats: This threat is a type of advanced cyber threat, like worms or Trojans, that can transform into a deadly one. Advancement of polymorphic threats may take place in diverse instances (e.g., alteration of the filename and compression of the files). Due to the evolution of polymorphic threats, it is almost impossible to identify by the signature-based defense system.
- Zero-day Threats: These threats are widely unknown to an operating system or application. As the name suggests, the attack was initiated on "day zero," which is previous to any public knowledge of the vulnerabilities. In certain circumstances, the vendor has previously acknowledged the susceptibilities; however, it has not exposed it widely since the vulnerability had not yet been patched. This attack is particularly effective, as it can be hidden for long periods and after detection, patching of the vulnerability requires days or even weeks.

- Composite Threats: Cyberattacks are categorized as syntactic and semantic attacks. However, the permutation of these two procedures is considered as blended or composite attacks [18–20]. Syntactic attacks utilize technical susceptibility in software and/or hardware, while semantic attacks take advantage of social vulnerabilities to acquire personal credentials. Recently, the two approaches have been utilized to realize complex attacks. This specifies a technical tool to facilitate social engineering for gaining privileged information to cause harm to network hosts and incorporates phishing attacks. These attacks recurrently employ emails to transfer a malicious attached harmless-appearing message to specifically selected victims that target zero-day vulnerabilities. In order to break the chain, phishing is deployed in primarily three steps. In this attack, any false message is sent to the victim that seems to be coming from legitimate organizations, typically from financial or banking services for disclosure of his/her personal or financial secret credentials by deception or else to install malicious applications for facilitating other security attacks like ransomware, credit card scams, identity theft, etc.

- The cyber threat phishing technique mostly considers the small number of receivers to whom an extremely personalized message is transmitted. Phishing predominantly abuses information retrieved from the social medium. Observably, the attack trace is dissimilar conditional on the intended circumstances, e.g., cyber crime might employ cautious APT to pilfer intellectual property during cyber war, which exploits botnets to perform Distributed Denial of Service (DDoS) attacks [21].

- Database Exposure: Database is exposed to hacking and security violation. Attackers may gain user credentials through social engineering to acquire entry. Since repositories are employed by several business organizations to hold records, any susceptibility to databases will definitely turn out to be a fatal problem.

- Deepfakes: Fake audios, videos, images, or files are generated with the help of deep learning and considered as Deep Fakes. This type of social-media-based emerging attack thoroughly goes into user details, including habits, speech, facial and personal characteristics, and activity to generate a fake identity of the user. Criminals may exploit these advantages to deliver fake biometric messages by making media that appear legitimate. Due to social media exposure, deep fakes can utilize actual data of the individual and create a more significant danger than other related email or text scams [22].

- COVID-19 Scenario-generated Attacks: Due to the COVID-19 pandemic, numerous organizations accept remote working situations. However, the shift of the working platforms of employees occurred so quickly that organizations were unable to plan sufficiently. The pandemic situation forces us to face the greatest challenges to cybersecurity since it was not the top priority at the time.

9.5 CYBER THREAT INTELLIGENCE SUB-DOMAINS

CTI is basically defined as any evidence-based knowledge about threats that may occur with the aim of resisting it or even shrinking the gap between identification and compromise. It actually assists to illuminate the risk landscape rather than taking any explicit decision. It is rigorous actionable information with the extreme potentiality for taking prompt response to gain some valuable outcome from business organizations [23–25]. It embraces threat indicators, context methods, suggestion, and actionable opinion about a preexisting or emerging threat as shown in Figure 9.4.

- Strategic Threat Intelligence: The purpose of this risk identification is to assist strategists to comprehend current risks and recognize additional risks about which they are not yet informed. It may have a financial impact on cyber activity or attack trends, historical data, or predictions regarding the threat's activity. Consequently, important information is regarded as the possible target for attacks. Strategic TI is usually in the form of reports, briefings, or conversations.
- Operational Threat Intelligence: This is information about detailed imminent attacks against the organization primarily consumed by high-level security employees, officials, or top personnel of an incident response team. Such intelligence is very rare. Sometimes it is mainly found in open source intelligence or sources with access to secure chat forums [26].
- Tactical Threat Intelligence: It is frequently referred to as Techniques, Tactics, and Procedures by the way at which threat actors accomplish attacks. Incident responders require this information to guarantee that their defenses and investigation are meant for current tactics.
- Technical Threat Intelligence (TTI): It provides the information that is generally consumed through technical resources. It typically refers to the investigative or monitoring functions of an organization such as mail filtering devices and provides some analytic tools for visualization of the logs [27, 28].

CTI Sub Domains	Depends On
Formal	Informal data gathering methods
Strategic, Operational	The analysis form inured to generate intelligence
Strategic, Tactical	The gathering methods
Tactical, Technical	The intelligence objective and target consumers

Figure 9.4 Subdivisions of threat intelligence.

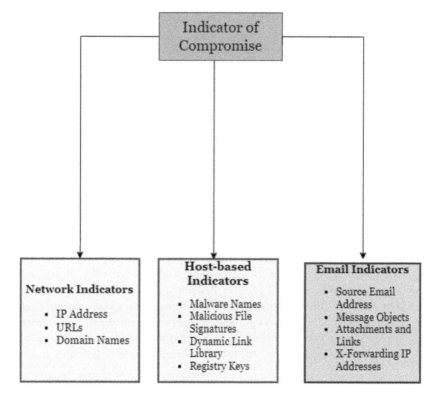

Figure 9.5 Indicators of compromise.

The defenders must be aware of the actor of cyber threats and must also know the nature of the risks they are suffering from. They must be knowledgeable about the data fundamentals related to these cyber breaches, which is called Compromise Indicators (CIs). The defender must be informed of the threat actors and the nature of the attacks the organizations will face. They must also be aware of the fundamentals of data connected with the cyber threats. These data are referred to as indicators of compromise (IOC). IOC is considered as the enabler of the Intelligence production and is closely related to CTI. The internal data is fed to the analyzer of the relevant organizations, and finally, the actionable decision is recovered. IOC is classified into three diverse groups: Network indicators, Host-based indicators, and Email indicators as shown in Figure 9.5.

- Network Indicators: These indicators are mostly located in domain names or URLs exploited for Command & Control (C&C) and Link-based malware surfing. It might be IP addresses required for attack detections from acknowledged compromised systems/servers, botnets, etc. Yet, the IOC has a short lifetime since the threat actors shift from one compromised server to another for getting hosting services from the cloud.

- Host-based Indicators: These indicators are mostly located in the investigation of any infected machine. It might be names of the malware entice documents or hashed files. The most frequently used malware IOC are SHA-1 or MD5 hashes of binaries. One of the soft targets for Dynamic Link Libraries is the Windows operating system, as attackers may restore Windows system files to ensure that the payload is executed every time Windows is initialized. Most often, registry keys may be added by any malicious code for allowing persistent keys which are adapted in computer registry settings. This technique is common for creating Trojans.

- Email indicators: These indicators are formed mostly when attackers use free email services to targeted organizations and individuals. These emails might be social engineering emails. The source address and subject of the mails appear to be of a recognized individual or organization, and the subject line must be of any intriguing current event highlighted and lured with featured links and attachments. X-originating and X-forwarding IP addresses are email headers categorizing the IP address of connecting mail servers, connecting web servers via a HTTP proxy server.

9.6 FUNDAMENTAL CONCEPT OF INCIDENT RESPONSE

The threat landscape is growing day by day, which is imposing additional skill, tools, intelligence, and defense policies to face them. Incident response (IR) is one of these approaches that can be incorporated to protect organizations from CTI. The key concept of each incident response format is briefly discussed here that allows categorization and assessment of each in this section. The basic concepts, categories, and supplementary capabilities are outlined in Table 9.1 with proper examples of IR. Essential requirements related to the core concepts are intended as supplementary capabilities, whereas earlier analyses of data formats in CTI are treated as diverse comparison criteria. We have emphasized core conceptual elements and incorporated the characterization and naming conventions. The incident response is a distinct area of identifying CTI and a completely novel and multi-fold concept. In this section we have categorized IR into four different building blocks, i.e., preliminary level concepts for fundamental understanding, structural level concepts for deeper understanding, technological level concepts for technical understanding, and finally, the security level concepts that are illustrated in Table 9.2. Each concept is described in Table 9.3 in short.

Table 9.1 Frequent data sources of CTI

CTI data source	Brief Description description	Source	Examples	Value
OSINT	Data that can be collected from the internet or other CTI companies	External	Vulnerability/exploit feeds, social media, Darknet data, public statements, threat feeds	Provides a comprehensive view of an organization's external threat landscape
Internal Intelligence	Data collected from internal cyber assets	Internal	Network logs, database access events, Intrusion Detection Systems (IDS) logs, Intrusion Prevention Systems (IPS) logs	Provides information about activities internal to an organization
Human Intelligence	Manual research and data collection	Internal and External	Direct hacker interactions	Provides very precise and deep knowledge
Counter Intelligence	Provides false information to deceive hackers	Internal and External	Honeypots, antihuman intelligence	Safely identifies tools and methods used by attackers
Finished Intelligence	Intelligence ready for dissemination	Internal and External	Commercial data feeds	Refines and analyzes intelligence

Table 9.2 Incident response for CTI and its derived capabilities

Category	Core concept	Derived capabilities
General	Aggregability	Information Sharing, Semantics
	Categorization	Comprehensibility, Delimitation
	Granularity	Structuring
	Versioning	Data Quality, Maintenance
	Referencing	Usability, Separation
	Extensibility	Customization, Sustainability
	Readability	Comprehensibility, Interpretability
	Unambiguous Semantics	Clarity, Interorganizational Understanding and Application
Structural	Workflow	Sequencing, Operations
	Actuator	Actionability
	Action	Atomicity
	Artifact	CTI Integration
Technological	Community	Usability, Acceptance, Maintenance
	Application	Technical Integration, Interoperability
Security	Serialization	Data Storage, Data Transfer
	Confidentiality	Information Sharing, Operations
	Authorization	Misuse Prevention, Operations
	Prioritization	Information Importance, Operations

Table 9.3 Description of the core concepts of IR

Core Concept	Description
Aggregability	Grouping of related incident response
Categorization	Distinguishable objectives of incident response
Granularity	Different levels of incident response
Versioning	Documenting incident response information updates and revocations
Referencing	Referral to incident response elements with unique IDs
Extensibility	Provision of additional IR information
Readability	Legibility of IR elements
Unambiguous Semantics	Distinct meaning of different incident response elements
Communality	Supporting elements of incident response standardizations
Applications	Technological dependencies of IR standardizations
Serializations	Encoding of incident response information
Confidentiality	Sensitivity aspect of IR information
Authorization	Control measures of IR procedures
Prioritizations	Urgency of IR actions

9.7 CYBER THREAT INTELLIGENCE FRAMEWORK FOR ENERGY CLOUD ENVIRONMENTS

A CTI-based security framework can develop better risk identification capabilities and an immediate response process of any smart city-based organization that uses the cloud. This framework is considered as the fundamental architecture of CTI-integrated security services of the organizations. It is composed of several nodes for generating a demand response system that performs production of essential intelligence based on IOCs. This framework follows several patterns in a hierarchical form, as shown is Figure 9.6.

CTI Sharing Procedure: This section demonstrates the data collection for the IoC with the purpose of generating a CTI in each layer of the framework. Each of the steps is mentioned in detail below and shown in Figure 9.7. The design of the final CTI report of the information is given in Figure 9.8.

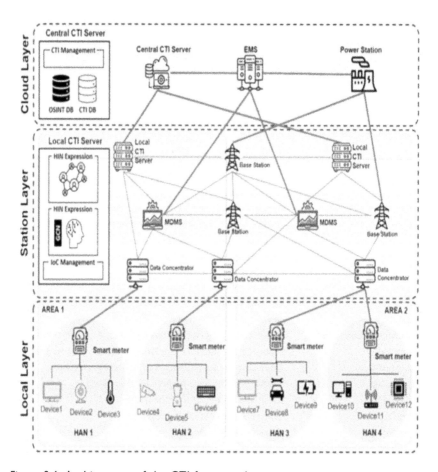

Figure 9.6 Architecture of the CTI framework.

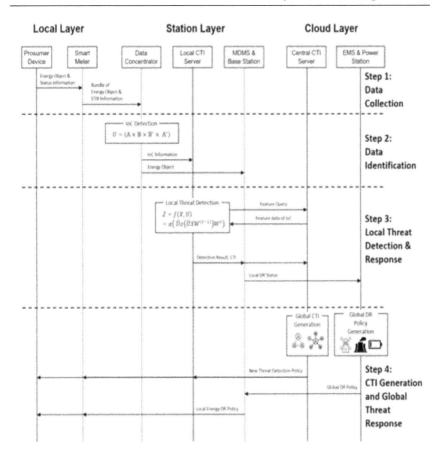

Figure 9.7 The dissemination process of policies on energy cloud if CTI.

- Step 1 (*Gathering of data from the devices*): The local layer incorporates multiple home area networks or HAN that transfers the functioning status, energy production, and consumption data to the smart meters. Then the status data and energy information of the diverse devices in the connected home area network (HAN) are collected and transmitted to the connected data concentrator. This communication requires small-range wired/wireless communications for communicating between devices, data concentrator, and smart meters.
- Step 2 (*Identification of compromise indicators from object data*): The data concentrators mark the received network data and action statuses of the device and further modify the data into CTI.
- Step 3 (*Threat identification in local range*): The local CTI server recognizes the IoC from the CTI data obtained from the data concentrator. Consequently, the local CTI server questions the database to the central CTI server to acquire data for the detected IoC data. After making the IoC attribute data secure, the local CTI server transforms

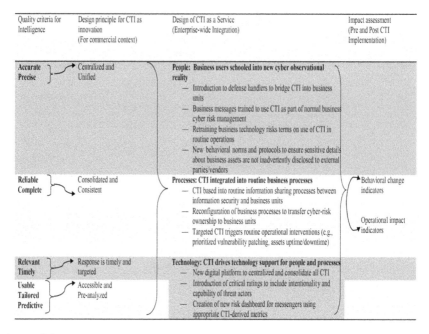

Quality criteria for Intelligence	Design principle for CTI as innovation (For commercial context)	Design of CTI as a Service (Enterprise-wide Integration)	Impact assessment (Pre and Post CTI Implementation)
Accurate Precise	Centralized and Unified	**People: Business users schooled into new cyber observational reality** — Introduction to defense handlers to bridge CTI into business units — Business messages trained to use CTI as part of normal business cyber risk management — Retraining business technology risks terms on use of CTI in routine operations — New behavioral norms and protocols to ensure sensitive details about business assets are not inadvertently disclosed to external parties/vendors	
Reliable Complete	Consolidated and Consistent	**Processes: CTI integrated into routine business processes** — CTI based into routine information sharing processes between information security and business units — Reconfiguration of business processes to transfer cyber-risk ownership to business units — Targeted CTI triggers routine operational interventions (e.g., prioritized vulnerability patching, assets uptime/downtime)	Behavioral change indicators Operational impact indicators
Relevant Timely	Response is timely and targeted	**Technology: CTI drives technology support for people and processes** — New digital platform to centralized and consolidate all CTI — Introduction of critical ratings to include intentionality and capability of threat actors — Creation of new risk dashboard for messengers using appropriate CTI-derived metrics	
Usable Tailored Predictive	Accessible and Pre-analyzed		

Figure 9.8 Design of CTI of energy cloud environment.

the CTI data into the HIN (Heterogeneous Information Network) format and calculates and checks the CTI data specifying the presence of a cyber threat applying a pre-learned Graph Convolutional Network (GCN) model; then the local CTI server sends the result and CTI data to the centrally present CTI server.

- Step 4 (*CTI triggering and response to threats in global prospect*): The central CTI server aggregates all the data received from numerous local CTI servers. It also collects added data from OSINT using the CTI's IoC resources delivered to collect a variety of cyber threat-related data. The action policy of the CTI is made by the core CTI servers that can directly be implemented by the devices and smart meters. It finally synthesizes the CTI analysis result that is received by the core server. These action policies are distributed in the form of a list of IPs that need to be blocked, domains updated, etc. The CTI synthesized by the core CTI server is distributed to local CTI servers.

9.8 BENEFITS OF CTI

Several groups of associations and partakers nowadays adopt the significance of threat information distribution for many significant causes. The interchange of crucial threat information failed to be exposed to avert the impending cyberattacks and to alleviate potential attacks. Benefits of sharing data embraces a better awareness of the threat vertical, a profound perception of threat actors and their TTPs, and a superior position to protect against surfacing risks [29].

Additionally, sharing threats perks up synchronization for a cooperative knowledge, response to original pressure, and reduction of the probability of cascading effects across complete sectors, system, industry, or across sectors [29–33]. The major benefits of CTI are:

- Offers a greater insight to possible cyber threats.
- Prevents loss of knowledge by identifying cause of knowledge discharge.
- Performs knowledge/data analysis to discover exploitable data points.
- Gathers and shares knowledge to spread threat awareness.
- Identifies security breaches at a preliminary stage.
- Utilizes the compromise indicators for modeling a proactive defense line before any system compromise.
- Boosts threat detection through prioritized event inspections.
- Leverages a comprehensive vision to the threat scenario.
- Situational awareness to potential threats in the enterprise.
- Forms a landscape that provides strategic decisions to the threat vertical.
- Associative approach for threat vertical for complete cyber protection.

CTI supports organizations to overcome severe threat and security breaches, facilitates threat information processing to identify and understand threat horizon, quickly reacts to any stressed situation, and anticipates any further operation of the adversary. It enables investors to intelligently invest in any enterprise by minimizing the risk for faster and efficient outcome. Alternatively, it assists the security team to make an effective judgement for revealing the approach, movement, techniques, and procedures that enable effective security by making the goals of the attackers unattainable. Additionally, it decreases the cost and resource requirement and thus enhances the accuracy of the analysis.

9.9 CHALLENGES OF CTI

Generally, security teams cannot formulate valuable use of their threat data because it presents lots of threat intelligence, which in turn causes inconvenience. The everyday deposit of indicators seems to become much distrustful occurrence in internet. It offers approximately 250 million indicators in a single day [30]. It enables consumers to assemble their own intelligence. The essential brain power is always required to examine the production speed of the threat data [34]. Timeliness or aptness of threat data is also crucial when defending against destructive attackers and zero-day utilizations.

A few attractive motivating and challenging results of experiments on attacks display are: 75% of attacks spread from Victim 1 to Victim 2 within a time period of 24 hours, and larger than 40% strike the next organization in less than an hour. These results exert immense pressure on researchers in security to accumulate and allocate CIs extremely fast to develop collective attentiveness. This section illustrates present issues and challenges that must be faced by producers and consumers of CTI [35].

> **Challenge 1: Overburden of Threat Information**: Diverse open and closed sources of threat data are available, and they are completely free to be used. Consumers must access those data in proper time and find out actionable threat intelligence to protect from cyberattacks. However, due to the availability of a huge volume of data and a lack of sincerity and ability of the security team, many enterprises fail to resist cyber breaches [36, 37].
>
> **Challenge 2: Quality of Threat Information**: According to a survey, it was discovered that approximately 73% of threat data is fake, vague, imprecise, and sketchy, and cannot be relied on. These data are irrelevant and of poor quality. It is required to assist in making decisions and to enrich the security support system.
>
> **Challenge 3: Legal Issues to Privacy**: To deal with CTI, enterprises must always consider the legal issues for sharing CTIs and govern how the data violates privacy terms. Many organizations are concerned about negative publicity or legal rules of the countries. Most of the time international regulations also prevent diverse sensitive information sharing, and thus limit the cooperation of the organizations doing information sharing [38].
>
> **Challenge 4: Lack of knowledge of the Victimized Enterprise**: Sometimes the analytics itself does not know about being compromised and occurrence of any cyberattacks. In that situation, it is quite natural not to share CTI information [39, 40].

9.10 CONCLUSION

The innovative incident response viewpoint on CTI widens the scope and reorients the focus on standardization approaches that outline how to employ CTI artifacts for efficient cyber protection. CTI itself intends to become a dominant weapon to defend against adversaries. The motivation for this chapter stems from the current emergence of sharing CTI and the involved challenges of automating its processes. The comprehensiveness of the CTI paradigm makes it best to muddle through threats to information security and information systems. The sharing of CTI is a crucial part of multi-layered tools used to defend organizations and systems from a variety of threats. Moreover, the nature of data supported by a range of formats and languages is linked with the data requirements for numerous use cases correlated to typical security operations. The key conclusion drew by us shows that there remain various standards of threat intelligent which are not up to the mark and gives very poor adaptation and performance. It is impossible to be accepted for identifying the threats in conventional or established easy formats.

REFERENCES

[1] Sarhan, M., Layeghy, S., Moustafa, N., & Portmann, M. (2023). Cyber threat intelligence sharing scheme based on federated learning for network intrusion detection. *Journal of Network and Systems Management, 31*, 3.

[2] Ahmad, A., Webb, J., Desouza, K. C., & Boorman, J. (2019). Strategically-motivated advanced persistent threat: Definition, process, tactics and a disinformation model of counterattack. *Computers & Security, 86*, 402–418.

[3] Ahmad, A., Maynard, S. B., Desouza, K. C., Kotsias, J., Whitty, M. T., & Baskerville, R. L. (2021). How can organizations develop situation awareness for incident response: A case study of management practice. *Computers & Security, 101*, 1–15.

[4] Schlette, D., Caselli, M., & Pernul, G. (2021). A comparative study on cyber threat intelligence: The security incident response perspective. *IEEE Communications Surveys & Tutorials, 23*, 2525–2556.

[5] Ramsdale, A., Shiaeles, S., & Kolokotronis, N. (2020). A comparative analysis of cyber-threat intelligence sources, formats and languages. *Electronics, 9*, 824.

[6] de Melo e Silva, A., Costa Gondim, J. J., de Oliveira Albuquerque, R. and García Villalba, L. J. (2020). A methodology to evaluate standards and platforms within cyber threat intelligence. *Future Internet, 12*, 1–23.

[7] Bauer, S., Fischer, D., Sauerwein, C., Latzel, S., Stelzer, D., & Breu, R. (2020). Towards an evaluation framework for threat intelligence sharing platforms. In *HICSS*, 1–10.

[8] Sillaber, C., Sauerwein, C., Mussmann, A., & Breu, R. (2016). Data quality challenges and future research directions in threat intelligence sharing practice. In *Proceedings of the 2016 ACM on Workshop on Information Sharing and Collaborative Security*, Vienna Austria, 24 October 2016, 65–70.

[9] Skopik, F., Settanni, G., & Fiedler, R. (2016). A problem shared is a problem halved: A survey on the dimensions of collective cyber defense through security information sharing. *Computers & Security, 60*, 154–176.

[10] Leite, C., den Hartog, J., Ricardo dos Santos, D., & Costante, E. (2023). Actionable Cyber Threat Intelligence for Automated Incident Response. In *Secure IT Systems: 27th Nordic Conference*, NordSec, Reykjavic, Iceland, 368–385.

[11] Ahrend, J. M., Jirotka, M., & Jones, K. (2016). On the collaborative practices of cyber threat intelligence analysts to develop and utilize tacit threat and defence knowledge. In *2016 International Conference On Cyber Situational Awareness, Data Analytics and Assessment (CyberSA)*, London, United Kingdom, 13–14 June 2016, 1–10.

[12] Zhang, K., Hu, Z., Zhan, Y., Wang, X., & Guo, K. (2020). A smart grid AMI intrusion detection strategy based on extreme learning machine. *Energies, 13*, 4907.

[13] De Souza, M. A., Pereira, J. L., Alves, G. D. O., de Oliveira, B. C., Melo, I. D., & Garcia, P. A. (2020). Detection and identification of energy theft in advanced metering infrastructures. *Electric Power Systems Research, 182,* 106258.

[14] Bendiab, G., Grammatikakis, K.-P., Koufos, I., Kolokotronis, N., & Shiaeles, S. (2020). Advanced metering infrastructures: Security risks and mitigation. In *Proceedings of the 15th International Conference on Availability, Reliability and Security,* 1–8.

[15] Yao, D., Wen, M., Liang, X., Fu, Z., Zhang, K., & Yang, B. (2019). Energy theft detection with energy privacy preservation in the smart grid. *IEEE Internet of Things Journal, 6,* 7659–7669.

[16] Bilali, V.-G., Kosyvas, D., Theodoropoulos, T., Ouzounoglou, E., Karagiannidis, L., & Amditis, A. (2022). IRIS Advanced Threat Intelligence Orchestrator–A way to manage cybersecurity challenges of IoT ecosystems in smart cities. In *Internet of Things: 5th The Global IoT Summit,* Dublin, Ireland, Revised Selected Papers, 315–325.

[17] Tounsi, W. & Rais, H. (2018). A survey on technical threat intelligence in the age of sophisticated cyber attacks. *Computers & Security, 72,* 212–233.

[18] Farnham, G. & Leune, K. (2013). Tools and standards for cyber threat intelligence projects. *SANS Institute, 3*(2), 25–31.

[19] Chismon, D. & Ruks, M. (2015). Threat intelligence: Collecting, analysing, evaluating. *MWR InfoSecurity Ltd, 3*(2), 36–42.

[20] Samtani, S., Abate, M., Benjamin, V., & Li, W. (2020). Cybersecurity as an industry: A cyber threat intelligence perspective. In T. J. Holt, A. M. Bossler (eds.), *The Palgrave Handbook of International Cybercrime and Cyberdeviance,* Springer, Switzerland, 135–154.

[21] Takahashi, T., Landfield, K., Millar, T., and Kadobayashi, Y. (2012). IODEF-extension to support structured cybersecurity information. *draft-ietf-mile-sci-05. txt, IETF.*

[22] Hernandez-Ardieta, J. L., Tapiador, J. E., & Suarez-Tangil, G. (2013). Information sharing models for cooperative cyber defence. In *2013 5th International Conference on Cyber Conflict (CYCON 2013),* 4–7 June 2013, Tallinn, Estonia, (pp. 1–28). IEEE.

[23] Irtija, N., Sangoleye, F., & Tsiropoulou, E. E. (2020). Contract-theoretic demand response management in smart grid systems. *IEEE Access, 8,* 184976–184987.

[24] Barnum, S. (2012). Standardizing cyber threat intelligence information with the structured threat information expression (stix). *Mitre Corporation, 11,* 1–22.

[25] Connolly, J., Davidson, M., & Schmidt, C. (2014). The trusted automated exchange of indicator information (taxii). *The MITRE Corporation,* 1–20.

[26] Liao, X., Yuan, K., Wang, X., Li, Z., Xing, L., & Beyah, R. (2016). Acing the IOC game: Toward automatic discovery and analysis of open-source cyber threat intelligence. In *Proceedings of the 2016 ACM SIGSAC Conference on Computer and Communications Security,* 24–28 October 2016, Vienna, Austria, 755–766.

[27] Gascon, H., Grobauer, B., Schreck, T., Rist, L., Arp, D., & Rieck, K. (2017). Mining attributed graphs for threat intelligence. In *Proceedings of the Seventh ACM on Conference on Data and Application Security and Privacy,* 15–22.

[28] Wang, S., Shi, H., Hu, Q., Lin, B., & Cheng, X. (2019). Moving target defense for Internet of Things based on the zero-determinant theory. *IEEE Internet of Things Journal, 7,* 661–668.

[29] Zhou, T. & Yang, B. (2022). Novel strategy to produce prenylated resveratrol by prenyltransferase iacE and evaluation of neuroprotective mechanisms. *Biochemical and Biophysical Research Communications*, *609*, 127–133.

[30] Sengupta, S., Chowdhary, A., Sabur, A., Alshamrani, A., Huang, D., & Kambhampati, S. (2020). A survey of moving target defenses for network security. *IEEE Communications Surveys & Tutorials*, *22*(3), 1909–1941.

[31] Sengupta, S., Chowdhary, A., Huang, D., & Kambhampati, S. (2019). General sum Markov Games for strategic detection of advanced persistent threats using moving target defense in cloud networks. In *Decision and Game Theory for Security: 10th International Conference, GameSec*, Stockholm, Sweden, October 30–November 1, 2019, 492–512.

[32] Gao, Y., Li, X., Peng, H., Fang, B., & Philip, S. Y. (2020). Hincti: A cyber threat intelligence modeling and identification system based on heterogeneous information network. *IEEE Transactions on Knowledge and Data Engineering*, *34*, 708–722.

[33] Zhao, H., Yao, Q., Li, J., Song, Y., & Lee, D. L. (2017). Meta-graph based recommendation fusion over heterogeneous information networks. In *Proceedings of the 23rd ACM SIGKDD International Conference on Knowledge Discovery and Data Mining*, New York, NY, United States, 13–17 August 2017, 635–644.

[34] Li, J., Ranka, S., & Sahni, S. (2011). Strassen's matrix multiplication on GPUs. In *2011 IEEE 17th International Conference on Parallel and Distributed Systems*, Tainan, Taiwan, 7–9 December 2011, 157–164.

[35] Mavroeidis, V., & Bromander, S. (2017). Cyber threat intelligence model: An evaluation of taxonomies, sharing standards, and ontologies within cyber threat intelligence. In *2017 European Intelligence and Security Informatics Conference (EISIC)*, 11–13 September 2017, Athens, Greece, 91–98.

[36] Mittal, S., Das, P. K., Mulwad, V., Joshi, A., & Finin, T. (2016). Cybertwitter: Using Twitter to generate alerts for cybersecurity threats and vulnerabilities. In *2016 IEEE/ACM International Conference on Advances in Social Networks Analysis and Mining (ASONAM)*, Davis, California, 18–21 August 2016, 860–867.

[37] Andrian, J., Kamhoua, C., Kiat, K., & Njilla, L. (2017). Cyber threat information sharing: A category-theoretic approach. In *2017 Third International Conference on Mobile and Secure Services (MobiSecServ)*, Miami Beach, USA, United States, 17–18 February 2017, 1–5.

[38] Sánchez-Zas, C., Villagrá, V. A., Vega-Barbas, M., Larriva-Novo, X., Moreno, J. I., & Berrocal, J. (2023). Ontology-based approach to real-time risk management and cyber-situational awareness. *Future Generation Computer Systems*, *141*, 462–472.

[39] Dog, S. E., Tweed, A., Rouse, L., Chu, B., Qi, D., Hu, Y., ... & Al-Shaer, E. (2016). Strategic cyber threat intelligence sharing: A case study of IDS logs. In *2016 25th International Conference on Computer Communication and Networks (ICCCN)*, Hawaii, USA, 1–4 August 2016, 1–6.

[40] Dondio, P., & Longo, L. (2014). Computing trust as a form of presumptive reasoning. In *2014 IEEE/WIC/ACM International Joint Conferences on Web Intelligence (WI) and Intelligent Agent Technologies (IAT)*, 26–29 October 2023, Venice, Italy, 274–281.

Chapter 10

Watermarking with blockchain

A survey

Om Prakash Singh
Indian Institute of Information Technology, Bhagalpur, India

Kedar Nath Singh
Jaypee Institute of Information Technology, Noida UP, India

Amit Kumar Singh
NIT Patna, Patna, India

Amrit Kumar Agrawal
Sharda University, Greater Noida, India

10.1 INTRODUCTION

With the rapid growth of computer and communication technologies, it is possible to share multimedia data over the public network for medical diagnosis, research and development, defense, business analytics, and more [1]. Images provide more critical information than other media data, making them the content format of choice. Unfortunately, the leakage of image privacy information and copyright violation has become a fundamental problem [2]. Therefore, we urgently need to find solutions to protect multimedia data, especially image forms. Digital watermarking is one promising method to achieve image data security. Watermarking embeds a specific message—a watermark—into a carrier media with remarkable invisibility and robustness [3]. By extracting the embedded message from a marked media, we can verify the ownership of the media. In this case, marked media may be attacked before message recovery; the watermarking system should be robust against attacks for reliable ownership verification. The basic concept of the embedding and extraction process is outlined in Figure 10.1.

Robustness, invisibility, and capacity are the basic requirements for watermarking systems. However, simultaneously obtaining satisfactory performance in basic requirements for any general watermarking systems is not easy. Although security and complexity are equally important, they are challenging to achieve in addition to the three basic requirements of watermarking systems [4]. The diagram of trade-off watermarking requirements is

DOI: 10.1201/9781003468974-10

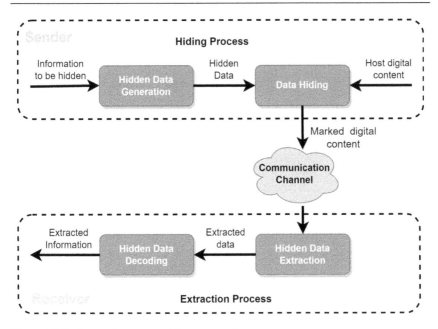

Figure 10.1 General watermarking concept.

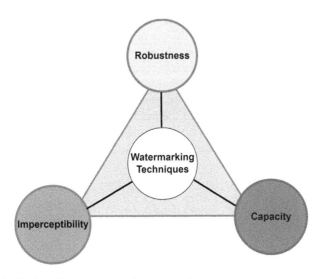

Figure 10.2 Trade-off properties of watermark system.

shown in Figure 10.2. All three properties of a watermark system contradict each other, and hence, it is a challenging task to maintain balance.

Watermarking with blockchain (BC) concepts have recently been used as an additional level of security and privacy for media documents with various applications [5]. The advantages of BC technology are decentralization, traceability, tamper-proof status, transparency, scalability, and immutability, which can resolve the security challenges of media data [6–7]. Each record contains a hash value stored in a BC environment, which helps to enhance better security in terms of media applications. The current generation of BC systems has been widely used in various applications such as Industry 4.0, cryptocurrency, the Internet of Things (IoT), information security, data provenance, 5G wireless network, healthcare, and the finance industry [8–10]. According to the market analysis report, BC technology's global market value was 10.02 billion dollars in 2022. BC technology is predicted to top 2022's annual growth rate of 87.7% from 2023 to 2030 [11]. In 2022, a global markets report [12] highlights that BC technology significantly improved the pharmaceutical industry. The initial stage of emerging BC technology and its development is shown in Figure 10.3.

This first generation of BC technology was designed and developed for public channels, known as Blockchain 1.0. In the initial stage of BC technology, Bitcoin and Cryptocurrency are the two most popular cryptocurrencies that ensure transaction security [13]. In 2013, the second phase of the BC system (Blockchain 2.0) was introduced with a smart contract to address the issue of mutual trust and user identity among participants [13]. Then the Hyperledger concept was employed in the BC system. It was associated with the smart contract to limit access to transactions to authorized participants [14].

Therefore, watermarking with BC is a promising method to achieve image security for practical applications.

The concept of watermarking with BC technology is outlined in Figure 10.4. First, the embedding procedure is employed to conceal confidential information inside a multimedia object of acceptable visual quality. A new transaction is created to store and upload the marked image, with its hash value on the BC framework, to enhance the additional security and authenticity.

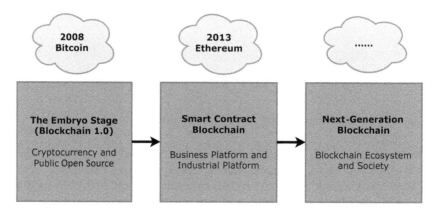

Figure 10.3 Development phases of BC system.

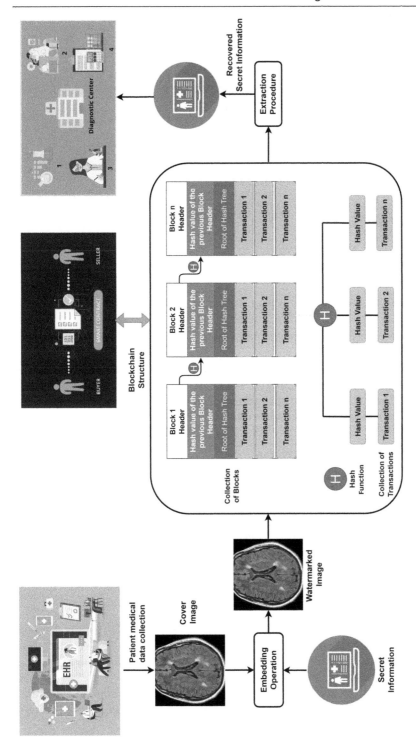

Figure 10.4 The concept of traditional watermarking scheme with novel BC technology.

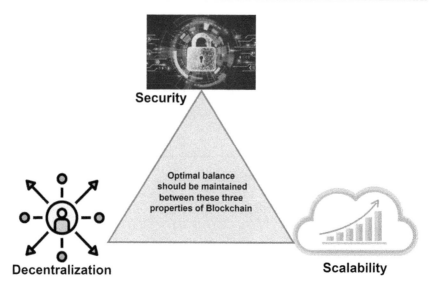

Figure 10.5 Relationship between three major attributes of BC system.

Lastly, a procedure is employed to extract confidential information for medical diagnosis.

Figure 10.5 shows the relationship between the critical attributes of the BC system. All three attributes of the BC system contradict each other. Hence, there should be an optimal trade-off between the scalability, security, and decentralization characteristics during BC development [15].

10.2 OUR CONTRIBUTION

Considering that using a combination of watermarking and BC is a relatively new area of research, current surveys on watermarking primarily concentrate on traditional algorithms. There are many existing surveys available based on watermarking for digital images. However, a comprehensive survey regarding digital watermarking with BC is still lacking. This study is the first survey to examine image security using watermarking with BC, including the extensive range of recent works. The contributions of this chapter are summarized as follows:

1. Introduce the background of watermarking and BC, including recent applications and essential characteristics.
2. Discuss recent developments and review existing techniques based on watermarking and BC for digital images.
3. Summarize and compare the most recent contributions in the literature, highlighting the significant challenges and suggestions for future directions in research.

The rest of this chapter is organized as follows. Section 10.3 details the classification of BC framework for digital content protection. Section 10.4 reviews the most recent works in the watermarking-blockchain domain using images. In Section 10.5, based on the survey, we mention some of the identified issues with watermarking-blochchain environments. Finally, in Section 10.6, we conclude the chapter.

10.3 CLASSIFICATION OF BC FRAMEWORK FOR DIGITAL CONTENT PROTECTION

This section describes the essential requirement for classifying the BC framework to provide digital content protection. The BC framework comprises seven parts, with several sub-divisions if required. The comprehensive classification of the BC framework for digital content protection is depicted in Figure 10.6.

10.3.1 Types of blockchain systems

The three major types of BC systems are as follows:

- **Public:** Any node can join the BC network with read and write access. It applies consensus protocol to ensure the BC network is trustworthy. This type of BC is termed permission-less. Bitcoin and Ethereum are the most common examples of public BC.
- **Private:** Only permissioned nodes can participate in the BC network in this mechanism. The trusted third party and encrypted database are performed to manage this permissioned node in the BC framework. This type of BC is termed permissioned. Multi-chain is an example of a private BC.
- **Hybrid:** This mechanism combines the features of public and private BCs. All operations are verified using a multi-party consensus protocol under hybrid BC. Hyperledger and Quorum are the most common examples of hybrid BC systems.

10.3.2 Types of transactions

The transaction signifies a transition state that modifies data from one value to another in the BC framework. Here, we have described three types of BC transactions.

- **On-chain:** This transaction type is visible to all the participants in the available network, and several details are captured on the blocks and distributed among entire BC networks.

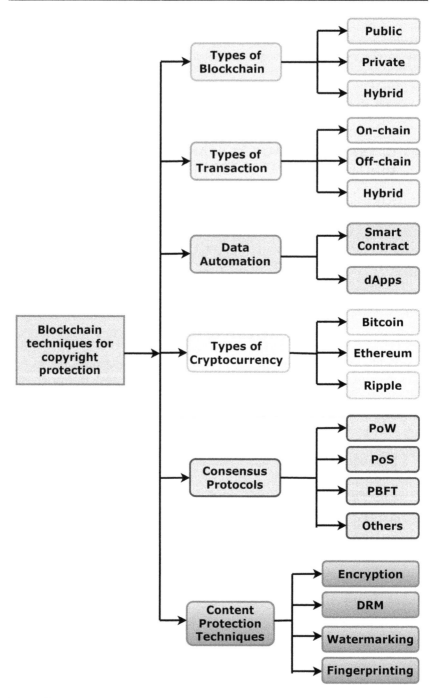

Figure 10.6 Classification of BC-based framework for copyright protection.

- **Off-chain:** This transaction type can occur outside the primary BC network, and involved parties can assign the agreement outside the network. Further, it includes a guarantor, which aims to ensure the completion of the transaction and certify the agreement.
- **Hybrid:** This transaction type combines specific features of both on-chain and off-chain transactions.

10.3.3 Data automation

A smart contract contains codes, account balances, and files. Users can create a transaction by applying the consensus protocol to perform various actions based on the smart contract code.

- **Smart contract:** Is created when the user uploads the transaction on the BC. During the execution of the transaction, a smart contract can efficiently perform the read or write operation to the IPFS storage system. The hash value of a smart contract is helpful for the identification of authorized users.
- **Distributed application (dApp):** Provides a better user interface, allowing the users to perform various operations on different smart contracts available in the BC.

10.3.4 Types of cryptocurrencies

Cryptocurrency has employed the concept of cryptography to verify and secure the transactions that the user creates. The idea applied to cryptocurrency is that funds can be transferred between two entities in a single transaction, using public and private keys to ensure security. In the early days of BC technology, Bitcoin and Ethereum were the two most popular cryptocurrencies to ensure transaction security, and now Ripple is the third most popular cryptocurrency used in the share market [14].

10.3.5 Consensus protocols

There is a consensus approach to the algorithms and protocols that ensure the establishment between two entities while creating a new transaction in the BC. Several types of consensus protocols are performed in the BC system.

- **PoW:** Various nodes participate in the procedure to complete the transaction to solve a complex problem. The selected node validates the block and establishes the transaction. Bitcoin and Ethereum 1.0 are the two most common approaches used in PoW.

- **PoS:** In this procedure, each node requires some finite amount of currency to claim the ownership of the given block during the mentioned transaction. PoW is shifted to the PoS platform to enhance the BC system's scalability and throughput.

10.3.6 Content protection mechanism

The content protection mechanism is applied to protect multimedia content from unauthorized users. This mechanism ensures copy protection, the authenticity of the multimedia object, medium transmission security, and digital rights [16]. It also offers an end-to-end content protection mechanism where only authorized users can access multimedia content. There are several types of content protection mechanisms.

- **Encryption:** This is one unique approach to data hiding. The original message is converted into an unreadable form (a ciphertext message) to maintain the confidentiality of multimedia data [17]. Further, the reverse procedure is performed on the ciphertext message to decipher the original message, known as decryption. This scheme offers the confidentiality, integrity, and authenticity of multimedia information.
- **Digital rights management (DRM):** DRM systems encrypt the multimedia content so only authorized users can access the confidential information, which protects unauthorized access to multimedia content [18]. The content is delivered to the authorized user, and it avoids content modification or illegal copying.
- **Digital watermarking:** Watermarking has been a widely used datahiding technique. This protection mechanism hides confidential information in multimedia objects to achieve copyright protection [19]. It extracts confidential information and can claim ownership and verify the authenticity of a multimedia object. The watermarking system focuses on robustness, security, payload, and visual quality features.

10.4 JOINT WATERMARKING AND BLOCKCHAIN-BASED TECHNIQUES

The integration of digital watermarking and BC framework has been used in various DRM systems to offer various solutions such as copyright management, content authentications, copyright transfers, and tracking the transaction status to digital media [20]. Digital watermarking plays a significant role in offering multimedia data copyright protection. However, a marked image can be tampered with when transmitted through an open channel. So, the watermarking method is insufficient to protect multimedia data completely. Nowadays, authors are motivated to exploit BC technology and watermarking protocols to solve these issues. This section briefly overviews the BC-based watermarking schemes, their attributes, and implementation.

In [21], Xu et al. proposed a lookup table-based secure watermarking scheme to provide secure information transmission and leakage tracking. Here, the BC technique is used for the fair distribution of multimedia content among clients without help from a trusted third party. Using Paillier encryption before embedding further increases the security of the digital marks. Meng et al. [22] presented a secure watermarking scheme with BC and perceptual hashing to provide copyright protection for digital images. The perceptual hash value of the cover image and the owner's personal information are taken as private marks and converted into QR codes, reducing the storage demand and improving robustness. The QR image is concealed within the cover image using the discrete cosine transform (DCT) technique, and the final marked image and its hash value are stored in the distributed interplanetary file system (IPFS) network. Sahoo et al. gave a novel BC-based watermarking scheme, BDmark, for providing copyright protection to big data [23]. Personal data are embedded at the granularity level of the basic data blocks.

Further, the given method is also evaluated against several types of attacks. The method is suitable for big data monetization and can provide a transparent and immutable audit trail on the receiver's side. In [24], Qureshi and Megias presented a multimedia distribution model based on BC and digital fingerprinting, which can provide data tracing, copyright protection, and secure data delivery. Prior to embedding, the original data is encrypted using the Paillier cryptosystem. Further, the fingerprint code words are embedded within the encrypted cover using the quantization index modulation-based watermarking scheme. Here, Ethereum smart contracts are used to keep all transaction records between the sender and the receiver to verify the integrity of the original content. Bhowmik and Feng [25] proposed a self-embedding watermark and BC-based framework for tamper-proof multimedia transmission. The transaction logs' cryptographic and image hash is considered a private mark.

Further, the lifting-based wavelet transformation technique embeds the marks within the lower frequency bands. Extracting the marks at the receiver's side will provide a transaction trail and details of the tamper regions. The authors of [26] proposed a fragile watermarking scheme to detect image tampering based on the localization method. Here, the Y component of the cover image is divided into 4×4 blocks and creates a cyclic chain of blocks with the concept of BC. The private marks are concealed within one of the blocks by measuring the information entropy and edge entropy values. According to the experimental result, the given method shows resistance against vector quantization and collision attacks.

Authors of [27] proposed a novel BC-based approach to provide security to the X-ray data at the time of storing in the cloud network. Here the cover X-ray image and patient personal data image are encrypted before embedding using a uniform quantization technique and chaotic encryption technique, respectively. Zhao et al. proposed an Ethereum-BC-based model, RobustCPS, to provide multi-platform copyright protection to audio signals [28]. The original signal is divided into blocks, and DCT-SVD is applied to the blocks to get the embedding coefficients. The proposed method provides superior results to existing BC schemes in the presence of typical processing and de-synchronization attacks. In [29], the authors developed a secure and decentralized IPFS-based model to check the copyright infringement of shared multimedia. The DCT technique captures the perceptual hash value from the cover image, which is further used as a private mark to detect the copyright. Experimental results show that the proposed method provides good resistance against different transformation operations. Li et al. [30] proposed a novel BC-based watermarking scheme to provide integrity, privacy, and availability of image big data. Here, the original cover image is encrypted using compressive sensing and then divided into blocks to add the original watermarks. Further, the marked data is stored on the IPFS server, and the hash value of the content is created. Finally, the hash value is uploaded to the blockchain to protect the privacy of the content.

In [31], Zhao et al. proposed a music copyright protection scheme, BMCprotector, based on BC and smart contracts. Multiple marks are inserted using the vector quantization method to verify the legitimate owner and receiver. Further, the marked data is encrypted using the AES algorithm before storing into the IPFS storage system. Authors of [32] developed an efficient and robust model based on BC, neural network, and watermarking schemes to provide copyright protection. Here, the convolutional neural network (CNN) is applied to the cover image to capture the latent image features, which is used to calculate the perceptual hash value. This hash value is used as the fingerprint of the cover image and securely stored in the BC. Garba et al. [33] proposed a secure DRM model to provide digital content authentication. Before embedding, the digital mark is encrypted using SPECK lightweight encryption to increase security and robustness. Further, DCT embeds the encrypted marks within the cover image. Finally, the data owner will upload the marked data in the cloud, storing the transaction records in the BC network.

The authors of [34] provided a secure watermarking-BC scheme, DRMchain, to detect internet misuse in artwork image DRM models. Arnold transformation technique is used to secure the watermarks before embedding. Further, a human visual system (HVS) is used to find appropriate embedding strength, and using the Watson DCT model, the private marks are invisibly concealed within the cover. The marked data is stored within the BC to provide access control and protect the users' privacy.

Franco [35] has presented a novel watermarking scheme combining buyer-friendly and mediated approaches and a BC network to avoid the direct involvement of trusted third parties in purchase transactions. BC generates the token that identifies the purchase of each transaction of digital content over the internet. This scheme ensures better security and is well suited for a web context. In [36], Yang et al. have illustrated a BC-based watermarking framework to provide copyright protection for big data. First, the watermarking scheme embeds the watermark information into big data. This scheme stores watermark copyright information and data-sharing records inside the BC and resists subset selection, alteration, and mix-and-match attacks. Wang et al. [37] have introduced an Ethereum-based watermarking framework for protecting digital images. The original image is transformed using DWT and SVD. Further, a chaotic map is performed on each original image block to obtain a scrambled feature image. The chaotic map scrambles the marked image and then inserts the scrambled feature image to obtain a zero watermark. IPFS is applied to solve the data expansion problem in the BC framework.

Wu et al. [38] have introduced a zero watermarking framework using BC technology for video copyright in the NSCT-SVD domain. First, a frame is chosen randomly in the given video frame and then separated into RGB components. Further, NSCT is applied to the scrambled RGB component, and the lower frequency component of NSCT is further transformed using SVD. Finally, a scrambled mark image is inserted inside a characteristic matrix of the selected frame to obtain the zero-mark image. Lou and Lu [39] introduced a data-hiding approach using the BC framework for delivering the authenticity and integrity of digital media. Before the embedding process, personal data is encrypted and embedded inside the multimedia object using multiple transforms (DWT-DCT-SVD). The marked image is transmitted through an open channel and stored inside the BC framework. Lastly, the extraction procedure pulls out confidential data to verify the authenticity and integrity of digital media.

Benkhaddra et al. [40] have used an optimization-based data hiding scheme in the BC environment to provide the secure transmission of confidential data. FIEO-based optimization is employed on the cover image to determine the optimal position for an embedding purpose. Wavelet transform is employed to embed the hidden data into an optimal position of the cover image. This scheme determines the robustness against selected attacks. Horng et al. [41] integrate the reversible watermarking scheme and BC technology to secure medical images. A medical record is encrypted using a symmetric key hidden inside the medical host image to maintain accepted visual quality. Marked data is stored within the consortium BC system to provide access control and protect the users' privacy. The payload of this scheme is extremely low. To verify the ownership of big data, Sahoo and Halder [42] proposed a watermarking approach using the BC system. LSB operation is performed for embedding the confidential information inside the cover image. Further, the marked image is uploaded on IPFS, and then the hash value of the marked image is generated for authentication. Xu et al. [43] introduced a watermarking scheme with BC and perceptual hashing to provide copyright protection to remote sensing images. The scrambled mark is hidden inside the cover image during the embedding step. The zero-mark image is stored on the BC, and the hash value of the zero-mark image is used for identifying copyright protection. In [44], Wang et al. focused on a zero watermarking framework using BC to protect copyright information. DWT and SVD transform the host image for the embedding process. A cat map and transformed cover images are employed on the mark to ensure additional security. The zero-marked image is obtained by performing the ex-or operation between the encrypted mark and the cover image. The zero-marked image is stored on the BC, and the zero-marked image's hash value is used to identify copyright protection.

Similarly, Bhadauria et al. [45] illustrated a watermarking scheme for protecting intellectual property in the BC environment. The fusion of DWT and SVD embeds confidential data inside the multimedia object. The marked image is uploaded inside the IPFS, and the hash value marked image is used for identifying the copyright protection of intellectual property. Peng et al. [46] introduced a data-hiding technique using the BC system to address the copyright issue of digital content. Firstly, the hash function is employed on image and text data to obtain a digital signature. Secondly, mark information in a QR code is embedded into acceptable visual quality cover media. Further, the hash value of the marked image and digital signature are uploaded on the smart contract. This scheme did not investigate any experimental analysis to measure the effectiveness of this method. In [47], Fei discussed a DRM system using the smart contract in the BC environment. This method employed the smart contract to ensure copyright management in terms of copyright registration and transactions of digital content. The sender creates a verified transaction; mark data is concealed inside the multimedia object. Furthermore, the encryption scheme is applied to the marked image and then the encrypted marked image, along with the private key, is uploaded to the IPFS database. However, this method applies to a single content owner.

Table 10.1 summarizes some notable BC-based watermarking techniques for methodology, objectives, cover type, watermark size, and limitations. The peak signal-to-noise ratio (PSNR) and structural similarity index (SSIM) were employed to evaluate the similarity between the cover and marked media [48]. The normalized correlation (NC) and bit error rate (BER) were used to determine the similarity between private and recovered marked images [49].

Further, Table 10.2 summarizes the BC techniques used for storage, consensus algorithm, smart contract, and framework.

Table 10.1 Summary of BC-based watermarking techniques

Ref no.	Objective	Methodology	Watermark size	Evaluation metric	Noticed limitation/Future work
[21]	Provides tracking of information leakage and fair distribution of contents.	Look-up table, Paillier encryption	1024 × 1024	Gas cost, Throughput, Computational cost	To protect the privacy of the transaction, zero-knowledge proof and ring signature protocols can be used.
[22]	Provides copyright protection to digital image contents and blind detection of watermarks.	Perceptual hashing, DCT, QR code, and IPFS	64 × 64	Hash value	In future, the proposed method can be used for other multimedia files like audio and video.
[23]	Provides immutable and transparent audit trail for big data monetization.	IPFS and granularity level insertion	NA	Gas cost	In future, this prototype model should be used to implement a real-time application.
[24]	To ensure copyright protection, secure delivery, transparent, data tracing, and privacy.	Quantization method, IPFS Hashing, Paillier encryption	NA	Hash value	The implementation part will be cover as future work.
[25]	To verify all the transaction records and detects content tampering.	LWT, hashing, and compressed sensing	8220 bytes	Gas cost, Hash value	The security of this scheme can be further improved.
[26]	To detect the location of image tampering and provide content security.	DCT and HVS	64 × 80	PSNR, SSIM, NC	In future, the proposed method will provide security for distorted images.
[27]	To provide privacy and security to the image information storing in cloud server.	Uniform quantization, chaotic encryption, and MQTT protocol	NA	PSNR, SSIM, SR	To improve the efficiency of the method, experimental study should be followed.

(Continued)

Table 10.1 (Continued) Summary of BC-based watermarking techniques

Ref no.	Objective	Methodology	Watermark size	Evaluation metric	Noticed limitation/Future work
[28]	To ensure cross-platform copyright protection for audio signals.	DCT and SVD	16 bits per sample	PSNR, Gas cost	The BC-based complete implementation of the method is not provided.
[29]	To detect breach of copyright for multimedia contents.	DCT, perceptual hash, and IPFS	64 bit	Hash value, Computational cost	The proposed hashing algorithm can be improved to enhance the performance.
[30]	Ensures the image big data integrity, privacy, and availability.	DWT, compressive sensing, IPFS	15 × 32	PSNR, SSIM, NC, BER	Payload of this scheme is very low.
[31]	Using the BC system and smart contract to protect music copyright and provides data tracking.	Vector quantization, IPFS, AES encryption	NA	Hash value	The proposed prototype can provide copyright protection for audio only.
[32]	Try to add multiple watermarks for authentication without depending on any third party.	CNN, perceptual hashing, and IPFS	NA	Hash value	The proposed method should be simulated and implemented for real applications.
[33]	Provides digital content authentication and resolves copyright issues.	SPECK light weight encryption and DCT	10 bits	Hash value, PSNR	To increase the security further, zero-knowledge proof protocol can be used.
[34]	Detects internet misuse and provides content protection in DRM model with good robustness and high security.	Arnold transformation, HVS, and DCT	250 × 250	PSNR, SSIM, BER, NC, Payload	Here, attacks are performed only on marked image. The robustness should be tested with some more attacks on the system.

Ref.	Objective	Technique	Size	Computational cost	Remarks
[35]	Design a BC-based system for web context application.	RA algorithm	128 bytes		The implementation part will be cover as future work.
[36]	To provide copyright protection of big data using watermarking.	LSB	16 bits	Payload	This scheme didn't measure the effectiveness of BC system.
[37]	To authenticate and secure the image copyright protection.	DWT, SVD, Cat map, and IPFS	512 × 512	NC, Gas cost	This scheme did not address the issue of supervision problems.
[38]	To design the watermark system to secure the video copyright.	NSCT, SVD, and Arnold cat map	256 × 256	NC, TPS	The proposed BC system can provide copyright protection for video files only.
[39]	Ensure the authenticity and integrity of digital information using data hiding scheme.	Hashing, DWT, DCT, and SVD	50 × 50	PSNR, SSIM	In future, this prototype model should be used to implement for text, drawing, and design.
[40]	To secure communication of digital data using BC system.	DWT, FIEO algorithm	256 × 256	PSNR, SSIM, Payload	The computational cost of the proposed system is high.
[41]	To secure medical images using BC-based data hiding scheme.	Hashing, AES, and consortium	12 bits	Gas cost	The proposed system didn't investigate the robustness analysis.
[42]	To develop a BC system to claim the ownership of big data.	LSB, Hashing	NA	Gas cost	It did not measure the effectiveness of watermark system.

(Continued)

Table 10.1 (Continued) Summary of BC-based watermarking techniques

Ref no.	Objective	Methodology	Watermark size	Evaluation metric	Noticed limitation/Future work
[43]	To provide copyright protection of remote sensing image.	NSCT, SVD, KL transform, and AT	NA	Hash value	In future, the proposed method can be implemented for different multimedia application.
[44]	To provide copyright protection using zero watermark.	DWT, SVD, IPFS, and AT	16 × 16	NC, Gas cost	The embedding capacity is very low.
[45]	To secure the intellectual information using BC system.	DWT, DCT, Hashing	256 × 256	Accuracy, Gas cost	In future, the proposed method can be applied to private BC to ensure the copyright issue.
[46]	To protect the copyright management system.	Digital Signature, ELGamal encryption scheme	QR Code	Hash value	This scheme didn't measure the effectiveness of watermarking system.
[47]	To secure the digital right management.	BDRM, digital Signature	NA	Hash value	This scheme didn't measure the effectiveness of BC system.

Table 10.2 Summary of the BC techniques used in the state-of-the-art

Ref. No.	Type of content	Type of BC sytem	Type of transaction	Type of framework used	Type of consensus algorithm	Type of storage	Use of smart contract
[21]	Multimedia	Consortium + private	Off-chain	Ethereum	PoA + PoW	BC	Yes
[22]	Image	NA	NA	Use online software	NA	BC+IPFS	No
[23]	Big data	Public	On-chain	Ethereum	PoA	BC+IPFS	Yes
[24]	Multimedia	Public	On-chain	Ethereum	PoW	BC +IPFS	Yes
[25]	Multimedia	Public	On-chain	Ethereum	PoW	BC	Yes
[26]	Image	NA	NA	NA	PoW	BC	No
[27]	Medical image	Public	On-chain	Fabric	NA	BC	Yes
[28]	Audio	Public	On-chain	Ethereum	NA	BC	Yes
[29]	Image and Video	Private	Off-chain	Ethereum	PoW	BC	No
[30]	Image big data	Public	On-chain	Ethereum	NA	BC+IPFS	Yes
[31]	Music	Public	On-chain	Ethereum	PoW	BC+ IPFS	Yes
[32]	Image	Public	On-chain	Ethereum	NA	BC+IPFS	No
[33]	Image	Private	Off-chain	Ethereum	PBFT	BC	Yes
[34]	Image	Consortium	Hybrid	Hyperledger Fabric	NA	BC	No
[35]	Web context	Public	On-chain	Use online software	NA	BC	No
[36]	Image	Public	On-chain	NA	NA	BC	No
[37]	Image	Private	Hybrid	Ethereum	PoW	BC+IPFS	Yes
[38]	Video	Private	On-chain	Fabric	PoW	BC	No

(Continued)

Table 10.2 (Continued) Summary of the BC techniques used in the state-of-the-art

Ref. No.	Type of content	Type of BC sytem	Type of transaction	Type of framework used	Type of consensus algorithm	Type of storage	Use of smart contract
[39]	Image	Private	Off-chain	Ethereum	PoW	BC+IPFS	Yes
[40]	Image	Public	On-chain	NA	PoW	BC+IPFS	Yes
[41]	Image	Consortium	Off-chain	Hyperledger Fabric	PoS	BC+IPFS	Yes
[42]	Image	Private	Hybrid	Ethereum	PoS	BC+IPFS	Yes
[43]	Color Image	Private	Off-chain	Hyperledger Fabric	PoW	BC+IPFS	No
[44]	Image	Public	Hybrid	Ethereum	PoS	BC+ IPFS	Yes
[45]	Image	Public	On-chain	Ethereum	PoS	BC+ IPFS	Yes
[46]	Image	Public	On-chain	Ethereum	NA	BC+IPFS	Yes
[47]	Image	Public	On-chain	Ethereum	PoS	BC+IPFS	No

10.5 POTENTIAL CHALLENGES

Some efficient BC-based digital watermarking techniques are already proposed for providing security to various domains. However, some challenges remain that limit the practical implementation of these models. Throughout this chapter, we have found numerous associated challenges and discussed further research direction in this area.

- The computational overhead and the storage demand of the BC model should be reduced using appropriate homomorphic encryption techniques.
- Most of the watermarking schemes did not maintain a balance between robustness, visual quality, and payload. The three properties of the watermark system contradict each other. Should one value increase, then another value must decrease simultaneously. Hence, an appropriate balance should be maintained between imperceptibility, embedding capacity, and robustness when embedding digital marks on the sender's side.
- Most authors did not focus on the security and complexity performance of the watermark system. The computational cost of the watermark system will increase to enhance its security. So, it is not suitable for a real-time-based application.
- The watermarking system must resist all attacks to evaluate its security and robustness.
- In permission-less BC frameworks, confidential information can be easily accessible in the open channel to different participants. However, the privacy of confidential information can be easily compromised.
- Various high programming languages can be applied to generate a smart contract. However, generating a programming language that can easily understand a human is not easy.
- A user's identity can be easily compromised in the public BC system.
- Appropriate compression techniques should also be used on the watermarked contents before uploading to the BC, as the size of the blocks is predefined.
- The consensus algorithms should be chosen based on the application, as it may increase computational expenses.
- A suitable external distributed storage provider (e.g., IPFS) can reduce the BC server's storage pressure.
- For resource-limited applications, using digital signature and encryption techniques will not be feasible, as it demands high computational power.
- Adding watermarking and encryption techniques on the BC may increase time complexity, as these techniques are time-consuming and complex.

- To protect the sender's and receiver's transaction records, ring signature and zero-knowledge proof protocol can be added to existing work.
- The scalability problem is one of the key issues in the BC system due to the limited block size of a transaction.
- An optimal trade-off should exist between the scalability, security, and decentralization characteristics during BC development. Figure 10.2 shows the relationship between these parameters.

10.6 CONCLUSION

We have discussed the basic need for multimedia security, challenges in existing watermarking methods, and how BC can be used with existing techniques to provide security solutions. Some existing joint watermarking-BC-based schemes are reviewed and compared in context to their methodology, objectives, cover type, and watermark size. Further, we have compared the BC techniques used in the chapter regarding BC type, storage type, smart contract, framework type, and consensus algorithm. In the end, potential issues and some research directions are suggested. It is concluded that the complete security of multimedia is still challenging for researchers. Therefore, existing systems indicate that much work is needed to manage the balance between security, storage, complexity, and usability for a real-time application.

REFERENCES

[1] B. Jiang, J. Yang, G. Ding, and H. Wang, "Cyber-physical security design in multimedia data cache resource allocation for industrial networks," *IEEE Transactions on Industrial Informatics*, vol. 15, no. 12, pp. 6472–6480, 2019.

[2] O. P. Singh, A. Singh, G. Srivastava, and N. Kumar, "Image watermarking using soft computing techniques: A comprehensive survey," *Multimedia Tools and Applications*, vol. 80, no. 20, pp. 30367–30398, 2020.

[3] D. K. Mahto, A. K. Singh, K. N. Singh, O. P. Singh, and A. K. Agrawal, "Robust copyright protection technique with high-embedding capacity for color images," *ACM Transactions on Multimedia Computing, Communications, and Applications*, pp. 1–12, 2023.

[4] O. P. Singh, A. Kumar Singh, and H. Zhou, "Multimodal fusion-based image hiding algorithm for secure healthcare system," *IEEE Intelligent Systems*, vol. 38, pp. 1–7, 2022.

[5] A. Qureshi and D. Megías Jiménez, "Blockchain-based multimedia content protection: Review and open challenges," *Applied Sciences*, vol. 11, no. 1, pp. 1, 2020.

[6] P. Shen, S. Li, M. Huang, H. Gao, L. Li, J. Li, and H. Lei, "A survey on safety regulation technology of blockchain application and blockchain ecology," *2022 IEEE International Conference on Blockchain (Blockchain)*, Espoo, Finland, pp. 494–499, 2022.

[7] S. Wang, L. Ouyang, Y. Yuan, X. Ni, and F.-Y. Wang, "Blockchain-enabled smart contracts: Architecture, applications, and future trends," *IEEE Transactions on Systems, Man, and Cybernetics: Systems*, vol. 49, no. 11, pp. 2266–2277, 2019.

[8] W. Liang, D. Zhang, X. Lei, M. Tang, K. Li, and K. Zomya, "Circuit copyright blockchain: Blockchain-based homomorphic encryption for IP circuit protection," *IEEE Transactions on Emerging Topics in Computing*, vol. 9, no. 3, pp. 1410–1420, 2021.

[9] E. J. de Aguiar, A. J. dos Santos, R. I. Meneguette, R. E. De Grande, and J. Ueyama, "A blockchain-based protocol for tracking user access to shared medical imaging," *Future Generation Computer Systems*, vol. 134, pp. 348–360, 2022.

[10] R. H. Kim, H. Noh, H. Song, and G. S. Park, "Quick block transport system for scalable hyperledger fabric blockchain over D2D-assisted 5G networks," *IEEE Transactions on Network and Service Management*, vol. 19, no. 2, pp. 1176–1190, 2022.

[11] Blockchain Technology Market Size & Share Report, 2030. Available at: https://www.grandviewresearch.com/industry-analysis/blockchain-technology-market (Accessed: 15 December 2023).

[12] Blockchain Technology Global Market Report 2022: Huge potential for blockchain technology in the pharmaceutical industry, GlobeNewswire News Room. Research and Markets. Available at: https://www.globenewswire.com/en/news-release/2022/08/19/2501524/28124/en/Blockchain-Technology-Global-Market-Report-2022-Huge-Potential-for-Blockchain-Technology-in-the-Pharmaceutical-Industry.html (Accessed: March 14, 2023).

[13] A. A. Monrat, O. Schelen, and K. Andersson, "A survey of blockchain from the perspectives of applications, challenges, and opportunities," *IEEE Access*, vol. 7, pp. 117134–117151, 2019.

[14] M. N. Bhutta, A. A. Khwaja, A. Nadeem, H. F. Ahmad, M. K. Khan, M. A. Hanif, H. Song, M. Alshamari, and Y. Cao, "A survey on blockchain technology: Evolution, architecture and security," *IEEE Access*, vol. 9, pp. 61048–61073, 2021.

[15] R. Huo, S. Zeng, Z. Wang, J. Shang, W. Chen, T. Huang, S. Wang, F. R. Yu, and Y. Liu, "A comprehensive survey on blockchain in Industrial Internet of Things: Motivations, research progresses, and future challenges," *IEEE Communications Surveys & Tutorials*, vol. 24, no. 1, pp. 88–122, 2022.

[16] B. Cao, Z. Wang, L. Zhang, D. Feng, M. Peng, L. Zhang, and Z. Han, "Blockchain systems, technologies, and applications: A methodology perspective," *IEEE Communications Surveys & Tutorials*, vol. 25, no. 1, pp. 353–385, 2023.

[17] K. N. Singh, O. P. Singh, N. Baranwal, and A. K. Singh, "An efficient chaos-based image encryption algorithm using real-time object detection for smart city applications," *Sustainable Energy Technologies and Assessments*, vol. 53, pp. 1–10, 2022.

[18] D. Mishra, M. S. Obaidat, S. Rana, D. Dharminder, A. Mishra, and B. Sadoun, "Chaos-based content distribution framework for Digital Rights Management System," *IEEE Systems Journal*, vol. 15, no. 1, pp. 570–576, 2021.

[19] O. P. Singh and A. K. Singh, "Image fusion-based watermarking in IWT-SVD domain," *Lecture Notes in Electrical Engineering*, pp. 163–175, 2022.

[20] R. Latypov and E. Stolov, "A new watermarking method to protect blockchain records comprising small graphic files," *2019 42nd International Conference on Telecommunications and Signal Processing (TSP)*, Budapest, Hungary, pp. 668–671, 2019.

[21] Y. Xu, C. Zhang, Q. Zeng, G. Wang, J. Ren, and Y. Zhang, "Blockchain-enabled accountability mechanism against information leakage in vertical industry services," *IEEE Transactions on Network Science and Engineering*, vol. 8, no. 2, pp. 1202–1213, 2020.

[22] Z. Meng, T. Morizumi, S. Miyata, and H. Kinoshita, "Design scheme of copyright management system based on digital watermarking and blockchain," *2018 IEEE 42nd Annual Computer Software Application Conference*, Tokyo, Japan, vol. 01, pp. 359–364, 2018.

[23] S. Sahoo, R. Roshan V. Singh, and R. Halder, "BDmark: A blockchain-driven approach to big data watermarking," *Asian Conference on Intelligent Information and Database Systems*, vol. 1178, pp. 71–84, 2020.

[24] A. Qureshi and D. Megías, "Blockchain-based P2P multimedia content distribution using collusion-resistant fingerprinting," *Asia-Pacific Signal and Information Processing Association Annual Summit and Conference (APSIPA ASC)*, Lanzhou, China, pp. 1606–1615, 2019.

[25] D. Bhowmik and T. Feng, "The multimedia blockchain: A distributed and tamper-proof media transaction framework," *22nd International Conference on Digital Signal Processing (DSP)*, London, UK, pp. 1–5, 2017.

[26] W. Fang, Y. Wang, and X. Wang, "Image tampering location and restoration watermarking based on blockchain technology," *International Conference on Big Data Analytics for Cyber-Physical-Systems*, vol. 1117, pp. 420–428, 2020.

[27] B. Liu, M. Liu, X. Jiang, F. Zhao, and R. Wang, "A blockchain-based scheme for secure sharing of X-ray medical images," *International Conference on Security with Intelligent Computing and Big-data Services (SICBS 2018)*, vol. 895, pp. 29–42, 2020.

[28] J. Zhao, T. Zong, Y. Xiang, L. Gao, and G. Beliakov, "Robust blockchain-based cross-platform audio copyright protection system using content-based fingerprint," *International Conference on Web Information Systems Engineering (WISE 2020)*, vol. 12343, pp. 201–212, 2020.

[29] R. Kumar, R. Tripathi, N. Marchang, G. Srivastava, T. R. Gadekallu, and N. N. Xiong, "A secured distributed detection system based on IPFS and blockchain for industrial image and video data security," *Journal of Parallel Distributed Computing*, vol. 152, pp. 128–143, 2021.

[30] M. Li, L. Zeng, L. Zhao, R. Yang, D. An, and H. Fan, "Blockchain-watermarking for compressive sensed images," *IEEE Access*, vol. 9, pp. 56457–56467, 2021.

[31] S. Zhao and D. O. Mahony, "BMCProtector: A blockchain and smart contract based application for music copyright protection," *Proceedings of the 2018 International Conference on Blockchain Technology and Application (ICBTA 2018)*, China, pp. 1–5, 2018.

[32] M. Zhaoxiong, M. Tetsuya, M. Sumiko, and K. Hirotsugu, "Perceptual hashing based on machine learning for blockchain and digital watermarking," *Third World Conference on Smart Trends in Systems Security and Sustainability (WorldS4)*, London, UK, pp. 193–198, 2019.

[33] A. Garba, A. D. Dwivedi, M. Kamal, G. Srivastava, M. Tariq, M. A. Hasan, and Z. Chen, "A digital rights management system based on a scalable blockchain," *Peer-to-Peer Networking and Applications*, vol. 14, pp. 2665–2680, 2021.

[34] M. Zhaofeng, H. Weihua, and G. Hongmin, "A new blockchain-based trusted DRM scheme for built-in content protection," *EURASIP Journal on Image Video Processing*, vol. 2018, pp. 1–12, 2018.

[35] F. Frattolillo, "A buyer-friendly and mediated watermarking protocol for web context," *ACM Transactions on the Web*, vol. 10, no. 2, pp. 1–28, 2016.

[36] J. Yang, H. Wang, Z. Wang, J. Long, and B. Du, "BDCP: A framework for big data copyright protection based on digital watermarking," *Security, Privacy, and Anonymity in Computation, Communication, and Storage*, pp. 351–360, 2018.

[37] B. Wang, S. Jiawei, W. Wang, and P. Zhao, "A blockchain-based system for secure image protection using zero-watermark," *IEEE 17th International Conference on Mobile Ad Hoc and Sensor Systems (MASS)*, Delhi, India, pp. 62–70, 2020.

[38] X. Wu, P. Ma, Z. Jin, Y. Wu, W. Han, and W. Ou, "A novel zero-watermarking scheme based on NSCT-SVD and blockchain for video copyright," *EURASIP Journal on Wireless Communications and Networking*, vol. 2022, no. 1, pp. 1–21, 2022.

[39] J. Lou and W. Lu, "Construction information authentication and integrity using blockchain-oriented watermarking techniques," *Automation in Construction*, vol. 143, pp. 1–14, 2022.

[40] I. Benkhaddra, A. Kumar, Z. E. Bensalem, and L. Hang, "Secure transmission of secret data using optimization based embedding techniques in blockchain," *Expert Systems with Applications*, vol. 211, pp. 1–15, 2023.

[41] J.-H. Horng, C.-C. Chang, G.-L. Li, W.-K. Lee, and S. O. Hwang, "Blockchain-based reversible data hiding for securing medical images," *Journal of Healthcare Engineering*, vol. 2021, pp. 1–22, 2021.

[42] S. Sahoo and R. Halder, "Traceability and ownership claim of data on big data marketplace using blockchain technology," *Journal of Information and Telecommunication*, vol. 5, no. 1, pp. 35–61, 2020.

[43] D. Xu, C. Zhu, and N. Ren, "A zero-watermark algorithm for copyright protection of remote sensing image based on blockchain," *International Conference on Blockchain Technology and Information Security (ICBCTIS)*, Huaihua City, China, pp. 111–116, 2022.

[44] B. Wang, S. Jiawei, W. Wang, and P. Zhao, "Image copyright protection based on blockchain and zero-watermark," *IEEE Transactions on Network Science and Engineering*, vol. 9, no. 4, pp. 2188–2199, 2022.

[45] S. Bhadauria, P. Kumar, and T. Mohanty, "Intellectual property protection using blockchain and digital watermarking," *IEEE International Conference on Advanced Networks and Telecommunications Systems (ANTS)*, Hyderabad, India, pp. 1–6, 2021.

[46] W. Peng, L. Yi, L. Fang, D. XinHua, and C. Ping, "Secure and traceable copyright management system based on blockchain," *IEEE 5th International Conference on Computer and Communications (ICCC)*, Chengdu, China, pp. 1243–1247, 2019.

[47] Xie Fei, "BDRM: A blockchain-based digital rights management platform with fine-grained usage control," *International Journal of Science*, vol. 6, no. 2, pp. 1–10, 2019.

[48] O. P. Singh and A. K. Singh, "Data hiding in encryption-compression domain," *Complex and Intelligent Systems*, vol. 9, pp. 2759–2772, 2023.

[49] O. P. Singh, A. K. Singh, A. K. Agrawal, and H. Zhou, "SecDH: Security of COVID-19 images based on data hiding with PCA," *Computer Communications*, vol. 191, pp. 368–377, 2022.

Chapter 11

No reference medical image quality assessment for image security and authorization

Sima Sahu
Malla Reddy Engineering College (Autonomous), Hyderabad, India

Nishita Priyadarshini
AIIMS Bibinagar, Hyderabad, India

Amit Kumar Singh
NIT Patna, Patna, India

11.1 INTRODUCTION

Medical image security and authorization ensures integrity, confidentiality, and availability of patient medical information. Quality assessment of medical images has a great role in evaluating the fidelity of medical images, tamper detection, and suitability for the intended purpose. The requirements of quality assessment in medical images in security and authentication are [1]:

- **Image Quality:** The quality of the medical images must be verified to ensure that the quality is sufficient for disease diagnosis, disease treatment, and research.
- **Authenticity:** Medical images must be authenticated that they are genuine and not altered or tampered.
- **Integrity:** Medical image integrity should be verified that they are not modified and corrupted during transmission, storage, and processing.
- **Confidentiality:** Medical images must be protected from unauthorized access and disclosure to maintain patient privacy.

Image quality is important to ensure that appropriate techniques and standards are applied to safeguard patient information and maintaining the trust of patients and healthcare providers. It helps in detecting distortions in an image, making it easier to analyze and detect any tampering or modifications [2]. Medical image authentication and security are important issues in the healthcare industry, as they play a crucial role in ensuring the privacy and confidentiality of sensitive patient information. Medical images contain a wealth of personal and confidential information that must be protected from unauthorized access and manipulation. There are several ways to address the challenge of medical image authentication and security [3]:

- **Encryption:** Medical images can be encrypted using various algorithms to protect the confidentiality of the information contained in the images. This makes it difficult for unauthorized users to access the data [4].
- **Access Control:** An access control mechanism such as user authentication and authorization can be put in place to ensure that only authorized individuals can access the medical images.
- **Digital Signature:** A digital signature can be used to verify the authenticity of medical images and ensure they have not been tampered with.
- **Watermarking:** Watermarking is a technique for embedding information in an image that can be used to track the origin and authenticity of the image.
- **Auditing and Logging:** Keeping track of who accesses the medical images, when and for what purpose can help detect and prevent unauthorized access.
- **Cloud Storage:** Storing medical images on secure, HIPPA-compliant cloud servers can help ensure the security of the data [1].

Keeping patient information secure and private is a very crucial task when communicating medical data through insecure channels. Medical data may be maliciously tampered with and illegally copied without authorization. These causes necessitate the application of integrity authentication and copyright protection in medical images. Many studies have been proposed for medical image authorization and security. These methods require a good robustness against noises and distortions like Gaussian noise, blur, and channel fading.

An approach for medical image security was introduced by Alqahtani et al. [4]. Their approach was based on Fractional Fourier Transform (FFT) and Jigsaw Transform (JT). They considered different noise effects like Gaussian noise, Salt and Pepper noise, Speckle noise, and Poisson noise in encryption and decryption efficiency.

A medical image authentication method was proposed by Sun et al. [5] by using wavelet packet decomposition. The authors verified the robustness of the result in resisting both additive and multiplicative noises.

The perceptual quality of medical images can be assessed automatically by using Image Quality Assessment (IQA) methods. Medical image quality assessment can be performed by subjective and objective approaches. A subjective assessment approach is carried out by measuring the image quality. Mathematical calculations are required for objective assessment approach. The objective approach results should match with the subjective approach results. Distortion in medical images may be caused due to several factors, such as operator mistake, fault in equipment, acquisition, compression, enhancement, and reconstruction process [6]. Due to the above reasons, subjective assessment may lead to inappropriate diagnosis. Therefore, objective assessment is highly recommended for medical image quality assessment [7]. Objective quality assessment can be Full Reference image quality assessment (FR-IQA) [8, 9], Reduced Reference image quality assessment (RR-IQA), and No Reference image quality assessment (NR-IQA). In FR-IQA, an undistorted image is used to determine the quality assessment. In RR-IQA, a part of the undistorted image should be available to determine the image quality assessment. In the case of NR-IQA, a reference image is not required to find the quality factor. In medical science, it is not possible to obtain an undistorted image. Therefore, FR-IQA and RR-IQA methods are not appropriate for medical images, while NR-IQA is a suitable technique to predict the quality of medical images [10]. Figure 11.1 shows the classification of image quality assessment techniques. The comparison of different image quality assessment methods is shown in Table 11.1.

NR-IQA is a method of accessing the quality of a digital image without reference to a "ground truth" or reference image. Traditional mage quality assessment methods compare an image to a reference image to determine quality. NR-IQA methods analyze the specific image features and attributes to impact image quality such as sharpness, contrast, and noise [11]. These methods use statistical models and machine learning algorithms to predict image quality based on these features. A NR-IQA was proposed by Omarova et al. [12] to contrast enhancement of poor quality X-ray image affected by environmental noise. They applied CLAHE and Gamma correction method for image enhancement and determined the quality of X-ray image by using NIQE and Blind Referenceless Image Spatial Quality (BRISQUE) functions. A NR-IQA method is proposed by Kumar et al. [13] to determine quality of the image by measuring the image sharpness. Difference of difference to edge was calculated to find the quality of the image. A NR-IQA method was proposed by Saad et al. [14] that used the Natural Scene Statistic (NSS) model for DCT coefficients. The quality score was predicted using the

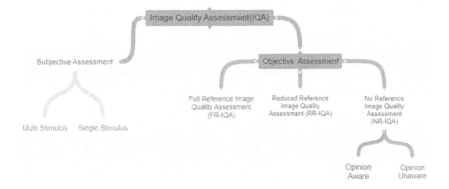

Figure 11.1 Classification of image quality assessment techniques.

Table 11.1 Comparison of image quality assessment approaches

Approach	Used methodology to predict Image quality
Subjective Assessment	Visual Inspection
Single Stimulus	Image is displayed to the observer for a short and fixed time
Multi Stimulus	Reference image and test images are displayed to the observer randomly
Objective Assessment	Mathematical calculation
Full Reference image quality assessment (FR-IQA)	Undistorted image is compared with distorted image
Reduced Reference image quality assessment (RR-IQA)	Part of undistorted image is compared with distorted image
No Reference image quality assessment (NR-IQA)	Unnatural image feature extraction from distorted image
Opinion aware NR-IQA	Model is trained by a database that is based on subjective opinion score of human-rated distorted images
Opinion unaware NR-IQA	Model is not trained by a database that is based on subjective opinion score of human-rated distorted images

Bayesian inference model. Mittal et al. [15] proposed a NR-IQA method based on statistical features, luminance coefficients of the image in statistical domain. Generalized Gaussian Distribution (GGD) was used to model the image features. This method was further extended by Chow et al. [16] to evaluate features of structural Magnetic Resonance Imaging (MRI) images. The MRI image feature was calculated from the image luminance coefficient and Difference Mean Opinion Score (DMOS).

A dual Convolutional Neural Network (CNN) structure-based NR-IQA technique was proposed by Li et al. [17]. Their method was based on calculating the quality parameter based on gray and color features of the image in Human Visual System (HVS) space. The quality assessment parameter was further used for de-noising the algorithm for image authorization and security. A blind image quality assessment method was proposed by Moorthy et al. [18] to judge the quality of natural scene by extracting the features of sub-band wavelet coefficients. Gaussian Scale Mixture (GSM) was used to model the wavelet coefficients and find the dependency between the wavelet coefficient and the neighbors. The rest of the state-of-the-art methods are discussed in Table 11.2.

The challenging task in the discussed state-of-the art NR-IQA methods is the estimation of image quality without any ground truth data. So, it is highly required that the extracted features from the distorted image must include all distortion types that determine the image quality efficiently for further processing. The proposed methodology utilizes the multiresolution approach to extract the features potentially. Image features not visible in

Table 11.2 State-of-the-art NR-IQA methods

Method	Feature	Classification and regression	Statistical modeling	Dataset	Other considerations
BLIINDS-II [14]	Natural Scene Statistics (NSS) of DCT Coefficients	SVM	Generalized Gaussian Distribution (GGD)	LIVE	• They suffer regression limitations because they require training to learn the prediction parameters. • High computational complexity
BRISQUE [15]	Luminance Coefficients	Support Vector Machine (SVM)	Generalized Gaussian Distribution (GGD)	Natural Image	• Simple Model • Lower Computational Complexity
DIVINE [18]	Wavelet Transform features	—	Gaussian scale mixture (GSM)	LIVE IQA	• Extracts statistical features. • Cannot compute specific distortion features.
CORNIA [19]	Local feature from raw image	Unsupervised Learning	—	LIVE, TID 2008	• Non-Linearity feature is improved using Max-pooling and image is represented using soft assignment coding for quality estimation.
BLIINDS [20]	DCT Coefficients	—	Multivariate Gaussian Model and Multivariate Laplacian Model	LIVE	• Do not consider any specific type of distortion.
NIQE [21]	NSS features	—	Multivariate Gaussian (MVG)	LIVE IQA	• Quality is expressed as deviation of statistical regularities.
Xue et al. [22]	Laplacian of Gaussian and Gradient Magnitude	ε-SVR	Weibull Distribution and GGD	LIVE, CSIQ, TID 2008	• Quality prediction accuracy is high. • Computational complexity is high.

(Continued)

Table 11.2 (Continued) State-of-the-art NR-IQA methods

Method	Feature	Classification and regression	Statistical modeling	Dataset	Other considerations
Liu et al. [23]	Curvelet Coefficients	SVM	AGGD	LIVE, TID 2008	• Cannot compute specific distortion features. • Can compute only statistics feature.
Hou et al. [24]	NSS	Deep Learning	Triangular and Uniform Distribution	LIVE, TID 2008, CSIQ, IVC, MICT	• Well to human valuation. • Strong in representing image quality. • Time Consuming • Features fail to express eccentric distortion.
Kang et al. [25]	Spatial feature	CNN	—	LIVE, TID 2008	• Can estimate quality in local region.
Kang et al. [26]	Spatial feature	Multitask CNN	—	LIVE, TID 2008, CSIQ	• Can identify distortion and find quality score of image.
PIQUE [27]	NSS features	—	—	LIVE IQA, TID & CSIQ	• Quality is predicted from local features. • Fast and Low computational complexity
BIECON [28]	Locally normalized image	Deep learning	—	LIVE, TID 2008	• Follow FR-IQA behavior
Fan et al. [29]	Spatial feature	Multi expert CNN	—	LIVEII, CSIQ	• High correlation with human visual system.
Bosse et al. [30]	Spatial feature	Deep Neural Network	—	LIVE, TID 2013	• High robustness of the learned features.

Method	Features	Classifier/Model	Distribution	Database	Advantages
Ma et al.[31]	Spatial feature	Multitask Deep Neural Network	—	TID 2013, CSIQ	• Ability to handle more distortion types.
Modified BRISQUE [16]	Luminance Coefficients	SVM	Asymmetric Generalized Gaussian Distribution (AGGD)	Osirix DICOM Viewer MRI database	• Statistically better than BRIQUE in terms of T-test and SROCC and RMSE.
WLBP [32]	Local Binary Pattern (LBP) of Wavelet Coefficients	Support Vector Regression	—	LIVE and TID2008	• LBP operator extracts structural features of wavelet coefficients. • Low computational complexity
Li et al. [17]	Gray and color features in HVS	CNN	—	LIVE	• Application in image security and authentication.
Yue et al. [33]	Entropy of intensity and Kullback-Leibler divergence	—	—	CSIQ,TID 2008,TID 2013	• Quality assessment of contrast distorted image. • Less run time than FR and NR methods.
Yan et al. [34]	Gradient features and non-linear distribution features	Deep Neural Network	—	LIVE, CSIQ, TID 2013, IVC	• Effective and Robust

one resolution can be determined in another resolution. The image features are extracted in wavelet domain by statistically modeling the coefficients. This chapter designed a NR-IQA method for medical images considering the various distortions in the image. The proposed method is based on statistical modeling of wavelet transform coefficients and extract features from the sub-band coefficients. Medical Image quality score is predicted using a Support Vector Machine Regression (SVR) method. The main contribution of the chapter is explained below:

1. A series of statistical feature vectors are extracted from medical image that is suitable for medical image security and authentication applications.
2. Wavelet coefficient features are evaluated and analyzed to estimate quality of medical image.
3. Noise features are combined with spatial image features that effectively estimate medical image quality for further process.

The remainder of this chapter is organized as mentioned follow. Section 11.2 discusses the proposed methodology for extracting feature vectors from medical images. The classification and regression procedure is also discussed in this section. Section 11.3 discusses the performance result of proposed method in NIH database. Finally, Section 11.4 concludes the chapter.

11.2 PROPOSED METHODOLOGY

This section discusses the proposed methodology to extract the medical image distortions in wavelet domain. The detailed network structure of the proposed methodology is explained in Figure 11.2 shown below. The input

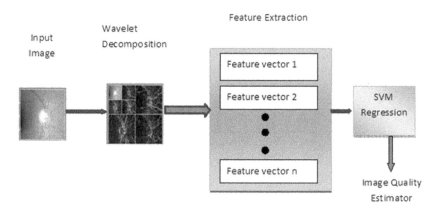

Figure 11.2 Proposed NR-IQA block diagram.

Table 11.3 List of features used to find IQA

Feature	Description	Computational process
$F_1 - F_9$	Variance of wavelet distribution in LL, HL, and LH sub-bands in all scales	Modeling wavelet sub-bands using NIG PDF
$F_{10} - F_{18}$	Location parameter of wavelet distribution in LL, HL, and LH sub-bands in all scales	Modeling wavelet sub-bands using NIG PDF
$F_{19} - F_{21}$	Noise variance in diagonal sub-band	Modeling diagonal sub-bands using Gaussian PDF
$F_{22} - F_{51}$	Spatial correlation across sub-bands	Fitting a 3rd order polynomial function to the correlation function
$F_{52} - F_{69}$	NSS feature in the Wavelet Domain	Calculating magnitude, variance, and entropy

distorted medical image is first converted from spatial domain into wavelet domain by applying wavelet decomposition technique. Next, a series of statistical features are extracted by utilizing the obtained wavelet coefficients in each sub-band. Further feature vectors are formed by arranging the calculated statistical features. Next, a regression model is designed using the SVM regression method. The regression model maps each feature into a quality measure index. Finally, the quality indexes resulting from distortion feature vectors are combined to produce a final image quality index. The feature vectors are shown in Table 11.3.

The steps of the proposed methodology are discussed below:

Steps:

1. Input distorted medical image $I\ (j,k)$.
2. Decomposition of medical image by 3 scale wavelet transforms results $W(j, k)$.
3. Extraction of features F_1 to F_{18} considering signal variances and location parameters in wavelet domain by modeling $W(j, k)$ using NIG PDF in LL, HL, and LH sub-bands.
4. Extraction of features F_{19} to F_{21} considering the noise variance in HH sub-bands, by modeling $W(j, k)$ using Gaussian PDF.
5. Extraction of features F_{22} to F_{51} considering spatial correlation and features F_{52} to F_{69} considering NSS features in wavelet domain.
6. Application of Support Vector Machine regression to find the final quality index.

11.2.1 Two-dimensional wavelet decomposition

Wavelet decomposition of digital image results in four sub-bands, Approximation sub-band (LL), Horizontal sub-band (HL), Vertical Sub-band (LH), and Diagonal sub-band (HH) [35], as shown in Figure 11.3 below.

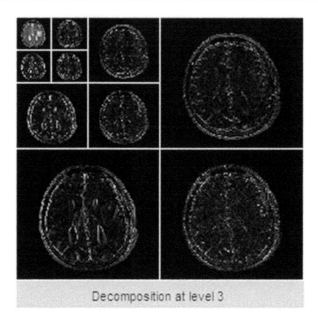

Decomposition at level 3

Figure 11.3 Three scale decomposition of medical image.

Distribution of wavelet coefficients is utilized to extract features in medical image. Empirical distribution of wavelet coefficients in LL, HL, and LH sub-bands are heavy tailed in structure. This chapter implements the 3 scale decomposition. The wavelet transform is applied in 3 scales, which results 12 sub-bands. The distribution of wavelet coefficients for the original medical image is shown in Figure 11.4. It can be seen from the figure that a heavy-tailed structure in LL, HL, and LH sub-band coefficients and a Gaussian structure in HH sub-band coefficients. The wavelet decomposition process for two dimensional of level L can be defined as follows:

$$
\begin{aligned}
W(j,k) = \frac{1}{\sqrt{JK}} \Bigg[&\sum_{a=1}^{J}\sum_{b=1}^{K} f_L^A(a,b) \times \Phi_L^A(j,k,a,b) \\
+ &\sum_{l=1}^{L} \sum_{M \in H,V,D} \sum_{a=1}^{J}\sum_{b=1}^{M} f_L^M \times (a,b) \Psi_L^M(j,k,a,b) \Bigg]
\end{aligned}
\tag{11.1}
$$

The size of the image $I(j,k)$ *is* $J \times K$. The approximation coefficients, diagonal detail coefficients, vertical detail coefficients, and horizontal detail coefficients are denoted by $f_L^A, f_L^{M\in D}, f_L^{M\in V}, f_L^{M\in H}$, respectively. The scaling and wavelet coefficients are denoted by Φ and Ψ and defined as:

$$
\Phi_L^A(j,k,a,b) = 2^{L/2} \phi\left(2^L j - a\right) \phi\left(2^L k - b\right)
\tag{11.2}
$$

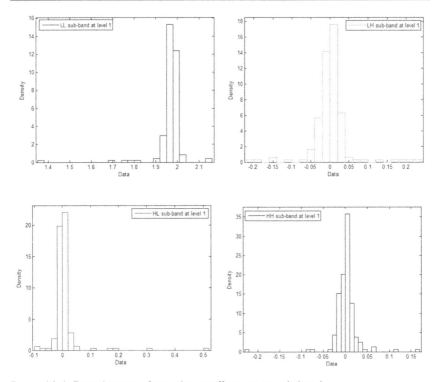

Figure 11.4 Distribution of wavelet coefficients in sub-bands.

$$\Psi_L^H\left(j,k,a,b\right)=2^{\frac{1}{2}}\psi\left(2^{l}j-a\right)\phi\left(2^{L}k-b\right) \tag{11.3}$$

$$\Psi_L^V\left(j,k,a,b\right)=2^{\frac{1}{2}}\varphi\left(2^{l}j-a\right)\psi\left(2^{L}k-b\right) \tag{11.4}$$

$$\Psi_L^D\left(j,k,a,b\right)=2^{\frac{1}{2}}\psi\left(2^{l}j-a\right)\psi\left(2^{L}k-b\right) \tag{11.5}$$

11.2.2 Wavelet coefficient modeling and feature extraction

In this chapter, Horizontal and Vertical Sub-bands (LL HL LH) in each scale are modeled using a Normal Inverse Gaussian (NIG) Probability Density Function (PDF). The diagonal sub-bands (HH) in each scale are modeled using Gaussian PDF, as this sub-band consists of all the noisy coefficients. It can find a heavy-tailed distribution of the wavelet coefficients, and the noise added to the medical image changes the shape of the distribution of wavelet coefficients. The extent of noise added can be found from the tail behavior of the distribution. NIG PDF fits the heavy-tailed wavelet distribution data and thus analytically tractable [36]. NIG PDF has been implemented in the modeling of the sub-band wavelet coefficients and results in effective feature extraction. The density function of NIG PDF is defined as:

$$P(C) = \left(\alpha\delta e^{\alpha\delta} k_j\left(\alpha\sqrt{\delta^2 + C^2}\right)\right) \Big/ \left(\pi\sqrt{\delta^2 + C^2}\right) \tag{11.6}$$

Where C denotes the random variable, k denotes modified Bessel function with j(index)=1. Tail heaviness of the distribution is defined by α and can control the steepness of the distribution. The scale parameter is denoted by δ. The shape of the distribution is controlled by α and δ. $\alpha \to \infty$ and $\delta \to \infty$ yields Gaussian distribution, and $\alpha \to 0$ yields Cauchy distribution [37]. Distribution parameters are estimated by fitting NIG PDF in all sub-bands (LL, LH, HL). Next, the variance information $\hat{\sigma}_c^2$ of the sub-bands is calculated using the following equation:

$$\hat{\sigma}_c^2 = \int\limits_{-\infty}^{+\infty} C^2 P(C) dc - \left(\int\limits_{-\infty}^{+\infty} cP(C) dc\right)^2 \tag{11.7}$$

A total of 18 features $F_1 - F_9$ are calculated corresponds to variance values, and $F_{10} - F_{18}$ corresponds to α values across the sub-bands.

11.2.3 Noise variance in diagonal sub-band

Diagonal sub-band in wavelet decomposition contains all the noisy data and gives important information regarding the noise present in the medical image. This concept motivates to extract image features $F_{19} - F_{21}$ corresponds to noise variance in HH sub-band in all scales. Orthogonal property of wavelet decomposition says that sub-band diagonal coefficient fits well by zero mean Gaussian PDF. By fitting the empirical wavelet distribution using Gaussian PDF, median is calculated from the distribution parameter, and next, a median estimator is applied to find the noise variance of the medical image. Noise variance $(\hat{\sigma}_n^2)$, calculated using a median estimator, is given by [38]:

$$\hat{\sigma}_n^2 = \left(\frac{\text{Median}(HH)}{0.6745}\right)^2 \tag{11.8}$$

11.2.4 Spatial correlation feature extractor

Medical images modify their structure in the presence of distortion. The smoothness of the image varies over the distance. The correlation between spatial structures of the sub-bands can be utilized to evaluate the quality factor. The following steps are implemented to find the correlation between the spatial structures.

Step 1: Calculation of joint empirical distribution $f_{x,y}(X, Y)$ between the coefficients at (l, k) and $N_8(l, k)$.

$N_8(i, j)$ is the distance $d \in \{1, 2, \ldots\ldots 25\}$

Step 2: Calculation of correlation between the variables X, Y using the following equation (11.9).

$$\rho_d = \frac{E_{xy}(X,Y)\left[X - E_x(X)\right]^T \left(Y - E_y(Y)\right)}{\sigma_X \sigma_Y} \tag{11.9}$$

Where E is the expectation operator and σ_X, σ_Y are the variances of X and Y vector, respectively.

Step 3: Parameterize the correlation ρ_d by fitting a 3rd order polynomial and calculation of coefficient of the polynomial.

Finally, the empirical value of correlation coefficient, fit error, and coefficient of the polynomial form the features $F_{22} - F_{51}$.

11.2.5 NSS feature extraction in the wavelet domain

Wavelet transform includes properties like multiresolution, locality, Gaussianity, and persistency. Self-similarity property of the scene is one of the most important properties of wavelet transform. The NSS feature in the wavelet domain changes irregularly with artifacts [24]. Magnitude of the wavelet coefficients exponentially decay across scale. This feature is utilized in this chapter for implementing quality detection. NSS feature is extracted from the image in wavelet domain. Sparse representation is implemented in this chapter to extract NSS features. Magnitude, variance, and entropy are calculated for the horizontal and vertical sub-bands for each scale as shown below:

$$magnitude_s = \frac{1}{N_s \times M_s} \sum_{k=1}^{N_s} \sum_{l=1}^{M_s} \log_2 |C_s(l,k)| \tag{11.10}$$

$$\vartheta ariance_s = \frac{1}{N_s \times M_s} \sum_{k=1}^{N_s} \sum_{l=1}^{M_s} \log_2 |C_s(l,k) - magnitude_s| \tag{11.11}$$

$$entopy_s = \sum_{j=1}^{N_s} \sum_{i=1}^{M_s} P(C_s(i,j)) \ln P(C_s(i,j)) \tag{11.12}$$

Where N_s and M_s are length and width of sth sub-band, $C_s(k, l)$ is the (k, l) coefficients of the sth sub-band, and $P(.) =$ Probability density function of the sub-band.

These features are averaged in the same sub-band and in the same scale and combined into a vector. For six sub-bands in three scales, the vector is defined as below.

$$
f = \begin{aligned}
&[m_{LH1}, m_{HL1}, m_{LH2}, m_{HL2}, m_{LH3}, m_{HL3}, \\
&\vartheta_{LH1}, \vartheta_{HL1}, \vartheta_{LH2}\vartheta_{HL2}, \vartheta_{LH3}, \vartheta_{HL3}, \\
&e_{LH1}, e_{HL1}, e_{LH2}, e_{HL2}, e_{LH3}, e_{LH3}]^T
\end{aligned}
\tag{11.13}
$$

Where m_{xy} is the magnitude of x sub-band at scale y, ϑ_{xy} is the variance of x sub-band at scale y, and e_{xy} is the entropy of x sub-band at scale y. A total of 18 features $F_{52} - F_{69}$ are calculated that correspond to magnitude, variance, and entropy values in sub-bands.

11.2.6 SVM regression and parameter selection

In our work, a standard regression is considered that works under general setting for predictive learning [39]. These method estimates a real value function as:

$$
y = r(f) + \delta
\tag{11.14}
$$

Where δ is the hyper parameter and f is a multi-valued input and y is the scalar output. Parameter selection is based on the finite number of features f and y values.

Let the features and their corresponding selection parameters are distributed jointly and defined by PDF as $P_{f,y}(F, Y)$. It can be written as:

$$
P_{f,y}(F, Y) = P_f(F) P_{f,y}(Y \mid F)
\tag{11.15}
$$

From equation (11.14) and (11.15) we can write the regression function as:

$$
r(f) = \int y P_{f,y}(Y \mid F) dy
\tag{11.16}
$$

The prime aim of the estimation procedure is to find the best model $f(f, \omega_0)$ from a sequence of models $f(f, \omega)$ for ω. The best model can be created by minimizing prediction risk as:

$$
R(\omega) = \int \left(L(y, f(f, \omega)) P(f, y) df dy \right)
\tag{11.17}
$$

Where $L\left(y,f\left(f,\omega\right)\right)=\left(y-f\left(f,\omega\right)\right)^{2}$ defines the loss function   (11.18)

Applying equation (11.18) in equation (11.17) results:

$$R(\omega)=\int\left(y-f\left(f,\omega\right)\right)^{2}P(f,y)dfdy \qquad (11.19)$$

In SVM regression method, a mapping scheme is used to map the input features to a multidimensional feature space. Next, a linear model in the feature space is created and can be written as:

$$f\left(f,\omega\right)=\sum_{i=1}^{n}\omega_{i}g_{i}\left(f\right)+b \qquad (11.20)$$

Where b is the bias term, g_i is the non-linear transform function, and n are the training samples. SVM regression is a linear regression in the high dimensional feature space consider the insensitive loss ε, and also reduces the complexity of the model $\|\omega\|^{2}$. The modified loss function can be written as:

$$L_{\varepsilon}\left(y,f\left(f,\omega\right)\right)=\begin{cases}0, \text{if } y-f\left(f,\omega\right)\le\varepsilon\\ \left|y-f\left(f,\omega\right)\right|-\varepsilon \text{ otherwise}\end{cases} \qquad (11.21)$$

The Risk function considering the insensitive loss is given by:

$$R_{\varepsilon}\left(\omega\right)=\frac{1}{n}\sum_{i=1}^{n}L_{\varepsilon}\left(y,f\left(f,\omega\right)\right) \qquad (11.22)$$

Thus, SVM regression minimizes the function $\frac{1}{2}\|\omega\|^{2}+c\sum_{i=1}^{n}\epsilon_{i}+\epsilon_{i}^{*}$

With constraints $\begin{cases}y-f\left(f,\omega\right)-b\le\epsilon_{i}+\epsilon_{i}^{*}\\ f\left(f,\omega\right)+b-y\le\epsilon_{i}+\epsilon_{i}^{*}\\ \epsilon_{i}\epsilon_{i}^{*}\ge0\end{cases}$ (11.23)

Where c is a positive constant, $\epsilon_{i},\epsilon_{i}^{*}$ are the slack variables, and n are the training samples.

11.3 EXPERIMENTAL RESULTS

This section discusses the performance results of the proposed method. The objective assessment is compared with human valuation. The proposed method is tested on National Institutes of Health (NIH) database [40] and simulated in MATLAB environment. All images are converted to 400×400 size for simulation. The proposed method requires approximately 50 seconds to produce the quality score. Compared to prediction time, SVR training time is negligible. The NIH database for different medical images such as Bone marrow Smear image lever, Brain MRI, Chest X-Ray, CT Scan of Brain, and Brian MRI images are shown in Figure 11.5. The proposed algorithm is compared with state-of-the-art methods including FR-IQA- and NR-IQA-based methods. Full reference methods include PSNR, SSIM [8], and IFC [9]. No reference methods include BRISQUE [15], CORNIA [19], DIIVINE [20], and WLBP [32]. The performance of the proposed algorithm

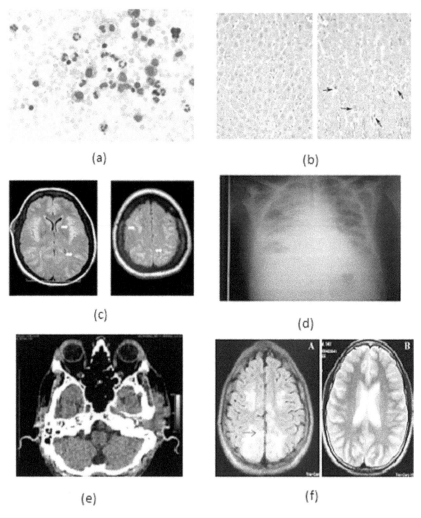

Figure 11.5 Medical images (a) Bone marrow smear (b) lever (c) Brain MRI (d) Chest X-Ray (e) CT Scan of Brain (f) Brian MRI.

is evaluated and analyzed by the Performance parameters. Those include Spearman Rank Ordered Correlation Coefficient (SROCC), Pearson Linear Correlation Coefficient (PLCC), and Root Mean Square Error (RMSE). These parameters are the most significant algorithm to evaluate NR-IQA [41]. Prediction monotonicity of the proposed method is measured through SROCC parameter and can be defined as:

$$SROCC\left(Q_{obj}, Q_{sub}\right) = 1 - \frac{6 \Sigma D_i}{N\left(N^2 - 1\right)} \tag{11.24}$$

Where Q_{obj} and Q_{sub} are predicted and actual score, respectively. Subjective score is the actual score predicted by human eye. D_i is the grade difference among Q_{obj} and Q_{sub} for sample i. And N is the number of images in the evaluation database.

PLCC defines the correlation between the subjective score and objective prediction score. Prediction accuracy is measured through PLCC parameter and can be defined as:

$$PLCC\left(Q_{obj}, Q_{sub}\right) = \frac{\text{cov}\left(Q_{obj}, Q_{sub}\right)}{\sigma\left(Q_{obj}\right)\sigma\left(Q_{sub}\right)} \tag{11.25}$$

The absolute deviation between subjective and objective score can be measured by RMSE and can be defined as:

$$RMSE = \sqrt{\frac{1}{N}\sum_{i=1}^{N}\left(S_i - O_i\right)^2} \tag{11.26}$$

Where S and O are subjective mean opinion score and objective mean opinion score, respectively. Subjective assessment is evaluated by large number of observers.

Tables 11.4–11.6 show that the performance results of proposed method in terms of SROCC, PLCC, and RMSE, respectively, for different destructions include JPEG 2000 (JP2K), JPEG, additive white noise (WN), Gaussian Blur (GB), and Fast Fading (FF). It is observed that the proposed method has a high measure of consistency with subjective qualitative assessment of human visual observation.

Table 11.4 shows the performance comparison of the proposed method with respect to SROCC. The proposed methods SROCC result is 0.952 considering all the distortions. We can see that the FR IQA methods are competitive with the proposed algorithm in terms of SROCC performance, and proposed method is statistically efficient than the state-of-the-art NR-IQA methods. Our proposed method improvements over SROCC score is 1.2% than WLBP [32] method in case of JP2K artifact, 0.73% than WLBP [32]

Table 11.4 SROCC performance comparison on NIH database on various distortions

Methods	JP2K	JPEG	WN	GB	FF	ALL
PSNR	0.842	0.861	0.935	0.725	0.855	0.846
SSIM [8]	0.938	0.953	0.964	0.853	0.936	0.887
IFC [9]	0.939	0.916	0.936	0.894	0.942	0.911
BRISQUE [15]	0.916	0.929	0.958	0.924	0.958	0.935
CORNIA [19]	0.906	0.876	0.961	0.946	0.923	0.916
DIIVINE [20]	0.923	0.935	0.976	0.935	0.905	0.932
WLBP [32]	0.926	0.939	0.971	0.939	0.961	0.944
Proposed	0.938	0.946	0.978	0.956	0.976	0.952

Table 11.5 PLCC performance comparison on NIH database on various distortions

Methods	JP2K	JPEG	WN	GB	FF	ALL
PSNR	0.883	0.871	0.976	0.731	0.886	0.834
SSIM [8]	0.936	0.913	0.971	0.835	0.913	0.873
IFC [9]	0.905	0.899	0.955	0.925	0.928	0.915
BRISQUE [15]	0.945	0.936	0.962	0.933	0.897	0.925
CORNIA [19]	0.923	0.925	0.958	0.946	0.935	0.921
DIIVINE [20]	0.937	0.932	0.961	0.953	0.853	0.932
WLBP [32]	0.939	0.941	0.953	0.955	0.845	0.935
Proposed	0.951	0.948	0.968	0.972	0.955	0.946

Table 11.6 RMSE performance comparison on NIH database on various distortions

Methods	JP2K	JPEG	WN	GB	FF	ALL
PSNR	7.116	8.108	3.658	9.055	7.883	9.204
SSIM [8]	5.314	6.923	3.855	7.321	5.325	8.843
IFC [9]	6.833	7.211	4.653	4.653	4.012	6.254
BRISQUE [15]	6.484	9.156	7.521	7.751	9.656	9.092
CORNIA [19]	8.332	9.287	7.615	7.521	8.921	9.321
DIIVINE [20]	8.585	9.632	8.202	8.202	10.246	9.998
WLBP [32]	7.969	9.129	9.116	9.116	10.004	9.634
Proposed	6.321	8.183	6.929	6.924	8.125	8.652

method in case of JPEG artifact, 0.20% than DIIVINE [20] method in case of WN distortion, 1.04% than CORNIA [19] method in case of GB distortion, 1.53% than WLBP [32] method in case of FF distortion, and 0.84% than WLBP [32] method considering all distortions. Table 11.5 shows the performance comparison of the proposed method with respect to PLCC. The proposed methods PLCC result is 0.946 considering all the distortions. Our proposed method improvements over PLCC score is 0.63% than

BRISQUE [15] method in case of JP2K artifact, 0.73% than WLBP [32] method in case of JPEG artifact, 0.61% than BRISQUE [15] method in case of WN distortion, 1.74% than WLBP [32] method in case of GB distortion, 2.09% than CORNIA [19] method in case of FF distortion, and 1.16% than WLBP [32] method considering all distortions. Table 11.6 shows the performance comparison of the proposed method with respect to SROCC. The proposed methods RMSE result is 8.652 considering all the distortions. Our proposed method improvements over RMSE score is 2.57% than BRISQUE [15] method in case of JP2K artifact, 11.48% than WLBP [32] method in case of JPEG artifact, 8.54% than BRISQUE [15] method in case of WN distortion, 8.62% than CORNIA [19] method in case of GB distortion, 9.79% than CORNIA [19] method in case of FF distortion, and 5.02% than BRISQUE [15] method considering all distortions.

11.4 CONCLUSION

A distortion generic No Reference Image Quality Assessment (NR-IQA) algorithm was developed in this chapter that operates in Wavelet domain. A NSS-based no reference quality assessment method was proposed for assessing quality of a medical image without using a reference image considering various distortions to be applied in image security and authorization. First, the features are extracted from the distorted image in wavelet domain and is then processed using SVR technique to estimate the image quality index. Experiments were performed on NIH database, and the proposed algorithm achieved a good performance over existing NR-IQA methods in terms of SROCC, PLCC, and RMSE parameters. Simulation results proved that the quality index of the proposed method is in line with FR-IQA methods and better than existing NR-IQA methods. In the future, a hybrid method may be developed considering the image features in various domains to extract more features from the medical images to produce a more accurate quality index.

REFERENCES

[1] Cao, F., Huang, H. K., & Zhou, X. Q. (2003). Medical image security in a HIPAA mandated PACS environment. *Computerized Medical Imaging and Graphics*, 27(2–3), 185–196.

[2] Herbadji, D., Belmeguenai, A., Derouiche, N., & Liu, H. (2020). Colour image encryption scheme based on enhanced quadratic chaotic map. *IET Image Processing*, 14(1), 40–52.

[3] Chow, L. S., & Paramesran, R. (2016). Review of medical image quality assessment. *Biomedical Signal Processing and Control*, 27, 145–154.

[4] Alqahtani, F., Amoon, M., & El-Shafai, W. (2022). A fractional fourier based medical image authentication approach. *CMC-Computers Materials & Continua*, 70(2), 3133–3150.

[5] Sun, T., Wang, X., Zhang, K., Jiang, D., Lin, D., Jv, X., ... & Zhu, W. (2022). Medical image authentication method based on the wavelet packet and energy entropy. *Entropy*, *24*(6), 798.

[6] Stępień, I., & Oszust, M. (2022). A brief survey on no-reference image quality assessment methods for magnetic resonance images. *Journal of Imaging*, *8*(6), 160.

[7] Marwan, M., Kartit, A., & Ouahmane, H. (2018). Security enhancement in healthcare cloud using machine learning. *Procedia Computer Science*, *127*, 388–397.

[8] Wang, Z., Bovik, A. C., Sheikh, H. R., & Simoncelli, E. P. (2004). Image quality assessment: From error visibility to structural similarity. *IEEE Transactions on Image Processing*, *13*(4), 600–612.

[9] Sheikh, H. R., & Bovik, A. C. (2006). Image information and visual quality. *IEEE Transactions on Image Processing*, *15*(2), 430–444.

[10] Jayageetha, J., & Vasanthanayaki, C. (2018). Medical image quality assessment using CSO based deep neural network. *Journal of Medical Systems*, *42*, 1–9.

[11] Padmapriya, R., & Jeyasekar, A. (2022). Blind image quality assessment with image denoising: A survey. *Journal of Pharmaceutical Negative Results*, *13*, 386–392.

[12] Omarova, G., Starovoitov, V., Myrzamuratova, A., Акzullakyzy, L., Takuadina, A., Tanirbergenov, A., ... & Sadirmekova, Z. (2023). No-reference quality assessment of medical images using contrast enhancement. *Journal of Theoretical and Applied Information Technology*, *101*(1), 267–281.

[13] Kumar, J., Chen, F., & Doermann, D. (2012, November). Sharpness estimation for document and scene images. In *Proceedings of the 21st International Conference on Pattern Recognition (ICPR2012)* (pp. 3292–3295). IEEE.

[14] Saad, M. A., Bovik, A. C., & Charrier, C. (2012). Blind image quality assessment: A natural scene statistics approach in the DCT domain. *IEEE Transactions on Image Processing*, *21*(8), 3339–3352.

[15] Mittal, A., Moorthy, A. K., & Bovik, A. C. (2012). No-reference image quality assessment in the spatial domain. *IEEE Transactions on Image Processing*, *21*(12), 4695–4708.

[16] Chow, L. S., & Rajagopal, H. (2017). Modified-BRISQUE as no reference image quality assessment for structural MR images. *Magnetic Resonance Imaging*, *43*, 74–87.

[17] Li, J., Yu, J., Xu, L., Xue, X., Chang, C.-C., Mao, X., & Hu, J. (2018). A cascaded algorithm for image quality assessment and image denoising based on CNN for image security and authorization. *Security and Communication Networks*, *2018*(2), 1–13.

[18] Moorthy, A. K., & Bovik, A. C. (2011). Blind image quality assessment: From natural scene statistics to perceptual quality. *IEEE Transactions on Image Processing*, *20*(12), 3350–3364.

[19] Ye, P., Kumar, J., Kang, L., & Doermann, D. (2012, June). Unsupervised feature learning framework for no-reference image quality assessment. In *2012 IEEE conference on computer vision and pattern recognition* (pp. 1098–1105). IEEE.

[20] Saad, M. A., Bovik, A. C., & Charrier, C. (2010). A DCT statistics-based blind image quality index. *IEEE Signal Processing Letters*, *17*(6), 583–586.

[21] Mittal, A., Soundararajan, R., & Bovik, A. C. (2013). Making a "completely blind" image quality analyzer. *IEEE Signal Processing Letters*, *20*(3), 209–212.

[22] Xue, W., Mou, X., Zhang, L., Bovik, A. C., & Feng, X. (2014). Blind image quality assessment using joint statistics of gradient magnitude and Laplacian features. *IEEE Transactions on Image Processing, 23*(11), 4850–4862.

[23] Liu, L., Dong, H., Huang, H., & Bovik, A. C. (2014). No-reference image quality assessment in curvelet domain. *Signal Processing: Image Communication, 29*(4), 494–505.

[24] Hou, W., Gao, X., Tao, D., & Li, X. (2014). Blind image quality assessment via deep learning. *IEEE Transactions on Neural Networks and Learning Systems, 26*(6), 1275–1286.

[25] Kang, L., Ye, P., Li, Y., & Doermann, D. (2014). Convolutional neural networks for no-reference image quality assessment. In *Proceedings of the IEEE Conference on Computer Vision and Pattern Recognition* (pp. 1733–1740).

[26] Kang, L., Ye, P., Li, Y., & Doermann, D. (2015, September). Simultaneous estimation of image quality and distortion via multi-task convolutional neural networks. In *2015 IEEE International Conference on Image Processing (ICIP)* (pp. 2791–2795). IEEE.

[27] Venkatanath, N., Praneeth, D., Bh, M. C., Channappayya, S. S., & Medasani, S. S. (2015, February). Blind image quality evaluation using perception based features. In *2015 Twenty First National Conference on Communications (NCC)* (pp. 1–6). IEEE.

[28] Kim, J., & Lee, S. (2016). Fully deep blind image quality predictor. *IEEE Journal of Selected Topics in Signal Processing, 11*(1), 206–220.

[29] Fan, C., Zhang, Y., Feng, L., & Jiang, Q. (2018). No reference image quality assessment based on multi-expert convolutional neural networks. *IEEE Access, 6*, 8934–8943.

[30] Bosse, S., Maniry, D., Müller, K.-R., Wiegand, T., & Samek, W. (2017). Deep neural networks for no-reference and full-reference image quality assessment. *IEEE Transactions on Image Processing, 27*(1), 206–219.

[31] Ma, K., Liu, W., Zhang, K., Duanmu, Z., Wang, Z., & Zuo, W. (2017). End-to-end blind image quality assessment using deep neural networks. *IEEE Transactions on Image Processing, 27*(3), 1202–1213.

[32] Rezaie, F., Helfroush, M. S., & Danyali, H. (2018). No-reference image quality assessment using local binary pattern in the wavelet domain. *Multimedia Tools and Applications, 77*, 2529–2541.

[33] Yue, G., Hou, C., Zhou, T., & Zhang, X. (2018). Effective and efficient blind quality evaluator for contrast distorted images. *IEEE Transactions on Instrumentation and Measurement, 68*(8), 2733–2741.

[34] Yan, Q., Gong, D., & Zhang, Y. (2018). Two-stream convolutional networks for blind image quality assessment. *IEEE Transactions on Image Processing, 28*(5), 2200–2211.

[35] Gonzalez, R. C. (2009). *Digital image processing*. Pearson Education India.

[36] Sahu, S., Singh, H. V., Kumar, B., & Singh, A. K. (2020). A Bayesian multi-resolution approach for noise removal in medical magnetic resonance images. *Journal of Intelligent Systems, 29*(1), 189–201.

[37] Bhuiyan, M. I. H., Ahmad, M. O., and Swamy, M. N. S., Wavelet based image denoising with the normal inverse Gaussian prior and linear MMSE estimator. *IET Image Processing, 2*(4), 203–217, 2008.

[38] S. Mallat, A theory for multiresolution signal decomposition: the wavelet representation. *IEEE Transactions on Pattern Analysis and Machine Intelligence* 11 (1989), 674–693.

[39] Cherkassky, V., & Ma, Y. (2004). Practical selection of SVM parameters and noise estimation for SVM regression. *Neural Networks*, 17(1), 113–126.

[40] Hutchins, B. I., Baker, K. L., Davis, M. T., Diwersy, M. A., Haque, E., Harriman, R. M., ... & Santangelo, G. M. (2019). The NIH open citation collection: A public access, broad coverage resource. *PLoS Biology*, 17(10), e3000385.

[41] Wang, L. (2021). A survey on IQA. arXiv preprint arXiv:2109.00347.

Chapter 12

Do digital images tell the truth?

A. Bruno
IULM Libera Università di Lingue e Comunicazione, Milan, Italy

P. Oza
Institute of Technology, Nirma University, Ahmedabad, India

F. Adedoyin
Bournemouth University, Poole, UK

M. Tliba, M.A. Kerkouri, A. Sekhri and A. Chetouani
Orleans University, Orleans, France

M. Gao
Shandong University of Technology, Shandong, China

12.1 INTRODUCTION

The advent of digital cameras brought many advantages in terms of the number of images and videos users can take due to the digital nature of the information stored in electronic devices. On top of that, digital cameras are embedded into smartphones, making photo-shooting an easy task. Understandably, many digital photos are now available online and on social media. Along with digital cameras, several image-editing tools were brought into the market. User-friendly interfaces and easy-to-use functions allow users to change image contents effortlessly [1, 2]. To quote *Star Wars*: "Twisted by the dark side, young Skywalker has become. The boy you trained, gone he is... Consumed by Darth Vader." Powerful tools may twist the proper side of a story, which is in an image and intertwine it with unauthentic contents.

Image tampering can significantly affect the trustworthiness of a digital image. When an image has been tampered with, it can no longer accurately represent the original scene or event. This can have severe consequences in a wide range of fields, such as law enforcement, journalism, and scientific research, where the integrity of an image is critical. Tampering can be used to hide or alter objects or information within the image, which can disseminate false or misleading information. This can sometimes lead to severe consequences, such as disseminating false information in news media or misidentifying suspects in criminal investigations [3].

DOI: 10.1201/9781003468974-12

247

In addition, tampered images can negatively impact the credibility and trustworthiness of the person or organization that created or distributed the image. This can lead to lost credibility and mistrust in their work, which can have long-term consequences in many fields.

Detecting image tampering is critical to maintaining the trustworthiness of digital images. Image forensics is a digital image processing field aiming to uncover any tampering or manipulation that may have occurred to an image [4]. Copy-move forgery (CMF) is one of the most common image-tampering techniques [5], where a portion of an image is copied and pasted elsewhere within the same image. This can be used to hide or alter objects within the image and can be difficult to detect without specialized techniques. Image alterations like CMF may change the semantic meaning of a given picture, undermining the reliability of digital images as proof. Other image tampering types, such as splicing and cloning, need to be mentioned, with the former being used to create a new image by combining two or more pictures [6]. Cloning is a process in which a portion of an image is copied and pasted elsewhere within the same image, but unlike copy-move forgery, it is used to hide or change the image's original content [7]. In Figure 12.1,

a)   b)

c)   d)

Figure 12.1 Some examples from the Copy-Move Forgery Dataset [8] are shown above; a) A portion of the image is copied and translated; b) the copy-moved region is graphically depicted with a binary mask; c) a region is copied, down-scaled, rotated, and pasted into another image area; d) the copy move forgery is shown in the binary mask.

two examples of copy-move forgery are given. Geometric transformations—such as translation, scaling, and rotation—allow moving the copied region somewhere else in the image. Some copy-move forgeries are easy to catch at first sight due to some artefacts that make them stand out from the image itself. Conversely, some more accurate copy fits the pasted region by not leaving any visible traces.

Copy-move forgery detection (CMFD) algorithms analyze the image for duplicated regions, which can then be flagged as potentially tampered areas. These algorithms often use feature extraction and pattern-matching techniques to identify duplicated regions. They can also be used with other image forensics techniques, such as error level analysis or digital watermarking, to increase the accuracy of forgery detection [9, 10].

CMFD methods aim to identify candidate duplicated regions in an image. This is typically done by analyzing the image at a pixel level and comparing the various regions.

Several techniques are commonly used in copy-move forgery detection. One of the most common sees the image getting divided into smaller regions or segments, which are compared using pixel-level feature descriptors (such as statistical moments, texture descriptors, contrast, and color). These features are then used in the next step, pattern matching. This is done by comparing the features of one segment to those of all the other segments in the image to identify any duplicated regions.

Even though image forensics is an active area of research, with new techniques and methods being developed to detect image forgery, no single technique or method can guarantee 100% detection of all forms of image forgery.

The main contribution of this chapter is to survey several CMFD methods spanning low-level image processing techniques through the most recent deep learning approaches. Since the topic is not new to the scientific literature, the chapter has been edited by bringing in the historical progress of methods, approaches, image features analysis, and performance assessment over publicly accessible datasets. On top of that, further investigations have been pursued about deep learning being or not being the top-scoring CMFD approach. The remainder of the chapter is organized as follows: Section 12.2 describes related techniques, which are grouped into three main categories (image processing, machine learning, and deep learning); Section 12.3 introduces some publicly available datasets for CMFD methods; Section 12.4 discusses the accuracy rates achieved by the SOTA (state-of-the-art) methods; Section 12.5 draws a line accounting for conclusions and future challenges in the topic.

12.2 RELATED TECHNIQUES

This section surveys the SOTA methods in CMFD spanning low-level image processing techniques, machine learning, and the most recent deep learning approaches.

12.2.1 Low-level image processing techniques

The first proposed approaches to countermeasure CMF were based on low-level image features. This subsection overviews some of the most popular techniques belonging to this category.

In 2003, Fridrich [11] proposed a block-based approach dividing the image into overlapping blocks. The latter undergo discrete cosine transformation (DCT) to be used as descriptors. Each block is then characterized by features that are then lexicographically arranged. Similarities between blocks are computed by comparing their description.

Another study by Zhao et al. [12] relies on overlapping blocks analysis. In particular, 2D-DCT is applied to the image blocks; the DCT coefficients are then quantized. Each block is divided into non-overlapping sub-blocks upon which SVD (Singular Value Decomposition) is applied. Last, the largest singular value out of each block is extracted to reduce the size of each block description.

Besides the previously mentioned methods, Lynch's approach [13] runs direct block comparisons rather than using block features. The first step has a given image divided into N small overlapping blocks with a sliding block approach. A dominant feature is computed for each block to avoid the bottleneck of way too many blocks to be compared.

The scientific literature counts several methods for CMFD that rely on local keypoint descriptors, such as SIFT, SURF, and BRISK [14].

Zhu et al. [15] presented a technique by introducing a Gaussian scale space, extracting the FAST keypoints and the ORB features in each scale space. The orientated FAST coordinates are projected onto the original image for a match analysis of the ORB features between every two different keypoints. Further refinement involves removing the false-matched keypoints with the RANSAC (Random Sample Consensus) algorithm [16].

By pairing SIFT descriptors with SVD (Single Value Decomposition), Chihauoi et al. [17] delved into the attempt to improve a SIFT-based copy-move detection by reducing the dimensionality of the corresponding descriptor.

Yeaps et al.'s approach [18] stands along the lines of SIFT-based methods. The authors tested the robustness of rotated BRIEF descriptors plus oriented FAST. Two Nearest Neighbor with Hierarchical Agglomerative Clustering were adopted for feature matching.

In a study by Wang et al. [19], the authors proposed a method using local keypoints and the SURF descriptor. A given image is segmented into non-overlapping and nearly uniform superpixel blocks. Local keypoints are extracted from each superpixel and are characterized with the superpixel contents and color invariance SIFER. Connected Delaunay triangles are drawn using the extracted image keypoints. Local image feature for each Delaunay triangle is computed by using FQRHFMs and gradient entropy.

Ardizzonet et al. [8] proposed a SIFT-based method for copy-move forgery detection. The method involved detecting local keypoints in the image using the SIFT (Scale Invariant Feature Transform) algorithm and computing SIFT descriptors for each keypoint. Delaunay triangulation, geometric features, and colors are considered to compare similar regions within the image.

In Khan et al.'s technique [20] DWT (Discrete Wavelet Transform) is applied to the input image resulting in a compressed representation. The compressed image is divided into overlapping blocks that are sorted. Phase Correlation is used as a similarity criterion to identify duplicated blocks.

Bi et al. [21] introduced a Multi-Level Dense Descriptor (MLDD) for feature extraction and a Hierarchical Feature Matching method. The employment of MLDD allows extracting dense feature descriptors consisting of a color texture descriptor and an invariant moment descriptor.

Davarzani et al. [22] employed MLBP (Multiresolution Local Binary Patterns) for copy-move forgery detection. The method proved robust against geometric distortions and illumination variations of duplicated regions.

Several low-level image features and descriptors were tested by Ardizzone et al. [23]: Statistical moments (mean, standard deviation, skewness, and kurtosis) of the pixels' gray values; Edge Histogram (filter blocks with four directional and non-directional Roberts-like operators); Tamura descriptors (Contrast, Coarseness, and Directionality properties from the Tamura set of features); Gabor descriptors (a bank of Gabor filters is applied to blocks); and Haralick descriptors (based on statistical moments and obtained from the co-occurrence matrix).

Noticeably, many methods based on low-level image features rely on the steps depicted in Figure 12.2: image decomposition into overlapped or partially overlapped blocks; feature extraction from each block; feature processing; feature matching; detection of candidate tampered patches.

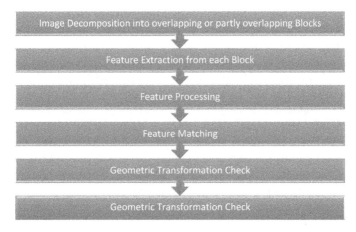

Figure 12.2 Some common steps involved in many methods for CMFD based on low-level image features.

12.2.2 Machine learning approaches

While the previous section is devoted to purely low-level image-processing techniques, this section approaches CMFD by surveying Machine Learning methods. For clarity's sake, Machine Learning here refers to AI approaches that do not rely on deep neural networks, which will be tackled in the Deep Learning subsection. The current subsection is further divided into two paragraphs focused on machine learning methods reliant on clustering and local descriptors.

12.2.2.1 Local descriptor-based techniques

Hussain et al. [24] utilized multiresolution Weber law descriptors as feature extractors and then trained support vector machine (SVM) to detect copy-move forgery. The approach could achieve about 91% detection accuracy. A similar approach by Muhammad et al. [25] relies on SVM to classify forged and original images. The authors used steerable pyramid transform to obtain multiscale and multi-oriented subbands. Then, a feature vector is generated by concatenating the histogram of sub-bands. Finally, SVM is used for image classification. Daniya et al. [26] proposed a method for copy-move forgery detection in videos using machine learning algorithms. In particular, they employed the statistical feature of noise remnant to detect forgeries in digital videos. The authors analyzed the temporal correlation of block-level noise remnants to find tampered sections in the video. Machine learning algorithms are then used for the classification process. Ferreira et al. [27] posed the issue in a multiscale behavior knowledge space. They combined the many aspects of copy-move detection techniques. First, using different scales on the training data, the process can encode the outcome combinations of various methods as prior probabilities. Then, generative models applied to the training data are used to predict the conditional probability of missing items accurately. Eventually, they provide several methods that use the data's multi-directionality to produce the final result detection map in a machine-learning decision-making manner. Experimental findings on complicated datasets demonstrate the proposed method's efficacy and applicability, which compare the proposed techniques with various copy-move detection approaches and other fusion strategies in the literature. Another work [28] proposed a two-step forgery detection system. The suggested method divides the suspect image into an authentic or counterfeit image in step one. Then, the optional second phase is used to identify the forged regions in the picture suspected of being fake. Performance of the suggested technique is evaluated using CoMoFoD [29] and CASIA [30] Datasets. The performance of the suggested approach demonstrates resilience even when post-processing assaults such as JPEG compression, scaling, and rotation are applied to the forged picture.

12.2.2.2 Clustering

A practical, efficient, and automatic copy-move forgery detection system based on a hybrid transform and a K-means clustering algorithm is described by the authors of [31]. This method operates without the need for prior information about the image. Initially, the picture dimensions are reduced using Discrete Wavelet Transform (DWT), then the feature vector elements' range is constrained using Discrete Cosine Transform (DCT). Finally, rapid k-means clustering is employed to cut down on calculation time. In addition, the FKM clustering algorithm helps avoid needless distance calculation by using trio inequality. The results make it evident that the provided algorithm overcomes other current and pertinent techniques in terms of both detection time and accuracy. In [32], the authors presented a matching technique to speed up detection and improve detection precision. This improvement is accomplished by grouping picture blocks into clusters and looking for identical blocks inside each cluster instead of looking for them all. The picture blocks are first clustered using k-means clustering, and then the blocks are matched using the Locality Sensitive Hashing (LSH) approach based on Zernike moments. According to the experimental findings, the processing time was cut by 10% while improving the detection accuracy. The study [33] presented a learning approach for forgery detection. The initial phase is image segmentation, where each block's histogram of angled slopes is functional, followed by feature extraction, which is concentrated to enable the dimension of similarity. Support vector machines are used to do the detection. The findings demonstrate that the proposed technique is efficient enough to recognize various examples of copy-move forgeries and be able to spot duplicate areas. Prewitt Filter with Generalized Action Selection (PFGAS) based Hybrid Artificial Bee Colony African Buffalo Optimization (HABC-ABO) technique was developed in the study [34] to detect tampered regions and identify forgeries. The CoMoFoD database with five distinct types of forged images was utilized in this work. The method would detect forgeries in digital photographs, even if they underwent resizing or rotation. According to experimental analysis, the suggested ECMFD technique performs better in Precision, F1-measure, and Recall. As a result, the proposed methodology has a higher detection accuracy of 99.82% than the other cutting-edge methods. An improved copy-move forgery detection pipeline using the k-means clustering approach for a better matching technique is developed by authors of [35]. The matching phase was individually performed within each cluster to group the overlapping blocks using k-means clustering, which sped up the matching procedure. Moreover, the feature vector clustering stage enabled the matching algorithm to identify the matches precisely. Therefore, Zernike moments and locality-sensitive hashing (LSH) were included to test the upgraded pipeline. The outcomes of the experiments show how significantly the suggested strategy can improve detection accuracy. Moreover, the proposed pipeline's LSH-based matching can shorten processing time. Chen et al. [36] worked on integrating clustering and SIFT keypoints by searching similar neighborhoods to locate tampered regions. As observed in the scientific literature, most machine-learning approaches rely on the steps depicted in Figure 12.2.

12.2.3 Deep learning approaches

Deep learning (DL) is a broad family of machine learning techniques relying on deep neural networks (DNN), which comprise multiple processing layers. The stack of the processing layers aims to extract progressively higher-level features from input data. Deep learning models performed well in almost all domains due to their generalization capabilities and automatic feature selection properties. Convolutional neural network (CNN) is one of the most successful networks of DL. Over time, CNNs have significantly improved due to new experiments, concepts, and the availability of processing and computational power. That has led to an increase in the number of CNN models and networks that are employed in the literature, such as VGG [37], ResNet [38], Efficientnet [39], etc. This section presents various DL-based methods for copy-move forgery detection. Krishnaraj et al. [40] developed a fusion model for copy-move forgery detection and localization. In particular, they fused GAN (Generative Adversarial Network) and DenseNet. An extreme learning classifier then ingests the outcomes. The authors performed parameter tuning of the model utilizing the Fish Swarm algorithm. Mallick et al. [41] developed a CNN-based method for copy-move and splicing forgery detection. First, the authors converted the input images to error-level analysis. Then, the feature extraction method relies on VGG (16 and 19) models and uses these pre-processed pictures. The pictures are finally classified using softmax with root mean squared propagation optimization. In another work [42], Chen et al. developed a DL detection and localization model. The authors connected two networks: a serial network with a copy-move similarity detection network and a source/target region distinguishment network. The first model was utilized to detect similar regions in the image, with the second distinguishing the tampered portions from the images out of the first model. A team of researchers proposed a two-stage copy-move forgery detection method in [43]: first, a self-deep matching network is designed as a backbone utilizing convolution integration, skip matching, and spatial attention methods. The backbone network generates a score map of suspected forged regions in the image. Spatial attention is used on self-correlation to strengthen the capacity to identify regions with similar appearances. The model is proposed to fix incomplete and eliminate false areas. Hosny et al. [44] presented an approach for copy-move forgery detection using a customized CNN model consisting of three convolutional layers and two max pooling layers for feature extraction. Fully connected layers are used to classify images as authentic or forged. Wu et al. [45] proposed an end-to-end DL model to predict the forgery mask. First, the authors used CNN to extract features and compute self-correlations between blocks. Then, they located matching points using a pointwise feature extractor. Finally, a forgery mask is reconstructed using a deconvolutional network. The authors concluded that the proposed method outperformed existing approaches dependent on several characteristics and matching algorithms for forgery detection. Furthermore, the proposed model is supposed to be robust against several known assaults, such as affine transformation, JPEG compression, and blurring. Muzaffer et al. [46] developed a DL-based framework for detecting and localizing copy-move forgeries. The method used AlexNet pre-trained model to obtain image sub-blocks features. After the matching process, they eliminated false matches. The method's pixel level F-measure (0,93) makes the technique stand out from other similar methods.

Another work [47] presented a two-stage DL approach to learning features to detect tampered images in different image formats. During the first stage, they used a stacked auto-encoder model to learn the complex feature of each image patch. In the second stage, the authors integrated the contextual information of each patch. The model could achieve an overall tampered region localization accuracy of 91.09% over both JPEG and TIFF images from the CASIA dataset. Elaskily et al. [48] developed a hybrid network comprising ConvLSTM and CNN for copy-move forgery detection. The main objective of the research was to classify an image into two classes: original and tempered. The experimental results revealed that 100 training epochs produced the best accuracy. For the databases MICC-F220 [49], MICC-F2000 [49], MICC-F600 [50], and combined databases, the accuracy is 100%, 98.89%, 98.14%, and 97.13%, respectively. One more work [51] used the DL-based method to distinguish between genuine and fake images. The dual-branch convolutional neural network retrieves multiscale information using various kernel sizes in each branch. A satisfactory accuracy, precision, and recall score are obtained using the extracted multiscale features. On the MICC F-2000 dataset, experiment analysis has been carried out using two alternative kernel size combinations. This method has resulted in 94% F1-score and 96% accuracy. Another study [52] investigated copy-move forgery detection utilizing a fusion processing model that included deep convolutional and adversarial models. The model was trained and tested on four datasets. The findings showed that the discriminator forgery detector and deep learning CNN presented high detection accuracy (95%). Rodriguez-Ortega et al. [53] developed two DL-based methods for the said task: a customized model and a model based on transfer learning. The effects of the network's depth are examined in each scenario using various performance indicators such as precision, recall, and F1 score. Additionally, images from eight different free-access datasets are used to address the generalization issue. Finally, evaluation measures, training and inference timeframes, and model performance are compared. The metrics achieved by the VGG-16 model by transfer learning are around 10% higher than those of the model with customized architecture.

12.2.4 Datasets

Several datasets with copy-moved forged images have been presented over the last few years. Some of the most popular datasets are described in this section. CASIA v2.0 [30] is a popular copy-move forgery detection research dataset. The Chinese Academy of Sciences created CASIA v2.0. It consists of 1050 images with copy-move forgeries. The dataset is divided into three subsets, each with different transformations.

The first subset, "CASIA v2.0 Subset 1," contains 435 images with simple copy-move forgeries. These forgeries involve copying a small patch of an image and pasting it onto another area of the same image. This subset tests the basic capabilities of copy-move forgery detection algorithms.

The second subset, "CASIA v2.0 Subset 2," contains 300 images with more complex copy-move forgeries. These forgeries involve rotating, scaling, or flipping the copied patch before pasting it onto another area of the same image. This subset is designed to test the robustness of copy-move forgery detection algorithms. The third subset, "CASIA v2.0 Subset 3," contains 315 images with more challenging copy-move forgeries. These forgeries involve copying a patch from one image and pasting it onto another. This subset allows testing the generalization ability of copy-move forgery detection algorithms. The images in CASIA v2.0 are in JPEG format with a resolution of 512×512 pixels. The dataset also includes ground-truth annotations specifying each image forgery location and type. Researchers can evaluate the performance of their copy-move forgery detection algorithms using objective metrics such as precision, recall, and F1 score.

CoMoFoD dataset [29] consists of 260 forged images grouped into two categories: small (512×512 pixels) and large (3000×2000 pixels). Furthermore, images are also stored according to the manipulation type: translation, rotation, scaling, combination, and distortion. Besides manipulations, different post-processing methods are run over the images: JPEG compression, blurring, noise adding, and color reduction. The forgeries are visually similar to the original images, and the tampering artefacts are not easily noticeable. This dataset is suitable for developing and evaluating copy-move forgery detection algorithms that detect visually similar forgeries.

COVERAGE [54] contains copy-move forged (CMFD) images and their originals with similar but genuine objects (SGOs). COVERAGE is designed to highlight and address tamper detection ambiguity of popular methods caused by self-similarity within natural images. In COVERAGE, forged-original pairs are annotated with (i) the duplicated and forged region masks and (ii) the tampering factor/similarity metric. For benchmarking, forgery quality is evaluated using (i) computer vision-based methods and (ii) human detection performance.

Copy Move Forgery Dataset [8]: It consists of medium-sized images (almost the entirety of them have dimensions 1000×700 or 700×1000 pixels), and it is subdivided into several groups (D0, D1, D2). D0 includes 50 not compressed images with copy moves relying on translation. D1 and D2 account for 20 non-compressed images depicting simple scenes (i.e., one object and a simple background) rather than complex scenes. The authors were primarily interested in studying the robustness against some specific attacks. Indeed, several images were altered using scaling, translation, rotation, and a mixed combination of the three to check on the CMFD methods' robustness. It should be noted that CMFD accounts for a wide range of attacks: 1) 50-degree rotations centered around zero degrees with steps of 5°; 30-degree rotations around 12 different angles in the full 360° range; 1-degree rotation around 11 different angles in $[-5°, 5°]$ range. Scaling factors also feature CMFD in the range $[0.25, 2]$. MICC Dataset [49]: Amerini et al. presented MICC in 2011. The dataset includes several subsets accounting for different image forgeries. MICC-F220 consists of 220 images equally grouped into original and forged categories. MICC-F2000 is composed of 700 tampered and 1300 original pictures. MICC-F8multi includes 8 tampered images with realistic multiple cloning. MICC-F600 is a collection of 440 original images, 160 tampered images, and 160 ground-truth images. Concerning MICC, it should be noted that the authors of MICC ran the following tampering transformations: rotations in the range $[0°, 90°]$ and scaling in the range $[0.5, 1.6]$.

12.2.5 Research challenges

This section overviews research questions and challenges involved in CMFD. The scientific literature features CMFD techniques accounting for diverse approaches, spanning low-level image properties through deep learning methods. Although recent progress in artificial intelligence highlights outstanding performances achieved by deep learning methods in CMFD, it is worth dissecting the results and the tampering transformations to analyze performances according to the following questions: Does DL address CMFD better than all other approaches as a whole? Are performances consistent over diverse datasets? Are there features or methodologies proving more robust against specific tampering transformations? Two publicly and highly cited datasets (MICC and CMFD) are employed to run comparisons to answer the research questions above.

12.3 DISCUSSION

It has been some time since the first papers on image forensics were presented. Here, some discussions about the methods' effectiveness are drawn. This section offers a specific case study by comparing some methods belonging to the three approaches. F1 scores for some state-of-the-art methods are compared over the datasets: CMFD and MICC (F2000, F220, F600). The F1-score (equation 1) is a meaningful metric for precision and recall. It is widely employed in evaluating methods' performances in the scientific literature. F1-score, Precision, and Recall are defined below in equations 12.2–12.3. Noticeably, F_1, Precision, and Recall refer to TP (True Positive), FP (False Positive), and FN (False Negative). Zooming in on the comparison methods, a deep learning method based on VGG-16 [53], a machine learning combining clustering and SIFT keypoint [36], a feature point-based technique [55], and a hand-crafted hybrid method [56] are compared using the F_1 score (see equation below). For clarity's sake, it should be noted that Chen et al. [36] method is referred to as 'Keypoint-based method'; Rodriguez et al.'s [53] as 'VGG-16 based method'; Yu et al.'s [55] as 'Hand-crafted feature point'; and Tinnathi et al.'s [56] is referred to as 'Hand-crafted hybrid method.' As shown in Figure 12.3, Keypoint-based method overcomes the VGG-16-based method [53] on the CMFD dataset. Conversely, the same deep learning approach outperforms two other state-of-the-art methods on the MICC dataset by at least 4% in the F1 score (see Figure 12.3). The effectiveness of the keypoints' descriptors is assessed through the comparison in Figure 12.5. Although both methods perform well on the CMFD dataset, keypoint descriptors plus clustering outperforms a deep learning approach. One of the possible reasons resides within the CMFD dataset, which pushes the bar of image alterations using combinations of scaling, translation, and rotation. With SIFT keypoints invariant

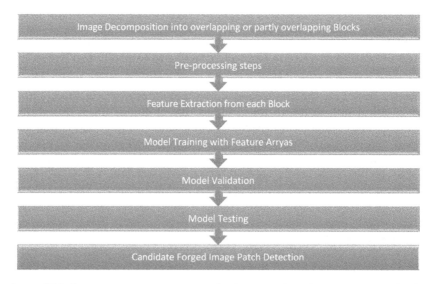

Figure 12.3 Some common steps involved in machine-learning methods for CMFD.

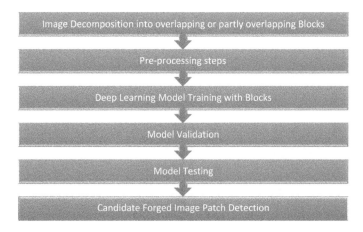

Figure 12.4 Some common steps involved in Deep Learning for CMFD.

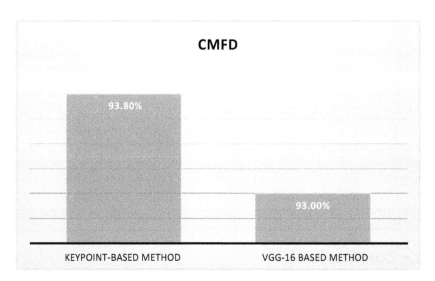

Figure 12.5 F1-score over the CMFD dataset for two state-of-the-art methods is depicted above.

to scale factors, the 'Keypoint-Based method' might have a higher catch on tampering detection.

$$F_1 = 2 \times \frac{\text{Precision} \times \text{Recall}}{\text{Precision} + \text{Recall}} = \frac{\text{TP}}{\text{TP} + \frac{1}{2}(\text{FP} + \text{FN})} \qquad (12.1)$$

$$\text{Precision} = \frac{\text{TP}}{\text{TP} + \text{FP}} \qquad (12.2)$$

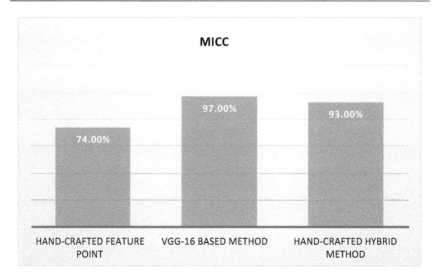

Figure 12.6 F1-score over the MICC dataset for three state-of-the-art methods is depicted in the diagram above.

$$\text{Recall} = \frac{\text{TP}}{\text{TP} + \text{FN}} \qquad (12.3)$$

At the same time, VGG-16-based Method proved more robust against image tampering in MICC when compared to 'Hand-Crafted Feature Point' and 'Hand-Crafted Hybrid Method.' MICC accounts for a larger number of images than CMFD. That could explain why 'VGG-16-based Method' overcomes the comparison methods. It might have inferred enough knowledge from original and forged images and thus be more suitable for the final goal.

12.4 CONCLUSION

The primary purpose of this chapter is to let readers approach copy-move forgery detection with a bottom-up strategy. Readers are first given an introductory section with background and context on the topic. Section 12.2 provides insights into the most common methods for CMFD: low-level image feature-based, machine learning, and deep learning methods. Each approach is characterized by different steps, as depicted in Figures 12.1–12.3. Noticeably, the deep learning pipeline does not include image feature extraction, as it is embedded within the convolutional layers. Section 12.3 outlines high-level and technical considerations about the methods' performances on publicly available datasets, such as MICC and CMFD, described in Section 12.2.4. Research questions are introduced in Section 2.5 to highlight the current challenges in the field and prompt readers to key factors concerning artificial intelligence-based methods and image processing techniques. In particular, a comparison between SOTA approaches is carried out by looking into F1-score and two publicly available datasets, such as MICC and CMFD (as in Figures 12.4 and 12.5). As can be noticed in Section 12.4, discussions and considerations have been drawn on the employment of diverse approaches consisting of different pipelines. For instance, low-level image feature methods can perform well, especially if they rely on robust descriptors such as SIFT and SURF (Figure 12.5) and when tampering transformations go beyond a certain scaling or rotating factor (as in the CMFD dataset). On the other hand, deep learning approaches reportedly outperform hand-crafted features and machine learning techniques over MICC. As well as in CMFD, the MICC dataset houses scaling, translation, and rotation in their forged images, except for geometrical transformation values being lower than in CMFD. The experimental results from the three SOTA methods suggest that keypoint descriptors might outperform some deep learning methods if tampered regions undergo scaling or rotation beyond certain threshold values.

REFERENCES

[1] Liad Kaufman, Dani Lischinski, and Michael Werman. Content-aware automatic photo enhancement. In *Computer Graphics Forum*, volume 31, pages 2528–2540. Wiley Online Library, 2012.

[2] Aparna Bharati, Mayank Vatsa, Richa Singh, Kevin W Bowyer, and Xin Tong. Demography-based facial retouching detection using subclass supervised sparse autoencoder. In *2017 IEEE International Joint Conference on Biometrics (IJCB)*, pages 474–482, 2017.

[3] Arfa Binti Zainal Abidin, Hairudin Bin Abdul Majid, Azurah Binti A Samah, and Haslina Binti Hashim. Copy-move image forgery detection using deep learning methods: a review. In *2019 6th International Conference on Research and Innovation in Information Systems (ICRIIS)*, pages 1–6. IEEE, 2019.

[4] Surbhi Gupta, Neeraj Mohan, and Priyanka Kaushal. Passive image forensics using universal techniques: A review. *Artificial Intelligence Review*, 55:1629–1679, 2022.

[5] Nor Bakiah Abd Warif, Mohd Yamani Idna Idris, Ainuddin Wahid Abdul Wahab, Nor-Syahidatul N Ismail, and Rosli Salleh. A comprehensive evaluation procedure for copy-move forgery detection methods: Results from a systematic review. *Multimedia Tools and Applications*, 81(11):15171–15203, 2022.

[6] Ruyong Ren, Shaozhang Niu, Junfeng Jin, Jiwei Zhang, Hua Ren, and Xiaojie Zhao. Multi-scale attention context-aware network for detection and localization of image splicing. *Applied Intelligence*, 53: 1–20, 2023.

[7] Amit Doegar, Maitreyee Dutta, and Gaurav Kumar. A review of passive image cloning detection approaches. In *Proceedings of 2nd International Conference on Communication, Computing and Networking: ICCCN 2018*, NITTTR Chandigarh, India, pages 469–478. Springer, 2019.

 [8] Edoardo Ardizzone, Alessandro Bruno, and Giuseppe Mazzola. Copy-move forgery detection by matching triangles of keypoints. *IEEE Transactions on Information Forensics and Security*, 10(10):2084–2094, 2015.

 [9] Nor Bakiah Abd Warif, Mohd Yamani Idna Idris, Ainuddin Wahid Abdul Wahab, and Rosli Salleh. An evaluation of error level analysis in image forensics. In *2015 5th IEEE International Conference on System Engineering and Technology (ICSET)*, pages 23–28. IEEE, 2015.

[10] Sanjay Kumar and Binod Kumar Singh. A review on digital watermarking-based image forensic technique. *Machine Vision and Augmented Intelligence—Theory and Applications: Select Proceedings of MAI 2021*, pages 91–100, 2021.

[11] Jessica Fridrich. Detection of copy-move forgery in digital images. In *Proc. Digital Forensic Research Workshop, 2003*, 2003.

[12] Jie Zhao and Jichang Guo. Passive forensics for copy-move image forgery using a method based on DCT and SVD. *Forensic Science International*, 233(1–3):158–166, 2013.

[13] Gavin Lynch, Frank Y Shih, and Hong-Yuan Mark Liao. An efficient expanding block algorithm for image copy-move forgery detection. *Information Sciences*, 239:253–265, 2013.

[14] Baheesa Fatima, Abdul Ghafoor, Syed Sohaib Ali, and M Mohsin Riaz. Fast, brief and sift based image copy-move forgery detection technique. *Multimedia Tools and Applications*, 81(30):43805–43819, 2022.

[15] Ye Zhu, Xuanjing Shen, and Haipeng Chen. Copy-move forgery detection based on scaled orb. *Multimedia Tools and Applications*, 75:3221–3233, 2016.

[16] Martin A Fischler and Robert C Bolles. Random sample consensus: A paradigm for model fitting with applications to image analysis and automated cartography. *Communications of the ACM*, 24(6):381–395, 1981.

[17] Takwa Chihaoui, Sami Bourouis, and Kamel Hamrouni. Copy-move image forgery detection based on sift descriptors and SVD-matching. In *2014 1st International Conference on Advanced Technologies for Signal and Image Processing (ATSIP)*, pages 125–129, 2014.

[18] Yong Yew Yeap, UU Sheikh, and Ab Al-Hadi Ab Rahman. Image forensic for digital image copy move forgery detection. In *2018 IEEE 14th International Colloquium on Signal Processing & Its Applications (CSPA)*, pages 239–244, 2018.

[19] Xiang-Yang Wang, Li-Xian Jiao, Xue-Bing Wang, Hong-Ying Yang, and Pan-Pan Niu. Copy-move forgery detection based on compact color content descriptor and Delaunay triangle matching. *Multimedia Tools and Applications*, 78:2311–2344, 2019.

[20] Saiqa Khan and Arun Kulkarni. An efficient method for detection of copy-move forgery using discrete wavelet transform. *International Journal on Computer Science and Engineering*, 2(5):2010, 1801.

[21] Xiuli Bi, Chi-Man Pun, and Xiao-Chen Yuan. Multi-level dense descriptor and hierarchical feature matching for copy-move forgery detection. *Information Sciences*, 345:226–242, 2016.

[22] Reza Davarzani, Khashayar Yaghmaie, Saeed Mozaffari, and Meysam Tapak. Copy-move forgery detection using multiresolution local binary patterns. *Forensic Science International*, 231(1–3):61–72, 2013.

[23] Edoardo Ardizzone, Alessandro Bruno, and Giuseppe Mazzola. Copy-move forgery detection via texture description. In *Proceedings of the 2nd ACM workshop on Multimedia in Forensics, Security and Intelligence*, pages 59–64, 2010.

[24] Muhammad Hussain, Ghulam Muhammad, Sahar Q Saleh, Anwar M Mirza, and George Bebis. Copy-move image forgery detection using multi-resolution weber descriptors. In *2012 Eighth International Conference on Signal Image Technology and Internet Based Systems*, pages 395–401. IEEE, 2012.

[25] Ghulam Muhammad, Munner H Al-Hammadi, Muhammad Hussain, and George Bebis. Image forgery detection using steerable pyramid transform and local binary pattern. *Machine Vision and Applications*, 25:985–995, 2014.

[26] T Daniya, Srilakshmi Aluri, S Velliangiri, and R Cristin. Copy-move forgery detection in videos using machine learning algorithm. In *2021 2nd International Conference on Smart Electronics and Communication (ICOSEC)*, pages 1502–1506. IEEE, 2021.

[27] Anselmo Ferreira, Siovani C Felipussi, Carlos Alfaro, Pablo Fonseca, John E Vargas-Munoz, Jefersson A Dos Santos, and Anderson Rocha. Behavior knowledge space-based fusion for copy-move forgery detection. *IEEE Transactions on Image Processing*, 25(10):4729–4742, 2016.

[28] SBG Tilak Babu and Ch Srinivasa Rao. An optimized technique for copy-move forgery localization using statistical features. *ICT Express*, 8(2):244–249, 2022.

[29] Dijana Tralic, Ivan Zupancic, Sonja Grgic, and Mislav Grgic. CoMoFoD—new database for copy-move forgery detection. In *Proceedings ELMAR-2013*, pages 49–54. IEEE, 2013.

[30] Jing Dong, Wei Wang, and Tieniu Tan. Casia image tampering detection evaluation database. In *2013 IEEE China Summit and International Conference on Signal and Iinformation Processing*, pages 422–426. IEEE, 2013.

[31] Tawheed Jan Shah et al. Enhanced k-means clustering technique based copy-move image forgery detection. *Turkish Journal of Computer and Mathematics Education (TURCOMAT)*, 12(12):37–47, 2021.

[32] Osamah M Al-Qershi and Bee Ee Khoo. Copy-move forgery detection using on locality sensitive hashing and k-means clustering. In *Information Science and Applications (ICISA) 2016*, pages 663–672. Springer, 2016.

[33] Amrita Parashar, Arvind Kumar Upadhyay, and Kamlesh Gupta. An effectual classification approach to detect copy-move forgery using support vector machines. *Multimedia Tools and Applications*, 78:29413–29429, 2019.

[34] Allu Venkateswara Rao, Chanamallu Srinivasa Rao, and Dharma Raj Cheruku. An enhanced copy-move forgery detection using machine learning based hybrid optimization model. *Multimedia Tools and Applications*, 81(18):25383–25403, 2022.

[35] Osamah M Al-Qershi and Bee Ee Khoo. Enhanced block-based copy-move forgery detection using k-means clustering. *Multidimensional Systems and Signal Processing*, 30:1671–1695, 2019.

[36] Haipeng Chen, Xiwen Yang, and Yingda Lyu. Copy-move forgery detection based on keypoint clustering and similar neighborhood search algorithm. *IEEE Access*, 8:36863–36875, 2020.

[37] Karen Simonyan and Andrew Zisserman. Very deep convolutional networks for large-scale image recognition. arXiv preprint arXiv:1409.1556, 2014.

[38] Kaiming He, Xiangyu Zhang, Shaoqing Ren, and Jian Sun. Deep residual learning for image recognition. In *Proceedings of the IEEE Conference on Computer Vision and Pattern Recognition*, pages 770–778, 2016.

[39] Mingxing Tan and Quoc Le. EfficientNet: Rethinking model scaling for convolutional neural networks. In *International Conference on Machine Learning*, pages 6105–6114. PMLR, 2019.

[40] N Krishnaraj, B Sivakumar, Ramya Kuppusamy, Yuvaraja Teekaraman, and Amruth Ramesh Thelkar. Design of automated deep learning-based fusion model for copy-move image forgery detection. *Computational Intelligence and Neuroscience*, 2022:8501738, 2022.

[41] Devjani Mallick, Mantasha Shaikh, Anuja Gulhane, and Tabassum Maktum. Copy move and splicing image forgery detection using CNN. In *ITM Web of Conferences*, volume 44, page 03052. EDP Sciences, 2022.

[42] Beijing Chen, Weijin Tan, Gouenou Coatrieux, Yuhui Zheng, and Yun-Qing Shi. A serial image copy-move forgery localization scheme with source/target distinguishment. *IEEE Transactions on Multimedia*, 23:3506–3517, 2020.

[43] Yaqi Liu, Chao Xia, Xiaobin Zhu, and Shengwei Xu. Two-stage copy-move forgery detection with self deep matching and proposal superglue. *IEEE Transactions on Image Processing*, 31:541–555, 2021.

[44] Khalid M Hosny, Akram M Mortda, Mostafa M Fouda, and Nabil A Lashin. An efficient CNN model to detect copy-move image forgery. *IEEE Access*, 10:48622–48632, 2022.

[45] Yue Wu, Wael Abd-Almageed, and Prem Natarajan. Image copy-move forgery detection via an end-to-end deep neural network. In *2018 IEEE Winter Conference on Applications of Computer Vision (WACV)*, pages 1907–1915. IEEE, 2018.

[46] Gul Muzaffer and Guzin Ulutas. A new deep learning-based method to detection of copy-move forgery in digital images. In *2019 Scientific Meeting on Electrical-Electronics & Biomedical Engineering and Computer Science (EBBT)*, pages 1–4. IEEE, 2019.

[47] Ying Zhang, Jonathan Goh, Lei Lei Win, and Vrizlynn LL Thing. Image region forgery detection: A deep learning approach. *SG-CRC*, 2016:1–11, 2016.

[48] Mohamed A Elaskily, Monagi H Alkinani, Ahmed Sedik, and Mohamed M Dessouky. Deep learning based algorithm (ConvLSTM) for copy move forgery detection. *Journal of Intelligent & Fuzzy Systems*, 40(3):4385–4405, 2021.

[49] Irene Amerini, Lamberto Ballan, Roberto Caldelli, Alberto Del Bimbo, and Giuseppe Serra. A sift-based forensic method for copy-move attack detection and transformation recovery. *IEEE Transactions on Information Forensics and Security*, 6(3):1099–1110, 2011.

[50] Irene Amerini, Lamberto Ballan, Roberto Caldelli, Alberto Del Bimbo, Luca Del Tongo, and Giuseppe Serra. Copy-move forgery detection and localization by means of robust clustering with J-Linkage. *Signal Processing: Image Communication*, 28(6):659–669, 2013.

[51] Nidhi Goel, Samarjeet Kaur, and Ruchika Bala. Dual branch convolutional neural network for copy move forgery detection. *IET Image Processing*, 15(3):656–665, 2021.

[52] Younis Abdalla, M Tariq Iqbal, and Mohamed Shehata. Copy-move forgery detection and localization using a generative adversarial network and convolutional neural-network. *Information*, 10(9):286, 2019.

[53] Yohanna Rodriguez-Ortega, Dora M Ballesteros, and Diego Renza. Copy-move forgery detection (CMFD) using deep learning for image and video forensics. *Journal of Imaging*, 7(3):59, 2021.

[54] Bihan Wen, Ye Zhu, Ramanathan Subramanian, Tian-Tsong Ng, Xuanjing Shen, and Stefan Winkler. Coverage—a novel database for copy-move forgery detection. In *2016 IEEE International Conference on Image Processing (ICIP)*, pages 161–165, 2016.

[55] Liyang Yu, Qi Han, and Xiamu Niu. Feature point-based copy-move forgery detection: Covering the non-textured areas. *Multimedia Tools and Applications*, 75:1159–1176, 2016.

[56] Sreenivasu Tinnathi and G Sudhavani. An efficient copy move forgery detection using adaptive watershed segmentation with AGSO and hybrid feature extraction. *Journal of Visual Communication and Image Representation*, 74:102966, 2021.

Chapter 13

A multi-layer encryption with AES and Twofish encryption algorithm for smart assistant security

S. Neelakandan
R.M.K. Engineering College, Chennai, India

S. Velmurugan
R.M.D. Engineering College, Chennai, India

M. Prakash
Vellore Institute of Technology, Vellore, India

D. Paulraj
R.M.K. Engineering College, Chennai, India

13.1 INTRODUCTION

According to Cisco, the Internet of Things (IoT) facilitates intelligent data flow between billions of devices in both physical and virtual environments. The endpoint electronics and communications market is anticipated to be valued at $21.3 billion by 2022 [1]. The smartphone, for example, has become a normal piece of technology in people's lives. The corporate and academic worlds, on the other hand, are deeply concerned about the Internet of Things' security [2, 3]. Insider threats [4], which allow attackers to access resources within an organization or network, are one of the most challenging difficulties for IoT applications. Users will lose direct control over their data once it is stored in the cloud, which may result in the leakage of sensitive information, particularly sensitive speech data. Before sending critical data to the cloud, users usually encrypt it. This method's purpose is to ensure data security and secrecy. When voice data is encrypted, however, the bulk of functions are often lost. This makes searching through massive amounts of ciphertext data and deciphering information included in encrypted conversations more difficult for consumers. The growing number of IoT devices indicates a successful industry, but many of them have resource constraints. The lightweight solutions are needed. IoT security is comprised of hardware, software, and networking limitations. Hardware imposes limitations on memory, power, compute, and storage capacities. The challenges of low-level embedded software and the complexities introduced

DOI: 10.1201/9781003468974-13

by low-power radios create difficulties in terms of mobility, scaling, and managing irregular network connections [5, 6].

Speech is important in the conveyance of information in recordings, particularly those used as evidence in court, orders in the military, and interpersonnel communications. Language proficiency is also required in the entertainment industry. The cloud must be used for the remote processing of all of these private and confidential data pieces, including speech retrieval, recognition, and authentication, as well as company and state secrets and personal data. Cloud computing's efficient and convenient data processing, sharing, and storage capabilities can be leveraged for this purpose. ME-AES is proposed as a potential solution to the problem of text recovery from encrypted cloud storage. The procedure in question is provided here as a solution to the retrieval problem.

The encryption strategy used, also known as the encryption algorithm approach, determines how much data transferred over an IoT network can be relied on. The key must be handled carefully and secretly for the cryptography procedure to work. In contrast, if a key is stolen, an attacker can steal confidential data and destroy the system [7]. The current implementation of SE technology relies on keyword matching, which is insufficient for decrypting voice data with perceptual redundancy. We express gratitude for the remarkable capabilities of automatic feature learning and detailed feature description exhibited in tasks such as for speech recognition [8–10], for speaker recognition [11], and for audio recognition [12–15] and retrieval.

The applied encryption mechanism, i.e., the designed encryption algorithm method, determines the security of the IoT information network. The key must be managed and processed in a way that maintains its confidentiality. Because of erroneous key management, including key loss and database corruption, it may be difficult for authorized users to perform encryption and decryption in real-world applications. However, if a key is taken, attackers may get access to sensitive data or even bring the system to a standstill. Key management is a cornerstone of cryptographic security and an important stage in the encryption process. It has an impact on several application solutions due to its important nature.

The objective of the research is to build a multilayer, reliable system of cloud sequences that uses cloud computing and the AES algorithm. This system can be used on cloud computers and integrated into the biological environment. By making a main key and a rule key, this method can protect the cloud sequence over cloud-based fog computing platforms from plaintext attacks. The study makes a number of contributions, such as (i) a multilayer encryption algorithm that uses both Identity-Based Encryption (IBE) and the AES algorithm; (ii) a reliable encryption technique for IoT-based smart assistant security systems; (iii) an encryption technique that reduces the length of messages and, therefore, the number of complex mathematical operations; and (iv) an encryption technique that improves encryption power and adds more security and complexity to multilayer AES and IBE.

IBE, an identity-based encryption scheme, makes use of elliptic curve and line elliptic curve cryptography. ECC keys are 163 bytes long, but RSA keys of the same level of security are 1024 bytes long. According to estimates, when compared to ECC, RSA is approximately 84% longer. Using the ECC encryption method can thus result in cost savings [16]. As a result, ECC encryption will significantly reduce the amount of storage time required [17]. Improving the security of the IBE algorithm and applying it to RFID devices and sensor networks used in the Internet of Things (IoT) with limited resources is consequently critical and has far-reaching implications. [18]

Our contributions are listed as follows:

- We present a multi-layer voice query strategy for the home voice system that preserves users' privacy while allowing them to retrieve other people's voices and transmit voice commands to servers.
- When requests are sent to the intelligent assistant, they are secured with Identity Based Encryption (IBE) and BLAKE2 hashing-generated keys. We can process these requests once they've been hashed. The IBE receives information from the user's email address and the serial number of the device.
- AES and Twofish are used to encrypt sensitive data and regular data, respectively. AES encryption is used for common data.
- Even if the attacker steals the ciphertext, it is difficult to decipher the data information of the receiver's identity from the ciphertext, so this chapter will propose an identity-based encryption algorithm.
- This layered approach to data protection secures data much more effectively and promptly.

The sections that follow are organized as follows. Section 13.2 will mostly detail our conclusions from the literature review. Section 13.3 provides a brief overview of the proposed system, which includes voice conversion, data encryption, and retrieval. In Section 13.4, we discuss F-score, encryption speed, and decryption speed, as well as its security. Section 13.5 concludes with our results and recommendations for additional investigation.

13.2 LITERATURE SURVEY

In this section, we show some of the most recent research on security and privacy of user surveys that has been published. This section evaluates previous efforts in data encryption in terms of energy consumption, processing speed, data type, throughput, avalanche effect, and packet size. This section provides a literature review on cryptography algorithm.

Hasan et al. [19] highlighted that the advent of the Internet of Things (IoT) has created the need to interconnect multiple devices within a network. There are also automobiles, sensors, and digital tools among these devices. The scale of the network of devices and the anonymity or uncontrollability of the internet structure must be taken into account. With IoT security, protecting data and communication networks is vital. In the studies, security problems have been solved by using neural network algorithms based on machine learning. Some other authors have looked at how well different security algorithms work on a single processor and in the cloud for different input sizes.

M. Shafiq et al. [20] aim to furnish quantitative terminology, like speedup ratios, that facilitate the use of cloud resources to develop safe algorithms (MD5, RSA, and AES), which businesses can utilize for encrypting substantial amounts of data. AES (symmetric encryption method), RSA (asymmetric encryption algorithm), and MD5 (hash algorithm) are the three different algorithms used.

Akhtaruzzaman et al. [21] reported that, based on their findings, employing algorithms in a cloud context (such as Google App) proves more efficient than deploying them on a single server. The least time-consuming algorithm for on-premises (single processor) and cloud (Appengine) systems is MD5, whereas RSA takes up the most time. The largest speedup in AES is possible for small input file sizes, and as the input file size increases, the speedup ratio rapidly decreases. For each input size, AES has the biggest speedup, followed by MD5, while RSA has the lowest speedup.

Indrasena Reddy et al. [22] suggests a novel approach for creating the key that differs from the AES algorithm and the flower pollination algorithm utilized in this chapter. (FPA). The combination in question is known as modified AES (MAES). An initial 128-bit plain string is provided as the method's input. An encrypted version of this text has been created. Key generation is required for the "S-box" generation (substitution box). Key generation for the intended task is done using the FPA. Using this method, the keys are constructed to increase the S-difficulties Boxes. The suggested work for data transmission via the internet is now more secure because of this. Later, encryption is completed. Decryption is the following stage. Lastly, 128-bit plaintext is acquired at the receiver's end. In this study, the flower pollination algorithm is used to generate the encryption key, which requires more time and raises only the S-box complexity, not the algorithm's overall complexity.

H. H. Ali and S. H. Shaker [23] proposed and put into practice an improved modification for the advanced encryption standard (AES) algorithm using an extra key generated using a linear feedback shift register (LFSR), which offers an effective method for pseudorandom number generation and reduces the number of rounds. The complexity of the algorithm depends on how the LFSR generates the keys. There isn't any more randomness displayed. The only thing different about the AES algorithm is how the keys are generated and scheduled.

Mohd Ariffin et al. [24] suggests a secured modified advanced encryption standard algorithm that lowers the AES round count from 32 to 14 to speed up the encryption and decryption processes while also boosting data security. Although the complexity is lowered in this investigation, the encryption time is not. It is clear from the earlier publications that none of them succeeded in striking a balance between speed and security.

Thabit et al. [25] have presented a new unique encryption strategy with the goal of boosting data security when stored in the cloud. This was done with the goal of increasing data security. These individuals suggested an entirely revolutionary new lightweight cryptographic technique based on a 16-byte block cypher and a 16-byte encryption key. Both bytes are kept in the same place. The algorithm is a simplified version of a block cypher. This proposed approach employs the Feistel and substitution-permutation algorithms to make the encrypting process more challenging. The substitution-permutation approach is also utilized.

Orobosade et al. [26] proposed a hybrid encryption system that protects users' privacy and safety in the cloud by using cryptographic algorithms that are built both symmetrically and asymmetrically. They created this hybrid encryption solution. They proposed a privacy paradigm that uses Elliptic Curve Cryptography (ECC), commonly known as the Advanced Encryption Standard (AES), as its principal security approaches. This model is likewise based on Elliptic Curve Cryptography (ECC).

Raghavendra et al. [27] conducted an inquiry into the Internet of Things safety issues as part of a research project. The objective was to assess challenges, constraints, requirements, and viable solutions, including communicative devices with the IoT framework. The three-layer Internet of Things architecture served as the organizing framework for their debate throughout its duration. This discussion centered on the Internet of Things. This served as the framework for their dialogue, which was built on this foundation.

Kallimani et al. [28] emphasized that Machine Learning and Deep Learning methodologies hold the potential to transform Internet of Things (IoT) security moving beyond merely facilitating secure communication between devices to the establishment of security-centric intelligent systems. Machine Learning and Deep Learning methodologies must evolve Internet of Things (IoT) security, transitioning from merely facilitating secure communication between devices to the establishment of security-centric intelligent systems. These approaches have the potential to revolutionize the security of the (IoT). This investigation investigated a broad of Internet of Things (IoT) system weaknesses and attack surfaces. Each one was taken apart and studied.

Wang et al. [29] established a paradigm for content-based privacy-preserving image retrieval, known as CBIR for short. Even when numerous users use it at the same time, this framework guarantees the anonymity of the query as well as the picture. CBIR is an abbreviation that stands for content-based image retrieval while protecting the user's privacy. In addition, they developed a key conversion method that allows several users to collect images using unshared keys while maintaining search accuracy. This was accomplished without forcing users to exchange their keys.

Li et al. [30] were successful in building a searchable encrypted voice system using granule computing. This allowed the researchers to secure the privacy of the users while still making the system searchable. It achieves this by first extracting speech features with MFCC and then concealing those features with fuzzy granules. This procedure is repeated until the desired result is reached. Before the voices are saved, the AES algorithm is used to encrypt the user's voices after they have been retrieved from the user's recording.

Peng An et al. [31] propose unsupervised ensemble autoencoders connected to the Gaussian mixture model (GMM) to adapt to multiple domains regardless of domain skewness. The attention-based latent representation and reconstructed features of the minimum error are used in the ensemble autoencoder's hidden space. In the GMM, the sample density is estimated using the expectation maximization (EM) algorithm. When the estimated sample density exceeds the learning threshold determined during the training phase, the sample is flagged as an outlier associated with an attack anomaly.

To lessen threats and create secure software, threat modeling has been suggested by Ramazanzadeh et al. [32] as a preventive measure during the software design phase. On the other hand, threat modeling is frequently criticized for being time-consuming, complicated, challenging, and error-prone. Automated Security Assistant of Threat Models (ASATM), the methodology used in this study, is an automated solution that can achieve a high level of security assurance. With the help of conceptual modeling, concept definition, automated security assistant algorithms, and secure software design, ASATM offers a fresh method for spotting threats, extracting security requirements, and creating secure software. The suggested approach shows how to quantitatively classify security at three levels (insecure, secure, and threat), twelve sublevels [33, 34] (nominal scale and color scale), and a five-layer depth (human understandability and conditional probability).

The modern world has entered a new phase with cloud computing. Many people and purposes have contributed to the development of cloud computing, depending on demand. The security risks have doubled as cloud technology has improved. So, we must address the security concerns with cloud computing. In this chapter, we covered cloud computing security measures and provided a comparison of many techniques.

13.3 PROPOSED SYSTEM

In this chapter, we have proposed a multi-layer encryption with AES and Twofish for the security of Smart Assistants, shown in Figure 13.1. The suggested paradigm, ME-AES, encrypts data at many levels and includes a security framework for intelligent assistants. Identity Based Encryption (IBE) and BLAKE2 hashing are used to generate the decryption keys for the

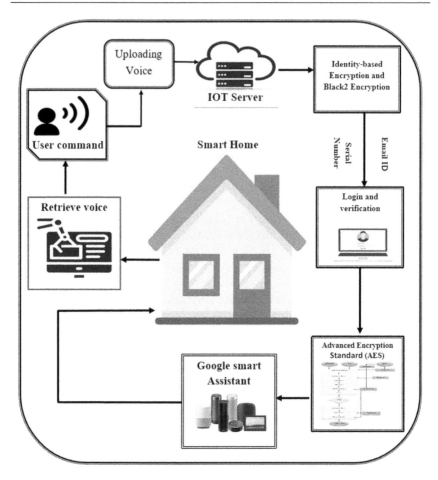

Figure 13.1 Proposed ME-AES method.

questions. The smart assistant receives the inquiries in encrypted form. IBE requires both the user's email address and the serial number of the device to which it is tied for it to function effectively. AES and Twofish are used to encrypt sensitive data, whereas AES is used to secure common data. This layered design provides substantially more efficient and rapid data security.

13.3.1 Uploading voice

Objects and keywords can be split as two independent components of a data structure throughout the voice uploading process. An "object" is the data from the user that will be transferred to the server. Class and attribute names can be used to identify an item. Each pair is represented on the server by a unique copy of the data set (objects and keywords) that it represents. The items are specifically encrypted and stored on the server. In contrast, the keywords are now recorded on the server as hidden attributes. Items and keywords may have many-to-many relationship. As a result, a keyword may be associated with many objects, or multiple items may be related to a keyword. For example, "apple, fruit" has two distinct meanings: "apple" refers to an item, while "fruit" refers to the class to which the object belongs. If the phrase "Apple, Red" is repeated, the server will append the latest crucial phrase "Red" to an item already identified as "Apple." During upload, the keyword is extracted using an obfuscation method using the Mel Frequency Cepstral Coefficient (MFCC). These two events happen at the same time. As a result, before sending the ciphertext to the server, this function encrypts the data to protect the privacy of users' sensitive data.

13.3.2 Retrieving voice

A user initiates the voice retrieval process by sending a query command to a server, which is followed by the ensuing activities. Home IoT Voice System (HIVS) is initially given the keyword and query instructions. After HIVS and masking have extracted features, the server receives them in an obscured state. The response is arranged in increasing order depending on the distance between these features within the encrypted response. After completion, HIVS receives the response with the least encrypted distance. The user will receive the original, unencrypted content once HIVS decrypts the encrypted version using AES. As a result, the user will hear the response.

13.3.3 Multi-layer feature characterizations

Smart home IoT devices are capable of a wide range of processing, storage, and communication functions. Bridges support IoT wireless protocols and TCP/IP and can connect to battery-powered devices like motion and water leak sensors. Smart TVs and Amazon Echoes use electricity and connect to the internet wirelessly or wired via household routers.

IoT Argos investigates a range of multi-layer properties derived from wireless packets gathered by sniffers and TCP/IP-based network flow records recorded by the SOFT FLOWD. Because most Internet of Things apps and services used in smart homes encrypt data transfers, IoT Argos focuses on behavioral elements such as data volumes, length, protocols, and remote end systems.

13.3.4 Identity-based encryption

The sender can encrypt communication using the recipient's identification in identity-based encryption systems. These benefits were initially emphasized. As a result, there is no longer a need for a centralized system to control the generation and distribution of public keys. An IBE scheme requires a trustworthy central authority. This is critical for us to achieve our goal.

Because the central authority of the IBE scheme has access to every private key, it is obvious that this type of scheme cannot guarantee non-repudiation. Remember that private keys must be securely held on the client or user's end or handed to them. This could be accomplished in the IoT by affixing a secret code put in the gadget during manufacturing or configuration.

The MasterKeyGen algorithm, the UserKeyGen method, the encryption strategy, and the decryption algorithm are used in IBE systems. UserKeyGen generates the ID, user private key, and master secret key, whereas MasterKeyGen generates the authority's key pair. Only the decryption and encryption algorithms must be run on the user's device; all other operations may take place in the secure environment supplied by the regulating body. It is possible to establish security proofs for a wide range of difficult situations using IBE systems. These issues include Ring Learning with Errors (RLWE) and the Bilinear Diffie-Hellman assumption [35, 36].

To implement the IBE approach and to evaluate its suitability for application to embedded Internet of Things devices. We present an overview of the necessary technical background here; the original work should be read for a more detailed explanation of the technical aspects and security proof. The master key must be generated by the central authority using the MasterKeyGen technique, which is detailed below (Algorithm 1). The entire cryptographic setup of the IBE system is determined by this way.

ALGORITHM 1:   Master Key Generation

1. $MasterKeyGen()$
2. do

3. $k, l \leftarrow D_{\sigma f}$ $\triangleright\ \sigma_f = 1.17\sqrt{\dfrac{q}{2n}}$

4. $while\ \max\left(\left\|(l, -k)\right\|, \left\|\left(\dfrac{qk}{f \times f + g\overline{g}}, \dfrac{q\overline{l}}{f \times f + g\overline{g}}\right)\right\|\right) > 1.17\sqrt{q}$

5. $U\ sin\ g\ EEA\ to\ compute\ \rho_k, \rho_l \in \Re\ and\ R_k, R_l \in \mathbb{Z}\ such$
6. $\rho_k.k = R_k\ mod\ x^n + 1\ and$
7. $\rho_k.l = R_k\ mod\ x^n + 1$
8. $If\ (GCD(R_k, R_l) \neq 1\ or\ GCD(R_k, q) \neq 1)\ Re\ start$
9. $U\ sin\ g\ EEA\ to\ compute\ u,\ v \in \mathbb{Z}\ such\ that\ u.R_k +$
          $v.R_l = l$
10. $K \leftarrow qv\rho_l$
11. $L \leftarrow qu\rho_k$

12. $o \leftarrow \left\lfloor \dfrac{K \times \overline{k} + 1 \times \overline{l}}{k \times \overline{k} + l\overline{l}} \right\rceil \in \Re$

13. $K \leftarrow K - o \times k$
14. $L \leftarrow L - o \times l$

```
15.    h←l×k⁻¹ mod q

16.    B ←  ⎛ A (l) − A (k) ⎞
             ⎝ A (L) − A (K) ⎠

17.    Return(so, po) = (B, h)
18. End
```

In order to produce a unique secret key for each user or device, the governing body will employ the UserKeyGen technique represented in Algorithm 2. This method is normally performed only once per embedded device during a secure system configuration phase.

ALGORITHM 2:   User Key Generation

```
1. UserKeyGeneration
2.      t ← H (ID) ∈ ℤ_q^n          ▷ H() is a hash function.
3.      s₁, s₂) ← (t, 0) − GaussianSampler(B, σ, (t, 0))
4.      Return so_ID = s₂
5. end
```

We will ignore the MasterKeyGen and UserKeyGen computations for field-installed embedded devices to pay attention to the following encryption and decryption methodologies for our implementation. As a result, we can disregard these computations (Algorithms 3 and 4, respectively). Encryption and decryption necessitate the use of three procedures: polynomial sampling, polynomial multiplication, and threshold encoding. An n-bit message can be transformed to a [0, 1] polynomial using the threshold encoding procedure. The polynomial has been encoded after being multiplied by q12 many times. The error-prone message polynomial [q 4], 3q 4] is obtained at completion of the decryption process. In this case, unlike in prior cases, the ciphertext bit will be set to 1.

13.3.5 BLAKE2 hash algorithm

The improved version of SHA-3, BLAKE2, decreases program performance. These techniques are used in cloud storage, versioning, detection, and intrusion detection. BLAKE2b and BLAKE2s are available for 64-bit platforms and smaller architectures, respectively. BLAKE2 consumes 32% less RAM than BLAKE thanks to its efficient MAC node and tree-hashing mode.

BLAKE2 carries out the following tasks: MasterKeyGen and UserKeyGen will not be used in our solution because they will not be implemented on field-deployed embedded devices. Instead, we will concentrate on encryption and decryption (Algorithms 3 and 4). Encipherment and decipherment will be discussed (Algorithms 3 and 4, respectively). Data encryption and decryption use threshold encoding, polynomial multiplication, and equally distributed ternary polynomials. A threshold encoding converts an n-bit message into a [0, 1] polynomial with n coefficients. The polynomial is encoded using the q12 technique. Use of polynomial decryption errors are then added to this polynomial, and each coefficient must match [q 4, 3q 4]. Otherwise, if the answer is no, set the ciphertext bit to 0.

1. Initialization: A 16-word state initialized so that different inputs result in different initial states.
2. Iteration of the Round Function: The round function will iterate 14 or 16 times (BLAKE-256) (BLAKE-512).
3. BLAKE only employs one basic function, the G function. The G function is repeated 128 times in BLAKE 512, compared to 112 times in BLAKE 256 (a 32-bit word) (64 bit word). Each column must be subjected to the G function. Apply the G function to each diagonal member in parallel.
4. Conclusion: The information supplied can be used to calculate a new chain value.

13.3.6 Advanced Encryption Standard (AES)

The Data Encryption Standard (DES), developed by the National Institute of Standards and Technology, was recommended for adoption. In 2001, the National Institute of Standards and Technology (NIST) replaced DES with the Advanced Encryption Standard (AES). Any database collection could benefit from AES. Prior to creating the encoded message, AES supports data lengths of up to 128 bits, with each bit split into at least four active basic blocks. Following processing as a single line of bytes, these elements are concatenated to generate the state, which is a 4 × 4 matrix. The initial phase in both encoding and decoding a cypher is the "Add round key stage." To get to the final round, the output must first go through the first nine fundamental rounds, where it experiences the four transformations listed below: The four subsequent actions are as follows: (1) adding a round key, (2) shifting rows, (3) mixing columns, and (4) sub-bytes. It is unable to use the mix column transformation in the ninth and final round. The full procedure is depicted in great detail in Figure 13.2. The inverse of encryption, decryption performs the opposite procedures:

1. Sub-byte
   The AES key is a data block of 128 bits. Each record in the database is made up of 16 bytes. The Rijndael S-box is an 8-bit substitution box used to change the sub-byte. Using this box, each data byte is transformed into a separate component during this transformation.

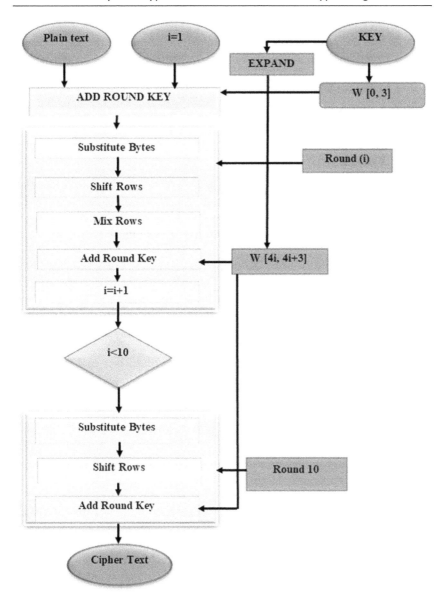

Figure 13.2 Advanced Encryption Standard (AES process).

2. Shift Rows

The transposition is a simple procedure; the bytes in the state's remaining three lines are modified based on their row placements. The second line of code does a one-byte circular shift. Circular shifts of two and three bytes happen consecutively in the third and fourth rows.

3. **Mix Columns**

At this stage, appending one stable matrix to each of the state vectors is functionally equal to running a duplicate set for each state vector column. This function treats sent bytes as if they had several names.

4. **Add Round Key Transformation**

The transformation results from performing a 128-bit XOR on the current state and the round key.

13.3.7 Twofish

Twofish employs a Feistel-like structure with 16 iterations and additional input and output whitening. Only 1-bit rotations can violate the Feistel equations. Moving the rotations within F generates Feistel structures without rotations. Before whitening the result, the text must be rotated once more.

Plaintext consists of four 32-bit words. Four keywords are used for input whitening. Then there are 16 rounds. The two leftmost words are used by the g functions in each cycle. (The first bit is 8-bit rotated.) The right-hand sentences have two consequences. To create the ciphertext, the four words are XORed with four new key words by inverting the previous round's swap.

Using the little-endian byte order, four words of 32 bits each are generated from the 16 bytes of plaintext $(p_0, p_1, \ldots, p_{15})$.

$$P_i = \sum_{j=0}^{3} p(4i+j)^{\cdot 2^{8j}} \quad i = 0, \ldots, 3 \tag{13.1}$$

The input whitening process will replace these words with four essential terms that are significantly larger.

$$R_0 = P_i \oplus K_i \quad i = 0, \ldots 3 \tag{13.2}$$

The first two words and the rounded integer are passed to the function F as parameters. This technique is repeated with each iteration. The character XORed has been added to the third word in place of the letter F, and it has also been slightly shifted to the right. The fourth word is XORed with the second word that is generated by F after being rotated left one bit. Both halves are switched around.

$$(F_{r,0}, F_{r,1}) = F(R_{r,0}, R_{1,r}) \tag{13.3}$$

$$R_{r+1,0} = ROR(R_{r,2} \oplus F_r 0, 1) \tag{13.4}$$

$$R_{r+1,1} = ROL(R_{r,3} 1) \oplus F_{r,1} \tag{13.5}$$

$$R_{r+1,2} = R_{r,0} \tag{13.6}$$

$$R_{r+1,3} = R_{r,1} \tag{13.7}$$

ROR and ROL rotate their first parameter, which is a 32-bit word, by their second argument when r equals 0, 1,... 15, respectively. The "swap" that was performed in the previous round is undone by output whitening, and the expanded key is used to XOR the data words.

$$C_i = R_{16}, (i+2) \bmod 4 \oplus K_{i+4} I = 0, \ldots 3 \tag{13.8}$$

When converted to little-endian format, the four ciphertext words result in the 16-byte sequence c0, ..., c15.

$$c_i = \left\lfloor \frac{C_{\lfloor \frac{i}{4} \rfloor}}{2^{8(i \bmod 4)}} \right\rfloor \bmod 2^8 i = 0, .., 15 \tag{13.9}$$

13.3.7.1 The function F

F recursively permutes 64-bit data based on a key. This function takes R_0, R_1, and the round integer r to choose subkeys. They are required for operation. T_0 is obtained by passing R_0 through g. After shifting R_1 to the left by 8 bits to generate T_1, the g function is applied to the newly generated value. After T_0 and T_1 are merged, two extra terms from the extended key are added to the Pseudo-Hadamard Transform (PHT).

$$T_0 = g(R_0) \tag{13.10}$$

$$T_1 = g(ROL(R_1, 8)) \tag{13.11}$$

$$F_0 = (T_0 + T_1 + K_{2r+8}) \bmod 2^{32} \tag{13.12}$$

$$F_1 = (T_0 + 2T_1 + K_{2r+9}) \bmod 2^{32} \tag{13.13}$$

F-result is represented as (F_0, F_1). In addition to F_0, which we define above, the analysis will make use of F_0. Unlike the F function, the F_0 function does not include whatever key in its output.

13.3.7.2 The function g

Twofish relies on g. The word X is divided into four bytes. Each byte is processed by its own key-dependent S-box. Each S-box can take an 8-bit input and output an 8-bit result. The calculations are carried out in the GF(28) field, and the four results are read as a four-element vector. It's also multiplied by the MDS matrix of dimension 4. G creates a vector that can be regarded as a 32-bit word.

$$x_i = \lfloor X/2^{8i} \rfloor \mod 2^8 i = 0,..3 \tag{13.14}$$

$$y_i = s_i[x_i] I = 0,...3 \tag{13.15}$$

$$\begin{pmatrix} z_0 \\ z_1 \\ z_2 \\ z_3 \end{pmatrix} = \begin{pmatrix} \bullet & \bullet \bullet \bullet & \bullet \\ & & \\ \bullet & \bullet \bullet \bullet & \bullet \end{pmatrix} MDS \cdot \begin{pmatrix} y_0 \\ y_1 \\ y_2 \\ y_3 \end{pmatrix} \tag{13.16}$$

$$Z = \sum_{i=0}^{3} z_i . 2^{8i} \tag{13.17}$$

where s_i are the key-dependent S-boxes and Z is the result of g. In some ways, this is the "natural" mapping because addition in GF (28) corresponds to a XOR of the bytes.

13.3.7.3 The key schedule

In addition to the four key-dependent S-boxes required by the g function, the key schedule must include Twofish support keys with N = 128, N = 192, and N = 256 bits for the four-word key $K_0,...,K_{39}$. The use of zero padding allows the use of keys with less than 256 bits.

k=N/64. M is made up of 8k bytes, which are m0, ..., m8k1. 2K 32-bit words are generated from bytes.

$$M_i = \sum_{j=0}^{3} m(4i + j) . 2^{8j} \quad i = 0,....2k - 1 \tag{13.18}$$

$$M_e = (M_0 M_2,..., M_{2k-2}) \tag{13.19}$$

$$M_o = (M_0 M_3,..., M_{2k-1}) \tag{13.20}$$

The key produces a second k-character word vector. The key bytes are segmented into eight-byte chunks, interpreted as vector over GF (28), and then subjected to multiplied by a 4 × 8 matrix incorporating a Reed-Solomon code.

Each 4-byte result is converted to a word using the 32-bit output. These words and phrases form the third vector in the equation.

$$\begin{pmatrix} s_{i,0} \\ s_{i,1} \\ s_{i,2} \\ s_{i,3} \end{pmatrix} = \begin{pmatrix} \bullet \; \bullet\bullet\bullet \; \bullet \\ RS \\ \bullet \; \bullet\bullet\bullet \; \bullet \end{pmatrix} \cdot \begin{pmatrix} M_{8i} \\ M_{8i+1} \\ M_{8i+2} \\ M_{8i+3} \\ M_{8i+4} \\ M_{8i+5} \\ M_{8i+6} \\ M_{8i+7} \end{pmatrix} \tag{13.21}$$

$$S_i = \sum_{j=0}^{3} s_{i,j} \cdot 2^{8j} \tag{13.22}$$

for $i = 0,\ldots,k-1$, and

$$S = \left(S_{k-1}, S_{k-2}, \ldots, S_0 \right) \tag{13.23}$$

Remember that S presented the terms in what appears to be a "backwards" order. The equation GF (2) [x]/w(x) signifies a degree 8 primitive polynomial over GF (28). This expression is employed by the RS matrix multiplication technique (2). The MDS matrix multiply has the same format as the mapping between byte values and GF elements (28).

13.4 RESULT AND DISCUSSION

13.4.1 Experimental setup

To put the technology to the test, a human voice was recorded. To put our technique to the test, we'll need numerous recordings of the same screenplay. This chapter compares the performance of the proposed scheme to existing schemes on key parameters. From the below table, it is clear that the Accuracy, Precision, and Recall values of the proposed scheme are high compared to existing methods LSTM, RSA, AES, DES, and Blowfish. The tests were carried out using a machine outfitted with a 2.20GHz Intel Core i5-5200U processor, 12GB of DRAM, and a 500GB SanDisk drive. There were 3,600 paragraphs written in Arabic, Chinese, and English. In English, Arabic, and Chinese, precision, recall, F-score, and search time were used. To compare with the proposed strategy, the techniques LSTM, RSA, AES, DES, and Blowfish were applied.

13.4.2 Assessment criteria

- True Positives (TP): An event that occurred and confirmed our predictions, including the actual yield. Another phrase for this is "good" consequences.
- True Negatives (TN): A situation we expected to be untrue but whose actual outcome was likewise false.
- Untrue Positives (FP): When a result was anticipated to be true but turned out to be untrue.
- Untrue Negatives (FN): Situations in which the expected conclusion was false but the actual outcome was also true.

Precision: This question is answered by dividing accurate predictions by accurate forecasts by the total number of accurate predictions.

$$\text{Precision} = \frac{TP}{TP + FP} \tag{13.24}$$

Recall: It is obtained by dividing the total number of conjugate samples by the number of correct positive outcomes (all samples that ought to have been identified as sure).

$$\text{Recall} = \frac{TP}{TP + FN} \tag{13.25}$$

F1-score: Computed by dividing conjugate samples by favorable results (all samples that ought to have been identified as sure).

$$F1 - \text{Score} = \frac{2TP}{2TP + FP + FN} \tag{13.26}$$

Accuracy: It estimates the proportion of samples used to create the model that match to all accurate predictions.

$$\text{Accuracy} = \frac{TP + TN}{TP + TN + FP + FN} \tag{13.27}$$

13.4.3 Encryption time

Encrypting data and converting it to ciphertext both take roughly the same amount of time. The efficiency of the technique is proportional to the amount of time required to encrypt the data.

There are two ways to evaluate this criterion:

- Compare input size and encryption time (100, 200, 300, 400, and 500 KB).
- The character count has the largest influence on how long it takes to encrypt and decrypt a message.

According to the findings, the time required for encryption grows linearly with the number of characters or file size, whereas decryption takes much less time. The proposed effort has reduced the level of computational complexity.

13.4.4 Time-based algorithm for decoding

The time necessary to decrypt the ciphertext and recover the original data is shown in the Decrypting Time column. The term "time complexity" refers to the amount of time required for decrypting a message using an algorithm. To calculate the time required to decrypt a file, use the following formula:

$$\text{Time consumed} = \text{end time} - \text{start time} \qquad (13.28)$$

The proposed approach decrypts much faster than prior encryption techniques. As a result, the presented paradigm is relevant and successful in providing secure communication.

1. **Precision**
   In Figure 13.3 and Table 13.1, a comparative precision analysis of the ME-AES approach against more traditional methods is presented. This illustration reveals that the IoT approach has yielded superior performance in terms of precision. For example, with 100 nodes, the precision value is 92.45% for ME-AES, whereas the LSTM, RSA, AES, DES, and Blowfish models have obtained precision of 62.56%, 56.67%, 71.56%, 85.78%, and 76.45%, respectively. However, the ME-AES model has shown maximum performance with different nodes. Similarly, under 600 nodes, the precision value of ME-AES is 95.76%, while it is 67.45%, 61.89%, 75.34%, 89.65%, and 81.21% for LSTM, RSA, AES, DES, and Blowfish models, respectively.

2. **Recall**
   Figure 13.4 and Table 13.2 compare ME-AES recall to other approaches. The graph shows that IoT increased recollection. For example, with 100 nodes, the recall value is 91.45% for ME-AES, whereas the LSTM, RSA, AES, DES, and Blowfish models have obtained recalls of 76.21%, 72.56%, 79.56%, 84.56%, and 81.89%, respectively. However, the ME-AES model has shown maximum performance with different nodes. Similarly, under 600 nodes, the recall value of ME-AES is

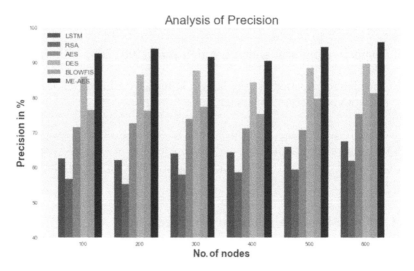

Figure 13.3 Precision analysis for ME-AES method with existing systems.

Table 13.1 Precision analysis for ME-AES method with existing systems

No of nodes	LSTM	RSA	AES	DES	BLOWFISH	ME-AES
100	62.56	56.67	71.56	85.78	76.45	92.45
200	62.11	55.32	72.56	86.45	76.21	93.89
300	63.89	57.89	73.88	87.56	77.34	91.56
400	64.21	58.61	71.22	84.34	75.32	90.44
500	65.89	59.44	70.67	88.42	79.66	94.32
600	67.45	61.89	75.34	89.65	81.21	95.76

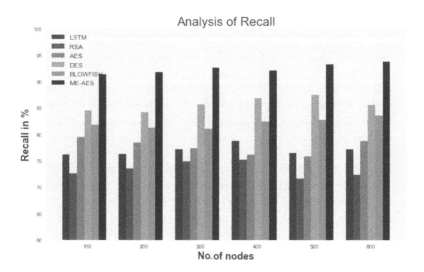

Figure 13.4 Recall analysis for ME-AES method with existing system.

Table 13.2 Recall analysis for ME-AES method with existing systems

No of nodes	LSTM	RSA	AES	DES	BLOWFISH	ME-AES
100	76.21	72.56	79.56	84.56	81.89	91.45
200	76.32	73.56	78.45	84.23	81.32	91.87
300	77.21	74.88	77.45	85.78	81.12	92.67
400	78.78	75.22	76.21	86.84	82.45	92.11
500	76.46	71.67	75.89	87.56	82.78	93.32
600	77.21	72.34	78.76	85.67	83.67	93.78

93.78%, while it is 77.21%, 72.34%, 78.76%, 85.67%, and 83.67% for LSTM, RSA, AES, DES, and Blowfish models, respectively.

3. **F-Score**

   Figure 13.5 and Table 13.3 compare ME-f-score AESs to other approaches. The figure illustrates that IoT has a higher f-score. For example, with 100 nodes, the f-score value is 92.34% for ME-AES, whereas the LSTM, RSA, AES, DES, and Blowfish models have obtained f-scores of 68.78%, 72.46%, 61.78%, 75.98%, and 83.56%, respectively. However, the ME-AES model has shown maximum performance with varied nodes. Similarly, under 600 nodes, the f-score value of ME-AES is 95.11%, while it is 71.42%, 74.78%, 66.42%, 75.13%, and 88.67% for LSTM, RSA, AES, DES, and Blowfish models, respectively.

4. **Encryption Time**

   A time analysis for ME-AES encryption is presented in Table 13.4 and Figure 13.6 with existing methods. The nodes clearly show that the

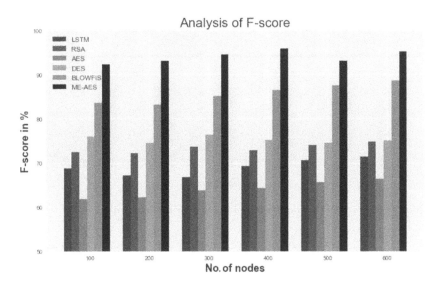

Figure 13.5 F-score analysis for ME-AES method with existing systems.

Table 13.3 F-score analysis for ME-AES method with existing system

No of nodes	LSTM	RSA	AES	DES	BLOWFISH	ME-AES
100	68.78	72.46	61.78	75.98	83.56	92.34
200	67.13	72.15	62.13	74.54	83.23	93.12
300	66.78	73.69	63.78	76.32	85.18	94.56
400	69.31	72.89	64.31	75.21	86.54	95.78
500	70.56	73.98	65.56	74.56	87.56	93.12
600	71.42	74.78	66.42	75.13	88.67	95.11

Table 13.4 Encryption Time analysis for ME-AES method with existing systems

No of nodes	LSTM	RSA	AES	DES	BLOWFISH	ME-AES
100	6.321	9.345	8.721	7.567	5.345	3.653
200	6.113	9.213	8.156	7.113	5.123	3.761
300	6.872	9.678	8.345	7.667	5.245	3.113
400	6.772	9.115	8.367	7.554	5.871	4.912
500	6.112	9.891	8.114	7.221	5.652	4.115
600	6.821	9.991	8.621	7.731	5.451	4.872

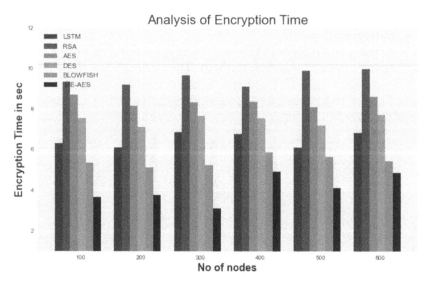

Figure 13.6 Encryption Time analysis for ME-AES method with existing systems.

ME-AES method has outperformed the other techniques in all aspects. For example, with 100 nodes, the ME-AES method has taken only 3.653 sec to encrypt, while the other existing techniques like LSTM, RSA, AES, DES, and Blowfish have an encryption time of 6.321 sec,

9.345 sec, 8.721 sec, 7.567 sec, and 5.345 sec, respectively. Similarly, for 600 nodes, the ME-AES method has an encryption time of 4.872 sec, while the other existing techniques like LSTM, RSA, AES, DES, and Blowfish have 6.821 sec, 9.991 sec, 8.621 sec, 7.731 sec, and 5.451 sec of encryption time, respectively.

5. **Decryption Time**

The decryption time of the ME-AES technique is examined in Table 13.5 and Figure 13.7 existing methods. The nodes clearly show that the ME-AES method has outperformed the other techniques in all aspects. For example, with 100 nodes, the ME-AES method has taken only 2.134 sec to decrypt, while the other existing techniques like LSTM, RSA, AES, DES, and Blowfish have a decryption time of 8.678 sec, 7.678 sec, 4.831 sec, 9.234 sec, and 6.567 sec, respectively.

Table 13.5 Decryption Time analysis for ME-AES method with existing systems

No of nodes	LSTM	RSA	AES	DES	BLOWFISH	ME-AES
100	8.678	7.678	4.831	9.234	6.567	2.134
200	8.566	7.566	4.321	9.456	5.789	2.456
300	8.431	7.431	4.678	9.123	6.661	3.876
400	8.234	7.234	4.897	9.652	6.567	3.112
500	8.872	7.872	5.431	9.156	6.431	4.245
600	8.912	7.912	5.667	9.567	7.112	4.211

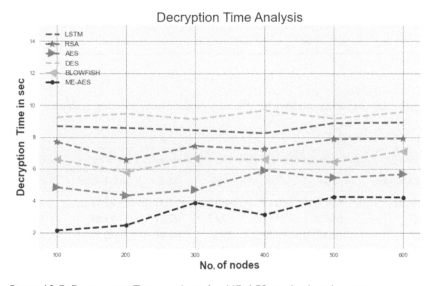

Figure 13.7 Decryption Time analysis for ME-AES method with existing systems.

Similarly, for 600 nodes, the ME-AES method has a decryption time of 4.211 sec, while the other existing techniques like LSTM, RSA, AES, DES, and Blowfish have 8.912 sec, 7.912 sec, 5.667 sec, 9.567 sec, and 7.112 sec of decryption time, respectively.

6. **Accuracy**

In Figure 13.8 and Table 13.6, a comparative examination of accuracy for the ME-AES approach is presented in contrast to more traditional methods. This illustration highlights that the IoT approach has delivered superior performance in terms of accuracy. For example, nodes with 100, the accuracy value is 95.14% for ME-AES, whereas the LSTM, RSA, AES, DES, and Blowfish models have obtained an accuracy of 85.77%, 73.67%, 88.15%, 92.45%, and 72.76%, respectively. However, the ME-AES model has shown maximum performance with different nodes. Similarly, under 600 nodes, the accuracy

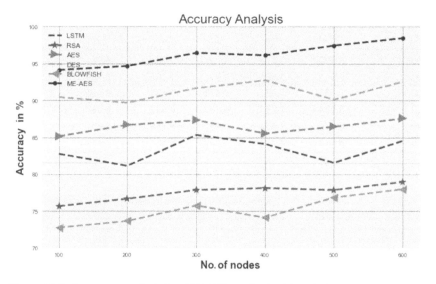

Figure 13.8 Accuracy analysis for ME-AES method with existing systems.

Table 13.6 Accuracy analysis for ME-AES method with existing systems

No of nodes	LSTM	RSA	AES	DES	BLOWFISH	ME-AES
100	85.77	73.67	88.15	92.45	72.76	95.14
200	86.13	74.67	89.67	92.67	73.67	95.67
300	86.33	75.87	89.32	93.67	75.77	96.45
400	87.12	76.13	89.55	94.76	74.13	96.13
500	87.56	77.87	90.45	94.12	76.87	97.45
600	87.55	78.98	91.56	93.56	77.98	98.45

value of ME-AES is 98.45%, while it is 87.55%, 78.98%, 91.56%, 93.56%, and 77.98% for LSTM, RSA, AES, DES, and Blowfish models, respectively.

7. **Search Time**

Table 13.7 and Figure 13.9 describe the search ME-AES time analysis vs. existing methods. The nodes clearly show that the ME-AES method has outperformed the other techniques in all aspects. For example, with 100 nodes, the ME-AES method has taken only 3.678 sec to search, while other existing techniques like LSTM, RSA, AES, DES, and Blowfish have a search time of 9.678 sec, 7.561 sec, 6.371 sec, 5.345 sec, and 4.235 sec, respectively. Similarly, for 600 nodes, the ME-AES method has a search time of 3.456 sec while other existing techniques like LSTM, RSA, AES, DES, and Blowfish have 9.912 sec, 8.211 sec, 7.421 sec, 6.256 sec, and 5.145 sec of search time, respectively.

Table 13.7 Search Time analysis for ME-AES method with existing systems

No of nodes	LSTM	RSA	AES	DES	BLOWFISH	ME-AES
100	9.678	7.561	6.371	5.345	4.235	3.678
200	9.566	8.631	7.431	6.761	5.456	3.764
300	9.431	8.773	7.671	6.721	5.123	2.921
400	9.234	8.841	6.821	5.812	4.782	3.762
500	9.872	8.457	7.321	6.145	4.881	3.621
600	9.912	8.211	7.421	6.256	5.145	3.456

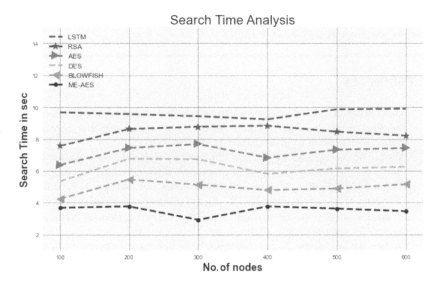

Figure 13.9 Search Time analysis for ME-AES method with existing systems.

13.5 CONCLUSION

This chapter discusses the different structures of Smart Homes and security issues. The Internet of Things has countless applications, but it is not without challenges. Privacy and security are crucial concerns. These constraints render IoT devices unsafe. Without IoT security, the internet is hazardous. We examined IoT security and the solutions that must be deployed to persuade customers that IoT is about more than simply low-cost gadgets, but also about security and privacy. This chapter describes a multi-user searchable encrypted speech system that increases the utility of home IoT voice searches while protecting users' privacy. We propose a Multi-layer Encryption with Advanced Encryption Standard (ME-AES) and a Twofish encryption algorithm in this chapter. The outline is as follows: The proposed model, ME-AES, consists of multiple encryption layers and a security architecture designed for the intelligent assistant. The queries directed to the intelligent assistant undergo a process of scrambling and encryption, employing key chaining with IBE and BLAKE2. IBE requires the gadget serial number and the user's email address. The sensitive data is secured with AES and Twofish, while non-sensitive data is safeguarded by the Advanced Encryption Standard (AES). This multilayer technique secures data in substantially less time and with significantly higher effectiveness. Our independent model ME-AES has conducted studies demonstrating that this threat is far more serious and devastating than previously anticipated. This is due to the operating system's functionality, the capabilities of the digital assistant, and the proximity of other IoT devices. The proposed model attains the optimal outcome, achieving an overall accuracy of 98.45% in predicting whether a user will belong to a specific group. We will pay more attention in the future to establishing the best effective technique for handling fuzzy queries and diverse keyword searches.

REFERENCES

1. Gartner report, 2021, https://www.gartner.com/en/newsroom/press-releases/2021-06-30-gartner-global-government-iot-revenue-for-endpoint-electronics-and-communications-to-total-us-dollars-21-billion-in-2022
2. W. Li, W. Meng, and M. H. Au, "Enhancing collaborative intrusion detection via disagreement-based semi-supervised learning in IoT environments," *Journal of Network and Computer Applications*, vol. 161, pp. 1–9, 2020.
3. W. Meng, W. Li, and L. F. Kwok, "Towards effective trust-based packet filtering in collaborative network environments," *IEEE Transactions on Network and Service Management*, vol. 14, no. 1, pp. 233–245, 2017.
4. X. Sun, H. Wang, and X. Fu, "Substring-searchable attribute based encryption and its application for IoT devices," *Digital Communications and Networks*, vol. 7, no. 2, pp. 277–283, 2021.

5. H. G. Li and F. G. Zhang, "A cloud storage method supporting speech encrypted search," *China Patent*, vol. 24, pp. 277–278, 2020.

6. C. Glackin, G. Chollet, N. Dugan, et al., "Privacy preserving encrypted phonetic search of speech data," in *Proceedings of the 2017 IEEE International Conference on Acoustics, Speech and Signal Processing (ICASSP)*, pp. 6414–6418, New Orleans, LA, USA, March 2017.

7. B. J. Lu, J. Zhou, and Z. F. Cao, "A multi-user forward secure dynamic symmetric searchable encryption with enhanced security," *Journal of Computer Research and Development*, vol. 57, no. 10, pp. 2104–2116, 2020.

8. B. L. Risteska Stojkoska and K. V. Trivodaliev, "A review of Internet of Things for smart home: Challenges and solutions," *Journal of Cleaner Production*, vol. 140, pp. 1454–1464, 2017.

9. M. A. Al Sibahee, S. Lu, Z. A. Abduljabbar, A. Ibrahim, et al., "Efficient encrypted image retrieval in IoT-cloud with multi-user authentication," *International Journal of Distributed Sensor Networks*, vol. 14, no. 2, pp. 5692–5716, 2018.

10. F. Zeng, S. Hu, and K. Xiao, "Deep hash for latent image retrieval," *Multimedia Tools and Applications*, vol. 78, no. 22, pp. 32419–32435, 2019.

11. Q. Qin, Z. Wei, L. Huang, J. Nie, and X. Ji, "A novel deep hashing method with top similarity for image retrieval," in *Proceedings of the 2019 IEEE International Conference on Acoustics, Speech and Signal Processing (ICASSP)*, pp. 2067–2071, Brighton, United Kingdom, May 2019.

12. M. Sridevi, S. Chandrasekaran, K. Murugeswari, T. B. Lingaiah, et al., "Deep learning approaches for cyberbullying detection and classification on social media," *Computational Intelligence and Neuroscience*, vol. 2022, pp. 1–13, 2022.

13. D. K. Jain, S. Neelakandan, T. Veeramani, S. Bhatia, and F. H. Memon, "Design of fuzzy logic based energy management and traffic predictive model for cyber physical systems," *Computers and Electrical Engineering*, vol. 102, 2022, 108135, https://doi.org/10.1016/j.compeleceng.2022.108135

14. D. Paulraj, P. Ezhumalai, & M. Prakash, (2022) "A Deep Learning Modified Neural Network (DLMNN) based proficient sentiment analysis technique on Twitter data." *Journal of Experimental & Theoretical Artificial Intelligence*, 2022. https://doi.org/10.1080/0952813X.2022.2093405

15. Q. Y. Zhang, Y. Z. Li, and Y. J. Hu, "A retrieval algorithm for encrypted speech based on convolutional neural network and deep hashing," *Multimedia Tools and Applications*, vol. 80, no. 1, pp. 1201–1221, 2021.

16. Z. Zhang, R. He, and K. Yang, "A bioinspired path planning approach for mobile robots based on improved sparrow search algorithm," *Advances in Manufacturing*, vol. 10, no. 1, pp. 114–130, 2022.

17. S. Pirbhulal, H. Zhang, M. E. Alahi, et al., "A novel secure IoT-based smart home automation system using a wireless sensor network," *Sensors*, vol. 17, no. 1, p. 69, 2016.

18. H. Cao, N. Tang, Y. Huang, W. M. Gan, and C. Zhang, "IIBE: An improved identity-based encryption algorithm for WSN security," *Security and Communication Networks*, vol. 2021, Article ID 8527068, 8 pages, 2021.

19. M. K. Hasan, "Lightweight encryption technique to enhance medical image security on Internet of Medical Things applications," *IEEE Access*, vol. 9, pp. 47731–47742, 2021.

20. M. Shafiq, Z. Tian, A. K. Bashir, X. Du, and M. Guizani, "CorrAUC: A malicious bot-IoT traffic detection method in IoT network using machine learning techniques," *IEEE Internet of Things*, vol. 8, no. 5, pp. 3242–3254, 2021.

21. M. Akhtaruzzaman, M. K. Hasan, S. R. Kabir, S. N. Abdullah, M. J. Sadeq, and E. Hossain, "HSIC bottleneck based distributed deep learning model for load forecasting in smart grid with a comprehensive survey," *IEEE Access*, vol. 8, pp. 222977–223008, 2020.

22. M. Indrasena Reddy and A. P. Siva Kumar, "A secure approach for data transmission in computer networks using modified advanced encryption standard algorithm," *Journal of Mechanics of Continua and Mathematical Sciences*, Special Issue, no. 3, pp. 14–28, 2019.

23. H. H. Ali and S. H. Shaker, "Modified Advanced Encryption Standard algorithm for fast transmitted data protection," in *Proceedings of the 2nd International Scientific Conference of Al-Ayen University (ISCAU-2020)*, IOP Conf. Series: Materials Science and Engineering, vol. 928, pp. 1–11, Nov 2020.

24. N. A. Mohd Ariffin and A. Y. Ahmed Ashawesh, "Enhanced AES algorithm based on 14 rounds in securing data and minimizing processing time," *Journal of Physics Conference Series*, vol. 1793, Article ID 012066, pp. 1–9, 2021.

25. F. Thabit, S. Alhomdy, H. A. Al-Ahdal, and S. Jagtap, "A new lightweight cryptographic algorithm for enhancing data security in cloud computing," *Global Transitions Proceedings* vol. 2, pp. 91–99, 2021.

26. A. Orobosade, T. A. Favour-Bethy, A. B. Kayode, and A. J. Gabriel, "Cloud application security using hybrid encryption," *Communications on Applied Electronics* vol. 7, pp. 25–31, 2020. ISSN 2394-4714.

27. S. Raghavendra, A. Harshavardhan, S. Neelakandan, R. Partheepan, R. Walia, and V. C. S. Rao, "Multilayer stacked probabilistic belief network-based brain tumor segmentation and classification," *International Journal of Foundations of Computer Science*, vol. 33, no. 06n07, pp.559–582, 2022. https://doi.org/10.1142/S0129054122420047

28. S. K. Perumal, J. S. Kallimani, S. Ulaganathan, S. Bhargava, and S. Meckanizi, "Controlling energy aware clustering and multihop routing protocol for IoT assisted wireless sensor networks," *Concurrency and Computation: Practice and Experience*, p. e7106, 2022. https://doi.org/10.1002/cpe.7106

29. C. Wang, T. Tai, J. Wang, A. Santoso, S. Mathulaprangsan, et al., "Sound events recognition and retrieval using multi-convolutional-channel sparse coding convolutional neural networks," *IEEE Transactions on Audio, Speech and Language Processing*, vol. 28, pp. 1875–1887, 2020.

30. Y. Z. Li, Q. Y. Zhang, and Y. J. Hu, "An encrypted speech retrieval scheme based on long short-term memory neural network and deep hashing," *KSII Transactions on Internet and Information Systems*, vol. 14, no. 6, pp. 2612–2633, 2020.

31. P. An, Z. Wang, and C. Zhang, "Ensemble unsupervised autoencoders and Gaussian mixture model for cyberattack detection," *Information Processing & Management*, vol. 59, no. 2, p. 102844, Article ID 102844, 2022.

32. M. A. Ramazanzadeh, B. Barzegar, and H. Motameni, "ASATM: Automated security assistant of threat models in intelligent transportation systems," *IET Computers and Digital Techniques*, vol. 16, no. 5–6, pp. 141–158, 2022.

33. K. Lakshmanna, N. Subramani, Y. Alotaibi, S. Alghamdi, O. I. Khalafand, and A. K. Nanda. "Improved metaheuristic-driven energy-aware cluster-based routing scheme for IoT-assisted wireless sensor networks," *Sustainability*, vol. 14, p. 7712, 2022. https://doi.org/10.3390/su14137712

34. K. Sreekala, C. P. D. Cyril, S. Neelakandan, S. Chandrasekaran, R. Walia, and E. O. Martinson, "Capsule network-based deep transfer learning model for face recognition," *Wireless Communications and Mobile Computing*, vol. 2022, https://doi.org/10.1155/2022/2086613

35. S. Neelakandan, M. Prakash, B. T. Geetha, A. K. Nanda, et al., "Metaheuristics with Deep Transfer Learning Enabled Detection and Classification Model for Industrial Waste Management," *Chemosphere*, vol. 308, part 1, p. 136046, 2022, https://doi.org/10.1016/j.chemosphere.2022.136046

36. D. K. Jain, X. Liu, S. Neelakandan, and M. Prakash, "Modeling of human action recognition using hyperparameter tuned deep learning model," *Journal of Electronic Imaging*, vol. 32, no. 1, p. 011211, 2022. https://doi.org/10.1117/1.JEI.32.1.011211

Chapter 14

Cancelable biometrics for fingerprint template protection

Vivek Singh Baghel and Surya Prakash
Indian Institute of Technology Indore, Indore, India

14.1 INTRODUCTION

Biometrics refers to the capability of recognizing an individual by means of physiological and behavioral characteristics. The physiological characteristics comprise fingerprint, face, ear, etc., whereas behavioral characteristics comprise gait, signature, voice, etc. These characteristics exhibit some distinct information for each individual, which is used to uniquely identify a person. In biometric systems, there are mainly two stages involved, viz., enrollment and verification or identification. At the time of enrollment, the biometric data of a person is collected, and a user template is constructed utilizing the distinct features present in a biometric trait. The computed user template is further stored in the database for verification and identification purposes. During the verification, the features extraction is performed to extract the features from the probe biometric image, and the user template is computed following the same procedure as followed during enrollment. Further, the generated probe template is compared/matched with the stored template to verify whether the probe user template is genuine or not. The difference between verification and identification is that one-to-one matching is performed for verification and one-to-many matching is performed for the identification stage.

Fingerprint biometrics is one of the widely used physiological biometric traits. It has been utilized to provide secure authentication in numerous recognition applications. The fingerprint data of a person is very distinct, and it remains permanent and unique for the complete life span of an individual. In addition, fingerprint biometrics provide good recognition performance, and they are easy to capture and process as compared to other biometric characteristics. A fingerprint constitutes continuous patterns of ridges and valleys. These patterns exhibit unique features that distinguish a person's identity from others. In fingerprint biometrics, feature extraction can be performed on three different levels [1], viz., global level, very-fine level, and local level. The ridge-flow represents a pattern of a fingerprint impression that wrapped around the singular points, and these patterns are considered

DOI: 10.1201/9781003468974-14

as global-level features. In the second-level features, i.e., very-fine level features, intra-ridge information is detected that includes width, curvatures, dots, etc., of the ridges in the fingerprint image. A very notable feature is sweat pores, which are distinct for identifying an individual. In the third-level features, i.e., local level, various minute ridge characteristics are present in the fingerprint impression. These minute details are susceptible to changes in the quality of fingerprint images. Nevertheless, among these minutiae points are prominent feature points in a fingerprint image, and these mainly include ridge end and bifurcation points. The points where ridges abruptly end are called ridge ends, whereas the points where the ridges bifurcate into two different ridges are called bifurcation points. For example, Figure 14.1 depicts an instance of a fingerprint image combined with the presentation of minutiae and singular points. Minutiae points are found to be very stable and robust against the change in the quality of fingerprint impression. Therefore, minutiae points become a natural choice to be considered as unique features for the computation of user templates, as compared to other features. The computed user templates that mainly constitute minutiae information are further stored in the database for identification and verification purposes.

Despite the security provided by a fingerprint authentication system to various resources and applications, the protection of the fingerprint user template present in the database is also essential, as the leakage of the stored template can cause the permanent identity theft of a person. Furthermore, it has been shown through various existing studies [2–4] from the literature that the fingerprint image reconstruction is feasible utilizing the stored template by employing reverse-engineering, if it is stolen by an adversary.

Figure 14.1 Representation of various feature points in a fingerprint image.

Therefore, it is necessary to protect the fingerprint user template before storing it in the database. The secure fingerprint template should be designed in a manner that the fingerprint reconstruction and even unauthorized access to the system are infeasible to perform utilizing the stolen fingerprint user template.

To protect the fingerprint template, numerous template protection strategies have been presented in the literature. When we look into these approaches, the main concept of these methods is to store the transformed/encrypted fingerprint template in the database in place of storing an original fingerprint template exhibiting the direct minutiae information. There are four important properties that need to be fulfilled by the designed fingerprint template protection approach, viz., revocability (renewability), diversity (unlinkability), security, and recognition performance. In an attack scenario, revocability allows the replacement of a compromised/leaked template with an entirely new fingerprint template for the same person. To support the revocability property, a template protection technique should generate diverse or unlinkable templates for the same person; thus, a technique should exhibit the property of diversity. Further, it must be infeasible to perform any kind of attack and reverse engineering to perform the fingerprint reconstruction from the secure fingerprint template; hence, the developed technique should provide a high level of protection. Lastly, the performance of the designed fingerprint system must not be degraded even after performing the transformation or encryption.

Furthermore, the methods utilized to protect fingerprint templates can be roughly divided into four types, viz., biometric cryptosystems [5, 6], homomorphic encryption [7], cancelable biometrics [8, 9], and hybrid approaches. Biometric cryptosystems make use of cryptographic keys and the concept of cryptography to secure the fingerprint template. In the second category, homomorphic encryption is utilized to secure fingerprint templates. In contrast to both categories, cancelable biometrics utilize invertible and non-invertible transformation of fingerprint features to compute the secure template. A user-defined keyset is usually used as transformation parameters in cancelable biometrics. In the fourth category, approaches that combine functionalities of more than one category have been explored. In the literature, approaches based on cancelable biometrics are extensively discussed template protection approaches. The reason is the high-level security of these approaches, along with the high performance of the designed system as compared to other categories of template protection approaches. In addition, there are many opportunities in cancelable biometrics for further developing effective and robust template protection approaches. Therefore, considering the significance of cancelable biometrics in fingerprint template protection research, this chapter provides a detailed discussion of cancelable biometrics, along with a few existing techniques related to cancelable biometrics. The discussion on existing techniques provides a comprehensive understanding of presented approaches, along with their result analysis considering the aforementioned various essential properties. Further, the significant contributions of this chapter are listed below.

- A detailed discussion on the working of cancelable biometrics along with its subcategories is presented in this chapter. In spite of considering various categories of fingerprint template protection approaches, this chapter mainly focuses on the discussion of approaches based on one of the prominent categories, i.e., cancelable biometrics, considering the most recent development in this area. Hence, this provides a novel discussion considering the cancelable biometrics.
- This chapter provides a detailed discussion of a few of the existing works considering their advantages and discusses their limitations and puts forth possible future directions, which can be useful for the research community in this area.

The remainder of this chapter is arranged as follows. Section 14.2 presents a detailed discussion on cancelable biometrics along with the subcategories. A few of the existing techniques are discussed considering the explanation of the proposed approach and the result analysis in Sections 14.3, 14.4, and 14.5. Section 14.6 presents the discussion on the significance of cancelable biometrics along with the open challenges. The chapter is concluded in Section 14.7.

14.2 CANCELABLE BIOMETRICS

Cancelable biometrics is one of the categories of fingerprint template protection. The concept of template protection approaches based on transformation, i.e., cancelable biometrics, was first presented by Ratha et al. [8]. In this work, various points of a biometric system were identified as potential points to be attacked, and a concept of cancelable biometrics was introduced. In cancelable biometrics, the original features extracted from the fingerprint are transformed before storing them in the database as a user template. The utilization of transformation is done in such a way that the distinctiveness of the unique features of fingerprint biometrics should be preserved. In other words, the inter-class dissimilarity and intra-class similarity should be preserved when we perform any kind of transformation of the actual information of the minutiae points or any texture-based features exist in the fingerprint impression. The computed secure template through the discussed transformation is stored in the database, which can be considered as a protected fingerprint user template. Now, the fingerprint image reconstruction should be unachievable by means of the protected template for an adversary even though the protected template is leaked from the database. In addition, the constructed templates should hold the revocability and diversity properties that enable the possibility of replacing a leaked template with the new

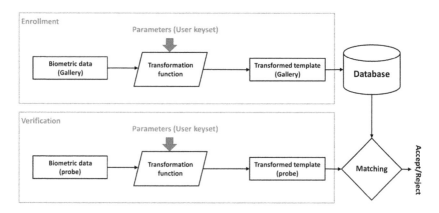

Figure 14.2 A generic working of a biometric system based on the cancelable biometrics.

fingerprint template, which does not have any linkage with the leaked one. Figure 14.2 shows a schematic block diagram illustrating the general operation of the template protection strategy based on cancelable biometrics. It becomes abundantly evident from Figure 14.2 that the secured/transformed user template is kept in the database and that the matching is carried out in the secured/transformed domain; therefore, there is no original information of the fingerprint image involved during the verification stage.

Furthermore, the cancelable biometrics can be categorized into the following types [10], i.e., biometric salting and non-invertible transformation, according to the existing research in the literature. In the existing approaches based on biometric salting [11], a transformation of biometric features is performed using user-specific keys/parameters. Reconstructing the original and unique biometric information by employing reverse-engineering and the protected template is challenging in these findings. However, the nature of the transformation process is invertible; therefore, it is necessary to protect the user-specific parameters as well because if the parameters are compromised, it is possible to invert the transformation. In contrast, when we see existing methods based on non-invertible transformation [9], a transformation process of non-invertible nature is adopted to construct the secure user template. Consequently, it is not possible to retrieve the original biometric data from the leaked user template even if the transformation parameters and the secure template are stolen. Due to this advantage of non-invertible transformation-based approaches, these are extensively discussed in the literature as compared to the biometric salting-based template protection approaches. A few of the prominent and recent existing works related to the biometric salting and non-invertible transformation-based cancelable biometrics technique for fingerprint biometrics are briefly discussed below.

A very few presented techniques are related to biometric salting in the literature, as compared to the approaches utilizing non-invertible transformation.

A brief discussion of some of the prominent existing approaches, which are related to salting, is provided as follows. Connie et al. [11] computed the revocable user template by means of the biometric salting technique. To construct the revocable and secure fingerprint user template, Fisher Discriminant Analysis (FDA) has been used for the extraction of features— and to compute the hash code, the binary discretization method has been utilized. Teoh et al. [12] presented a new approach to prevent the leakage of the original information from the stored fingerprint template, and the formulation is called BioPhasor in this work. Essentially, the BioPhasor is constructed by combining the fingerprint features with the user-specific pseudo-random numbers in an iterative way, and the generated BioPhasor is in the form of binary code. Jin et al. [13] presented an approach called Minutia Vicinity Decomposition (MVD). In MVD, minutiae triplets were computed, which is, in a way, the decomposition of local minutia vicinity. Further, unique features from the computed triplets were extracted, which are geometrical invariants. Further, these features were secured utilizing a salting-based transformation mechanism.

In the literature, several approaches utilizing non-invertible transformation have been discussed due to the multiple advantages over the salting-based approaches as discussed earlier. Hence, to depict the recent development of the approaches for protecting the user template based on non-invertible transformation, a few of the recent existing works are briefly discussed as follows. Wang et al. [14] obtained a secure fingerprint user template using a partial Hadamard transform. In this work, the Discrete Fourier Transform (DFT) of binary vectors equivalent to fingerprint features was transformed for generating the protected fingerprint user template. In [15], a novel technique termed dense registration of the fingerprint image was developed to remove intra-subject variances such as distortions caused by skin elasticity. The presented technique in this work was also based on a transformation function that is non-invertible in nature for the construction of a protected fingerprint template. Lee et al. [16] proposed a secure biometric authentication mechanism for partial fingerprint biometrics. In this work, a novel feature, i.e., ridge shape features, from the fingerprint image along with the minutiae points were considered for computing the secure user template for partial fingerprint images. Wang et al. [17] used a unique local structure formed by means of minutiae, which is extracted from the zoned minutia-pairs for the purpose of constructing the cancelable user template for fingerprint biometrics. In this work, the DFT was utilized to carry out a non-invertible transformation of extracted features from the fingerprint impression. Moujahdi et al. [18] introduced an approach known as a fingerprint shell to protect the fingerprint template. This work utilized the Euclidean distances of a singular point from the minutiae to construct a fingerprint shell, which visually looks like spiral curves when we plot the final template points. Further, Jain and Prasad [19] presented a fingerprint indexing technique for a biometric system by means of a fingerprint shell and a clustering approach. Although fingerprint shell [18] computed a secure fingerprint template, secure templates computed in this work exhibit a prominent issue. The Euclidean distances between minutiae and a singular point considered for generating the spiral curves can possibly be derived from the stored template in the database if it is compromised. Therefore, the leakage of these distances can be used for the reconstruction as the distances are between the original minutiae and a singular point of a fingerprint image. To overcome this issue of the existing fingerprint shell approach, Ali and Prakash [20, 21] presented an enhancement of the fingerprint shell using the transformed distance by means of user-specific keysets. The work proposed in [20, 21] furthermore improved, considering the recognition performance (i.e., Equal Error Rate [EER]) in [22, 23]. Ali et al. [24] presented a fingerprint template protection method that utilized translation/ rotation-invariant features for the computation of a protected fingerprint template. In this work, minutiae locations were altered by means of the non-invertible transformation along with user-specific keys/parameters. Even though the presented approach is secure enough to protect the fingerprint template, the expected performance was not achieved in this work. Hence, Ali et al. [25] further improved the performance without compromising the security of the original fingerprint features. Trivedi et al. [26] suggested a method for generating a non-invertible fingerprint template using minutiae triplet information of a fingerprint image. Here, the Delaunay triangulation was used as minutiae triplets, and the geometrical characteristics of these triplets were considered to construct the secure template. In this study, the generated template appears secure; nevertheless, sufficient analysis has not been conducted, and performance is not significantly improved when compared to state-of-the-art approaches. Yang et al. [27] presented a multi-biometric system that was based on fingerprint and finger-vein biometric traits. The fused multi-biometric template is constructed utilizing the geometric characteristics of minutiae pairs from fingerprints and vein pattern features from finger-vein. This technique was also evaluated for fingerprint biometrics alone, and the effectiveness is not noteworthy as compared to previous methodologies in the literature. However, the presented method functioned well in the multi-biometric case. Ali et al. [28] presented the polynomial vault framework, which is built on polynomial curves. The polynomial curve in this work was constructed by transforming the distances of a singular point from minutiae. Trivedi et al. [29] presented a template protection approach adopting Delaunay triangulation. The internal angles of Delaunay triangles and minutiae orientation values were used to generate the feature vector, which is then secured by employing the function for transformation that uses user-specific keys as the transformation parameters. Lahmidi et al. [30] discussed a method that computed tetrahedron structures from the combination of four minutiae. The retrieved characteristics from the tetrahedron structures were then altered for constructing the protected fingerprint template. Although the constructed templates using the presented technique appear to be secure, the chance of missing minutiae exists since performance degrades for poor-quality fingerprints. In [31], the extracted minutiae were grouped into four disjoint parts centered at the singular point. To generate the transformed information of minutiae, the user-specific keys that were too specific for each group were adopted in this work. Despite the fact that the secure templates in this study don't reveal anything regarding the original and unique biometric information, the performance is demonstrated to be quite low. To secure minutiae-pair characteristics of fingerprint impressions, Yang et al. [32] presented a novel strategy based on feature-adaptive projection. A novel projection system was used in this study, although the performance was poor and it was not tested on hard protocols. To protect the fingerprint template, Bedari et al. [33] presented a feature transformation method comprised of two different stages. Although the recognition performance is superior to previous works, the approach computes the secure template using more than one sample. Furthermore, a few recent works [34–36] that come under the area of fingerprint template protection have been discussed. These works presented the alignment-free and non-invertible transformation-based method for the purpose of protecting the fingerprint template. The presented approaches performed significantly better than the previous existing approaches. In this chapter, we have considered these three of the existing recent works and discussed them in detail as provided in further sections.

14.3 GENERATION OF ALIGNMENT-FREE AND NON-INVERTIBLE FINGERPRINT TEMPLATE USING PAIR-POLAR STRUCTURES OF MINUTIAE

In this work [34], the pair-polar structures of minutiae points are exploited to construct a protected fingerprint user template. The presented technique is alignment-free and there is no need of a singular point, which is usually utilized in existing work for fingerprint alignment purposes. This eliminates the chances of incorrect extraction of the singular point due to the change in the quality of fingerprint images and due to the type of fingerprint images, i.e., arc-type. A schematic block diagram that shows the various steps of this work is shown in Figure 14.3. Further, a brief description of how each stage in the transformation process works is presented below, starting with the extraction of minutiae and ending with the final matching phase. It can be seen from Figure 14.3 that the presented technique consists of the following steps: the extraction of minutiae, computation of pair-polar structures, the transformation of pair-polar structures, and computation of the protected fingerprint template, which is the collection of binary vectors.

Minutiae extraction: The presented technique utilizes the minutiae information that mainly includes the orientation and location values of minutiae. The minutiae locations provide the position of minutiae in Cartesian space,

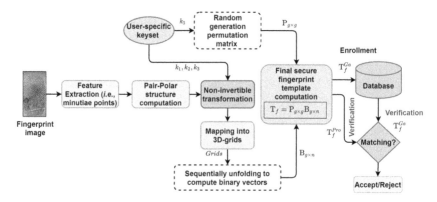

Figure 14.3 A block diagram representing the working of the presented work in [34].

whereas orientation indicates the direction of ridges at the minutia point with respect to the reference axis. Verifinger-SDK (Demo version) [37] has been utilized in this work for the purpose of minutiae extraction from a fingerprint impression. Let us suppose the total number of minutiae points is n, then these n number of minutiae points are used to compute the pair-polar coordinates/structures by employing each minutia as the reference minutia point.

Computation of pair-polar structure: In this step, each minutia is chosen as the reference minutia to generate the pair-polar structures [38, 39] of the set of remaining minutiae for a fingerprint impression. Here, minutiae are represented in the form of polar space, where the reference minutia depicts the center of space (i.e., origin) and its orientation value would be the X-axis. Further, with respect to remaining minutiae except for reference minutia, pair-polar coordinates are evaluated. In this work, the pair-polar coordinates consist of three values, which are the distance between a minutia and reference minutia point, the difference between minutia's orientation and the orientation of the reference minutia, and the direction of a minutia respecting to the orientation of the reference minutia. An instance of depicting the pair-polar coordinate for a minutia m_j and considering m_i as reference is given in Figure 14.4. Hence, the figure clearly shows that the representation of a pair-polar coordinate of a minutia m_j with respect to m_i can be given as $\{d_{ij}, \alpha_{ij}, \beta_{ij}\}$. Similarly, employing each minutia as a reference minutia, pair-polar coordinates are evaluated. Therefore, the total of n sets having $n - 1$ values each are computed in this process. Further, these computed pair-polar structure values are transformed to compute the secure template.

Transformation of pair-polar structures: In this work, many-to-one mapping is utilized for the computation of the final template; however, pair-polar coordinates are transformed before the computation of the final secure template. The non-invertible transformation is used in this work, and the

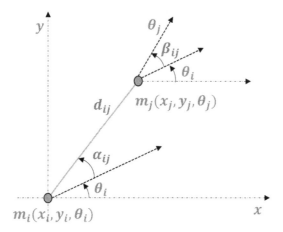

Figure 14.4 Representation of pair-polar structures of the minutiae points.

user keyset $\{k_1, k_2, k_3\}$ is adopted as transformation parameters. The non-invertible transformation of the pair-polar coordinates is performed by following three different steps. First, a value v_{ij}, i.e., an integer value, is computed using the pair-polar coordinate value and the user keyset. Second, a vector r of s-dimensions having integer values in a certain range, i.e., 0 to $s - 1$, is randomly generated. One of the user keys, i.e., k_3, is used as a seed for the random generation process. Further, the binary equivalent of value v_{ij} (i.e., s-bits) is computed and element-wise multiplied with the vector r having integer values, then the sum of resultant vector gives the intermediate transformed value h_{ij}. In the third step, the value of h_{ij} is rescaled between the range of 0 to the maximum dimension of the given fingerprint image. This eventually gives the transformed value d_{ij}^T of the actual distance d_{ij} value. Similarly, the transformation is performed for all the pair-polar coordinates corresponding to the minutiae points. Further, these transformed pair-polar coordinates are utilized to compute the secure fingerprint template in the form of binary vectors.

Computation of the secure fingerprint template in the form of binary vectors: The computed secure pair-polar structures are further utilized for the generation of the binary vectors by mapping into a 3D-grid having dimensions with respect to d_{ij}^T, α, and β. If a transformed pair-polar coordinate of a minutia is mapped into a cell, then the respective cell value in a grid is kept 1. There may be a possibility that more than one secured pair-polar coordinates gets to be mapped into a single cell; in that situation, the value of that cell still remains 1 in order to enable the many-to-one mapping strategy. Here, the n number of 3D-grids are produced that is equivalent to the total minutiae extracted from a fingerprint impression. Once the n 3D-grids are obtained, the sequential unfolding is performed to generate the n binary strings. The length of a binary string fully depends on the dimension of the grid, so a grid of size $g_d \times g_\alpha \times g_\beta$ (e.g., $8 \times 16 \times 16$) will generate the binary string of length $1 \times g$, where $g = g_d g_\alpha g_\beta$ (e.g., 1×2048), and so the size of the template will be given as $n \times g$ (e.g., 30×2048, if number of minutiae $n = 30$). Further, these binary strings are permuted using a randomly generated permutation matrix denoted as $P_{g \times g}$ to get the final protected fingerprint template that will be stored in the database for verification purposes.

Matching score: The matching process will take place between the probe and gallery template in a transformed domain, which makes the matching process completely secure. Suppose a probe template consists of m number of binary strings and gallery template contains the n number of binary strings. Thus, to match the probe and gallery templates, each binary string of probe template is matched with every binary string present in a gallery secure template, and the best score is considered corresponding to each probe binary string. Here, the matching score between two binary strings is essentially the bitwise *and* operation between the binary strings. Finally, the mean of all the best or maximum scores obtained with respect to probe binary strings after matching with the gallery template is the contemplated final matching score.

Experimental analysis: This work has been analyzed considering four essential properties of an approach for protecting the fingerprint template, which are revocability (renewability), diversity (unlinkability), security, and recognition performance. Six fingerprint databases taken from Fingerprint Verification Competitions (FVC), i.e., FVC2002 [40] and FVC2004 [41], are utilized to verify the proposed approach considering the aforementioned properties. The revocability property of a proposed technique guarantees that a leaked/stolen template is easily replaceable by a completely new template that does not have any linkage with the stolen one for the same user. In this work, two existing frameworks [42, 43] are used to show the revocable characteristics of the computed secure templates. The experimental analysis with respect to these frameworks clearly shows the remarkable revocable characteristics of the generated secure fingerprint templates and hence depicts the feasibility of generating a revocable template employing the presented method. The diversity/unlinkability property of a method to protect the fingerprint user template ensures that the generated protected templates for a person through the presented approach are unlinkable to each other or, in other words, do not have any linkage between each other. This work utilizes a recent existing framework [44] to analyze the presented approach in terms of unlinkability. The presented approach follows the favorable conditions as discussed in [44] to show the highly unlinkable nature of the computed template and thus depicts the diversity property. In this work, the presented approach has been evaluated against the various attack scenarios such as non-invertibility analysis and brute force attack. The presented approach is found to be robust against reverse engineering to retrieve the original features and brute force attack to get unauthorized access into a biometric system. Further, the presented approach has also been tested considering the recognition performance, where EER and

Receiver Operating Characteristics (ROC) curves are adopted as performance measures. In this work, the presented approach outperformed the existing techniques in spite of the scenario of challenging fingerprint databases that contain poor-quality fingerprint images.

14.4 GENERATION OF ALIGNMENT-FREE AND SECURE FINGERPRINT TEMPLATE USING DFT FOR CONSUMER ELECTRONICS DEVICES

In this work [35], a transformation function of non-invertible characteristics is used to secure fingerprint templates that consist of minutiae points using DFT. Local association of minutiae (i.e., pair-polar structures [38, 39]) considering the values of distances and angles have been utilized in this work. Adaptation of local structures of minutiae in the form of pair-polar structures eliminates the need of fingerprint alignment and makes the presented technique an alignment-free approach. This work presented an application of the presented approach for Consumer Electronics (CE) devices, and the various steps of the presented technique can be seen in Figure 14.5. Firstly, the acquisition of the fingerprint impression is performed by means of the sensor provided in the CE device. Further, the minutiae are extracted and the Verifinger SDK (Demo) [37] has been utilized in this work for the minutiae extraction. By utilizing the extracted minutiae and the multiple steps of the presented approach, as depicted in Figure 14.5, the final protected fingerprint templates are computed. In order to enable the revocability of the generated template, a user key or seed s is used that can be independently provided by a user or randomly generated by the system for multiple users. Furthermore, a brief description of the different steps and experimental analysis of this work is provided below.

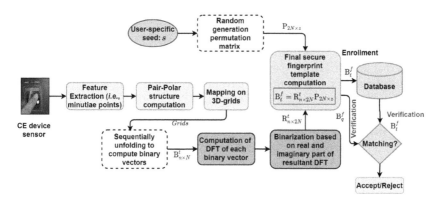

Figure 14.5 A block diagram representing the working of the presented work in [35].

Computation of pair-polar structures: Assume a set of n number of minutiae points having the Cartesian location and orientation values of minutiae. Now, to construct pair-polar structures of the given set of minutiae points, each minutia m_i is considered a reference minutia, and with respect to m_i (i.e., reference minutia), the pair-polar structures are given as $\{(d_{ij}, \alpha_{ij}, \beta_{ij}): 1 \leq j \leq n$ and $j \neq i\}$ for all the remaining minutiae points. Here, the distance between a reference minutia m_i and a minutia m_j is given as d_{ij}, α_{ij} depicts the direction of the minutia m_j respecting the orientation of the minutia m_i, and β_{ij} depicts the difference between the orientation values of the reference minutia m_i and a minutia m_j. An instance of illustrating pair-polar coordinates/structures considering minutia m_i as a reference minutia is shown in Figure 14.4.

Generation of binary fingerprint template: While considering each minutia point as the reference minutia, n sets of pair-polar structures are computed. Further, the mapping of pair-polar structures is performed into the 3D-grid representing the quantities d, α, and β towards all three dimensions, respectively. The 3D-grids are computed separately corresponding to each reference minutia; therefore, there will be total n 3D-grids, which is equivalent to the n number of minutiae points present in a fingerprint impression. Further, there may be possibilities that more than one value is mapped to a single cell of grid; hence, in this scenario as well, the cell value is still set to one instead of incrementing it. This will eventually generate the 3D-grid having values either 0 or 1 and so the resultant binary string by performing the sequential unfolding of the generated 3D-grid. After sequentially unfolding 3D-grids, a total of n binary vectors corresponding to each reference minutia are generated and the size of each binary vector is $1 \times N$, where $N = g_d g_\alpha g_\beta$. Further, these n binary vectors combined form the final binary fingerprint template computed from this step.

Securing the generated binary fingerprint template: Once the binary fingerprint user template is constructed, it is secured by employing the N-point DFT followed by the second stage of the binarization process that makes use of real and imaginary parts of the resultant Fourier transform values. To do that, first, the N-point DFT of each binary vector is computed, and these resultant complex vectors are further converted into the binary strings based on the real and imaginary part of the complex values. If the value of real or imaginary part is positive, then the resultant binary value is set to 1 else set to 0. Therefore, if the length of binary vector computed in the previous step is N, then the length becomes $2N$ after performing the second stage binarization using N-point DFT. Now, if we look into this binarization scheme, it makes it impossible for an adversary to get the inverse DFT in order to retrieve the quantized cell positions of pair-polar structures when the template has been compromised. The reason behind this phenomenon is that the infinite number of possibilities will be there to guess the real and imaginary part from the binary vectors. Furthermore, to compute the final secure template, the computed binary stings are randomly permuted by means of permutation matrix of size $2N \times z$, where $z < 2N$. Here, due to the condition $z < 2N$, infinite possibilities are there to revert-back the binary strings that were generated using DFT-based binarization. Finally, the computed protected fingerprint template is stored into the database for purposes of the verification.

Computation of matching scores between secure fingerprint templates: The bit-error is computed between the binary strings from the secure template to get the matching score between probe and gallery templates. The matching process is completely secure, as matching is carried out between the transformed templates and there is no original information involved in this process. Suppose a probe template has m number of secure binary vectors and a gallery template has n number of secure binary vectors. Then, the bit-error is computed between each binary vector from the probe template and binary vectors from the query template. Now, out of n error values, the minimum is selected as the bit-error corresponding to a binary vector from a probe template. Further, the same process is repeated for all the remaining binary vectors from the probe template, and the minimum of all the minimum values of error corresponding to binary vectors of probe template gives the final bit-error for a probe template. To compute the final matching score, the compute bit-error is subtracted from the maximum length of the binary vector in either of the probe or gallery template. The computation of the matching score can be also understood through the following equation.

$$score = z - \min_{b_q^k \in B_q^f}\left\{ \min_{b_t^i \in B_t^f}\left\{ BitErr\left(b_q^k, b_t^i\right)\right\}\right\}$$

Protecting a fingerprint user template in a CE device: When we look into the application of the presented fingerprint template protection approach for a CE device, the computed secure template using the presented approach is stored in the device. The system will randomly generate a key/seed (i.e., s) while registering a new user, and the key will be employed for generating a protected fingerprint template. Suppose, if an attack is performed by an adversary to get the stored template, then a user will only lose a transformed template and it is not possible to retrieve original information employing the stolen template. At the same time, the stolen template can be replaced with the new one by changing the seed s for the same user. This clearly illustrates the complete protection of user's fingerprint information in the CE device and prevents against the permanent loss of an individual's identity.

Experimental analysis: The presented approach has been evaluated on publicly available fingerprint databases and taken from the Fingerprint Verification Competitions (FVC) 2002 [40] and 2004 [41]. Furthermore, to show the feasibility of the presented approach with respect to the CE devices having small-size fingerprint sensors, a fingerprint database consisting of partial fingerprints extracted from the FVC2002 DB1 is employed, and the generated partial fingerprint database is denoted as PL-02DB1. The partial fingerprint size is taken as 181×181, where each partial fingerprint impression should contain at least 10 minutiae. Two different types of enrollment strategies are utilized for the verification of the presented approach for the partial fingerprint database, viz., single-patch and multi-patch enrollment processes. In the first strategy, a single patch is used during enrollment as a gallery template, and a single patch is used as a probe template to match with the gallery template for the verification purposes. In contrast, the multiple gallery patches are enrolled for a fingerprint image in the multi-patch evaluation procedure, and a single patch is utilized as a probe template and matched for the verification purposes. In this work, the presented approach has been evaluated considering the essential requirements of any template protection approach, which are revocability (renewability), diversity (unlinkability), security, and recognition performance. In order to analyze the revocability property of the presented approach, an existing revoked template attack framework [42] is utilized. In this framework, the leaked template is utilized to perform the attack on a biometric system, while an entirely new template is stored in the database in place of the leaked one for the same user considering two different attack strategies, viz., Type-I and Type-II attack strategies. It is found in this work that not a single leaked/stolen template was able to get unauthorized access to the system when the stolen template is revoked from the database. Therefore, this clearly depicts the revocability property of the presented approach. In order to support the revocability, the secure templates generated for a person should be unlinkable to each other, which is enabled by the diversity property of the presented approach. To analyze the same, an existing framework [44] has been utilized. This framework [44] suggests that if the non-mated and mated score distributions are overlapping with each other, and the global measure for unlinkability denoted as $D_{\leftrightarrow}^{sys}$ attains value near to zero, then the designed system generates completely unlinkable templates. This work exhibits all the favorable properties as discussed in the framework [44], which clearly depicts the diversity property of the presented approach.

In this work, to show the security of the generated template against reconstruction, a non-invertibility analysis has been presented. In addition, to show the infeasibility of getting illegitimate access to the system, brute force attack and cross-match attack scenarios have been analyzed considering the presented approach. It is found from the analysis that the reconstruction of the original unique features from the leaked template is computationally not possible as well as infeasible to get unauthorized access into the biometric system. Further, the recognition performance of the proposed technique is assessed considering EER as a performance measure and using ROC curves. The obtained performance measures clearly illustrate that the presented approach attained significant EER values while comparing it with the existing techniques. The presented approach not only performed significantly better in the case of poor-quality fingerprint images and challenging protocols, but it performed significantly for the fingerprint database containing partial fingerprint images. This clearly depicts the feasibility of the presented approach for the CE devices having small-size fingerprint sensors.

14.5 GENERATION OF ALIGNMENT-FREE AND SECURE FINGERPRINT TEMPLATE USING ENHANCED FINGERPRINT SHELL

This work [36] presented a fingerprint template protection approach that generates the non-invertible, singular point-independent, and alignment-free fingerprint user template. The principal idea of this work is to build a fingerprint shell-based secure user template, which eliminates the shortcomings of the existing fingerprint shell-based implementation [18, 22]. Figure 14.6 illustrates a block diagram showing the various stages of the presented approach. In order to generate the secure fingerprint shell, the basic salient features are the transformed pair-polar coordinates extracted out of the set of minutiae by considering every minutia one after another as a reference point of the polar representation. An illustration of the transformation process of the pair-polar coordinates has been given in Figure 14.7. The various stages that come under the presented work along with the experimental analysis are briefly discussed below.

Minutiae extraction: Minutiae points from the captured fingerprint impression are extracted by means of the VeriFinger SDK (Demo) [37]. The location of each minutia point, i.e., (x_i, y_i), and the orientation value, i.e., θ_i, is used as the feature set to compute the transformed salient features using the pair-polar coordinates of minutiae. Further, these salient features are utilized to construct the protected fingerprint shell-based fingerprint user template.

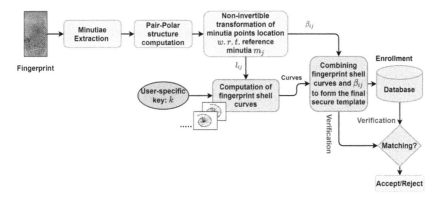

Figure 14.6 A block diagram representing the working of the presented approach in [36].

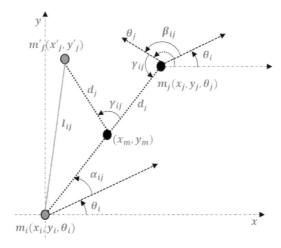

Figure 14.7 Computation of secure and transformed features for the construction of fingerprint shell.

Feature computation: In order to compute the local alignment-free feature from the minutiae, each minutia point is taken as a reference point, and with respect to this point, the following three features are computed for other remaining minutiae. First feature is β_{ij}, i.e., an angle formed between the orientation of reference minutia m_i and a minutia m_j. Second feature is γ_{ij}, i.e., an angle formed between the line segment $m_i m_j$ and the orientation value of minutia m_j. Third feature is a distance l_{ij}, i.e., a secure and transformed distance computed between minutiae m_i and the transformed location m_j'. The computation of the transformed and secure distance l_{ij} can be clearly seen in Figure 14.7. Here, the set of these three features is computed by employing each minutia point as the origin or reference point; hence, the total of n sets is generated. Further, the secure distances l_{ij} and angles β_{ij} are adopted for the computation of the secure fingerprint shell-based fingerprint template. Here, again the total number of fingerprint shells computed are similar to n minutiae points. The secure distances are used to compute the fingerprint shell, whereas the angles β_{ij} are stored in the database along with the fingerprint shell, which eventually improve the recognition performance.

Generation of the secure fingerprint shell: In this step, the obtained secure distances for minutiae points with respect to each reference minutia point are used to construct the fingerprint shell. Here, the fingerprint shell is a spiral curve, which is computed by utilizing the transformed distances as the hypotenuse of continuous right-angle triangles. An example of representing the computed fingerprint shell in the form of spiral curve is shown in Figure 14.8. Further, to compute the fingerprint shell, a set that contains the combination of secure distances l_{ij} and user-specific key k, denoted as $\{k \cup (l_{ij} + k): 1 \leq j \leq n \text{ and } j \neq i\}$ is used. Now, the values of this set are sorted in ascending order, and then the secure fingerprint shell is computed,

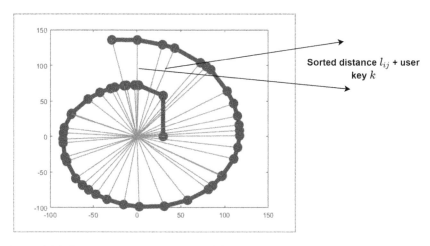

150

100

50

0

-50

-100
-100   -50   0   50   100   150

Sorted distance l_{ij} + user
key k

Figure 14.8 Representing an example of fingerprint shell spiral curve respecting a reference minutia.

where the sorted values are used as the hypotenuses of the contiguous right-angle triangles. It is observed evidently from Figure 14.8 that the spiral curve is a collection of points; hence, these points, along with corresponding values of β angle, are stored in the database, which is a secure fingerprint template. Here, the secure distances have been computed by employing each minutia an origin or reference minutia; therefore, the total number of spiral curves in the final protected template will be n, i.e., number of minutiae. Finally, the computed set of spiral curves, which is essentially the set of points, is stored in the database along with the corresponding angles β for verification purposes.

Computation of matching score: This work developed a two-stage matching approach to compute the matching score between gallery and probe template. To verify a probe fingerprint template using this approach, each spiral curve from a probe fingerprint template is first compared with all the spiral curves of a gallery or enrolled fingerprint impression. If the Euclidean distance between a probe curve point and a gallery curve point is less than a given threshold value, the associated β values of those points are additionally compared during the matching of two curves. If the matching requirements are met in both phases, the two-point matching is termed successful. The following equation depicts the final score of matching between the probe and gallery fingerprint template, where the number of minutiae in probe template is m and in gallery template is n.

$$score = \frac{\sum_{i=1}^{m}\left[\max_{j \in n}\left(\frac{count_{ij}}{m}\times 100\right)\right]}{m}$$

Here, $count_{ij}$ depicts the count of points, which fulfills the two-step matching condition when the matching is performed between i^{th} probe curve to the jth gallery curve.

Experimental analysis: The presented approach has been evaluated by considering the essential characteristics of the template protection technique, viz., revocability (renewability), diversity (unlinkability), security, and recognition performance. To analyze the proposed technique based on these properties, multiple existing frameworks have been utilized. A total five number of fingerprint databases have been utilized for experimental analysis, which are taken from the FVC2002 [40], FVC2004 [41], and FVC2006 [45]. To analyze the revocability property, an existing framework [42] based on revoked template attack has been utilized. The findings obtained clearly demonstrate that not even a single leaked template has indeed been recognized as a legitimate template, while every stolen template has been replaced with an entirely new template and saved in the database. Now, a framework [44] is utilized in this work to analyze the diversity of the computed fingerprint templates through the presented approach. It is evident from the obtained result in this work that the non-mated and mated score distributions are overlapping with each other that is the favorable condition for the diversity/unlinkability of a presented approach. In this work, the security of the generated template has been analyzed considering four different attack scenarios, which are non-invertibility analysis, false accept attack, brute force attack, and Attack via Record Multiplicity (ARM). The presented technique demonstrated the infeasibility to perform these attack scenarios in this work. At last, when we consider the recognition performance, the presented technique has performed significantly better comparing it with the existing approaches considering the values of EER for different fingerprint databases. In addition, a statistical analysis, i.e., Kolmogorov Smirnov (KS)-test [46] has been also performed to illustrate the significant difference between genuine and imposter score distributions. According to the KS-test, if the test value is near to 1, that means the input distributions are significantly different from each other. It has been found in the results of the presented approach with respect to the KS-test that the values are near to 1 for all the databases, which clearly depict the significant difference between genuine and imposter distributions.

14.6 DISCUSSION

It is well established by the above discussion that cancelable biometrics provides a robust and effective way to protect the fingerprint template without compromising the overall recognition performance of the fingerprint system. This is the reason that cancelable biometrics-based approaches have been extensively explored in the literature as compared to other fingerprint template protection approaches such as biometric cryptosystems, homomorphic encryption, and hybrid approaches. Figure 14.9 depicts the prominence of

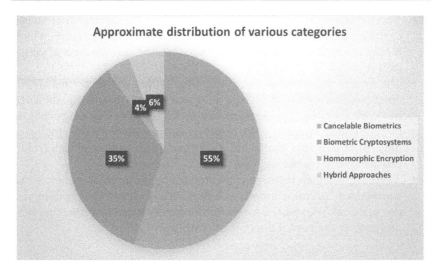

Figure 14.9 Representation of approximate distribution for the various categories of fingerprint template protection.

cancelable biometrics-based approaches in the field of fingerprint template protection as compared to other categories of fingerprint template protection. This chapter has presented the generic working of cancelable biometrics along with a comprehensive discussion of recent existing approaches to protect the fingerprint template, which can be helpful to understand and start with this area for further development.

Although the existing approaches have shown robustness to secure the fingerprint template against identity theft and various attack scenarios to access the systems, a few limitations still exist. Considering the various existing approaches and especially discussed in Sections 14.3, 14.4, and 14.5, a few of the limitations are provided as follows. First, the recognition performance is poor in the case of challenging databases having low-quality fingerprint images; hence, novel approaches can be developed to further improve the performance in the case of challenging databases. Second, the size of the final secure template becomes larger in the existing approaches to make the template alignment-free; therefore, approaches can be developed that not only generate the alignment-free secure fingerprint template but also compute the small-size protected fingerprint template, which can be easily used in small-size consumer devices. Furthermore, a few of the open issues in the overall area of cancelable biometrics are provided below.

- Even though numerous template protection approaches performed quite well to protect the fingerprint template, there is still scope to develop novel approaches that can protect the template without compromising the recognition performance of the system while considering the fingerprint databases containing poor-quality fingerprint images.

- There is scope to develop fingerprint template protection approaches based on cancelable biometrics that are inter-sensor operable, which means the different sensors can be used for the enrollment and verification stages.
- The fingerprint template protection approaches can be further developed considering the size of the final secure fingerprint template without compromising the performance and alignment-free properties of the computed template. The approaches that generate the small-size fingerprint template can be utilized to provide secure access control in consumer devices having a small size of memory.
- There is not much research presented in the literature to generate the cancelable fingerprint template for the partial fingerprint images; hence, this area can be explored for the development of such approaches that can protect the partial fingerprint template.

14.7 CONCLUSION

Due to the advantages in biometric recognition systems over traditional authentication systems—along with a surge in interest—there has been huge growth in the use of these systems in the wide variety of multi-functional applications. Meanwhile, an evident increase in the problem of identity theft has been seen, which is a great security concern regarding biometric recognition systems. In the biometric system based on fingerprint biometrics, usually, a user template containing the information of minutiae points is stored in the database. It has been quite evident from the studies presented in the literature that the fingerprint image reconstruction is feasible by means of the stored template if it is compromised by an adversary. Therefore, it is necessary to protect the original fingerprint data before storing it in the database. To protect the fingerprint template, numerous fingerprint template protection methods have been discussed in the literature. Among them, cancelable biometrics is one of the categories of fingerprint template protection that has been widely discussed as compared to the other categories. This chapter has provided a comprehensive understanding of the working of cancelable biometrics, including a brief discussion on recent developments in the area of cancelable biometrics to protect the fingerprint template. In addition, a detailed discussion of three of the recent approaches has been given. These approaches presented the fingerprint template protection techniques based on non-invertible transformation and dealt with the various issues in the area of fingerprint template protection and fingerprint biometric systems in general. In the future, fingerprint template protection approaches based on cancelable biometrics can be developed to improve the recognition performance for challenging databases containing poor-quality fingerprint images. The hybrid approaches that combine cancelable biometrics with other categories are less explored in the literature; therefore, further exploration of hybrid approaches can be performed for fingerprint template protection approaches. In addition, the cancelable biometrics approaches that enable the sensor inter-operability can be also developed in the future to secure the fingerprint template.

REFERENCES

[1] Maltoni, D.; Maio, D.; Jain, A. K.; Prabhakar, S. *Handbook of Fingerprint Recognition*, 2nd ed.; Springer Publishing Company, Incorporated, 2009.

[2] Ross, A. A.; Shah, J.; Jain, A. K. Toward Reconstructing Fingerprints from Minutiae Points. In *Proc. of SPIE Conf. on Biometric Technology for Human Identification*; 2005; pp. 68–80.

[3] Ross, A.; Shah, J.; Jain, A. K. From Template to Image: Reconstructing Fingerprints from Minutiae Points. *IEEE Trans. Pattern Anal. Mach. Intell.*, 2007, *29* (4), 544–560.

[4] Feng, J.; Jain, A. K. Fingerprint Reconstruction: From Minutiae to Phase. *IEEE Trans. Pattern Anal. Mach. Intell.*, 2010, *33* (2), 209–223.

[5] Juels, A.; Wattenberg, M. A Fuzzy Commitment Scheme. In *Proc. of Computer and Communications Security*, Singapore; 1999; pp 28–36.

[6] Baghel, V. S.; Prakash, S.; Agrawal, I. An Enhanced Fuzzy Vault to Secure the Fingerprint Templates. *Multimed. Tools Appl.*, 2021, *80* (21), 33055–33073.

[7] Gomez-Barrero, M.; Maiorana, E.; Galbally, J.; Campisi, P.; Fierrez, J. Multi-Biometric Template Protection Based on Homomorphic Encryption. *Pattern Recognit.*, 2017, *67*, 149–163.

[8] Ratha, N. K.; Connell, J. H.; Bolle, R. M. Enhancing Security and Privacy in Biometrics-Based Authentication Systems. *IBM Syst. J.*, 2001, *40* (3), 614–634.

[9] Ratha, N. K.; Chikkerur, S.; Connell, J. H.; Bolle, R. M. Generating Cancelable Fingerprint Templates. *IEEE Trans. Pattern Anal. Mach. Intell.*, 2007, *29* (4), 561–572.

[10] Jain, A. K.; Nandakumar, K.; Nagar, A. Biometric Template Security. *EURASIP J. Adv. Signal Process*, 2008, *2008*.

[11] Connie, T.; Teoh, A.; Goh, M.; Ngo, D. PalmHashing: A Novel Approach for Cancelable Biometrics. *Inf. Process. Lett.*, 2005, *93* (1), 1–5.

[12] Teoh, A. B.; Ngo, D. C. Biophasor: Token Supplemented Cancellable Biometrics. In *Proc. of 9th International Conference on Control, Automation, Robotics and Vision*; 2006; pp 1–5.

[13] Jin, Z.; Jin, A. T. B. Fingerprint Template Protection with Minutia Vicinity Decomposition. In *Proc. of International Joint Conference on Biometrics (IJCB)*; 2011; pp 1–7.

[14] Wang, S.; Deng, G.; Hu, J. A Partial Hadamard Transform Approach to the Design of Cancelable Fingerprint Templates Containing Binary Biometric Representations. *Patt. Recogn.*, 2017, *61*, 447–458.

[15] Si, X.; Feng, J.; Yuan, B.; Zhou, J. Dense Registration of Fingerprints. *Patt. Recogn.*, 2017, *63*, 87–101.

[16] Lee, W.; Cho, S.; Choi, H.; Kim, J. Partial Fingerprint Matching Using Minutiae and Ridge Shape Features for Small Fingerprint Scanners. *Expert Syst. Appl.*, 2017, *87*, 183–198.

[17] Wang, S.; Yang, W.; Hu, J. Design of Alignment-Free Cancelable Fingerprint Templates with Zoned Minutia Pairs. *Patt. Recogn.*, 2017, *66*, 295–301.

[18] Moujahdi, C.; Bebis, G.; Ghouzali, S.; Rziza, M. Fingerprint Shell: Secure Representation of Fingerprint Template. *Patt. Recogn. Lett.*, 2014, *45*, 189–196.

[19] Jain, A.; Prasad, M. V. N. K. A Novel Fingerprint Indexing Scheme Using Dynamic Clustering. *J. Reliab. Intell. Environ.*, 2016, *2*, 159–171.

[20] Ali, S. S.; Prakash, S. Enhanced Fingerprint Shell. In *Proc. of SPIN 2015*; 2015; pp. 801–805.

[21] Ali, S. S.; Prakash, S. Fingerprint Shell Construction with Prominent Minutiae Points. In *Proc. of COMPUTE 2017*; ACM, 2017; pp. 91–98.

[22] Ali, S. S.; Prakash, S. 3-Dimensional Secured Fingerprint Shell. *Patt. Recogn. Lett.*, 2019, *126*, 68–77.

[23] Ali, S. S.; Ganapathi, I. I.; Prakash, S. Fingerprint Shell Construction with Impregnable Features. *J. Intell. & Fuzzy Syst.*, 2019, *36* (5), 4091–4104.

[24] Ali, S. S.; Ganapathi, I. I.; Prakash, S. Robust Technique for Fingerprint Template Protection. *IET Biometrics*, 2018, *7* (6), 536–549.

[25] Ali, S. S.; Ganapathi, I. I.; Prakash, S.; Consul, P.; Mahyo, S. Securing Biometric User Template Using Modified Minutiae Attributes. *Patt. Recogn. Lett.*, 2020, *129*, 263–270.

[26] Trivedi, A. K.; Thounaojam, D. M.; Pal, S. A Robust and Non-Invertible Fingerprint Template for Fingerprint Matching System. *Forensic Sci. Int.*, 2018, *288*, 256–265.

[27] Yang, W.; Wang, S.; Hu, J.; Zheng, G.; Valli, C. A Fingerprint and Finger-Vein Based Cancelable Multi-Biometric System. *Pattern Recognit.*, 2018, *78*, 242–251.

[28] Ali, S. S.; Ganapathi, I. I.; Mahyo, S.; Prakash, S. Polynomial Vault: A Secure and Robust Fingerprint Based Authentication. *IEEE Trans. Emerg. Top. Comput.*, 2019, *9*, 612–625.

[29] Trivedi, A. K.; Thounaojam, D. M.; Pal, S. Non-Invertible Cancellable Fingerprint Template for Fingerprint Biometric. *Comput. & Secur.*, 2020, *90*, 101690.

[30] Lahmidi, A.; Minaoui, K.; Moujahdi, C.; Rziza, M. Fingerprint Template Protection Using Irreversible Minutiae Tetrahedrons. *Comput. J.*, 2022, *65* (10), 2741–2754. https://doi.org/10.1093/comjnl/bxab111

[31] Lahmidi, A.; Moujahdi, C.; Minaoui, K.; Rziza, M. On the Methodology of Fingerprint Template Protection Schemes Conception: Meditations on the Reliability. *EURASIP J. Inf. Secur.*, 2022, *2022* (1), 1–13.

[32] Yang, W.; Wang, S.; Shahzad, M.; Zhou, W. A Cancelable Biometric Authentication System Based on Feature-Adaptive Random Projection. *J. Inf. Secur. Appl.*, 2021, *58*, 102704.

[33] Bedari, A.; Wang, S.; Yang, J. A Two-Stage Feature Transformation-Based Fingerprint Authentication System for Privacy Protection in IoT. *IEEE Trans. Ind. Informatics*, 2022, *18* (4), 2745–2752.

[34] Baghel, V. S.; Ali, S. S.; Prakash, S. Adaptation of Pair-Polar Structures to Compute a Secure and Alignment-Free Fingerprint Template. *IEEE Trans. Ind. Informatics*, 2023, *19* (2), 1947–1956.

[35] Baghel, V. S.; Prakash, S. Generation of Secure Fingerprint Template Using DFT for Consumer Electronics Devices. *IEEE Trans. Consum. Electron.*, 2022, *69* (2), 118–127. https://doi.org/10.1109/TCE.2022.3217234

[36] Baghel, V. S.; Ali, A.; Prakash, S. A Robust and Singular Point Independent Fingerprint Shell. *Appl. Intell.*, 2023, *53*, 9270–9284. https://link.springer.com/article/10.1007/s10489-022-04038-6

[37] Neurotechnology, VeriFinger SDK. [last accessed: 31 March 2023], Link: https://www.neurotechnology.com/verifinger.html

[38] Li, C.; Hu, J. A Security-Enhanced Alignment-Free Fuzzy Vault-Based Fingerprint Cryptosystem Using Pair-Polar Minutiae Structures. *IEEE Trans. Inf. Forensics Secur.*, 2016, *11* (3), 543–555.

[39] Ahmad, T.; Hu, J.; Wang, S. Pair-Polar Coordinate-Based Cancelable Fingerprint Templates. *Patt. Recogn.*, 2011, *44* (10), 2555–2564.

[40] Fingerprint Verification Competition 2002 Database. [last accessed: 31 March 2023], Link: http://bias.csr.unibo.it/fvc2002/

[41] Fingerprint Verification Competition 2004 Database. [last accessed: 31 March 2023], Link: http://bias.csr.unibo.it/fvc2004/

[42] Ferrara, M.; Maltoni, D.; Cappelli, R. A Two-Factor Protection Scheme for MCC Fingerprint Templates. In *Proc. of BIOSIG 2014*; 2014; pp 1–8.

[43] Dwivedi, R.; Dey, S.; Singh, R.; Prasad, A. A Privacy-Preserving Cancelable Iris Template Generation Scheme Using Decimal Encoding and Look-up Table Mapping. *Comput. & Secur.*, 2017, *65*, 373–386.

[44] Gomez-Barrero, M.; Galbally, J.; Rathgeb, C.; Busch, C. General Framework to Evaluate Unlinkability in Biometric Template Protection Systems. *IEEE Trans. Inf. Forensics Secur.*, 2018, *13* (6), 1406–1420.

[45] Cappelli, R.; Ferrara, M.; Franco, A.; Maltoni, D. Fingerprint Verification Competition 2006. *Biometric Technol. Today*, 2007, *15* (7), 7–9.

[46] Wilcox, R. Kolmogoro-Smirnov Test. In P. Armitage, T. Colton (eds.), *Encyclopedia of Biostatistics*; John Wiley & Sons, Ltd, 2005.

Chapter 15

Computational intelligence

An optimization perspective for data privacy against adversaries

Vandana Bharti
Indian Institute of Technology, Dharwad, India

Anshul Sharma and Amit Kumar Singh
National Institute of Technology Patna, Patna, India

15.1 INTRODUCTION

Connectivity plays a pivotal role in the current landscape of smart services and digital communication trends, facilitating the rapid exchange of data across various communication channels. These data encompass diverse formats, ranging from text to video, collected and shared using multiple sensors. Within the health care domain, the utilization and sharing of image data are prevalent. However, these medical data sets contain private and sensitive patient information, necessitating robust measures to ensure protection against unauthorized access. With the increasing instances of data breaches, data security has emerged as a critical and challenging concern, particularly in industries like health care, where even minor alterations in data can lead to erroneous diagnoses and life-threatening consequences.

To address these challenges, researchers from diverse fields, including Artificial Intelligence (AI), Cybersecurity, and optimization, are continuously striving to develop efficient solutions for data preservation [1–3]. Computational Intelligence (CI) has gained significant popularity in solving optimization problems characterized by varying complexities and natures, such as from convex to non-convex, unimodal to multi-modal, and single objective to multi-objective [4–7]. The inherent flexibility, randomization, derivative-free nature, and ability to handle tasks with incomplete information make optimization techniques well-suited for NP-hard problems.

This chapter provides insights into the application of CI for maintaining data privacy. While encryption techniques have been widely employed in data privacy preservation, most existing methods are tailored for text data and reliant on specific keys. However, in health care, a significant portion of data comprises images, necessitating further modifications to encryption schemes to make them suitable for image data. Additionally, to enhance security, a shift from fixed secret keys, which are vulnerable to adversarial attacks, to an optimization-based approach for key generation is recommended.

DOI: 10.1201/9781003468974-15

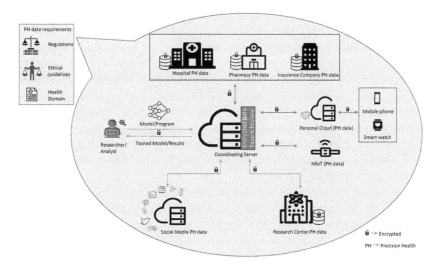

Figure 15.1 An outline of secure data sharing in the precision health care system [8].

The introduction of randomization in optimal key generation adds an extra layer of difficulty for adversaries attempting to gain unauthorized access.

This chapter emphasizes the importance of medical data security, providing an overview of traditional security measures for medical data, as well as the role of CI in data security. Furthermore, it presents information on optimal key generation using Evolutionary Computation (EC). To provide a visual representation, Figure 15.1 offers an overview of secure data publishing in precision health care.

15.1.1 Importance of medical data security

The rapid advancement of Industry 4.0 has brought about a transformative impact on industrial applications, empowering them with a competitive advantage in the market. Its influence extends across diverse sectors, including health care, agriculture, and digital imaging, among others. The integration of this technology has facilitated efficient data transmission over public networks, opening up new opportunities and challenges across various fields. However, alongside these advancements, concerns regarding data security and integrity have taken center stage for almost every industry, from finance to medicine and the digital world. As IoT devices, sensors, and fast connectivity evolve and improve, the demand for reliable and secure data transmission becomes increasingly vital [9].

Within the medical sector, where the exchange of patient reports and sensitive information is frequent, ensuring secure data transmission is of utmost importance. To deliver high-quality health care services at a reduced cost, mobile cloud-based e-health services have made significant strides, leveraging cutting-edge technologies such as big data, medi-cloud, blockchain, and IoT in health care [10]. IoT devices play a pivotal role in the advancement of smart HealthTech, enabling the achievement of numerous objectives. However, these systems are susceptible to data theft and security breaches, posing additional risks. Cyberattacks primarily target critical national infrastructure, including hospitals, banks, and electric power grids, which rely on SCADA and industrial control systems for their operations management [11]. Such attacks have resulted in major breaches, exemplified by the ransomware attack on the Pacific Alliance Medical Center in Los Angeles on June 14, 2017, compromising sensitive data belonging to 266,123 patients, among other similar incidents [12, 13].

Consequently, the prevalence of data manipulation attacks, such as health information tampering, manipulation, and theft, presents one of the most challenging aspects of smart health care: data privacy and security. While Industry 4.0 has significantly improved operational efficiency and productivity in various industries, it is crucial to address concerns surrounding data security as technology continues to advance. By doing so, we can ensure that these technological advancements benefit society as a whole. In summary, the key points highlighted are:

> Medical data security is of utmost importance in the health care industry as it involves the sensitive personal information of patients. Medical data includes various types of information such as medical history, diagnosis reports, test results, insurance details, and personal identification information. Unauthorized access or misuse of this data can lead to various adverse consequences, including identity theft, financial loss, and reputational damage.
>
> In addition to privacy concerns, medical data security is also important for maintaining the integrity and accuracy of the data. Inaccurate or manipulated medical data can lead to misdiagnosis, incorrect treatment, and other medical errors, which can have serious implications for patient health.
>
> Medical data security is a legal requirement in many countries, with regulations such as HIPAA in the United States and GDPR in the European Union. Failure to comply with these regulations can result in hefty fines and legal repercussions.
>
> Overall, medical data security is crucial for protecting patient privacy, maintaining data integrity, and complying with legal requirements. Thus, it is important that health care organizations must take proactive measures to ensure the confidentiality, integrity, and availability of medical data throughout its lifecycle, from collection and storage to transfer and disposal.

The privacy and security concerns of health care have been thoroughly investigated and are presented in [14]. Figure 15.2 displays some frequent

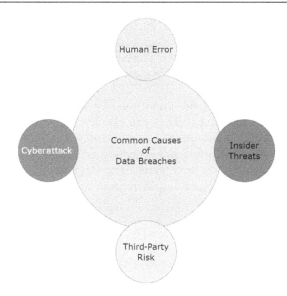

Figure 15.2 Common causes of data breaches.

reasons why data breaches happen. The following section discusses several security techniques that have been used in IoMT based on their effectiveness.

15.1.2 Security measures of medical data

Extensive research and development efforts have been dedicated to designing and studying various traditional and modern AI schemes with the objective of ensuring sensitive data security. In the context of health care organizations, several traditional security measures can be employed to safeguard sensitive data. These measures include:

Access Control: Access control mechanisms limit access to medical data to authorized personnel only. This can be done by implementing role-based access control, where users are assigned access privileges based on their job responsibilities.

Authentication: Authentication mechanisms such as passwords, biometrics, or smart cards can be used to ensure that only authorized personnel are accessing the medical data.

Encryption: Encryption is the process of converting data into a code or cipher to prevent unauthorized access. Medical data can be encrypted when stored, transferred, or accessed, making it difficult for unauthorized users to understand.

Information Hiding: Information hiding techniques are used to protect secret data inside the cover image or video. It also provides content authentication, data ownership verification, and copyright protection. Watermarking and steganography also come under this scheme.

Backup and Recovery: Regular backups of medical data can help in ensuring that sensitive data is not lost due to accidental deletion, system failures, or other disasters. The backup data can be used to restore lost or damaged data in case of a security breach or other incidents.

Employee Training: Regular training and awareness programs can help employees understand the importance of medical data security and their role in protecting it. They can also learn about security policies and best practices.

Physical Security Measures: Implementing physical security measures, such as access controls, surveillance systems, and secure storage facilities, can protect physical infrastructure and prevent unauthorized access to sensitive data.

These traditional security measures, when implemented effectively, can help health care organizations protect medical data from unauthorized access, data breaches, and other security threats. However, as technology advances, new security measures may need to be implemented to keep up with evolving threats. Additionally, AI solutions are in high demand in almost every area. Here are some AI-based solutions that can be used to preserve medical data privacy:

Intrusion Detection Systems (IDS): IDS [15] is an AI solution that detects and responds to cyberattacks. It uses machine learning algorithms to analyze network traffic and identify abnormal activity that may indicate an attack.

Malware Detection: AI-based malware detection systems [16] can identify malicious software and prevent it from infecting systems. These systems use machine learning algorithms to analyze patterns in code and behavior to identify malicious software [14].

User Behavior Analytics: It uses AI to identify abnormal user behavior that may indicate a security threat. For example, it can detect when a user logs in from an unusual location or attempts to access sensitive data outside of their normal working hours.

Data Loss Prevention: These systems use AI to monitor data usage and prevent sensitive data from being accessed or transmitted to unauthorized parties. These systems can identify patterns in data usage and flag any unusual activity that may indicate a data breach.

Access Control: AI can be used to manage access to medical data by implementing intelligent access control policies. This can involve analyzing user behavior to detect anomalies and flag suspicious activity.

Differential Privacy: AI can be used to implement differential privacy, which adds noise to the data to protect individual privacy while allowing for useful insights to be derived. Differential privacy is a mathematical framework that ensures an individual's data is protected even when combined with other data sets. Recent work [1] has presented secure medical data classification by employing differential privacy in an AI-based classification model.

Homomorphic Encryption: AI can be used to implement homomorphic encryption, which allows data to be encrypted while still being processed. This allows for sensitive medical data to be securely analyzed without the need to decrypt it first.

Data Masking: AI can be used to mask sensitive data in medical records, such as names and addresses, while still allowing for other useful information to be analyzed. This can be done through techniques such as tokenization or hashing.

Natural Language Processing (NLP): AI can be used to develop NLP models that can scan medical documents for sensitive information such as patient names or addresses and redact or remove such information automatically.

Federated Learning: Federated learning is another paradigm that allows multiple clients to train AI models securely without sharing sensitive data with other participants [2, 17].

Advanced AI Models: Instead of sharing original data for model training, artificial data can be created and translated from one medical domain to another by cyclic GAN and can be further utilized for knowledge distillation purposes [18].

Optimal Key Generation for Data Encryption: By utilizing CI with appropriate objective functions, random and optimal keys can be generated, which are less vulnerable to attackers due to the high search space of the key. It can be utilized for encryption purposes. They can be further extended to information hiding.

Overall, AI can be an effective tool to preserve medical data privacy. However, it is important to ensure that AI systems are secure and are implemented in accordance with privacy regulations and best practices to prevent the misuse of sensitive data.

15.2 OVERVIEW OF CI

CI is a dynamic field encompassing the theory, design, development, and application of computational paradigms inspired by biological and linguistic processes. Neural Networks [19], Fuzzy systems [20], and EC [6] have traditionally been considered the three primary pillars of CI. These paradigms are designed to emulate the behavior of natural intelligence and provide powerful tools for solving complex problems in a wide range of domains, including machine learning, robotics, data analytics, and optimization. By harnessing the power of CI, researchers and practitioners can develop novel algorithms and models that can learn, adapt, and evolve in response to changing environments and data inputs, leading to new insights and discoveries that can benefit society as a whole. Among all these, our primary focus is on EC.

15.2.1 Evolutionary computation

EC is an exciting subfield of AI that draws inspiration from biological evolution and natural events performed by organisms. By modeling the principles of evolution, EC methods aim to solve complex optimization problems efficiently. The primary goal of EC is to create novel computing methods that mimic natural intelligence discovered in physical, chemical, and biological systems. Unlike other optimization techniques, EC methods have been proven effective as a global optimization method for multiple problems. EC methods are population-based approaches that generate a random initial population and utilize variation operators, such as mutation and crossover, to create the next population or offspring. The natural selection process is then used to refine the population for the next generation. By following these steps, EC methods mimic the process of natural selection to create increasingly better solutions to the optimization problem at hand.

EC has a rich history dating back to the 1960s when researchers proposed Genetic Algorithms (GA), Genetic Programming (GP), and Evolution Strategies (ES) to solve global optimization problems [21]. Since then, other methods such as Differential Evolution and Estimation Distribution Algorithms have been developed, all falling under the umbrella of evolutionary algorithms. In the 1990s, researchers also explored the simulation of natural intelligent phenomena of ants and swarms to create optimization methods, giving rise to the field of Swarm Intelligence [22]. GDWCNPSO [3], QL-SSA [7], MDO [23], and Golden Jackle optimization [24] are a few recent developments in this category. These methods are all subclasses of EC [25] and have greatly expanded the scope of EC. EC algorithms are particularly well-suited to non-convex and black-box optimization problems where the mathematical form of the objective function is not known. The mutation and crossover operations are based on guided randomness, and the method, as a whole, typically does not require any gradient knowledge about the objective function being optimized. Their derivative-free nature makes them a popular choice for solving challenging problems. Due to the versatility of EC methods, they have become the center of attention in the optimization field and have led to numerous innovations. These techniques are also effective for solving multi- and many-objective optimization issues. A broad overview of these intelligent optimization methods is presented in Figure 15.3. Further, different subclasses are shown in Figure 15.4.

Overall, EC is an innovative approach to solving complex optimization problems that draws inspiration from biological evolution. Its population-based characteristics and natural selection processes make it a powerful tool for creating efficient algorithms that can adapt to changing environments. With ongoing research and development, the potential for EC to solve increasingly complex problems continues to expand.

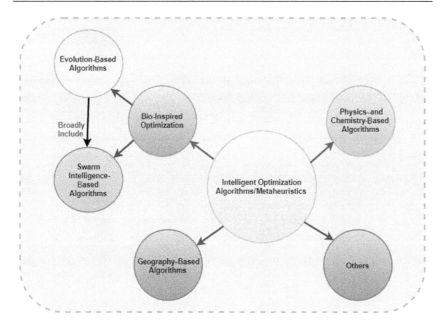

Figure 15.3 Pictorial representation of Intelligent Methods.

15.3 CI AND DATA SECURITY

The health care industry plays a crucial role in promoting people's well-being, but unfortunately, it has become one of the most vulnerable sectors to malicious attacks. The impact of these attacks can be detrimental to patients' lives and the overall functioning of the health care environment. To address the pressing issue of health care data security, researchers have developed various techniques, including watermarking, encryption, compression, and steganography [26–29]. While these techniques have been widely researched, few studies have specifically focused on securing health care data within the context of IoT networks. One notable work in this area is the development of a security microvisor middleware (SμV) for IoT devices by Daniels et al. [30]. This middleware utilizes software virtualization and low-overhead assembly code verification to enable customized security operations and memory isolation, while maintaining minimal impact on memory and battery life. Similarly, Manogaran et al. [31] proposed a secure industrial IoT-based Meta cloud redirection (MC-R) framework for collecting data from medical sensors embedded in patients' bodies. These sensors collect clinical measurements such as heart rate, body temperature, respiratory rate, blood pressure, and blood sugar. If these measures exceed their normal value, the framework sends a warning message containing these clinical measures to doctors via a wireless sensor network. To ensure the secure transmission of large data, the researchers implemented a key management security mechanism.

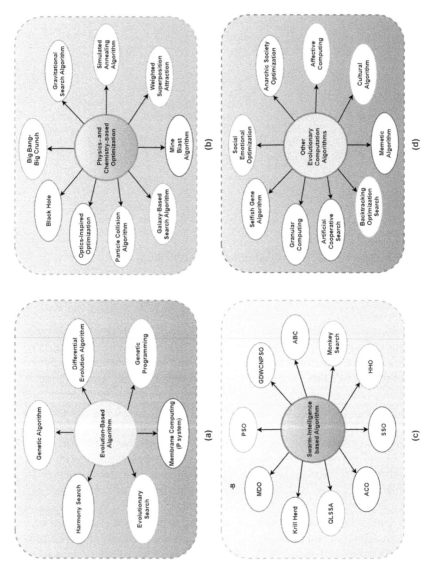

Figure 15.4 (a) CI based on Evolution theory (b) CI inspired by physics (c) Swarm Intelligence approaches (d) Other approaches.

In recent years, researchers have explored new approaches to enhance the security of IoT systems. One promising solution is the development of blockchain-based technologies that integrate hardware security with physical unclonable functions (PUFs), hashing modules, and blockchain. In [32], the authors present a novel blockchain, called PUFchain, that uses PUFs to provide robust data security and device security. They also propose a new consensus algorithm that can be easily integrated into resource-constrained IoT environments, addressing issues such as energy consumption, scalability, and latency.

Another approach to enhancing health care data security is the use of watermarking techniques. Naheed et al. [33] developed a reversible interpolation-dependent watermarking technique using GA and particle swarm optimization (PSO) for medical and standard data. In a similar study, Alphonsa et al. [34] used grasshopper optimization with GA to create an optimal key for data sanitization and restoration processes. The authors found this approach to be more effective than other methods in terms of convergence and performance on medical data. These studies offer promising insights into the development of innovative techniques for enhancing the security of health care data.

Further, encryption is a commonly used technique to ensure secure storage of sensitive data such as medical records and reports. Traditional encryption methods like Data Encryption Standard (DES) [35], Triple DES (3DES) [36], and Advanced Encryption Standard (AES) [37] are based on standard cryptography and are widely used for text data. However, these techniques are not ideal for medical images that are primarily used for analysis. To address this, various initiatives have been taken in recent years.

One such initiative proposed in [10] involves using a hybrid algorithm of grasshopper-PSO to enhance the security of encryption and decryption processes for medical data. This algorithm selects the optimal key to ensure the highest possible security. Another promising approach is Elliptic Galois Cryptography (EGC), proposed in [38], which is based on cryptography and steganography for secure data transmission over an IoT network. The elliptic curve theory is used to generate the key, and an EGC protocol with adaptive firefly optimization is proposed for hidden and secure data in IoTs. Various parameters such as mean square error, carrier capacity, and peak signal-to-noise ratio are considered to ensure the security and effectiveness of the EGC protocol.

In recent years, there have been several advancements in the field of medical data encryption. Authors [39] presented a resource optimization model for clinical data transmission that ensures low processing time and energy consumption. They also proposed a biometric-based security model that extracts heartbeats from ECG signals to generate a unique biometric key. Binary features were extracted from the encoded bits of the heartbeat, concatenated, and evaluated as a biometrically generated key, which was initially 128-bit and sufficient to encrypt the original medical information using logical operations. This approach enables efficient and secure transmission between patients and remote doctors.

Other techniques for medical image encryption have also been proposed. Authors in [40, 41] proposed techniques for preserving a single medical image based on the serial mode, while Hua et al. [42] used high-speed scrambling and pixel adaptive diffusion for image encryption. To improve the diffusion effect, Chai et al. [40] proposed a bi-directional adaptive technique that changed all pixel values in a single round of diffusion. Chen et al. [41] used hierarchical diffusion in a non-sequential manner after evaluating the bit distribution of medical images. They showed that only two rounds of encryption were capable of delivering satisfactory encryption. Another work [43] addressed the limitations of low-dimensional chaotic maps for medical data encryption by proposing a technique that uses 2D chaotic maps. Finally, Song et al. [44] presented a faster and more practical cryptosystem for image encryption using parallel computing and chaotic encryption. They used a permutation and substitution architecture of chaotic encryption to encrypt the medical image.

In addition, there has been a recent focus on developing efficient optimization techniques for generating optimal keys for image encryption while minimizing the loss of information while retrieving the original image [3, 23]. These works have also experimented with unique objective functions for optimal key generation. Such advancements are crucial in ensuring that encrypted medical images can be securely stored and transmitted while maintaining their integrity and minimizing the risk of losing or corrupting sensitive medical information. In a similar spirit, another work [45] presented a hybrid optimization technique for optimal key generation.

To summarize, while traditional encryption methods are often used for text data, they may not always be the most appropriate for medical images that are primarily used for analysis. However, recent advancements in hybrid algorithms and techniques, such as EGC, offer promising solutions for secure medical data storage and transmission. Additionally, biometric-based security, adaptive diffusion, optimal key-based encryption, and chaotic encryption have demonstrated potential for ensuring efficient and secure transmission of medical data. These recent developments highlight the importance of exploring new techniques to enhance the security of sensitive medical information.

15.4 OPTIMAL KEY GENERATION FOR MEDICAL DATA SECURITY

Using EC methods for optimal key generation in medical data security can result in more secure and robust systems that provide better protection for sensitive medical data while being adaptable to changing needs and environments. EC-based approaches offer several benefits, such as personalized

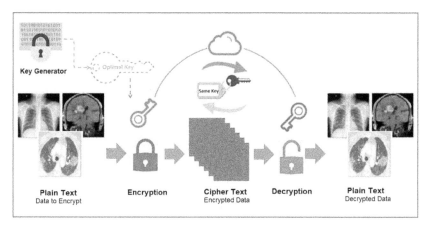

Figure 15.5 An overview of image encryption using an optimal key generated by the EC method.

security for medical data, faster and more efficient key generation, and easy integration with other security techniques, enabling the design of more robust and secure mechanisms for medical data security. By leveraging the power of EC, it is possible to enhance the security of medical data and ensure that it remains protected against potential threats, including cyberattacks and unauthorized access. An overview of image encryption using an optimal key is shown in Figure 15.5, where for encryption, we can choose any cryptography method like DES, AES, etc.

15.4.1 Advantages of EC for key generation

Medical data security can benefit from the use of EC for key generation in a number of ways, including:

Increased Security: EC can generate highly secure keys by optimizing objective functions that are more resistant to attacks than traditional key generation methods.

Flexibility: Intelligent algorithms can adapt to changing environments and situations, making them more flexible and adaptable than traditional key generation methods.

Scalability: EC algorithms can handle large search spaces and optimize complex functions, making them well-suited for generating keys for large-scale medical data systems.

Speed: Efficient EC algorithms can quickly converge on optimal solutions, making them efficient for key generation in medical data security.

Robustness: EC algorithms can continue to function even when some agents fail or leave the system, making them more robust and fault-tolerant than traditional key generation methods.

15.4.2 How to implement EC methods for optimal key generation in medical data security?

Implementing the EC approach for optimal key generation involves a structured process of problem definition, algorithm selection, population generation, fitness evaluation, reproduction, and optimal solution selection. The specific steps and details may vary depending on the problem and algorithm. In short, the process of creating an optimum key using EC techniques involves the following essential steps:

Problem Specification: The first step is to define the problem, including the type of key to be generated and the specific requirements and constraints of the problem domain.

Choosing EC Approach: An appropriate optimization technique must be selected based on the problem and its characteristics.

Generating the Initial Population: The next step is to generate an initial population of potential keys or solutions. This may involve randomly generating a set of keys or using other methods, such as hill climbing or local search, to generate a starting point.

Fitness Evaluation: Once the initial population is generated, each key is evaluated based on its fitness or suitability for the problem. The fitness function is defined based on the problem and may involve performance evaluation metrics such as mean squared error, efficiency, or robustness. It may be designed using statistical measures. Fitness functions or objective functions need to be carefully designed or chosen. These functions are optimized using optimization techniques, and the overall performance quality is solely dependent on these functions and the optimization technique's ability to optimize them.

Reproduction and Variation: The fittest individuals in the population are selected for reproduction, and new solutions are generated through variation and mutation. This process continues for a number of generations or until a stopping criterion is met.

Selection of Optimal Solution: The final step is to select the optimal key or solution based on the fitness function and other constraints of the system. The selection of the final optimal solution also depends on the formulation of the optimal key generation problem, which may be a single-objective or multi-objective optimization problem. Thus, selecting optimal solutions/equally good solutions may involve comparing the fitness values of different solutions or using other methods, such as Pareto optimization to find the best compromise between different objective values.

15.4.3 Limitations of EC approaches

EC approaches have some limitations that need to be addressed in the context of security, despite the fact that they are efficient at solving complex optimization problems. These limitations can be addressed with the help of interdisciplinary concepts and careful consideration of the specific context like data security. Major limitations of EC while integrating with other security measures are discussed as follows.

Computational Expensive: Usually, the termination criteria for EC approaches are a number of iterations. As these methods follow different steps within a single iteration and when EC methods are integrated with other security mechanisms and advanced deep learning models, it becomes computationally expensive and thus limits its performance. Further, these algorithms can be time-consuming, especially when generating a large number of keys. This can be a significant limitation in real-time medical data processing and analysis, where time is often critical. Hence, required, an efficient EC approach for such an application.

Parameter Tuning: Algorithms belonging to EC require setting various parameters, such as the population size, mutation rate, and selection criteria, that can impact the quality of the generated keys. Selecting optimal values for these parameters can be challenging.

Scalability: The effectiveness of optimization approaches for key generation can be limited by the size of the data and the complexity of the problem. This can be a limitation when dealing with large-scale medical data, where the number of keys required can be significant.

Generalizability: The effectiveness of EC algorithms can depend on the specific data and problem at hand. Therefore, it can be challenging to generalize these algorithms across different medical data settings and applications. However, careful design of objective functions can solve this problem.

Addressing these challenges requires a multidisciplinary approach involving expertise in computer science, mathematics, and medical data security. Further, designing self-adaptive and efficient EC methods requires overcoming the aforementioned issues.

15.5 FUTURE DIRECTIONS

EC has the potential to offer significant benefits for medical data security. Some potential future applications of this approach include:

Personalized Medicine: EC can be used to generate personalized security keys for medical data unique to each patient. This could help protect sensitive medical data while allowing for personalized medical treatments based on individual patient data.

Secure Predictive Analytics: EC can be used to generate a predictive model or for robust optimal model creation that helps identify potential security threats before they occur in combination with the cryptography method. This could help improve medical data security by allowing for proactive measures to prevent data breaches.

Integrative Approach with Other Advanced Security Techniques: Watermarking and other information-hiding techniques can be combined with EC to design a more robust system. Further, a combination of EC with federated learning as well as differential privacy can be another potential direction.

Remote Health Care: The COVID-19 pandemic has highlighted the importance of remote health care, and EC could be used to develop secure remote health care solutions. This could include secure transmission of medical data, secure remote consultations with health care providers, and secure storage and retrieval of medical records.

Blockchain-Based Medical Data Security: Blockchain technology offers a secure and decentralized way to store and manage medical data. EC could be used to develop secure key generation algorithms that could be integrated with blockchain-based medical data management systems as shown in Figure 15.6.

Multi-Objective Optimization: Traditional key generation methods focus on a single objective, such as maximizing security or minimizing key length. However, EC can be used to optimize multiple objectives simultaneously, such as security, key length, and computational efficiency. This approach can result in key generation algorithms that are more efficient and effective than traditional methods.

Improved Fitness Functions: The fitness function used in EC approaches determines how well a particular key performs in a given context. Recent research has focused on developing more sophisticated fitness functions that take into account factors such as the specific requirements of medical data security, the complexity of the data set, and the potential threats to the data.

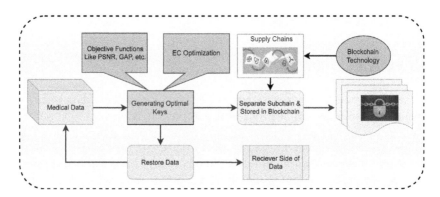

Figure 15.6 Architectural representation for blockchain-based medical data security.

Parallel Computing: EC can be computationally intensive, particularly for large data sets. Recent advancements in parallel computing have made it possible to speed up the key generation process by running multiple instances of the algorithm simultaneously on multiple processors or in a distributed computing environment.

15.6 CONCLUSION

The field of medical data security is of paramount importance and requires constant attention to ensure that patient information remains confidential, secure, and available when needed. Key generation is a critical aspect of medical data security, as it determines the level of protection afforded to sensitive data. EC methods represent a promising avenue for generating optimal keys for medical data security. By leveraging the power of evolutionary algorithms and Swarm Intelligence, this approach can offer personalized and adaptive solutions that can handle large data sets and complex security requirements. While EC has shown great promise in this area, there is still much to be explored in terms of its potential applications and limitations. Future research could focus on developing new algorithms and techniques to further optimize the key generation process, as well as exploring how EC methods can be integrated with other security measures to provide even greater protection for medical data. This chapter highlights the need for medical data security, challenges, and possible solutions by using CI. This chapter mainly focuses on a specific CI method, which are EC approaches and possible future directions in the context of medical data security that are still in the early stages or unexplored. Overall, the potential benefits of using EC methods for key generation in medical data security are substantial, and continued research and development in this area will be critical to ensuring the continued safety and security of sensitive patient information.

REFERENCES

1. Abhinav Kumar, Sanjay Kumar Singh, K Lakshmanan, Sonal Saxena, and Sameer Shrivastava. A novel cloud-assisted secure deep feature classification framework for cancer histopathology images. *ACM Transactions on Internet Technology (TOIT)*, 21(2):1–22, 2021.
2. Abhinav Kumar, Vishal Purohit, Vandana Bharti, Rishav Singh, and Sanjay Kumar Singh. MediSecFed: Private and secure medical image classification in the presence of malicious clients. *IEEE Transactions on Industrial Informatics*, 18(8):5648–5657, 2021.
3. Vandana Bharti, Bhaskar Biswas, and Kaushal Kumar Shukla. A novel multi-objective GDWCN-PSO algorithm and its application to medical data security. *ACM Transactions on Internet Technology (TOIT)*, 21(2):1–28, 2021.

4. Vandana Bharti, Bhaskar Biswas, and Kaushal Kumar Shukla. Recent trends in nature inspired computation with applications to deep learning. In *2020 10th International Conference on Cloud Computing, Data Science & Engineering (Confluence)*, Noida, India, pages 294–299. IEEE, 2020.

5. Vandana Bharti, Bhaskar Biswas, and Kaushal Kumar Shukla. Computational intelligence in Internet of things for future healthcare applications. In *IoT-Based Data Analytics for the Healthcare Industry*, pages 57–78. Elsevier, 2021.

6. Vandana Bharti, Bhaskar Biswas, and Kaushal Kumar Shukla. Swarm intelligence for deep learning: Concepts, challenges and recent trends. In *Advances in Swarm Intelligence: Variations and Adaptations for Optimization Problems*, volume 1054, pages 37–57. Springer, Cham, 2023, https://link.springer.com/book/9783031098345

7. Vandana Bharti, Bhaskar Biswas, and Kaushal Kumar Shukla. QL-SSA: An adaptive Q-learning based squirrel search algorithm for feature selection. In *2022 IEEE Congress on Evolutionary Computation (CEC)*, Padua, Italy, pages 1–7. IEEE, 2022.

8. Chandra Thapa and Seyit Camtepe. Precision health data: Requirements, challenges and existing techniques for data security and privacy. *Computers in Biology and Medicine*, 129:104130, 2021.

9. Carlo Puliafito, Enzo Mingozzi, Francesco Longo, Antonio Puliafito, and Omer Rana. Fog computing for the Internet of Things: A survey. *ACM Transactions on Internet Technology (TOIT)*, 19(2):1–41, 2019.

10. Mohamed Elhoseny, K Shankar, SK Lakshmanaprabu, Andino Maseleno, and N Arunkumar. Hybrid optimization with cryptography encryption for medical image security in Internet of Things. *Neural Computing and Applications*, 32:10979–10993, 2018.

11. Leandros A Maglaras, Ki-Hyung Kim, Helge Janicke, Mohamed Amine Ferrag, Stylianos Rallis, Pavlina Fragkou, Athanasios Maglaras, and Tiago J Cruz. Cyber security of critical infrastructures. *ICT Express*, 4(1):42–45, 2018.

12. Kurt Thomas, Frank Li, Ali Zand, Jacob Barrett, Juri Ranieri, Luca Invernizzi, Yarik Markov, Oxana Comanescu, Vijay Eranti, Angelika Moscicki, et al. Data breaches, phishing, or malware? Understanding the risks of stolen credentials. In *Proceedings of the 2017 ACM SIGSAC Conference on Computer and Communications Security*, Dallas, Texas, pages 1421–1434, 2017.

13. Corey M Angst, Emily S Block, John D'Arcy, and Ken Kelley. When do IT security investments matter? *Accounting for the Influence of Institutional Factors in the Context of Healthcare Data Breaches (January 24, 2016)*. pages 1–601, 2020. https://papers.ssrn.com/sol3/papers.cfm?abstract_id=2858549

14. Antonio López Martínez, Manuel Gil Pérez, and Antonio Ruiz-Martínez. A comprehensive review of the state-of-the-art on security and privacy issues in healthcare. *ACM Computing Surveys*, 55(12):1–38, 2023.

15. Ayoub Si-Ahmed, Mohammed Ali Al-Garadi, and Narhimene Boustia. Survey of machine learning based intrusion detection methods for Internet of Medical Things. *Applied Soft Computing*, 140:110227, 2023.

16. Anshul Sharma and Sanjay Kumar Singh. A novel approach for early malware detection. *Transactions on Emerging Telecommunications Technologies*, 32(2):e3968, 2021.

17. Hao Li, Chengcheng Li, Jian Wang, Aimin Yang, Zezhong Ma, Zunqian Zhang, and Dianbo Hua. Review on security of federated learning and its application in healthcare. *Future Generation Computer Systems*, 144:271–290, 2023.

18. Vandana Bharti, Bhaskar Biswas, and Kaushal Kumar Shukla. QEMCGAN: Quantized evolutionary gradient aware multiobjective cyclic GAN for medical image translation. *IEEE Journal of Biomedical and Health Informatics*, PP:1–12, 2023.

19. Abhinav Kumar, Sanjay Kumar Singh, Sonal Saxena, K Lakshmanan, Arun Kumar Sangaiah, Himanshu Chauhan, Sameer Shrivastava, and Raj Kumar Singh. Deep feature learning for histopathological image classification of canine mammary tumors and human breast cancer. *Information Sciences*, 508:405–421, 2020.

20. Abhinav Kumar, Sanjay Kumar Singh, Sonal Saxena, Amit Kumar Singh, Sameer Shrivastava, K Lakshmanan, Neeraj Kumar, and Raj Kumar Singh. CoMHisP: A novel feature extractor for histopathological image classification based on fuzzy SVM with within-class relative density. *IEEE Transactions on Fuzzy Systems*, 29(1):103–117, 2021.

21. Agoston E Eiben and Jim Smith. From evolutionary computation to the evolution of things. *Nature*, 521(7553):476–482, 2015.

22. Eric Bonabeau, Marco Dorigo, and Guy Theraulaz. Inspiration for optimization from social insect behaviour. *Nature*, 406(6791):39–42, 2000.

23. Vandana Bharti, Bhaskar Biswas, and Kaushal Kumar Shukla. MDO: A novel murmuration-flight based dispersive optimization algorithm and its application to image security. *Journal of Ambient Intelligence and Humanized Computing*, 14:4809–4826, 2023.

24. Nitish Chopra and Muhammad Mohsin Ansari. Golden jackal optimization: A novel nature-inspired optimizer for engineering applications. *Expert Systems with Applications*, 198:116924, 2022.

25. Jun Zhang, Zhi-hui Zhan, Ying Lin, Ni Chen, Yue-jiao Gong, Jing-hui Zhong, Henry SH Chung, Yun Li, and Yu-hui Shi. Evolutionary computation meets machine learning: A survey. *IEEE Computational Intelligence Magazine*, 6(4):68–75, 2011.

26. A Mullai and K Mani. Enhancing the security in RSA and elliptic curve cryptography based on addition chain using Simplified Swarm Optimization and Particle Swarm Optimization for mobile devices. *International Journal of Information Technology*, 13:551–564, 2021.

27. Baiying Lei, Ee-Leng Tan, Siping Chen, Dong Ni, Tianfu Wang, and Haijun Lei. Reversible watermarking scheme for medical image based on differential evolution. *Expert Systems with Applications*, 41(7):3178–3188, 2014.

28. Vipul Kumar Sharma and Roohie Naaz Mir. An enhanced time efficient technique for image watermarking using ant colony optimization and light gradient boosting algorithm. *Journal of King Saud University–Computer and Information Sciences*, in press, 34:615–626, 2019.

29. Kedar Nath Singh, Naman Baranwal, Om Prakash Singh, and Amit Kumar Singh. SIELNet: 3D chaotic-map-based secure image encryption using customized residual dense spatial network. *IEEE Transactions on Consumer Electronics*, PP(99):1–1, 2022.

30. Wilfried Daniels, Danny Hughes, Mahmoud Ammar, Bruno Crispo, Nelson Matthys, and Wouter Joosen. S μ v – the security microvisor: A virtualisation-based security middleware for the internet of things. In *Proceedings of the 18th ACM/IFIP/USENIX Middleware Conference: Industrial Track*, pages 36–42, Las Vegas, Nevada, ACM, 2017.

31. Gunasekaran Manogaran, Chandu Thota, Daphne Lopez, and Revathi Sundarasekar. Big data security intelligence for healthcare industry 4.0. In

L Thames, D Schaefer (eds.) *Cybersecurity for Industry 4.0*, pages 103–126. Springer International Publishing, Cham, 2017.

32. Saraju P Mohanty, Venkata P Yanambaka, Elias Kougianos, and Deepak Puthal. PUFchain: A hardware-assisted blockchain for sustainable simultaneous device and data security in the Internet of Everything (IoE). *IEEE Consumer Electronics Magazine*, 9(2):8–16, 2020.

33. Talat Naheed, Imran Usman, Tariq M Khan, Amir H Dar, and Muhammad Farhan Shafique. Intelligent reversible watermarking technique in medical images using GA and PSO. *Optik*, 125(11):2515–2525, 2014.

34. MM Annie Alphonsa and N MohanaSundaram. A reformed grasshopper optimization with genetic principle for securing medical data. *Journal of Information Security and Applications*, 47:410–420, 2019.

35. Don Coppersmith. The Data Encryption Standard (DES) and its strength against attacks. *IBM Journal of Research and Development*, 38(3):243–250, 1994.

36. R Ratnadewi, Roy Pramono Adhie, Yonatan Hutama, A Saleh Ahmar, and MI Setiawan. Implementation cryptography Data Encryption Standard (DES) and Triple Data Encryption Standard (3DES) method in communication system based Near Field Communication (NFC). *Journal of Physics: Conference Series*, 954:1–8, 2018. Makassar, Indonesia, IOP Publishing.

37. NIST FIPS PUB. 197: Advanced encryption standard (AES). *Federal Information Processing Standards Publication*, 197:441–0311, 2001.

38. Manju Khari, Aditya Kumar Garg, Amir H Gandomi, Rashmi Gupta, Rizwan Patan, and Balamurugan Balusamy. Securing data in Internet of Things (IoT) using cryptography and steganography techniques. *IEEE Transactions on Systems, Man, and Cybernetics: Systems*, 50(1):73–80, 2019.

39. Sandeep Pirbhulal, Oluwarotimi Williams Samuel, Wanqing Wu, Arun Kumar Sangaiah, and Guanglin Li. A joint resource-aware and medical data security framework for wearable healthcare systems. *Future Generation Computer Systems*, 95:382–391, 2019.

40. Xiuli Chai, Jitong Zhang, Zhihua Gan, and Yushu Zhang. Medical image encryption algorithm based on Latin square and memristive chaotic system. *Multimedia Tools and Applications*, 78(24):35419–35453, 2019.

41. Junxin Chen, Lei Chen, Leo Yu Zhang, and Zhi-liang Zhu. Medical image cipher using hierarchical diffusion and non-sequential encryption. *Nonlinear Dynamics*, 96(1):301–322, 2019.

42. Zhongyun Hua, Shuang Yi, and Yicong Zhou. Medical image encryption using high-speed scrambling and pixel adaptive diffusion. *Signal Processing*, 144:134–144, 2018.

43. Shanshan Li, Li Zhao, and Na Yang. Medical image encryption based on 2D zigzag confusion and dynamic diffusion. *Security and Communication Networks*, 2021:1–23, 2021.

44. Wei Song, Chong Fu, Yu Zheng, Lin Cao, and Ming Tie. A practical medical image cryptosystem with parallel acceleration. *Journal of Ambient Intelligence and Humanized Computing*, 14:9853–9867, 2023.

45. Yogesh R Kulkarni, Balaso Jagdale, and Shounak R Sugave. Optimized key generation-based privacy preserving data mining model for secure data publishing. *Advances in Engineering Software*, 175:103332, 2023.

Index

Pages in *italics* refer to figures and pages in **bold** refer to tables.

Milton Keynes UK
Ingram Content Group UK Ltd.
UKHW031127141024
449569UK00006B/383